From Small Screen to Vinyl

From Small Screen to Vinyl

A Guide to Television Stars Who Made Records, 1950–2000

Bob Leszczak

ROWMAN & LITTLEFIELD
Lanham • Boulder • New York • London

Published by Rowman & Littlefield
A wholly owned subsidiary of The Rowman & Littlefield Publishing Group, Inc.
4501 Forbes Boulevard, Suite 200, Lanham, Maryland 20706
www.rowman.com

16 Carlisle Street, London W1D 3BT, United Kingdom

British Library Cataloguing in Publication Information Available

Library of Congress Cataloging-in-Publication Data

Leszczak, Bob, 1959–
  From small screen to vinyl : a guide to television stars who made records, 1950–2000 / Bob Leszczak.
    pages cm
  Includes bibliographical references and index.
  ISBN 978-1-4422-4273-9 (hardback : alk. paper) — ISBN 978-1-4422-4274-6 (ebook) 1. Television actors and actresses—Discography. 2. Television personalities—Discography. I. Title.
  ML158.L47 2015
  016.78164026'6—dc23

                                                                    2015002443

∞™ The paper used in this publication meets the minimum requirements of American National Standard for Information Sciences—Permanence of Paper for Printed Library Materials, ANSI/NISO Z39.48-1992.

Printed in the United States of America

To all of the multitalents and multitaskers who double dabbled
in my favorite writing subjects—music *and* television,
my personal raison d'être.
Rock and roll, as well as television, flourished in the 1950s.
The two of them made great companions, and despite many naysayers,
their marriage has harmoniously withstood the test of time.

Contents

List of Entries

Sheb Wooley
Tom Wopat
Jo Anne Worley
Tina Yothers
John Zacherley
Efrem Zimbalist Jr.

APPENDIX A: HONORABLE MENTIONS

Bill Anderson
Lucie Arnaz
Desi Arnaz Jr.
Jim Backus
Robby Benson
Lisa Hartman Black
Jimmy Boyd
Ruth Brown
George Burns
Michael Callan
Les Crane
James Darren
Hannah Dean
Rick Dees
Dick Dodd
Leif Garrett
Barry Gordon
Andy Griffith
Bill Hayes
Burl Ives
Mabel King
Gladys Knight
James Komack
L. L. Cool J.
Patti LaBelle
Michele Lee
Julie London
Tina Louise
James MacArthur
Patty McCormack
Marilyn Michaels
Hayley Mills

Bill Mumy
Ozzie Nelson
Joe Pesci
Della Reese
Burt Reynolds
Kurt Russell
Susan Silo
The Smothers Brothers
Marcia Strassman
Paul Sylvan
Tracey Ullman
Miyoshi Umeki
Billy Vera
Adam Wade
Robert Wagner
Robert Walden
Deborah Walley
Tuesday Weld
Marie Wilson
Hattie Winston
Edward Woodward
Chuck Woolery

APPENDIX B: DEBUNKED TV STARS' RECORDS

Don Adams
Wally Cox
Donna Douglas
Linda Evans
Brian Keith
Chuck Norris

APPENDIX C: VINYL FROM ANIMATED AND COSTUMED CHARACTER SHOWS

The Archies
The Banana Splits
Barney and Friends

Preface

Did you know that Lorne Greene, the actor who portrayed Ben Cart-wright of the Ponderosa on the long-running NBC western series called *Bonanza*, also had a number 1 hit record titled "Ringo" in 1964? Were you aware that Walter Brennan had a Top Five single while portraying Amos McCoy on *The Real McCoys*? Do you remember Bruce Willis's Top Five remake of the Staple Singers' "Respect Yourself" (a hit while he was playing David Addison on *Moonlighting*)? How about Don Johnson, who, while fighting crime in pastel colors and no socks as Sonny Crockett on *Miami Vice*, reached the Top Ten with a song called "Heartbeat"? Remember child star Johnny Crawford, who portrayed Mark McCain alongside Chuck Connors on *The Rifleman*? He made Top Ten with a ballad titled "Cindy's Birthday" and had a couple of other songs that just missed.

Beginning in television's infancy, the networks and the television studios discovered another avenue to increase revenue, while padding the popularity of their programs. They released phonograph recordings by the stars of said programs. This practice was especially prevalent in studios that also owned record companies, such as Screen Gems (and its CBS, Colpix, Columbia, Colgems, and Epic labels), ABC-Paramount, MGM, United Artists, and Warner Bros. What better way was there to promote a recording than on a hit TV series? What better way was there to promote a TV series than with a hit record?

A few of the TV stars who made records proved to be very proficient singers and were pleasing to both your rabbit ears and the ears on your head. Many others, however, were wise to keep their day jobs. Yes, in-deed, a few of them did go from flat screen to flat notes. In many cases, the celebrity was pressured into entering the recording studio against his or her own better judgment. Some had big hits, but so many didn't. You'll get to read about the experience, positive or negative, in quotes from many of these TV pseudo songbirds, such as Whispering Bill Anderson, Julie Budd, Joyce Bulifant, Carol Burnett, Leo De Lyon, Donna Douglas, Louise Duart, Bobbie Eakes, John Eimen, Rosey Grier, Dwayne Hickman, Tab Hunter, Tom Kennedy, Stanley Livingston, Gloria Loring, Johnny Mann, Andrea Marcovicci, Jerry Mathers, Marilyn Michaels, Bill Mumy, Butch Patrick, Paul Petersen, Susan Silo, Rex Smith, Paul Sylvan,

Billy Vera, Johnny Whitaker, and Mason Williams. All of these stars had a double date with fame, and doubled our pleasure much like Doublemint Gum. Additionally, Stephen Burnette, Bill Funt, and David Narz shared memories of their famous TV fathers and the recordings released.

A goodly number of celebrities, such as Frankie Laine, Mac Davis, Perry Como, and Sonny and Cher, experienced things in reverse—they had hit records and parlayed their musical success story into small-screen stardom. For that reason, they are excluded from this volume. Arthur Godfrey is not included because his recording career began while he was enjoying success on radio. Also omitted are motion picture and Broadway soundtrack stars such as Judy Garland, Eddie Albert, and Eddie Bracken. Those who made their mark after 2000 (Miley Cyrus, Hillary Duff, Selena Gomez, iCarly, Demi Lovato, Laura Marano, Renee Olstead) are not included. Presented from A to Z (Nick Adams to the recently deceased Efrem Zimbalist Jr.) are those who got to make records/music as a result of their TV fame *during* their TV successes. In most instances, the "Oh, wow" factor in this work will be epic. Appendix A lists a few exceptions—examples of those whose TV and music careers didn't exactly align, but are nonetheless worthy of a mention. I simply couldn't exclude them. In appendix B you will find a short list of debunked artists—TV stars long believed to have made phonograph records but who in fact did not. Finally, appendix C lists animated and costumed character programming that also yielded vinyl platters. Calling up all of these "tube tunes" on YouTube doubles your thrill while reading about them.

A note regarding the information at the beginning of each entry: Because so many programs, especially in television's early days, switched networks two, sometimes three times, said networks are listed alphabetically. Where the word *respectively* appears after the years, it connects the shows to their respective years on TV and not to the networks. The same applies to the record labels. Specific songs and their respective label numbers and chart positions are also linked with the word *respectively*, but the labels themselves are listed alphabetically, rather than chronologically.

As far as the entry headings themselves go, in each case I went with the name(s) listed on the record, whether the group or TV character (e.g., the Blues Brothers), the actor (e.g., Carroll O'Connor and Jean Stapleton), or both.

Borrowing a few lines from the sci-fi TV classic *The Outer Limits*— "There is nothing wrong with your television set. Do not attempt to adjust the picture. We are controlling transmission. . . . You are about to experience the awe and mystery" of those who made the transition *From Small Screen to Vinyl, 1950–2000*.

Acknowledgments

Dual thanks go out to Whispering Bill Anderson, Julie Budd, Joyce Bulifant, Carol Burnett, Leo De Lyon, Donna Douglas, Louise Duart, Bobbie Eakes, John Eimen, Rosey Grier, Dwayne Hickman, Tab Hunter, Tom Kennedy, Stanley Livingston, Gloria Loring, Johnny Mann, Andrea Marcovicci, Jerry Mathers, Marilyn Michaels, Bill Mumy, Butch Patrick, Paul Petersen, Susan Silo, Rex Smith, Paul Sylvan, Billy Vera, Johnny Whitaker, and Mason Williams—dual talents who did double duty and shared dual memories of their TV *and* musical careers. Special thanks to Stephen Burnette, Bill Funt, and David Narz for sharing memories of their famous TV fathers and their vinyl releases. Also, much gratitude goes to Matt Ottinger, Roger Reinhart, Mark Rothman, David Schwartz, and especially Vincent Terrace for their double vision.

A

Nick Adams brought his popular Johnny Yuma character from *The Rebel* to vinyl.

NICK ADAMS

Most Famous TV Role: Johnny Yuma on *The Rebel*; **Network:** ABC; **Years:** 1959–1961; **Hit Recording:** none; **Labels:** Mercury, RCA Victor; **Release Years:** 1960–1962; **Matrix:** "Born a Rebel" (Mercury #71579), "Johnny Yuma, the Rebel" (Mercury #71607), "Tired and Lonely Rebel" (RCA Victor #8073); **Chart:** none

Nick Adams was born as Nicholas Aloysius Adamschock in Nanticoke, Pennsylvania, on July 10, 1931. Nick's father was a coal miner. When Nick was five, the Adamschock family moved to Jersey City, New Jersey. Nick had an opportunity to play minor league baseball, but because of the low wages, he turned down the offer. He decided to try to become an actor, shortened his surname to Adams, and developed a kinship with actor Jack Palance, who was also the son of a coal miner. After several small parts in films such as *Mister Roberts*, *Pillow Talk*, and *Rebel without a Cause*, he landed the role that would define him—Johnny Yuma on the ABC western from Mark Goodson and Bill Todman (best known for their hit game shows) titled *The Rebel*. Johnny Yuma, the rebel, was a former Confederate soldier who roamed the West. Johnny Cash performed the famous theme song. To cash in on the show's brief popularity, Adams landed a recording contract with Mercury Records and later RCA Victor, releasing a few singles about his famous TV character, Johnny Yuma. Neither the Mercury nor the RCA Victor singles made the charts.

After the cancellation of *The Rebel*, Adams earned one other starring role—as newspaper man Nick Alexander on the short-lived NBC drama series called *Saints and Sinners*. The program costarred Richard Erdman and Barbara Rush. When this series was cancelled after 18 episodes, Adams's career hit quite a lull. He became extremely distraught when a picture to be filmed in Rome called *Murder in the Third Dimension* was nixed, and he allegedly committed suicide in his Beverly Hills home as a result on February 7, 1968, at the age of 36.

LOLA ALBRIGHT

Most Famous TV Role: Edie Hart on *Peter Gunn*; **Networks:** ABC, NBC; **Years:** 1958–1961; **Hit Recording:** none; **Labels:** Columbia, Kem; **Release Years:** 1958–1959; **Matrix:** "Think of Me" (Kem #2744), "Goodbye, My Lover" (Kem #2745), "Candy" (Kem #2772), *Lola Wants You* (Kem LP #101), *Dreamsville* (Columbia LP #1327); **Chart:** none

"What Lola wants" is for you to "Think of Her" and her show, *Peter Gunn*.

Lola Jean Albright was born in Akron, Ohio, on July 20, 1925. She began as a model and parlayed that into numerous small roles in films throughout the 1950s. In 1958, she secured a recurring role as Edie Hart, the nightclub singer at Mother's, on the Blake Edwards crime drama titled *Peter Gunn*. She sang often on the show and also served as Gunn's main squeeze. The popularity of the film noir program led to a recording contract with the Kem label. Playing on the title of the famous song "Whatever Lola Wants, Lola Gets," she recorded an album titled *Lola Wants You* and several singles. However, Kem Records was known mostly for risqué novelty records, and it's likely Albright's efforts on vinyl weren't taken seriously. Her Columbia album titled *Dreamsville*, featuring the Henry Mancini

Orchestra (Mancini also wrote the *Peter Gunn* theme song), had a better chance of succeeding, but failed to catch on. Along with numerous guest-starring roles on episodic TV programs and a big part as Dolly Fletcher in the 1962 Elvis Presley classic titled *Kid Gallahad*, Albright briefly took over the role of Constance McKenzie Carson on the popular prime-time soap opera *Peyton Place* when Dorothy Malone required surgery (1965–1966). Albright endured three failed, childless marriages and nowadays prefers her own company.

REX ALLEN

Most Famous TV Roles: Dr. Bill Baxter on *Frontier Doctor*, cohost of *Five Star Jubilee*; **Network:** syndicated; **Years:** 1958–1959, 1961, respectively; **Hit Recording:** "Don't Go Near the Indians"; **Label:** Mercury; **Release Year:** 1962; **Matrix:** Mercury #71997; **Chart:** #17 *Billboard* Hot 100

Rex Elvie Allen was born in Willcox, Arizona, on New Year's Eve 1920. He moved to Hollywood in the late 1940s to seek success on the silver screen. He found roles in numerous movie westerns until they began to go out of vogue. Westerns and singing cowboys were still big on the small screen, and Rex secured the lead role of Dr. Bill Baxter on a syndicated series titled *Frontier Doctor* from 1958 to 1959. In 1961, he became one of the five stars on NBC's *Five Star Jubilee* summer series. His visibility on that series led to a Top Twenty pop single (Top Five country) titled "Don't Go Near the Indians" (Mercury #71997). The song told the bizarre story of a father who warned his son to stay away from the nearby Native Americans. The son didn't listen and fell in love with an Indian girl who, it turned out, was his sister.

Allen amassed quite a lengthy discography with releases for labels such as Buena Vista, Decca, Disneyland, Hacienda, Musicor, and Mercury, but didn't score any other pop hits. After a career lull, Allen made a comeback as the narrator for the popular motion picture *Charlotte's Web* and performed the theme song for the very funny but short-lived 1981 western ABC TV sitcom titled *Best of the West*. He got his star on the Hollywood Walk of Fame in 1983. Allen died of a massive heart attack on December 17, 1999, only days before his 79th birthday. His son, Rex Allen Jr., recorded successfully for Warner Bros. in the 1970s and '80s.

STEVE ALLEN

Most Famous TV Role: host of *The Steve Allen Show*, *I've Got a Secret*, and *The Tonight Show*; **Networks:** CBS, NBC, syndicated; **Years:** 1954–1967; **Hit Recordings:** "The Autumn Leaves," "The Gravy Waltz"; **Labels:** Coral, Dot; **Release Years:** 1955, 1962, respectively; **Matrix:** "The Autumn Leaves" (Coral #61485), "The Gravy Waltz" (Dot #16457); **Chart:** #38, #64, respectively, *Billboard* Hot 100

Steve Allen was born in New York City on December 26, 1921. He started in radio, but became a star on television. After a stint on *Arthur Godfrey's Talent Scouts*, he made history as the first host of *The Tonight Show* beginning in 1954. He was also very musically inclined and proficient on the piano, releasing a number of records during his lifetime. His first and only Top Forty single was a version of Roger Williams's "Autumn Leaves" on the Coral label in 1955, during his run on *The Tonight Show*. His only Top Ten album in that same year was *Music for Tonight* (Coral LP #57004)—it was laden with old standards. He also wrote a bevy of songs, including one that became his theme song, "This Could Be the Start of Something Big."

His quick wit was very endearing, and after Jack Paar took the reins of *The Tonight Show* in 1957, Allen hosted a number of popular eponymous variety and talk shows—*The Steve Allen Show*, *The New Steve Allen Show*, *The Steve Allen Plymouth Show*, and *The Steve Allen Westinghouse Show*. He was also a regular panelist on *What's My Line?* and took over as host of *I've Got a Secret* when Garry Moore bowed out. While doing the late-night shows for Westinghouse, Steve recorded a jazz piece called "The Gravy Waltz" for Dot Records in 1963. While not a major chart hit, it did get attention and garnered Allen a Grammy Award. His TV shows made stars of many of his regulars such as Pat Harrington Jr., Don Knotts, Gabe Dell, Tom Poston, and Louis Nye. Allen also made a couple of motion pictures—*The Benny Goodman Story* and *Down Memory Lane*. He was married twice, most notably to Jayne Meadows from 1954 until his passing from a massive heart attack (suffered shortly after an automobile accident) on October 30, 2000. He had four children—three with his first wife and one with Meadows. He has two stars on the Hollywood Walk of Fame—one for radio and one for television.

Fran Allison of *Kukla, Fran and Ollie* "pulled some strings" to get on vinyl.

FRAN ALLISON

Most Famous TV Role: Fran on *Kukla, Fran and Ollie*; **Networks:** ABC, NBC, PBS; **Years:** 1948–1957, 1961–1962, 1969–1971; **Hit Recording:** none; **Labels:** Decca, Mercury, RCA Victor; **Release Years:** 1950–1966; **Matrix:** "Punky Punkin'" (RCA #0253), "The Doughnut Song" (RCA #971), "The Christmas Tree Angel" (RCA #3938), "Too Young" (RCA #4105), "The Girls in My Little Boy's Life" (RCA #8767), "Water Tumbler Tune" (Decca #29452), "Galway Bay" (Mercury #70806); **Chart:** none

Frances Helen Allison was born in La Porte City, Iowa, on November 20, 1907. After graduating from Coe College she found work as a teacher before her radio broadcasting career began locally. She then moved to Chicago and worked for NBC Radio before venturing into television in its infancy. A local puppeteer friend named Burr Tillstrom was putting together a kids' show and asked Fran to join in as the program's lone human. The *Kukla, Fran and Ollie* program was a huge success and initially ran for a decade, returning with new episodes in 1961 and 1969 with much less success. She also hosted an eponymous talk show as well as *The CBS Children's Film Festival*, but is best known for her work with the Kuklapolitan Players. During her most successful years on the small screen, Allison also recorded numerous youth-oriented songs for major labels such as Decca, Mercury, and RCA Victor. Even though they didn't make the charts, her seasonal songs such as "Punky Punkin'" and "The Christmas Tree Angel" were quite popular perennial favorites. She also recorded the answer to Mike Douglas's "The Men in My Little Girl's Life" (Epic #9876) titled "The Girls in My Little Boy's Life." Allison has a star on the Hollywood Walk of Fame, and a postage stamp was issued in her honor on August 11, 2009. She died of a rare bone marrow disorder at the age of 81 on June 13, 1989.

ED AMES

Most Famous TV Role: Mingo on *Daniel Boone*; **Network:** NBC; **Years:** 1964–1968; **Hit Recording:** "My Cup Runneth Over"; **Label:** RCA Victor; **Release Year:** 1967; **Matrix:** RCA Victor #9002; **Chart:** #8 *Billboard* Hot 100

Ed Ames was born as Edmund Dantes Urick in Malden, Massachusetts, on July 9, 1927—the youngest of nine children. Four of the five boys (Ed, Joe, Gene, and Vic) formed a pop vocal group in the 1950s and performed locally in the Boston area. They dropped the surname of Urick and were first known as the Amory Brothers and then finally the Ames Brothers. After recording a few sides for Coral Records, they really hit it big with three Top Ten records on RCA Victor—"The Naughty Lady of Shady Lane" (#5897), "Tammy" (#6930), and "Melodie D'Amour" (#7046).

Surging rock and roll records put the kibosh on the old sound of the Ames Brothers, and their chart success conquests were few and far between after 1957. Ed Ames opted to pursue acting in the new decade of the 1960s, and he earned a role in the new NBC adventure series called *Daniel Boone* in 1964. Fess Parker (see the entry under his name) played the title character, and Ames portrayed Native American Mingo on the program. He also portrayed Mingo's evil twin Taramingo on occasion. At this same time, Ames was revving up a solo singing career and struck gold in 1967 with a Top Ten ballad called "My Cup Runneth Over" from the musical *I Do, I Do*. The *My Cup Runneth Over* album (RCA Victor #3774) reached the Top Five and earned a gold record. Later that same year, he reached Top Twenty yet again with a song titled "Who Will Answer?" (RCA Victor #9400). Once again, the *Who Will Answer? and Other Songs of Our Time* (RCA Victor #3961) LP peaked at number 13 and garnered another gold record for Ames.

Ames achieved TV immortality in an episode of *The Tonight Show Starring Johnny Carson* when, as a Native American expert, he was involved in a now legendary tomahawk toss. He was supposed to hurl a tomahawk at a picture of a man on a wooden board and, completely innocently, the tomahawk landed and lodged in a most sensitive region of the male anatomy. The clip became a staple and a favorite on Carson's yearly *Tonight Show* anniversary specials on NBC. Ames has been married twice, and both marriages ended in divorce.

MOREY AMSTERDAM

Most Famous TV Role: Buddy Sorrell on *The Dick Van Dyke Show*; **Network:** CBS; **Years:** 1961–1966; **Hit Recording:** none; **Label:** Roulette; **Release Year:** 1962; **Matrix:** *The Next One Will Kill You* (Roulette LP #25196); **Chart:** none

Moritz "Morey" Amsterdam was born in Chicago on December 14, 1908. He was performing as a straight man and cellist in vaudeville in his early teens. He developed a reputation for having jokes for any and every subject, and was dubbed "the Human Joke Machine." It's not well known, but Morey is credited with penning the lyrics for the Andrews Sisters' hit "Rum and Coca Cola" in 1945. After years of work in radio, Amsterdam made the transition to television and had hosted the live *Morey Amsterdam Show* on the short-lived DuMont Television Network from 1948 to 1950. A young Art Carney and a yet-unknown Jacqueline Susann were regulars on the show. After the demise of this series, Morey moved on to *Broadway Open House* on NBC from 1950 to 1951. A decade later, he happened upon his most famous and enduring role—joke writer Buddy Sorrell for *The Alan Brady Show* on the classic *Dick Van Dyke Show*. It was during the run of this show that Morey released an album for the Roulette Records label titled *The Next One Will Kill You*. The album cover shows Amsterdam against a dart board eyeing a dart that just missed his left ear. The LP featured a song for which he had become synonymous—"Yuk-a-Puk," first performed on his old DuMont series. He had previously recorded the song on the small Apollo Records label out of New York (Apollo #1042) during the run of *The Morey Amsterdam Show*. Van Dyke left the show at the peak of its popularity, and Amsterdam and Rose Marie became regulars on the game show circuit. Amsterdam was seen on *The Hollywood Squares*, *The Match Game*, and especially *Can You Top This?* He died of a heart attack at the age of 87 on October 28, 1996, leaving behind his wife of 47 years, Kay Patrick, and two children, Cathy and Gregory.

SUSAN ANTON

Most Famous TV Role: Jackie Quinn on *Baywatch*; **Network:** syndicated; **Years:** 1993–1994; **Hit Recording:** "Killin' Time"; **Label:** Scotti Brothers; **Release Year:** 1979; **Matrix:** Scotti Brothers #609; **Chart:** #28 *Billboard* Hot 100

Susan Anton was born on Columbus Day 1950 in Oak Glen, California. She was named Miss California in 1969 and parlayed that achievement into a career in movies, television, and music. After countless appearances on *The Merv Griffin Show*, Anton earned a couple of short-lived music series—*Mel and Susan Together* (with Mel Tillis) on ABC in 1978 and *Presenting Susan Anton* on NBC in 1979. Her visibility led to a contract with Scotti Brothers Records and one lone Top Thirty hit single, a duet with country star Fred Knoblock called "Killin' Time" in 1980. She also secured movie roles in *Cannonball Run II*, *Spring Fever*, and *Goldengirl*. Anton found her greatest success in Las Vegas, with a long run at the Flamingo Hilton. As of this writing, Anton still lives in Vegas with her second husband, Jeff Lester. Her longest run on television came with the recurring role of Jackie Quinn on the syndicated David Hasselhoff series titled *Baywatch* from 1993 to 1994. She has also enjoyed a couple of runs in the Broadway version of *Hairspray*.

DESI ARNAZ

Most Famous TV Role: Ricky Ricardo on *I Love Lucy*; **Network:** CBS; **Years:** 1951–1960; **Hit Recording:** "I Love Lucy"; **Label:** Columbia; **Release Year:** 1954; **Matrix:** Columbia #43997; **Chart:** none

Desi Arnaz sang this on the May 11, 1953, episode of *I Love Lucy* titled "Lucy's Last Birthday."

Desiderio Alberto Arnaz y de Acha III was born in Santiago, Cuba, on March 2, 1917. The family moved to Miami, Florida, in 1934 and it was there he attended high school. In 1939, once he had become more fluent in English, he sought work in show business and quickly found work on Broadway in *Too Many Girls* at the age of 22. His next stop was Hollywood to perform in the movie version, and it was there he met Lucille Ball, whom he eventually married on November 30, 1940. Because of a bad knee he was assigned to limited duty in the U.S. Army during World War II. After being discharged, Arnaz and his orchestra recorded several singles for RCA Victor Records—"In Santiago, Chile" backed with "Rumba Rumbero" (RCA Victor #2827), "Cuban Pete" backed with "Tabu" (RCA Victor #2865), "Babalu" backed with "Brazil" (RCA Victor #2866), and "Peanut Vendor" backed with "Tico Tico" (RCA Victor #2867).

In 1951, only a couple of years after these somewhat popular singles, Arnaz and Ball sold a TV sitcom pilot to CBS and the legend that is *I Love Lucy* was born. During the show's original six-year run, Arnaz performed many of these songs on the program (with "Babalu" becoming the most famous). During the program's peak popularity, Arnaz got to release the show's theme song, with lyrics, on CBS's record label, Columbia (#43997). In fact, that song, "I Love Lucy," was backed with another song from the series, "There's a Brand New Baby at Our House" (performed after the "expectant" Ball gave birth to little Ricky). In 1957, the weekly episodes of *I Love Lucy* came to an end, but the story continued over the next three seasons in a series of hour-long specials originally called *Westinghouse Desilu Playhouse*, but later renamed *The Lucy Desi Comedy Hour* in syndication. These episodes came at a time when Ball and Arnaz's marriage was nearing an end. Arnaz is credited with inventing the three-camera filming method still used today on programs with a studio audience. After divorcing, Ball returned to television in *The Lucy Show* (Arnaz is credited as executive producer on the early black-and-white episodes) and then *Here's Lucy*. He took his shares of Desilu Productions and formed his own company called Desi Arnaz Productions (which gave us *The Mothers-in-Law* from 1967 to 1969 on NBC). Ball and Arnaz did remain on friendly terms, however, even after each remarried. Both Lucie and Desi Jr. also made records (see the entries for them in appendix A). Desi Sr. died of lung cancer on December 2, 1986, at the age of 69. He has two stars on the Hollywood Walk of Fame—one for motion pictures and one for TV. His 1976 autobiography was simply called *A Book*.

CLIFF ARQUETTE (CHARLEY WEAVER)

Most Famous TV Role: occupied lower left square on *The Hollywood Squares*; **Network:** NBC; **Years:** 1965–1974; **Hit Recordings:** none; **Label:** Columbia; **Release Year:** 1959; **Matrix:** "Christmas in Mount Idy" (Columbia #41504); **Chart:** none

Cliff Arquette, alias Charley Weaver, was born in Toledo, Ohio, on December 28, 1905. By the time he was in his late teens, he was performing as a comic and pianist. After working extensively in radio, Arquette was seasoned in time for the advent of television. He appeared on numerous shows, including the live daily daytime sitcom *Dave and Charley* on NBC in 1952 (with longtime friend Dave Willock). He also had a several-season run on the prime-time NBC sitcom *The Dennis Day Show* from 1952 to 1954. His Charley Weaver character became a regular on Jack Paar's *The Tonight Show* between 1958 and 1962, and said character's popularity led to the release of a Columbia 45 rpm record for the holiday season in 1959—"Christmas in Mount Idy" backed with "Happy New Year, Happy." Mount Idy was the fictional "assisted living home for the elderly" in which Charley Weaver resided. As Charley Weaver, Arquette enjoyed a long and very visible run on NBC's original *Hollywood Squares* from 1965 to 1974. Charley occupied the lower left square and was joined by fellow regulars Wally Cox and Paul Lynde. Arquette suffered a serious stroke in 1973 and his square was filled by George Gobel. Arquette was able to return to the program, briefly, looking very frail. He died a short time later on September 23, 1974, leaving behind a talented Arquette family consisting of Rosanna, David, and Patricia.

JOHN ASHLEY

Most Famous TV Role: Clipper Hamilton on *Straightaway*; **Network:** ABC; **Years:** 1961–1962; **Hit Recording:** none; **Labels:** Capehart, Dot, Intro, Silver; **Release Years:** 1957–1962; **Matrix:** "Little Lou" (Capehart #5006), "Born to Rock" (Dot #15775), "Let the Good Times Roll" (Dot #15878), "The Hang Man" (Dot #15942), "Let Yourself Go Go Go" (Intro #6097), "Seriously in Love" (Silver #1002), "One Love" (Silver #1005); **Chart:** none

John Ashley was born John Atchley in Kansas City, Missouri, on Christmas Day in 1934. He was discovered by John Wayne while visiting a movie set, and a contract with American International Pictures followed. However, they typecast Ashley with juvenile delinquent roles in *Dragstrip Girl* and *Motorcycle Gang*. He made the transition to television, with guest-starring roles on *Frontier Doctor* and *The Beverly Hillbillies*, eventually garnering the costarring role of Clipper Hamilton on the ABC drama about a garage for race car drivers titled *Straightaway*. The program was originally to be called *The Racers*, but the program's sponsor, Autolite Spark Plugs (a division of Ford), wanted the racing aspect of the show to be deemphasized and the title was changed. Ashley, a rockabilly singer and guitarist, also got to perform a tune in each episode. Ashley's career slowed after *Straightaway* was cancelled in 1962, but he managed to resurrect his career making movies in the Philippines.

Upon returning to the United States years later, Ashley turned to producing, and among his credits are *Walker Texas Ranger* and *The A-Team*. Ashley was also the narrator on the latter. He was married three times and his first bride was fellow actor/singer Deborah Walley of *The Mothers-in-Law* (see the entry under her name). Ashley suffered a heart attack and died on a movie set on October 3, 1997, at the age of 63.

JOHN ASTIN

Most Famous TV Role: Gomez Addams on *The Addams Family*; **Network:** ABC; **Years:** 1964–1966; **Hit Recording:** none; **Label:** United Artists; **Release Year:** 1965; **Matrix:** "Wallflower Pete" (United Artists #942); **Chart:** none

John Astin was born in Baltimore, Maryland, on December 30, 1930. He majored in mathematics at Johns Hopkins University, but eventually followed his passion for the theater instead. A small role in *West Side Story* got his career in gear. In 1962, he was cast as one of the stars of the very funny but short-lived slapstick-laden ABC sitcom titled *I'm Dickens, He's Fenster*. His most famous TV role was as the eccentric Gomez Addams, patriarch of the creepy, spooky, and all-together ooky *Addams Family*. Many will be surprised to learn that the series only lasted two seasons on ABC, but has enjoyed a lucrative life in reruns. During the run of *The Addams Family*, Astin released one single for United Artists titled "Wallflower Pete" backed with "Querido Mia." Astin didn't really sing on the record; it was more of a recitation. Apparently United Artists had hopes of "Wallflower Pete" becoming a hit, and Astin lip-synched the song on several teen music programs, but it failed to chart. Astin continued to find recurring roles on television, but *The Phyllis Diller Show*, *Operation Petticoat*, and *Mary* all had very short runs. In recent years, Astin returned to his alma mater, Johns Hopkins, where he teaches method acting. He resides in the Baltimore area with his third wife, Valerie.

CHRISTOPHER ATKINS

Most Famous TV Role: Peter Richards on *Dallas*; **Network:** CBS; **Years:** 1982–1984; **Hit Recording:** "How Can I Live without Her?" **Label:** Polydor; **Release Year:** 1982; **Matrix:** Polydor #2210; **Chart:** #71 *Billboard* Hot 100

Christopher Atkins Bomann was born February 21, 1961, in Rye, New York. He was discovered while working as a lifeguard and was cast in one of his most famous movie roles as Richard Lestrange in the 1980 blockbuster titled *The Blue Lagoon*, for which he received a Golden Globe nomination. He is best known for his movie roles, but he did have a run as swimming instructor Peter Richards on the long-running CBS drama *Dallas* from 1982 to 1984. During this period, he also costarred with Kristy McNichol in *The Pirate Movie*. A song from that film—"How Can I Live without Her?"—was released as a single and cracked the Hot 100 in 1982. A follow-up release from the film, "First Love" backed with "Girl, You Really Got Me Goin'" (a duet with Kristy McNichol—Polydor #2217), failed to chart. Atkins and his *Blue Lagoon* costar Brooke Shields reunited briefly on her NBC sitcom *Suddenly Susan* in 1999.

DAN AYKROYD. *See* THE BLUES BROTHERS.

B

SCOTT BAIO

Most Famous TV Roles: Chachi Arcola on *Happy Days*, Charles on *Charles in Charge*; **Network:** ABC, CBS, syndicated; **Years:** 1977–1984, 1984–1990, respectively; **Hit Recording:** none; **Label:** RCA Victor; **Release Years:** 1982–1985; **Matrix:** "What Was in That Kiss?" (RCA Victor #13256), "Woman, I Love Only You" (RCA Victor #13356), "Some Girls" (RCA Victor #13553); **Chart:** none

Scott Vincent James Baio was born in Brooklyn, New York, on September 22, 1960. He became active as an actor at age 11. By the time he was 16, he scored a recurring role on *Happy Days* as the Fonz's cousin, Chachi Arcola. (By the way, the surname of Arcola was the street on which the program's creator, Garry Marshall, lived in Toluca Lake, California.) Baio was a cast member for seven seasons and also got a short-lived spinoff called *Joanie Loves Chachi*. During his *Happy Days* run, Baio was given a recording contract from RCA Victor Records. The record deal resulted in two LPs (*The Boys Are Out Tonight*—RCA Victor #4696 and *Scott Baio*—RCA Victor #8025) and three singles ("What Was in That Kiss?" backed with "Looking for the Right Girl," "Woman, I Love Only You" backed with "Wanted for Love," and "Some Girls" backed with "Heartbreaker"). The *Scott Baio* album peaked at number 181 on the charts. None of the singles reached the Hot 100, despite a push from the record label. Even though the recording career never took off, Baio remained busy in television on the popular *Charles in Charge, Diagnosis: Murder*, and most recently the Nick at Nite series titled *See Dad Run*. Baio and his wife, Renee, have one child.

PAMELA BAIRD

Most Famous TV Roles: Mary Ellen Rogers on *Leave It to Beaver*, Gloria on *The Danny Thomas Show*; **Network:** ABC; **Years:** 1959–1961, 1962, respectively; **Hit Recording:** none; **Label:** Dynasty; **Release Year:** 1960; **Matrix:** "My Second Date" (Dynasty #641); **Chart:** none

Pam Baird was born as Pamela Beaird in Bexar County, Texas, on April 6, 1945. Her acting career spanned 10 years, but was over before her 20th birthday. Her first recurring role was as Hildy Broeberg on *My Friend Flicka* during the 1955–1956 TV season. Then came a stint as Nancy, one of Kelly Gregg's friends from school on *Bachelor Father*. From there, she assumed the role of Wally Cleaver's main squeeze, Mary Ellen Rogers, on *Leave It to Beaver*. Pam's last name was sometimes listed as Baird and sometimes listed as Beaird. It was never consistent (neither was her first name—sometimes Pamela, sometimes Pam). On her lone 45 rpm record for the Dynasty label, affiliated with Imperial Records, she is listed as Pam Beaird. That record, "My Second Date" backed with "Oh Why?" was not a hit. She was a decent vocalist and possessed a rather mature voice for a 15-year-old. It's surprising that this was her only single release. After guest-starring roles on *Mr. Novak* and *Perry Mason* in 1964, Baird called it a career. She is married with five children and is now known as Pamela Beaird Hensley.

RONA BARRETT

Most Famous TV Role: gossip columnist on *Good Morning America* and *Entertainment Tonight*; **Networks:** ABC, syndicated; **Years:** 1975–1991; **Hit Recording:** none; **Label:** Miss Rona; **Release Year:** 1975; **Matrix:** *Miss Rona Sings Hollywood's Greatest Hits* (Miss Rona LP #1001); **Chart:** none

Rona Barrett was born Rona Burstein on October 8, 1936, in New York City. She was the president of the Eddie Fisher fan club as a teenager, and later worked with teen idols Frankie Avalon and Fabian as their manager's assistant. Always infatuated with show business folk, she began her gossip columnist career in the middle 1960s for KABC-TV in Los Angeles and parlayed her popularity into numerous TV specials, successful magazine columns, and eventually national exposure on *Good Morning, America* and *Entertainment Tonight*. Just as she was catching on, she released an album on her own Miss Rona label. That album, *Miss Rona Sings Hollywood's Greatest Hits*, was not a big hit, but did help with the necessary exposure to further her career. It proved to be her only recording and contained many standards, including "Over the Rainbow." She was also signed to work on Tom Snyder's popular late-night NBC series *The Tomorrow Show*, but a well-publicized feud with Snyder put the kibosh on that deal. Barrett penned numerous books in her heyday, including her autobiography titled *Miss Rona*. She also made a few guest appearances on episodic TV programs such as *Mannix* and *The Odd Couple*. She opted to retire to her ranch in California in 1991, and became devoted to nonprofit causes, including her own Rona Barrett Foundation, which aids the elderly. She was married to Bill Trowbridge for 28 years, until his passing in 2003. She then married Daniel Busby on Valentine's Day of 2008. She received her star on the Palm Springs Walk of Stars the following year.

CHUCK BARRIS

Most Famous TV Role: host of *The Gong Show*; **Network:** NBC; **Years:** 1976–1980; **Hit Recording:** none (however, Barris wrote "Palisades Park" for Freddy Cannon on Swan Records); **Labels:** Capitol, Dot, Gong Show, MCA, Swan; **Release Years:** 1962–1980; **Matrix:** "Palisades Park" (Swan #4106); **Chart:** #3 *Billboard* Hot 100

Charles Hirsch Barris was born in Philadelphia, Pennsylvania, on June 3, 1929. He began his long show business career as a page for NBC, and then worked behind the scenes on Dick Clark's *American Bandstand*. Barris, ever the multitasker, also took an interest in writing songs. He penned one called "Amusement Park" with Dion in mind. Dion never did record the song, but Barris's connections at *American Bandstand* helped him land the song with the local Swan Records label. Freddy "Boom Boom" Cannon was in need of a hit to get him back into the Top Ten, and "Amusement Park" became "Palisades Park" to cash in on the popularity of the New Jersey attraction of the same name. It became Cannon's third and final Top Ten single and became a timely hit during the summer of 1962. Barris attempted his own recording career in 1968. In that year, he released "Too Rich" backed with "I Know a Child" (Capitol #2536) and "Baja, California" backed with "Donnie" (Dot #17137). Neither single caused much excitement.

Proving to be a man of many varied talents, Barris achieved his greatest success when his focus turned to creating fun and memorable game shows beginning in the middle 1960s, such as *How's Your Mother-in-Law?*

The Dating Game, The Newlywed Game, and later *The New Treasure Hunt* and *The $1.98 Beauty Show.* He became a star when he opted to host his own off-kilter talent series titled *The Gong Show* from 1976 to 1980. During the show's run, Barris released two more singles—"Sometimes, It Just Don't Pay to Get Up" backed with "Why Me, Oh, Lord?" and one on his own Gong Show label called "The Theme from Gene Gene" (a running bit on *The Gong Show*) backed with "Lovee" (Gong Show #100). Just like his earlier recordings, they failed to chart. Barris's autobiography titled *Confessions of a Dangerous Mind,* in which he alleges that he was an assassin for the CIA, was brought to the silver screen by George Clooney in 2002. Attempts to revive *The Gong Show* have never equaled the popularity of the original.

GENE BARRY

Most Famous TV Roles: Bat Masterson on *Bat Masterson,* Amos Burke on *Burke's Law;* **Network:** NBC; **Years:** 1958–1961, 1963–1965, respectively; **Hit Recording:** none; **Labels:** Capitol, Felsted; **Release Years:** 1962–1976; **Matrix:** "Mountain Gambler" (Felsted #8648), "I Want the Whole World to Love Me" (Capitol #4330); **Chart:** none

Gene Barry was born as Eugene Klass in New York City on June 14, 1919. He was a violin virtuoso as a child. He began performing on Broadway in 1942 in *The New Moon.* After a run in numerous other Broadway shows, Barry made the smooth transition to television. His first recurring role was as Gene Talbot in the long-running Eve Arden sitcom, *Our Miss Brooks* in the middle 1950s. From there he scored starring roles in numerous TV series—*Bat Masterson* (ABC, 1958–1961), *Burke's Law* (ABC, 1963–1966), *The Name of the Game* (NBC, 1968–1971), *The Adventurer* (syndicated, 1972–1973), and a remake of *Burke's Law* (CBS, 1994–1995). While still filming *Bat Masterson,* in 1961 Barry recorded a single for the small Felsted Records label (#8648)—"Mountain Gambler" backed with "Red Silk Stockings and Green Perfume." He had been in a few musicals on Broadway, but the single was not a success. He tried again in 1976 for Capitol Records (#4330) with "I Want the Whole World to Love Me" backed with "Soon," but it, too, failed to catch on. In 1983, Barry got to be part of the *La Cage aux Folles* original cast soundtrack album (RCA Victor #4824). It garnered a gold record. Barry portrayed Georges in the show and was nominated for a Tony Award, but did not win. His wife of 58 years, Betty, died in 2003. Barry died on December 9, 2009, in Woodland Hills, California, at the age of 90, leaving behind two sons and a daughter.

JACK BARRY

Most Famous TV Roles: host of *Winky Dink and You, Juvenile Jury, Twenty One, High Low,* and *The Joker's Wild;* **Networks:** CBS, NBC, syndicated; **Years:** 1953–1984; **Hit Recording:** none; **Label:** Decca; **Release Year:** 1955; **Matrix:** "Winky Dink and You" (Decca #88174); **Chart:** none

Jack Barry was born Jack Barasch in Lindenhurst, New York, on March 20, 1918. He got his start in radio, and it was there he met his future game show partner, Dan Enright. With the advent of television, Barry hosted a couple of very popular children's programs—*Juvenile Jury* and *Winky Dink and You.* The latter show, likely TV's first interactive program, offered kids (for a price) a plastic see-through screen to be placed over the set. Kids could then use a felt-tip pen to draw and write on the screen. Many TV sets were ruined, however, by kids who didn't own that special screen, but wished to participate (to the chagrin of their parents). During the show's run, Jack Barry and Mae Questel released a couple of songs from the show on Decca 45 rpm singles—"Boola, Walla Winkle" (Decca #319) and the "Winky Dink and You" theme song (Decca #88174). Neither record made the charts, but almost everyone from that era knows all the words to the program's catchy theme.

Barry and Enright's next venture, game shows, started strongly. However, when it was discovered that answers were supplied to some of the contestants, Barry and Enright became embroiled in the infamous "quiz show scandal." Suddenly, immensely popular game shows such as *Twenty One, Tic Tac Dough,* and *Dotto* disappeared under a cloud of shame. Robert Redford directed an Oscar-nominated 1994 film called *Quiz Show* about these unsavory events in TV's history. Luckily for Barry and Enright, the public was quick to forget, and their return to television with *The Joker's Wild* and *Break the Bank* in the 1970s earned millions. Barry hosted *The Joker's Wild* from 1972 until his passing on May 2, 1984, and Bill Cullen took over until the program was cancelled in 1986.

JENNIFER BEALS

Most Famous TV Role: Perry Quinn on *2000 Malibu Road;* **Network:** CBS; **Year:** 1992; **Hit Recording:** none; **Label:** IRS/Capitol; **Release Year:** 1992; **Matrix:** "How Will I Know Him?" (IRS #13825); **Chart:** none

Jennifer Beals was born December 19, 1963, on the south side of Chicago, Illinois. Her father was African American and her mother was Irish. Her first job was as a soda jerk in an ice cream parlor. After discovering a passion for acting and appearing in numerous high school productions, she attended Yale University with a major in literature. She suspended her studies when she landed the lead role in *Flashdance*. After filming, she resumed her schooling. Refusing to disrupt her schooling yet again, she turned down a role in *St. Elmo's Fire*. After a part in *Vampire Kiss*, Beals moved to television and starred in CBS's short-lived *2000 Malibu Road* as a lawyer named Perry Quinn in 1992. At this same time, she released a single for the IRS/Capitol label (#13825) titled "How Would I Know Him?" backed with "One Girl in a Million." It wasn't a hit, and Beals went back to her day job, making movies, including *Devil in a Blue Dress*, *The Grudge 2*, and *The Book of Eli*. She also returned to television as Bette Porter in *The L Word* on Showtime. She has surfaced yet again on a web series titled *WIGS* in recent years. She is a practicing Buddhist and has been married twice—first to Alexandre Rockwell (1986–1996, ending in divorce) and then to Ken Dixon, to whom she is still married and with whom she has a daughter.

JOHN BELUSHI. *See* THE BLUES BROTHERS.

BARBI BENTON

Most Famous TV Role: a regular on *Hee Haw*; **Network:** syndicated; **Years:** 1971–1976; **Hit Recordings:** "Staying Power," "Brass Buckles"; **Label:** Playboy; **Release Year:** 1976; **Matrix:** "Staying Power" (Playboy #6078), "Brass Buckles" (Playboy #6032); **Chart:** #108 *Billboard* Bubbling Under, #5 Country, respectively

Barbi Benton was born Barbara Lynn Klein in New York City on January 28, 1950. She became a *Playboy* model and posed nude a couple of times beginning in 1970 and first appeared under her real name of Barbara Klein. She became a regular on the syndicated version of *Hee Haw* from 1971 to 1976. While appearing on the program, she also pursued a recording career for, appropriately, the Playboy Records label. She only reached number 108 on the Pop charts with "Staying Power" in 1976, but she fared better on the Country charts with "Brass Buckles" in 1975, reaching number 5. "Brass Buckles" is a coming-of-age song about a young girl who quickly outgrew brass buckles on her shoes and then found love. Benton composed many of her own songs, and one of them, "Ain't That Just the

Way" (Playboy #6056), became a big hit in Sweden. Her *Something New* album (Playboy LP #411) peaked at number 208.

Benton left *Hee Haw* in 1976 to pursue other opportunities and became one of the stars of the short-lived James Komack–produced ABC sitcom titled *Sugar Time*. The program, about a musical girl group, was supervised by composer Paul Williams and began with a trial run during the summer of 1977. It did well enough to be brought back for a second shot in the spring of 1978, but ratings were abysmal and it quickly disappeared from ABC's schedule. Benton's career hit a lull in the late 1970s, and an attempted comeback album titled *Kinetic Voyage* (Takoma #72876) in 1988 failed to catch on. She has been married to the same man, George Gradow, since 1979. They have two grown children—Alexander and Ariana. Benton and Gradow have homes in Aspen, Colorado, and Los Angeles, California. Benton has been in semiretirement since 1990.

CRYSTAL BERNARD

Most Famous TV Role: Helen Chapel on *Wings*; **Network:** NBC; **Years:** 1990–1997; **Hit Recording:** none; **Label:** River North; **Release Years:** 1996–1999; **Matrix:** *The Girl Next Door* (River North LP #1207), *Don't Touch Me There* (River North LP #1403); **Chart:** none

Crystal Lynn Bernard was born September 30, 1961, in Garland, Texas. Her dad was a Baptist televangelist, and she began singing gospel at a very early age. Her acting studies were split between the Alley Theatre and Baylor University. Her first recurring TV role was as waitress Amy Tompkins in the syndicated version of *It's a Living*. She then scored the role of the emotional and sarcastic airport lunch counter waitress and cello virtuoso Helen Chapel on NBC's *Wings* for seven seasons (1990–1997). During the show's run, Bernard recorded her first country album, *The Girl Next Door*, for the small River North label. It wasn't a big hit, nor was its sequel, titled *Don't Touch Me There*. She also wrote "If I Were Your Girl" for Paula Abdul's *Head over Heels* album, and sang a duet titled "Forever Tonight" with Chicago's Peter Cetera on his *One Clear Voice* album. This duet became her biggest hit single, cracking the Adult Contemporary Top Thirty in 1995.

Bernard's career hit quite a lull after the cancellation of *Wings*. A long-awaited sequel called *Forget Paris 2* costarring Bernard was in postproduction as of this writing. Crystal's older sister, Robyn Bernard, enjoyed a long run as Terry Brock on ABC's *General Hospital*.

JAMES BEST

Most Famous TV Role: Sheriff Roscoe P. Coltrane in *The Dukes of Hazzard*; **Network:** CBS; **Years:** 1979–1985; **Hit Recording:** none; **Label:** Scotti Brothers; **Release Year:** 1982; **Matrix:** "Flash" (Scotti Brothers #02957); **Chart:** none

James Best was born Jules Guy in Powderly, Kentucky, on July 26, 1926. His mother died when he was very young and he was put up for adoption. A family named Best, Essa and Armen, took him in (thus the name change). He appeared in dozens of motion pictures, mostly westerns, and guest starred on dozens upon dozens of episodic TV shows, but is best known for his long run as Sheriff Roscoe P. Coltrane on CBS's popular *Dukes of Hazzard* series. During the show's run, the sheriff acquired a basset hound named Flash—the subject of a 45 rpm record by Best released in 1982 on the Scotti Brothers label. That song called simply "Flash" was backed with another song related to the TV series, "The Ballad of General Lee" by Doug Kershaw. Best also took part in recording the album *The Dukes of Hazzard TV Cast Sings* (Scotti Brothers #37712). Best died on April 6, 2015. His autobiography, *Best in Hollywood: The Good, the Bad, and the Beautiful*, was published in 2009 by Bear Manor Media. He left behind his third wife, Dorothy (since 1986). Through marriage, he was related to Don Everly of the Everly Brothers and actor/singer Michael Damian.

JOEY BISHOP

Most Famous TV Roles: Joey Barnes on *The Joey Bishop Show* (sitcom), host of *The Joey Bishop Show* (talk show); **Networks:** ABC, CBS, NBC; **Years:** 1961–1965, 1967–1969, respectively; **Hit Recording:** none; **Label:** ABC; **Release Year:** 1968; **Matrix:** *Joey Bishop Sings Country and Western* (ABC LP #656); **Chart:** none

Joseph Abraham Gottlieb was born February 3, 1918, in the Bronx, New York, but raised in Philadelphia. Joseph became a sergeant in the army. After being discharged, he pursued stand-up comedy and worked the Borscht Belt. He eventually became a popular fill-in host for Johnny Carson on *The Tonight Show*. He also landed his own sitcom beginning in 1961 called *The Joey Bishop Show* (a spinoff of *The Danny Thomas Show*). In the first season, Bishop portrayed Joey Barnes, who still lived at home with his mother and sister (played by a young Marlo Thomas). In season 2, the format changed, and Joey Barnes was married to Abby Dalton and was now host of a popular late-night talk and variety show. That second format lasted for three years (two on NBC and one on CBS).

Bishop's sitcom may have been cancelled in 1965, but a short time later he became host of a real talk show similar to the one his Joey Barnes character had hosted. Up against Johnny Carson, *The Joey Bishop Show* consisted of a young Regis Philbin as Bishop's sidekick (see the entry for Philbin) and Johnny Mann as the bandleader (see the entry for Mann). During this show's run on ABC, Bishop was appropriately signed to ABC Records and released one LP titled *Joey Bishop Sings Country and Western*. Among the cuts—"Born to Lose," "Your Cheatin' Heart," "Cold, Cold Heart," "It Keeps Right on a Hurtin'," and "Take These Chains from My Heart." Bishop performed all of the tunes in his usual deadpan manner, but his picture on the cover in a baby blue cowboy outfit (including boots and a ten gallon hat) belies the serious tone of these cuts. The album was not a success, and there weren't any follow-ups. Bishop continued to perform on stage and numerous game shows into the late 1980s, and was the last surviving member of the legendary rat pack that also consisted of Frank Sinatra, Dean Martin, Sammy Davis Jr., and Peter Lawford. After years of failing health, Bishop died of heart failure on October 17, 2007, at the age of 89. His eponymous sitcom was most recently aired on the TV Land and Retro TV cable networks.

BILL BIXBY

Most Famous TV Roles: Tim O'Hara on *My Favorite Martian*, Tom Corbett on *The Courtship of Eddie's Father*, Dr. David Banner on *The Incredible Hulk*; **Networks:** ABC, CBS; **Years:** 1963–1966, 1969–1972, 1978–1982, respectively; **Hit Recording:** none; **Label:** MGM; **Release Year:** 1970; **Matrix:** "Best Friend" (MGM #14198); **Chart:** none

Bill Bixby was born Wilfred Bailey Everett Bixby III on January 22, 1934, in San Francisco, California. He attended the University of California, Berkeley, and later joined the U.S. Marine Corps. After being discharged, he moved to Hollywood to pursue a career as an actor and snagged numerous guest-starring roles on episodic TV sitcoms such as *Hennesey*, *The Many Loves of Dobie Gillis*, and *The Andy Griffith Show*. He then found a short-lived recurring role on *The Joey Bishop Show* as Charles Raymond

(1962) on NBC. A year later, he was starring in his own series on CBS titled *My Favorite Martian*, as newspaper reporter Tim O'Hara who shared an apartment with his "Uncle" Martin, the Martian. That series lasted three seasons, and Bixby then found work in two Elvis Presley films, *Clambake* and *Speedway*. He was offered a regular role on *That Girl* with Marlo Thomas (they had worked together earlier on *The Joey Bishop Show*), but he turned it down. Much like *My Favorite Martian*, his next venture—the TV version of the classic Glenn Ford film *The Courtship of Eddie's Father*—lasted three seasons. On this series, Bixby portrayed a widowed magazine publisher, caring for and raising his young son, Eddie, with the help of his housekeeper, Mrs. Livingston (Miyoshi Umeki—see the entry for her). The program's theme song was written and performed by Harry Nilsson, but in 1970 MGM released a version of that theme song called "Best Friend" as performed by Bill Bixby. The flip side, "Daddy What If?" was a duet between Bixby and his young costar Brandon Cruz (Eddie Corbett), and featured Eddie asking the kinds of life questions incorporated into the opening and closing of each episode of the series. The record was not a hit and no follow-ups were released. Years later, Cruz teamed up with a rock band called Doctor Who.

Bixby continued to find work in television—first as Anthony Blake on *The Magician* on NBC (1973–1974) and then as Dr. David Banner on *The Incredible Hulk* on CBS (1978–1982). Bixby and Brandon Cruz remained friends, and Cruz did a guest spot on *The Incredible Hulk*, and gave his own son the middle name of Bixby. After one more short-lived series, *Goodnight, Beantown* with costar Mariette Hartley on CBS (1983–1984), Bixby turned his attention to directing numerous episodes of ABC's *Sledge Hammer* and NBC's *Blossom*. He was married to actress Brenda Benet from 1971 to 1980 (she committed suicide the following year). Two other marriages (Laura Michaels and Judith Kliban) followed, both ending in divorce. In 1991, he was diagnosed with prostate cancer, and shortly after making his condition public in 1993, he collapsed on the set of *Blossom* and died on November 21, 1993, at the age of 59. A biopic about Bixby's life has long been bandied about, but as of this writing has never come to fruition.

HONOR BLACKMAN

Most Famous TV Role: Catherine Gale on *The Avengers*; **Network:** ABC (Associated British Corporation, London); **Years:** 1962–1964; **Hit Recording:** "Kinky Boots"; **Label:** Decca; **Release Year:** 1964; **Matrix:** Decca #11843; **Chart:** #5 BBC Radio 1 Music

Honor Blackman was born August 22, 1925, in Plaistow, West Ham, Essex, England. A gift of acting lessons for her 15th birthday changed her life. Blackman appeared in dozens of films throughout the 1940s and 1950s before making the transition to television. Her first series was the syndicated 1959 program called *The Four Just Men*, on which she portrayed Nicole. After the program's cancellation, Blackman landed the role of Catherine Gale on the original *Avengers* in the early 1960s. The program, which starred Patrick Macnee, began very differently than the 1966 version that aired on CBS. It was initially a live program on iTV in the United Kingdom. This version of the program wasn't shown in the United States for over two decades. These "lost" episodes were recently shown on the COZI TV network. During the show's initial run, Blackman and Macnee recorded a single for Decca Records called "Kinky Boots" (not related to the Broadway musical of same name) and it became an unexpected hit in England, reaching the Top Five on BBC Radio 1. In that same year, Blackman attained immortality as Pussy Galore in the James Bond classic titled *Goldfinger*. Blackman didn't release any other singles but did attempt solo success with an LP in 1968 for London Records (#3408). It was titled *Everything I've Got*, but it failed to match the success of its predecessor and she kept her main focus on her acting skills. She portrayed Veronica Barton in the short-lived series called *Never the Twain* (1981–1982) and Laura West in *The Upper Hand* (1990–1996). Blackman has been married and divorced twice, has two children by her second marriage, and nowadays prefers her own company.

THE BLUES BROTHERS

Most Famous TV Role: Jake (John Belushi) and Elwood (Dan Aykroyd) Blues on *Saturday Night Live*; **Network:** NBC; **Years:** 1975–1979; **Hit Recordings:** "Soul Man," "Gimme Some Lovin'"; **Label:** Atlantic; **Release Years:** 1978–1980; **Matrix:** "Soul Man" (Atlantic #3545), "Gimme Some Lovin'" (Atlantic #3785); **Chart:** #14, #18, respectively, *Billboard* Hot 100

Dan Aykroyd was born in Ottawa, Ontario, Canada, on July 1, 1952. He initially had interest in the ministry, but after a promising run in the Second City comedy troupe, his future was sealed. He gained fame quickly on television as one of the original cast members of *Saturday Night Live* on NBC, where he also served as the program's youngest writer. John Belushi was born in Chicago, Illinois, on January 24, 1949. The eldest of four children, he joined the Second City comedy troupe in the early 1970s, and from there rose quickly in the business. He became a sensation on

Saturday Night Live, and then his star shone even brighter in the wildly popular *National Lampoon's Animal House* in 1978. A recurring sketch on the TV program as the Blues Brothers led to a success on the silver screen and several hit records. Belushi and Aykroyd as Jake and Elwood Blues scored two Top Twenty national hits with remakes of 1960s classics "Soul Man" (originated by Sam and Dave) and "Gimme Some Lovin'" (originated by the Spencer Davis Group). Their *Briefcase Full of Blues* album (Atlantic LP #19217) reached number 1 and went platinum.

After a long list of motion picture successes, in 1997 Aykroyd returned to television in ABC's short-lived sitcom, coincidentally titled *Soul Man,* on which he portrayed Reverend Mike Weber, harkening back to his original career choice. In recent years, he has costarred in the musical biopics *Behind the Candelabra* about the final years of Liberace, and *Get on Up* about the "Godfather of Soul," James Brown. Aykroyd is also the cofounder and part owner of Crystal Head Vodka. Sadly, the whirlwind of talent known as John Belushi was silenced in Hollywood on March 5, 1982, after a combined dose of cocaine and heroin known as a speedball. Had he lived, he would have been one of the stars of *Ghostbusters.* He has a star on the Hollywood Walk of Fame.

DANNY BONADUCE

Most Famous TV Role: Danny Partridge on *The Partridge Family;* **Network:** ABC; **Years:** 1970–1974; **Hit Recording:** none; **Label:** Lion; **Release Years:** 1972–1973; **Matrix:** "Dreamland" (Lion #145), "I'll Be Your Magician" (Lion #151), *Danny Bonaduce* (Lion LP #1015); **Chart:** none

Danny Bonaduce was born August 13, 1959, in Broomall, Pennsylvania. Danny's dad, Joe Bonaduce, wrote scripts for countless TV sitcoms (many filmed for Screen Gems) and *may* have had some influence in his son becoming a regular on *The Partridge Family* in 1970. Bonaduce actually made his TV debut in an extremely short-lived Jerry Van Dyke sitcom titled *Accidental Family* in 1967 in an episode titled "Halloween's on Us." Even though Danny doesn't sing on any of the Partridge Family hits, he rode their pastel bus to fame during the show's four-season run. During that run, the Lion Records label attempted to cash in on the young man's popularity, and Bonaduce recorded an entire album of pop songs for them. The album was appropriately titled *Danny Bonaduce* and yielded two singles, neither of which garnered much attention—"Dreamland" in 1972 and "I'll Be Your Magician" in 1973.

One must grant Bonaduce a great deal of credit for being able to reinvent himself in adulthood as a radio personality (in Philadelphia, Seattle, and Detroit), a reality show star (*Breaking Bonaduce* and *I Know My Kid's a Star*), and a daytime TV talk show host (*The Danny Bonaduce Show* and *The Other Half*). There was also the very forgettable series, *Hulk Hogan's Celebrity Championship Wrestling*, on which Bonaduce was a major player. Like so many child stars of the era, Bonaduce battled years of drug addiction, arrests, and even homelessness, but managed to conquer his demons and successfully bounce back. On November 22, 2010, he took his third bride, Amy Railsbeck (23 years his junior). As of this writing, they are still together and have homes in Los Angeles and Seattle. Bonaduce's autobiography, *Random Acts of Badness*, was released in 2002.

RANDY BOONE

Most Famous TV Role: Randy Benton on *The Virginian*; **Network:** NBC; **Years:** 1964–1966; **Hit Recording:** none; **Labels:** Decca, Gregar, Just Good; **Release Years:** 1964–1967; **Matrix:** "Tennessee Stud" (Decca #31755), "It's So Hard to Tell Mama Goodbye" (Gregar #00105), "Let's Go Out Tonight" (Just Good #101); **Chart:** none

Clyde Randall Boone was born January 17, 1942, in Fayetteville, North Carolina. He played football in high school, but after graduation began to pursue a career in music. He got to play his guitar quite often as Vern Hodges in the short-lived 1963 NBC sitcom *It's a Man's World*, on which he and several friends lived aboard a houseboat named *The Elephant*. Quickly after the show's cancellation, Boone was thrust into the role of Randy Benton on the long-running NBC western called *The Virginian*—a weekly 90-minute program that ran for nine seasons. Boone stayed with the show for two seasons.

During that time, Boone also scored a recording contract with Decca Records, resulting in one single—"Tennessee Stud" backed with "Just Waitin'." He was also part of two Decca LPs—one, a solo album titled *Ramblin' Randy* (Decca #4663), and one a promotional vehicle for his TV show called *Singing Stars of the Virginian* (Decca #4619) with Roberta Shore (see the entry for her). After leaving *The Virginian*, Boone surfaced on yet another series—CBS's *Cimarron Strip*, another 90-minute western. Boone portrayed photographer Francis Wilde on the show, and his visibility on the program scored him yet another record deal—this time with Gregar Records. This resulted in one single—"Tennessee Stud" backed with "It's So Hard to Tell Mama Goodbye," and a couple of LPs—*Randy Boone Country* (Gregar #7001) and *Star of TV's Cimarron Strip* (Gregar #7005) in 1968. None of these releases sold especially well, and Boone (related to Pat and Debby Boone) tried one more time with a single on the Just Good label titled "Let's Go Out Tonight" backed with "Whiskey," but it had absolutely no impact.

After *Cimarron Strip* was cancelled and westerns began to disappear from prime time, Boone was relegated to being a guest star on episodic TV programs such as *Kolchak: The Night Stalker* and *Emergency!* He was inducted into the Fayetteville Music Hall of Fame in 2011. *The Virginian* frequently runs on classic cable TV channels such as COZI and MeTV.

WAYNE BRADY

Most Famous TV Role: host of *Let's Make a Deal*; **Network:** CBS; **Years:** 2009–present; **Hit Recording:** *A Long Time Coming*; **Label:** Peak; **Release Year:** 2009; **Matrix:** Peak LP #23066; **Chart:** #20 *Billboard* R&B Albums

Wayne Alphonso Brady was born June 2, 1972, in Columbus, Georgia, but grew up in Orlando, Florida, with his grandmother. Originally opting for a career in the military, Brady discovered a knack for improvisational comedy and performed in Orlando area improv groups before moving to Hollywood. He first came to the attention of the American public during his long run on the Drew Carey version of *Whose Line Is It Anyway?* This led to recurring roles on *Girlfriends* and *How I Met Your Mother*. Brady also had his own eponymous daytime talk show from 2002 to 2004. Since 2009, he has taken over as host of the classic TV game show *Let's Make a Deal*, originally emceed by Monty Hall. Brady has always done his share of singing on both *Whose Line Is it Anyway?* and *Let's Make a Deal*, and as a result got a record deal with Peak Records. His 2009 album, *A Long Time Coming*, reached the R&B Top Twenty. A new CD collection of songs released for Walt Disney Records in 2011 titled *Radio Wayne* was far less successful. Brady has been married and divorced twice, and is the father of a little girl from his second marriage named Maile Masako Brady. In 2014, Brady revealed that he was attempting to deal with recurring bouts of depression.

THE BRADY BUNCH

Most Famous TV Role: cast of *The Brady Bunch*; **Network:** ABC; **Years:** 1969–1974; **Biggest Hit Recording:** *Merry Christmas from the Brady Bunch*; **Labels:** MCA, Paramount; **Release Years:** 1971–1973; **Matrix:** Paramount LP #5026; **Chart:** #6 *Billboard* Top Pop Albums

The Brady Bunch in its original form aired on ABC from September 26, 1969, to March 8, 1974. The program starred Florence Henderson as Carol Brady, Robert Reed as Mike Brady, Maureen McCormick as Marcia, Eve Plumb as Jan, Susan Olsen as Cindy, Barry Williams as Greg, Christopher Knight as Peter, Mike Lookinland as Bobby, and Ann B. Davis as Alice. The program spent its entire prime-time run on Friday nights and was never a ratings bonanza—it never finished in the Top Thirty for any of its five seasons, yet managed to get renewed year after year. During the show's run, the cast recorded several albums for Paramount Records—a division of Paramount Studios that produced the program. The most successful of these was the Christmas album released late in 1971 titled *Merry Christmas from the Brady Bunch*. Among the tracks on the Christmas LP are "The First Noel," "Jingle Bells," "Silver Bells," "Silent Night," "Frosty the Snowman," "Rudolph the Red-Nosed Reindeer," "Santa Claus Is Coming to Town," and "We Wish You a Merry Christmas." A follow-up album called *Meet the Brady Bunch* charted as well, but peaked at number 108. There was also *Kids from the Brady Bunch* (Paramount LP #6037) and *Phonographic Album* (Paramount LP #6058). None of the other albums cracked the 200 Top Pop Albums. All six kids participated, but none of the adults. The kids also performed the show's theme song during seasons 2–5.

After the original show ended in March of 1974, its 117 episodes enjoyed a very healthy run in syndication. The show was so popular in reruns that several attempts were made to recapture the magic in revivals such as *The Brady Brides*, *The Brady Bunch Hour*, *The Brady Kids*, and *The Bradys*. All of them failed. There have also been numerous TV reunions and even a motion picture, starring Shelley Long and Gary Cole as Carol and Mike Brady, respectively. The only awards the program has ever won were part of the yearly *TV Land Awards* broadcasts, including "Favorite Made-for-TV Maid," "Favorite Guest Appearance by a Musician" (Davy Jones), and "Favorite TV Food" (pork chops and applesauce). Additionally, Barry Williams released a single in 1970 called "Sunny" backed with "Sweet Sweetheart" (Paramount #0122), and Christopher Knight released two singles for the label in 1972—"Over and Over" backed with "Good for Each Other" (Paramount #0177) and "Little Bird" backed with

"Just Singin' Alone" (Paramount #0292—a duet with Maureen McCormick). Chris and Maureen also recorded an album of duets called *Chris Knight and Maureen McCormick* for Paramount (#6062) in 1973. Even Mike Lookinland took a solo shot. He released one single in 1973 for Capitol Records (#3914) titled "Love Doesn't Care Who's in It" backed with "Gum Drop." Much like his costars, he failed to catch on as a recording artist.

BRANDY

Most Famous TV Role: Moesha Mitchell on *Moesha*; **Network:** UPN; **Years:** 1996–2001; **#1 Hit Recordings:** "The Boy Is Mine" (with Monica), "Have You Ever?"; **Label:** Atlantic; **Release Year:** 1998; **Matrix:** "The Boy Is Mine" (Atlantic #84089), "Have You Ever?" (Atlantic #84198), **Chart:** both #1 *Billboard* Hot 100

Brandy Norwood was born February 11, 1979, in McComb, Mississippi (but raised in Southern California). An affinity for the performing arts was encouraged beginning at a young age, and by 14 Brandy scored her first recurring role on the single season ABC sitcom called *Thea*. It was during the run of that series, on which Brandy portrayed Thea Vidale's daughter Danesha, that she had her first Top Ten hit for the Atlantic Records label, "I Wanna Be Down" (Atlantic #87225). A short time later, the upstart UPN TV network granted young Brandy her very own series titled *Moesha*, and it enjoyed a successful five-season run. The TV exposure greatly enhanced her visibility, and Brandy landed five singles in the Top Twenty. Her biggest hit, the Grammy-winning multiplatinum "The Boy Is Mine," was a duet with Monica that stayed at number 1 for an impressive thirteen weeks. Brandy hit number 1 yet again on her own a short time later with "Have You Ever?" This multitasker also conquered the silver screen with the role of Karla Wilson in *I Still Know What You Did Last Summer* (1998). In the new millennium, she made the transition to reality TV and served as a celebrity judge on *America's Got Talent* (2006), and had a nice run on the 2010 edition of *Dancing with the Stars*, but didn't win the competition. She also joined the cast of BET's sitcom *The Game* in the recurring role of a bartender in 2012. After a couple of less-than-successful albums on the Epic Records label, Brandy signed with Chameleon Records and, as of this writing, was working on a new comeback CD.

The *Real McCoys* boy, Walter Brennan, harvested a few hit singles.

WALTER BRENNAN

Most Famous TV Role: Amos McCoy on *The Real McCoys*; **Networks:** ABC, CBS; **Years:** 1957–1963; **Hit Recording:** "Old Rivers"; **Label:** Liberty; **Release Year:** 1962; **Matrix:** Liberty #55436; **Chart:** #5 *Billboard* Hot 100

Walter Andrew Brennan was born July 25, 1894, in Lynn, Massachusetts. He discovered an interest in performing at an early age, and by his 15th birthday was on stage in vaudeville. He served in the U.S. Army during World War I, and afterward made a fortune in the real estate market, only to lose it all during the Depression. At that point, he began taking any small movie roles he could find. He became proficient at his craft very quickly, and garnered three Best Supporting Actor Oscars between 1936 and 1940. He was especially adept at playing elderly characters—a talent that served him extremely well when he made the move to television in 1957 as the star of the ABC sitcom *The Real McCoys*. On the program, Brennan portrayed the stubborn grandfather of the McCoy clan consisting of grandson Luke (Richard Crenna) and Luke's wife, Kate (Kathy Nolan). After five seasons on ABC, the series spent its final season on CBS. In those latter episodes, Luke was a widower who had started dating again.

During the run of *The Real McCoys*, Brennan scored a recording contract with Dot, and then Liberty Records. While with Liberty, he scored a surprise Top Five hit titled "Old Rivers." The song was narrated rather than sung and told the story of an old, very diligent worker on a farm. The narrator reflects upon the passing of the old man, fond memories of the old guy, and faith in the afterlife. It proved to be Brennan's only major hit, although two other singles, "Dutchman's Gold" (Dot #16066) and "Mama Sang a Song" (Liberty #55508), cracked the Top Forty. A short time after the cancellation of *The Real McCoys*, Brennan starred in another series, a single-season ABC sitcom called *The Tycoon*. On the series, Brennan portrayed Walter Andrews, the stubborn millionaire chairman of the board of the Thunder Corporation. He attempted success in an ABC western next—*The Guns of Will Sonnett*, again on ABC where it ran for two seasons—and he rounded out his TV work as a regular on season two of the CBS John Forsythe sitcom *To Rome with Love*. Brennan has a star on the Hollywood Walk of Fame. He was married to the same woman, Ruth Wells, for 54 years. They had three children together. Brennan died of emphysema on September 21, 1974, at the age of 80. As of this writing, *The Real McCoys* runs five days a week on the COZI cable TV channel.

JAMES BROLIN

Most Famous TV Role: Dr. Stephen Kiley on *Marcus Welby, M.D.*; **Network:** ABC; **Years:** 1969–1976; **Hit Recording:** none; **Label:** Artco; **Release Year:** 1974; **Matrix:** "California on My Mind" (Artco #5011), *James Brolin Sings* (Artco LP #1099); **Chart:** none

James Brolin was born as Craig Kenneth Bruderlin on July 18, 1940, in Los Angeles, California. He was inspired by longtime childhood friend Ryan O'Neal to become an actor. His early credits on episodic TV were mostly for drama shows such as *Voyage to the Bottom of the Sea* and *Twelve*

Hopefully California wasn't on James Brolin's mind while in the operating room on *Marcus Welby, M.D.*

O'Clock High, but he also made a visit to *The Patty Duke Show* as the new neighbor with whom both Patty and Cathy were infatuated. His first recurring role came on the short-lived 1966 ABC series called *The Monroes,* on which he portrayed Dalton Wales. He also secured a movie contract with 20th Century Fox, but none of the motion pictures in which he appeared became hits and his contract was not renewed. This proved to be a lucky break, because he then signed at Universal Studios, and was almost immediately cast in the role of Dr. Stephen Kiley on Robert Young's new ABC drama series, *Marcus Welby, M.D.* The series had a seven-season run and established Brolin as a star and a heartthrob. Smack dab in the middle of the program's reign on the Tuesday night schedule, Brolin recorded a single for the Artco Records label—"California on My Mind" backed with "Rodeo Rider." It wasn't a hit, but an entire album titled *James Brolin Sings* was released by the label (Artco #1099). Brolin's singing career never did take off, but he didn't much care, as he was about to embark on another long TV run as Peter McDermott on ABC's *Hotel* from 1983 to 1988. Brolin has been married three times and has three children. Famous acting son Josh Brolin is from James's first marriage to Jane Cameron Agee. After Jane came actress Jan Smithers (1986–1995) and Barbra Streisand (since 1998). James is the grandfather of two.

JAMES E. BROWN

Most Famous TV Role: Lieutenant Rip Masters on *The Adventures of Rin Tin Tin*; **Network:** ABC; **Years:** 1954–1959; **Hit Recording:** none; **Label:** MGM; **Release Years:** 1955–1957; **Matrix:** "Ballad of Davy Crockett" (MGM #11941), "The Berry Tree" (MGM #11987), "The Man from Laramie" (MGM #12011), "Ghost Town" (MGM #12350), "Wagon Train" (MGM #12384); **Chart:** none

James E. Brown, not to be confused with "the Godfather of Soul," was born in Desdemona, Texas, on March 22, 1920. Brown almost pursued a career as a professional tennis player until the acting bug hit him, and bit him hard. By the time he reached his 20s, he found steady work in motion pictures, including the classic *Going My Way* with Bing Crosby. With the advent of television, he smoothly made the transition to the small screen and his most famous role of Lieutenant Rip Masters on ABC's *The Adventures of Rin Tin Tin*—the tale of a boy and his German shepherd. During the run of the series, Brown recorded numerous singles for MGM between 1955 and 1957. All of his singles had a country flair ("The Man from Laramie," "Ghost Town," "Wagon Train"), but none of them caught on, despite the popularity of his TV series. When the series ended, Brown stayed busy with countless guest appearances on episodic TV shows such as *The Virginian, Laramie,* and *Daniel Boone.* He found a recurring role as Luke on ABC's short-lived western sitcom called *The Rounders* in 1966. He remained very visible in the 1980s with a long list of guest shots on *Dallas* as police detective Harry McSween. Only a short time after his final guest appearance on an episode of *Murder She Wrote,* Brown died of lung cancer on April 11, 1992, in Woodland Hills, California.

PETER BROWN

Most Famous TV Role: Deputy Johnny McKay on *Lawman;* **Network:** ABC; **Years:** 1958–1962; **Hit Recording:** none; **Label:** Warner Bros.; **Release Year:** 1959; **Matrix:** *We Wish You a Merry Christmas* (Warner Bros. LP #1337); **Chart:** none

Many will be amazed to know that Peter Brown's real name is Pierre Lind de Lappe. He was born October 5, 1935. His mother, Mina, was a radio actress on the *Terry and the Pirates* program. While in the army, Peter Brown became interested in pursuing a career in the performing arts after receiving a great response while entertaining the troops. His lucky break came when he met one of the Warner brothers at a filling station, leading to an audition and a role (Deputy Johnny McKay) in the long-running western titled *Lawman* on ABC.

During the late 1950s and early 1960s, Warner Bros. Studios capitalized on the popularity of their TV programs by having cast members release recorded material on their Warner Bros. label. Some of these stars, such as Connie Stevens and Edd Byrnes, had big hit singles as a result. Peter Brown wasn't quite so lucky, and his only release for the label was as part of a seasonal album titled *We Wish You a Merry Christmas* (Warner Bros. #1337). Brown was not very disappointed that his recording career didn't jell because he found more TV work after the cancellation of *Lawman* on series such as *Laramie, The Bold and the Beautiful,* and *Days of Our Lives.* Brown has been married five times and has two sons named Matt and Josh. He is not to be confused with the Peter Brown who had a disco hit with "Dance with Me" in 1978.

EDGAR BUCHANAN

Most Famous TV Role: Uncle Joe Carson on *Petticoat Junction;* **Network:** CBS; **Years:** 1963–1970; **Hit Recording:** none; **Label:** Dot; **Release Year:** 1967; **Matrix:** "Phantom 309" (Dot #17047); **Chart:** none

William Edgar Buchanan was born in Humansville, Missouri, on March 20, 1903. He studied dentistry like his father, and the family moved to Southern California in the 1930s, along with the dental practice. Buchanan caught the acting bug while there, and appeared in his first film when he was almost 40. He most often portrayed characters much older than his actual age. After a series of films such as *Cheaper by the Dozen* and *McClintock*, and then an enviable list of episodic TV credits on *Leave It to Beaver, Route 66, Twilight Zone, The Rifleman, Maverick,* and *Bringing up Buddy*, Edgar got to costar in what became a seven-season sitcom run on *Petticoat Junction* as Uncle Joe Carson (who moved kind of slow at the junction). Upon the passing of the program's star, Bea Benaderet, Buchanan became the show's main focus (until June Lockhart was added to the cast). During the run of the program, Buchanan recorded one 45 rpm record on the Dot Records label—"Phantom 309" backed with "Cotton Picker" in 1967. It's actually more of a recitation, in the manner of "Old Rivers" by Walter Brennan. The record was not a hit and there weren't any follow-up singles.

After the cancellation of *Petticoat Junction*, Buchanan was quickly cast in another CBS series—a western starring Glenn Ford called *Cade's County*. Despite the star power, the show only lasted one season. One of Buchanan's final roles, the blockbuster hit *Benji*, reunited him with one of his costars from *Petticoat Junction*—Higgins (who portrayed Dawg on the TV series and became the top dog in the motion picture). The dog was trained by Frank Inn, who also worked with Arnold the pig on *Green Acres*. Buchanan was married to the same woman, Mildred, for 51 years. They had one son together. Buchanan died of a stroke in Palm Desert, California, on April 4, 1979, at the age of 76. (See the entries for Rufe Davis, Gunilla Hutton, Meredith MacRae, Mike Minor, and Pat Woodell).

JULIE BUDD

Most Famous TV Role: Regular on *Showcase '68;* **Network:** NBC; **Year:** 1968; **Hit Recording:** "One Fine Day"; **Label:** Tom Cat; **Release Year:** 1976; **Matrix:** Tom Cat #10454; **Chart:** #93 *Billboard* Hot 100

Julie Budd was born as Edith Erdman on May 4, 1954, in New York City. Much like Judy Garland, Brenda Lee, Wayne Newton, Stevie Wonder, and Michael Jackson, her incredible voice and talent became evident at a very young age. Budd recalled,

As a child I was inspired by the great Julie Andrews (I loved everything about her), and while entering a talent show in the Catskills, I was fortunate to meet Herb Bernstein, who became my mentor and producer, and whom after all these years, still remains my conductor. As a producer and orchestrator, Herb has had hits with Laura Nyro, Tina Turner, the Four Seasons, and many other gifted and noted artists. While Herb was also producing Merv Griffin's new album, Herb took that opportunity to have me there at that session, and on one of the breaks, had Merv listen to me sing. Immediately, Merv took a real liking to me and wanted me on his show right away. I was only twelve, and all of this was very exciting. Merv had just one problem with me. He thought that my name, Edith, sounded too old, and Edie was too associated with Gorme and Adams. The name Julie Budd was inspired by a terrific and talented man who worked for Herb named Bud Julius Rehak (he composed "Navy Blue" for Diane Renay, was extremely gifted, and I adored him). Two days later, I was on *The Merv Griffin Show*, and my new life began.

In 1968, Budd released her first LP, *Child of Plenty*, on the MGM label (#4545). That same year, she became a regular on the NBC TV series titled *Showcase '68*, saying,

> That was a crazy time. The show was hosted by Lloyd Thaxton. Sly and the Family Stone, the Chambers Brothers, the American Breed, Andrea Marcovicci, and I, were all finalists on the show. Andrea and I became great lifelong friends. And we shared the journey. We were all sent to Ohio for the "Final Concert." It was so hot, and we worked our brains out. Plus, the performances were all outdoors. We were there for an entire week. Finally, out of nowhere, Sly Stone and his band flew in late and walked away with the award. What an experience! But looking back, it was great fun. Think about it. . . .That's what you do when you're starting out—you pay your dues, and learn how to perform. I knew that I was so lucky to be there.

Sadly, TV variety shows are a thing of the past. Budd reflected, "When I was getting started, there were so many great ones. There was a place for everyone to work, famous, or not-so-famous. There was all kinds of variety entertainment. And, I was so fortunate and worked with great legends. I learned from the best. Among the highlights—of course, Merv Griffin, Johnny Carson (who was beyond wonderful to me), Ed Sullivan (loved him), Carol Burnett (a total lady and great pro), and the terrific Jim Nabors (more gifted than so many have given him credit for, and a true sweetheart)."

Regarding the films *The Devil and Max Devlin* and *Two Lovers*, Budd said, "Having the opportunity to work for the Disney Company was a life changer for me. At Disney, they always do it right. I met Marvin Hamlisch while working on *The Devil and Max Devlin*, and continued working with him for the next thirty years. On *Two Lovers*, I worked with the brilliant and very original director James Gray. We had an outstanding cast, and it was a tremendous learning experience—the kind that lives with you forever."

One of her biggest hit singles was a cover version of the Chiffons' "One Fine Day," and Budd added, "I was so young at the time. And I was mostly associated with standards and music that was very dramatic and orchestrated. This was an attempt to record material that was more contemporary. And it really paid off, too! I also hit the disco charts with that song, and that was a real thrill for me." However, recently when asked to pick her favorite recording, Budd said, "I recorded so many songs that have meant a lot to me, but there is one which stands out as very special. It's on my *If You Could See Me Now* CD. Herb Bernstein wrote it, and it's called, 'When a Piano Plays.' I love that recording."

Never one to slow down, Budd shared, "I'm in the studio right now recording my new CD. I know that a lot of people say this about new projects, but I believe it to be my best work. And I'm so excited about it. I am also very busy working on my new book as well. It's a process that has taken forever, but I keep changing those chapters. What can I say? It just has to be right, and you always know when it's right."

JOYCE BULIFANT

Most Famous TV Role: Mrs. Murray Slaughter on *The Mary Tyler Moore Show*; **Network:** CBS; **Years:** 1971–1977; **Hit Recording:** none; **Label:** Edge; **Release Year:** 1975; **Matrix:** "Why's My Daddy Gone?" (Edge #108); **Chart:** none

Perpetually perky Joyce Bulifant, besides a very memorable role in the motion picture comedy classic *Airplane* and frequent guest appearances on the 1970s incarnation of *The Match Game*, has long been a familiar TV presence on sitcoms such as *Tom, Dick and Mary*, *The Bill Cosby Show*, *Love Thy Neighbor*, and *The Mary Tyler Moore Show* (as Murray's wife, Marie Slaughter). In 1975, she also released a 45 rpm record on the Edge Records label (#108) with a country feel to it. Bulifant remembered, "It was a song that I wrote called 'Why's My Daddy Gone?' A guy named Barry Adems is listed as cowriter of the song because he helped me with the music. It was such fun recording it, and going on the road where I was interviewed by numerous DJs. But, if people wanted to buy it, they were not able to because the distributor went out of business. That's show biz."

Today, Bulifant is married to seasoned actor Roger Perry, lives in the Palm Springs area, and as of this writing is involved in a big project. Bulifant elaborated, "I have written over 100 pages of my autobiography, tentatively to be called *My Four Hollywood Husbands*." In fact, one of the four, actor James MacArthur, also made a 45 rpm record titled "The Ten Commandments of Love" (see the entry under his name).

GARY BURGHOFF

Most Famous TV Role: Corporal Walter "Radar" O'Reilly on *M*A*S*H*;
Network: CBS; **Years:** 1972–1979; **Hit Recording:** none; **Label:** Shalom; **Release Year:** 1977; **Matrix:** *Just for Fun* (Shalom LP #651); **Chart:** none

Gary Burghoff was born May 24, 1943, in Bristol, Connecticut. He took up the drums as a young man, as well as tap dancing. He was the first Charlie Brown in the original Broadway production of *You're a Good Man, Charlie Brown* in 1967. He also performed in nightclubs with a band called the Relatives. His biggest break came when he was cast as Radar O'Reilly in the motion picture version of *M*A*S*H*, and then in the long-running TV series of the same name. In 1977, during the show's run, he released an LP of jazz music and old standards for the Shalom label. Backed by the Mardi Gras Celebration Jazz Band, the album was recorded in New Orleans and was appropriately titled *Just for Fun*. There was also one unsuccessful single for the Showcase Records label at the same time titled "Rainbow" backed with "As I Am" (Showcase #401). Burghoff won one Emmy for the show, and stayed until 1979. An attempt at a spinoff series titled *W*A*L*T*E*R* never got past the pilot stage. That pilot aired in the eastern and central time zones, but was preempted on the West Coast for the Democratic National Convention on July 17, 1984. Burghoff remained visible with frequent guest shots on celebrity game shows such as *The Match Game*, *$20,000 Pyramid*, and *Tattletales*, as well as a series of BP Gasoline commercials. He is an avid fisherman and stamp collector. He's been married twice with one child from his first and two from his second. Both marriages ended in divorce.

CHRIS BURKE

Most Famous TV Role: Corky on *Life Goes On*; **Network:** ABC; **Years:** 1989–1993; **Hit Recording:** none; **Label:** BMG; **Release Years:** 1990–1992; **Matrix:** *Forever Friends* (BMG CD #000008MO8); **Chart:** none

Christopher Joseph Burke was born with Down syndrome August 26, 1965, in Point Lookout, New York. His parents were urged to institutionalize him, but they opted to raise him at home and encourage his talents. After his schooling, he found work as an elevator operator. He took an interest in acting and began attending auditions, earning his first role in the ABC TV movie *Desperate* in 1987. He so impressed the powers-that-be at ABC that he was then cast in the role of Corky Thatcher in 1989 on the new series titled *Life Goes On*. The program featured the Beatles song "Ob-La-Di, Ob-La-Da" as its theme, and Burke stayed with the show for its entire four-season run. He was nominated for a Golden Globe for his work on the show, but did not win. After the program was cancelled, Burke stayed busy in episodic TV, and cowrote his own autobiography titled *A Special Kind of Hero* in 1991. Burke is also a member of the band Forever Friends (with Joe and John DeMasi) and recorded an album of songs for BMG Music, including the signature song titled "Celebrate" (not to be confused with the Three Dog Night classic). All of the songs on the album are very upbeat, positive, and fun.

CAROL BURNETT

Most Famous TV Role: star of *The Carol Burnett Show*; **Network:** CBS; **Years:** 1967–1978; **Hit Recording:** "I Made a Fool of Myself over John Foster Dulles"; **Label:** ABC-Paramount; **Release Year:** 1957; **Matrix:** ABC-Paramount #9850; **Chart:** none

Carol Creighton Burnett was born in San Antonio, Texas, on April 26, 1933. Her parents divorced while she was still very young and she was sent to live with her grandmother. Her first job in the theater was as an usherette in Hollywood. She then caught the acting bug while performing in school plays. She secured a few minor roles on television, and while collecting unemployment, which was $36 a week at the time, she got a call to read for a part in a new Max Liebman live sitcom on NBC called *Stanley*. The sitcom starred Buddy Hackett, and they were seeking a girlfriend for Buddy on the series. Burnett won the role of Celia Howard and was on her way to stardom. The show's ratings weren't very good, and several "plants" were placed in the audience—paid laughers to make the program appear to be funnier than it was. The ploy didn't work and the live sitcom only lasted one season, despite having staff writers such as Neil Simon and Woody Allen. Burnett then got to record for ABC-Paramount Records, and even though it didn't make the charts, one of her singles garnered a lot of attention. Burnett shared,

> It was called "I Made a Fool of Myself over John Foster Dulles." Dulles was the secretary of state at the time and lived up to his last name. He was a dull guy—very dour. It seemed as though he never smiled. Well, at the time,

A treasured, autographed photo of the singer of "I Made a Fool of Myself over John Foster Dulles," Carol Burnett.

Elvis Presley was all the rage, and young girls were swooning over him. Composer/writer Ken Welch came up with the idea of having me perform a song in which I swooned over Dulles. By the way, Welch has gone on to win five Emmy Awards. At that time, I was performing stand-up at the Blue Angel in New York City. I wasn't especially comfortable doing stand-up, but Ken's hilarious song made for a great opening for my act. When I first heard it I couldn't stop laughing. The song began getting a lot of attention and Jack Paar wanted me to sing it on his program. I jumped at the opportunity, and it went over extremely well. In fact, a member of Dulles's staff, a gentleman named David Waters called and asked if I might perform it again on Paar's show and again I obliged. That led to my being asked to sing it on *The Ed Sullivan Show*. The Sullivan clip, by the way, is posted on YouTube. The following Sunday, Dulles was a guest on *Meet the Press* and he was asked what he thought about my song. That very staid and dour man suddenly developed a twinkle in his eye and a half smile and said, "I make it a policy never to discuss matters of the heart in public." It was a wonderful and memorable moment in my life.

A comedic song called "Puppy Love," complete with Carol barking, howling, and panting, was placed on the flip. Burnett added, "Ken Welch wrote that one for me, too."

Garry Moore took notice of Burnett's unparalleled comedic talents and snagged her to be a regular on *The Garry Moore Show*. At this same time she found success on Broadway in *Once upon a Mattress*. While on Moore's variety show, Carol recorded a few singles for Decca Records—"Ten Cents a Dance" backed with "Happiness Is a Thing Called Joe" (Decca #25527) and "Sweet Georgia Brown" backed with "Nobody" (Decca #25594). After leaving Moore's show in 1962, Carol's soundtrack album from her two woman show with Julie Andrews called *Julie and Carol at Carnegie Hall* (Columbia LP #2240) made *Billboard*'s Top Pop Album chart. Burnett said, "Julie and I are attempting to get our three TV specials released on a DVD box set. One was in black-and-white and two were in color. The hardest part is getting clearance for the music."

Burnett was also a cast member on a series called *The Entertainers* on CBS in 1964. When *The Entertainers* was cancelled, Burnett still had the option on her contract with CBS for another series. She wanted to do a variety show. Reportedly CBS wasn't initially too keen on the idea, but the results proved to be legendary and epic. *The Carol Burnett Show* became a sensation and had an 11-year run. The program is best remembered for its comedy sketches, but Burnett and her musical guests did sing often on the program. After the program left prime time, its comedy sketches were repackaged for syndication as half-hour shows and called *Carol and Friends*. Burnett surprised many with a much lauded serious role in the TV movie *Friendly Fire* in 1980. She returned to series television in a recurring role as Theresa Stemple, portraying Helen Hunt's mother on NBC's *Mad about You*. Carol wrote her memoirs in 2010, and they were appropriately titled *This Time Together*—lyrics from the song with which she closed her long-running weekly variety series. She has won six Emmys and two Golden Globes, and has a star on the Hollywood Walk of Fame. This sweet, kind, and generous lady was deservedly honored by the Kennedy Center in 2003.

SMILEY BURNETTE. *See* RUFE DAVIS AND SMILEY BURNETTE.

RONNIE BURNS

Most Famous TV Role: himself on *The George Burns and Gracie Allen Show* and *The George Burns Show*; **Network:** CBS, NBC; **Years:** 1955–1959; **Hit Recording:** none; **Label:** Verve; **Release Year:** 1958; **Matrix:** "Kinda Cute" (Verve #10125); **Chart:** none

Ronnie Burns performed his new 45 on the debut episode of *The George Burns Show* in 1958.

Ronald Jon Burns was born July 9, 1935, in Evanston, Illinois. He was adopted by very famous parents, George Burns and Gracie Allen, at the age of two months and took on the surname of Burns. They had already adopted a girl, Sandra Jean, a while earlier. Ronnie joined his parents' sitcom at the age of 17 and portrayed himself. When Gracie retired because of health reasons in 1958, George ventured out on his own in *The George Burns Show* on NBC. It began as a sitcom with all the same players as *The George Burns and Gracie Allen Show*—that is, except for Gracie. This new program was not a ratings winner, and George Burns changed to a variety show format midseason. This change lasted seven weeks, and then suddenly *The George Burns Show* was once again a sitcom. All versions of the series failed to attract a large audience, and the program was cancelled after a truncated first season. On the debut episode of *The George Burns Show*, Ronnie Burns had the opportunity to lip-synch along with his brand new 45 release on the Verve Records label—"Kinda Cute" backed with "Double Date." One of his background singers in the episode was a very young Joby Baker, later one of the stars of CBS's *Good Morning, World* sitcom in 1967.

Ronnie Burns was following in the footsteps of Ricky Nelson, who had his first two out of a long, long string of hits with Verve Records. However, Burns was not quite as fortunate, and that lone 45 rpm release failed to make a big splash. Any notions of a follow-up single were quickly tabled. A short time later, Burns got to star in his own sitcom on NBC called *Happy*. Set in Palm Springs, the program allowed us to hear the thoughts of his new baby nicknamed Happy. The show was able to hang on by its fingertips and was invited back for a truncated second season before disappearing forever. After *Happy* was cancelled, Burns made very few public appearances. After a lengthy retirement, Ronnie died of cancer on November 14, 2007, at the age of 72, leaving behind Janice, his wife; three children; and six grandchildren. (See the entry in appendix A for George Burns.)

RED BUTTONS

Most Famous TV Role: host of *The Red Buttons Show*; **Networks:** CBS, NBC; **Years:** 1952–1955; **Hit Recording:** "Strange Things Are Happening (the Ho Ho Song)"; **Label:** Columbia; **Release Year:** 1953; **Matrix:** Columbia #39981; **Chart:** #9 *Billboard* Hot 100

Red Buttons was born Aaron Chwatt on February 5, 1919, in New York City. He realized his lot in life was to entertain while still a child, and by the time he was 16, he was a bellhop slash entertainer in the Bronx, New York. Allegedly, his bellhop uniform with its "red buttons" led to his stage name. He played the Borscht Belt as a comic, and then sought success on Broadway. He was drafted into the army in 1943, and, as one would expect, he entertained the troops. In television's infancy, he was given his own eponymous weekly variety series on CBS. It was a huge hit early on, and Buttons was given the opportunity to record for CBS's own record label, Columbia. This venture spawned a big hit called "Strange Things Are Happening (the Ho Ho Song)." The program, however, was unable to sustain the quality of that wildly successful first season (writers came and went quickly), and it was cancelled by CBS in 1954. NBC gave it another chance, but it had run its course and was gone by 1955.

Buttons failed to connect with any more hit singles, but he could seemingly do everything well and won a Best Supporting Actor Oscar for his portrayal of Airman Joe Kelly in *Sayonara* in 1957. Other great movie roles in *The Longest Day*, *They Shoot Horses Don't They?* and *The Poseidon Adventure* kept him on the silver screen for decades. He also became a favorite member of the dais on *The Dean Martin Celebrity Roasts* of the 1970s with his immensely funny signature "never got a dinner" routine. His one misstep was in giving another series a try. In 1966, he starred in the ABC spy spoof sitcom titled *The Double Life of Henry Phyfe*, but it failed to find an audience and quickly disappeared. His final recurring role was that of a homeless person on the long-running *Knots Landing* on CBS. He married three times, with number 3 lasting the longest—37 years. Buttons died on July 13, 2006, after complications of severely high blood pressure.

RUTH BUZZI

Most Famous TV Role: Gladys Ormphby on *Rowan and Martin's Laugh-In;* **Network:** NBC; **Years** 1968–1973; **Hit Recording:** none; **Labels:** Reprise, United Artists; **Release Years:** 1969, 1977; **Matrix:** "Don't Futz Around" (Reprise #0753), "You Oughta Hear the Song" (United Artists #951); **Chart:** none

Ruth Buzzi was born July 24, 1936, in Westerly, Rhode Island, but was raised in Wequetequock, Connecticut. As a cheerleader in high school, she discovered how much she enjoyed performing in front of people and pursued an acting career. After working on the road with Rudy Vallee and Dom De Luise, her biggest break came when she snagged a role in the Broadway production of *Sweet Charity*. Her exposure in that show earned her a recurring role as Ann Marie's friend Pete (yes, Pete) on *That Girl* and then an audition for a new TV program to be called *Rowan and Martin's Laugh-In*. She remained with the latter program for its five-and-a-half-year run on NBC.

During the show's ratings reign, Buzzi and costar Arte Johnson released a single for Reprise Records called "Don't Futz Around" backed with "Very Interesting"—the latter being one of the many catch phrases mined from the TV show. Buzzi and Johnson worked together on the program in a recurring skit about a dirty old man who, in his attempts to pick up the homely Gladys Ormphby, gets pummeled with repeated blows from her purse. That single was not a hit, and Buzzi got another chance to record a decade later—this time for United Artists Records. This 1977 release titled "You Oughta Hear the Song" was not a comedy record, but rather a serious attempt at a hit single. It was not a hit, but at this same time, Buzzi began a long and lucrative career supplying voices for animated TV characters on a long list of successful shows such as *Alvin and the Chipmunks, Cro, Baggy Pants and the Nitwits, Pound Puppies,* and *Sheep in the City.* Buzzi is very active with Texas-based charities and also paints and collects automobiles (for Pete's sake). She was nominated five times for an Emmy Award, but has yet to win. She has been married to Kent Perkins since 1978.

Edd "Kookie" Byrnes "combed" many sources and then found success with both Warner Bros. Television and Warner Bros. Records.

EDD "KOOKIE" BYRNES

Most Famous TV Role: Edd "Kookie" Byrnes on *77 Sunset Strip*; **Network:** ABC; **Years:** 1958–1963; **Hit Recording:** "Kookie, Kookie, Lend Me Your Comb"; **Label:** Warner Bros.; **Release Year:** 1959; **Matrix:** Warner Bros. #5047; **Chart:** #4 *Billboard* Hot 100

Edward Byrne Breitenberger was born July 30, 1933, in New York City. In his 20s, he opted to give acting a try, and was cast in the pilot episode for a new Warner Bros. series titled *77 Sunset Strip*. Strangely, he portrayed a serial killer in that pilot episode, but proved to be so popular with viewers, he was brought back as a "good guy" hipster parking attendant named Gerald Lloyd Kookson III (a.k.a. "Kookie"). He usually wore a windbreaker and was constantly combing his hair. Byrnes remained on the show from 1958 to 1963 and even scored a hit record during the show's run. At the time, Warner Bros. was cashing in on the popularity of its TV stars with its record division, and released material by a majority of its stars on vinyl. Teaming Byrnes with *Hawaiian Eye*'s Connie Stevens resulted in a Top Ten 1959 single titled "Kookie, Kookie, Lend Me Your Comb." Byrnes wasn't much of a singer, however, and attempts at follow-ups such as "Like I Love You" (Warner Bros. #5087), "Kookie's Love Song" (Warner Bros. #5114), and a holiday release called "Yulesville" (Warner Bros. #5121) failed to crack the Top Forty.

Because he was under a long-term contract with Warner, Byrnes had to turn down many major movie offers and, as a result, was typecast as the "Kookie" character. After a long dry spell, he got to host the pilot episode of *Wheel of Fortune* in 1974, but the original hosting job instead went to Chuck Woolery. Byrnes finally achieved a comeback of sorts as Vince Fontaine, the host of *National Bandstand* in the motion picture version of *Grease* in 1978. The following year, he portrayed the emcee in a new *Love Boat*–styled hour-long NBC program called *Sweepstakes*, but it lasted only two months. He was married to Asa Maynor from 1962 to 1971, and they had one child together—a boy named Logan, who today is a newscaster. Byrnes can often be seen at autograph conventions held across the United States.

C

SEBASTIAN CABOT

Most Famous TV Role: Mr. Giles French on *Family Affair*; **Network:** CBS; **Years:** 1966–1971; **Hit Recording:** none; **Label:** MGM; **Release Year:** 1966; **Matrix:** *Sebastian Cabot Reads Bob Dylan* (MGM LP #4431); **Chart:** none

Charles Sebastian Thomas Cabot was born July 6, 1918, in London, England. It will surprise many that at age 14 he got his very first job in an automotive garage. However, his next job as a valet and chauffeur for a British actor planted the seed for his own interest in the performing arts. He also developed an affinity for cooking and eventually found work as a chef while seeking work as an actor. After finding work in British films throughout the 1930s and 1940s, he turned to television and in 1956 secured his first recurring role as Monsieur Cerveaux in the Wally Cox–filmed NBC sitcom called *The Adventures of Hiram Holliday*. After that show was cancelled, he found steady work in episodic TV and, of special note, is his appearance as Mr. Pip in *The Twilight Zone* episode titled "A Nice Place to Visit" from 1960. At the same time, he garnered a regular role as Carl Hyatt on the two-season crime drama called *Checkmate* (1960–1962) on CBS. In 1962, he jumped to another series called *The Beachcomber* as Commissioner Crippen. That syndicated series lasted only one season. He filled the gap between *The Beachcomber* and *Family Affair* as a regular on the celebrity charades-like game show called *Stump the Stars*.

Speaking of *Family Affair*, Cabot's earlier work as a valet, chef, and chauffeur served him well as the butler/manservant in the Davis family's penthouse apartment. His dulcet tones were also put on record in 1966 on a reading of the Bob Dylan and Turtles classic hit titled "It Ain't Me, Babe" on the MGM label (#13650). It was a single release from the MGM album (#4431) titled *Sebastian Cabot Reads Bob Dylan*. It was not a hit, but the following year, Cabot was part of another album—the soundtrack from Walt Disney's *The Jungle Book* (Disneyland #3948). While it was great to have steady work, he was typecast in that role of Mr. French, and his career definitely suffered as a result in the 1970s. His considerable girth narrowed his acting possibilities as well, and he was forced to take the role of Santa Claus in the 1973 TV version of *The Miracle on 34th Street*. With fewer and fewer roles coming his way, Cabot and his wife and three children settled in British Columbia, Canada. Cabot suffered a stroke on August 22, 1977, and died at the age of 59.

RORY CALHOUN

Most Famous TV Role: Bill Longley on *The Texan*; **Network:** CBS; **Years:** 1958–1960; **Hit Recording:** none; **Label:** MGM; **Release Year:** 1958; **Matrix:** "Kiss of Love" (MGM #12359); **Chart:** none

Rory Calhoun was born Francis Timothy McCown in Los Angeles, California, on August 8, 1922. He was the son of a professional gambler who died when young Francis was less than a year old. His mother remarried, and young Francis had a troubled childhood and did time in a youth reformatory after stealing a revolver. He escaped and got in some more trouble and was charged with several felonies and imprisoned. At the age of 21, he was released and went straight, opting to find work in motion pictures. Despite his checkered past, his rugged good looks got him numerous movie roles with Betty Grable, Susan Hayward, and even Marilyn Monroe. He was given the new identity of Rory Calhoun in the movies, but the tabloids still found out about his time in the slammer. When the news of his youthful indiscretions broke, however, his bad boy image and his career were actually enhanced. He formed his own production company and produced and starred in his own CBS western titled *The Texan*, on which he portrayed Bill Longley. During the show's run, Calhoun released one single record for MGM titled "Kiss of Love" backed with "Flight to Hong Kong" (MGM #12359). It was his only recording, and it was not a success.

When the show was cancelled, he returned to the silver screen in numerous European-made films and guest starred on countless episodic American TV programs. In the 1970s, he received some bad advice and turned down a role on *Dallas*, but bounced back with a recurring role on the daytime soap opera *Capitol* on CBS. His final role came in the 1992 motion picture titled *Pure Country*. He was married twice and had five daughters. He was a longtime smoker—in fact, his nickname among friends was "Smoke." His last years were spent in Burbank, California, where he died from emphysema on April 28, 1999, at the age of 76.

HENRY CALVIN

Most Famous TV Role: Sergeant Demetrio Lopez Garcia on *Zorro*; **Network:** ABC; **Years:** 1957–1961; **Hit Recording:** none; **Label:** Disneyland; **Release Year:** 1957; **Matrix:** "Here's to a Soldier of the King" backed with "The *Zorro* Theme" (Disneyland #77); **Chart:** none

Henry Calvin was born as Wimberly Calvin-Goodman on May 25, 1918, in Dallas, Texas. He sang in his church choir and sought a career as an actor. He found work on Broadway and on radio in the 1940s. Already nearing 40, he briefly portrayed Big Ben on TV's *Howdy Doody*, but achieved his greatest success on Disney's television version of *Zorro* on ABC as Sergeant Demetrio Lopez Garcia. During the show's first year, Calvin released a single in 1957 on the new Disneyland Records label—"Here's to a Soldier of the King" backed with his own version of "The *Zorro* Theme." The biggest hit version of the program's theme came from the Chordettes in 1958 (Cadence #1349). Calvin was also part of the soundtrack albums for *Kismet* (Columbia #4850), *Peter Pan* (Disneyland #1206), and *Babes in Toyland* (Buena Vista #4022). He made numerous guest appearances on episodic TV shows such as *The Dick Van Dyke Show*, *Petticoat Junction*, and *The Man from U.N.C.L.E.* in the 1960s. On October 6, 1975, Calvin died at the young age of 57 from throat cancer in his native Dallas.

HAMILTON CAMP

Most Famous TV Role: Andrew Hummel, the fix-it man on *He and She*; **Network:** CBS; **Years:** 1967–1968; **Hit Recording:** "Here's to You"; **Label:** Warner Bros.; **Release Year:** 1968; **Matrix:** Warner Bros. #7165; **Chart:** #76 *Billboard* Hot 100

Hamid Hamilton Camp was born in London, England, on October 30, 1934. He was evacuated to the United States with his family during World War II. He became a child actor on this side of the pond, first as Bob Camp. In the early 1960s he was half of a folk duet with Bob Gibson, and together they played the Newport Jazz Festival. A couple of his compositions were later recorded by Gordon Lightfoot, the Quicksilver Messenger Service, and Simon and Garfunkel. While maintaining an interest in music, Bob Camp became Hamilton Camp and guest starred on dozens upon dozens of episodic TV shows such as *The Andy Griffith Show; Gomer Pyle, U.S.M.C.; The Twilight Zone;* and *Bewitched* in the 1960s. He was cast in the regular role of Andrew Hummel, the inept handyman for the building on the sitcom called *He and She* in 1967–1968. During the show's single season, Camp got to record for Warner Bros. Records and charted with a song titled "Here's to You." It became his only chart single, although he later recorded an album for Elektra Records as the leader of a group called the Skymonters in the early 1970s. He remained busy as a sitcom guest star in the 1970s (including a memorable episode of *The Mary Tyler Moore Show*), and eventually became a very prolific voice actor in cartoon series such as *The Flintstone Kids, The Smurfs, Ducktales, Darkwing Duck, The Pirates of Dark Water, The All New Dennis the Menace,* and *Aladdin.* Camp died suddenly on October 2, 2005, at the age of 70. He married only once and left behind six children.

DIANA CANOVA

Most Famous TV Role: Corinne Tate on *Soap;* **Network:** ABC; **Years:** 1977–1980; **Hit Recording:** none; **Label:** 20th Century Fox; **Release Year:** 1980; **Matrix:** "Who You Foolin'?" (20th Century Fox #2486); **Chart:** none

Diana Canova Rivero was born in West Palm Beach, Florida, on June 1, 1953, but was raised in Southern California. Mirroring Lucie Arnaz, Diana had a comedienne mother, Judy Canova, and her father was Cuban musician Filberto Rivero. She made her acting debut on episodic TV programs such as *Happy Days, Starsky and Hutch, Barney Miller,* and *Chico and the Man.* She became a regular on *Soap* as Corinne Tate, and stayed with the program until 1980 when she got her own series called *I'm a Big Girl, Now*—an ABC sitcom that costarred Danny Thomas, Sheree North, and Martin Short. Diana performed the theme song for the sitcom, and during the run of this series, she also got a recording contract with 20th Century Fox's label. The result was one single titled "Who You Foolin'?" backed with "I Did It Again." It was not a hit. Her series was cancelled after one season—it was also not a hit. After two more short-lived sitcoms—*Throb* and *Home Free*—Canova turned her considerable talents to cartoon voice work and video shorts. As of this writing, she lives in Connecticut with her husband and two children.

CAPTAIN KANGAROO

Most Famous TV Role: keeper of the Treasure House on *Captain Kangaroo*; **Networks:** CBS, PBS; **Years:** 1955–1984; **Hit Recording:** none; **Label:** Everest; **Release Year:** 1960; **Matrix:** *Peter and the Wolf* (Everest LP #3043); **Chart:** none

Bob Keeshan was born in Lynbrook, New York, on June 27, 1927. After attending Fordham University in the Bronx, New York, Keeshan found work in television's infancy as the first Clarabelle, the silent clown on *Howdy Doody*. After a couple of other short-lived TV programs geared toward children, Keeshan got to star in an innovative new daily show for CBS called *Captain Kangaroo*. The program debuted in 1955 when Keeshan was only 28, but in his costume and makeup he always appeared much older. The show had a cast of characters that included Mr. Green Jeans, Mister Moose, Bunny Rabbit, Grandfather Clock, Dancing Bear, Magic Drawing Board, and Bee Bee the sheepdog. The program became immensely popular, and in 1958 Keeshan narrated an album called *Captain Kangaroo's Treasure House of Best Loved Children's Songs* (Golden Records LP #25). Then, in 1960 Keeshan released an album on which he narrated the entire story of *Peter and the Wolf* for the Everest label. The album didn't chart, but was popular among young fans of the show. Keeshan also released, for Columbia (the Columbia Broadcasting System's record label), a seasonal single and perennial favorite titled "The Littlest Snowman" (Columbia #4291). Like Keeshan's album, it was also narrated. Keeshan remained with the show until 1984 when he opted out of his contract because CBS had been placing more and more restrictions on the content. Reruns of the show then ran on PBS for several years. Keeshan died at the age of 76 on January 23, 2004, leaving behind three children.

JUDY CARNE

Most Famous TV Role: the "Sock-It-to-Me Girl" on *Rowan and Martin's Laugh-In*; **Network:** NBC; **Years:** 1968–1970; **Hit Recording:** none; **Label:** Reprise; **Release Year:** 1969; **Matrix:** "Sock It to Me" (Reprise #0680); **Chart:** none

Judy Carne was born Joyce Audrey Botterill in Northampton, England, on April 27, 1939. Some of her first work was on the British TV series *Dan-*

ger Man, but in the United States her start was on the short-lived sitcom *Fair Exchange* in 1962 on CBS. It began as an hour-long sitcom, but was cancelled midseason because of low ratings. A deluge of mail brought the program back in a half-hour format, but once again the numbers just weren't there, and it was soon gone for good.

Once again on CBS, Carne portrayed Barbara Wyntoon, the love interest of Les Brown Jr.'s character of Jim Bailey in a handful of episodes of the forgettable sitcom called *The Baileys of Balboa*. Then came *Love on a Rooftop* on ABC with costar Peter Duel (sometimes spelled Deuel), set in San Francisco in 1966. It was never explained why Carne's character of Julie Willis had a British accent, but her parents did not. Carne's next venture, however, proved to be one for which she is best remembered— the "Sock-It-to-Me Girl" on *Rowan and Martin's Laugh-In* on NBC. During the show's run, Carne released a single titled "Sock It to Me" (chock-full of sound effects) backed with "Right, Said Fred" on the Reprise label in 1969. "Here Come the Judge," another catch phrase from the show, became a big hit for both Shorty Long (Soul #35044) and Pigmeat Markham (Chess #2049), but not Carne's "Sock It to Me," and no follow-ups were released. Carne's brief marriages to Burt Reynolds and Robert Bergmann comprised a large part of her autobiography titled *Laughing on the Outside, Crying on the Inside: The Bittersweet Saga of the Sock-It-to-Me Girl* in 1985. It also covered her bisexuality and her public battle with drug addiction. After a small handful of guest starring roles in the early 1970s, Carne all but disappeared from public view.

DARLEEN CARR

Most Famous TV Role: Cindy Smith on *The Smith Family*; **Network:** ABC; **Years:** 1971–1972; **Hit Recording:** none; **Label:** RCA Victor; **Release Year:** 1971; **Matrix:** "Shades" (RCA Victor #8974); **Chart:** none

Darleen Carr was born Darleen Farnon on December 12, 1950, in Chicago, Illinois. One of her earliest TV roles came in the short-lived TV sitcom titled *The John Forsythe Show* on NBC in 1965. On the show Forsythe was the head of an all-girls school, and 14-year-old Darleen portrayed one of the students, Kathy. Her next role was as the middle child to Henry Fonda and Janet Blair in *The Smith Family*, a Don Fedderson TV show somewhere in between a comedy and a drama series (what was much later termed a dramedy). During the two seasons of that series, Carr scored a recording contract with RCA Victor Records and released a single titled "Shades,"

Even with Lee Hazlewood and Perry Botkin Jr. behind her, *The Smith Family*'s Darleen Carr failed to have a hit single.

written by famous singer/songwriter/musician Lee Hazlewood, backed with "Through the Looking Glass." By the time the record was released, however, the TV show's ratings had begun a quick descent and, thus, the record failed to catch on. Almost a decade later, Carr got to star in a groundbreaking CBS sitcom called *Miss Winslow and Son*, on which she portrayed an unwed mother, but the subject matter was just a bit ahead of the times, and it was gone from the prime-time lineup within a couple of months. She was nominated for a Golden Globe for her work on the mini-series titled *Once an Eagle*, and a while later secured a recurring role on the new 1980s TV version of *Maverick*. However, like so many others, in the 1990s she became a successful voice actress for movie and TV animation.

DAVID CARRADINE

Most Famous TV Role: Kwai Chang Caine on *Kung Fu*; **Network:** ABC; **Years:** 1972–1975; **Hit Recording:** none; **Labels:** Billy, Coop; **Release Year:** 1975; **Matrix:** "You and Me" (Billy #103), "Walk the Floor" (Coop #5585); **Chart:** none

David Carradine was born John Arthur Carradine into an acting family on December 8, 1936, in Hollywood, California. After studying drama and music theory in San Francisco, Carradine appeared in some 100 films over a long career, but is best known for his TV work. His first series was the short-lived 1966 ABC TV version of the classic Alan Ladd movie *Shane.* His biggest break came in 1972 when he was cast as the half Chinese, half Caucasian Shaolin monk named Kwai Chang Caine on the ABC series called *Kung Fu.* As a student of martial arts, Carradine was the perfect choice for this role. This original version of the show was cancelled after three seasons. In its final year, Carradine had the opportunity to release a few single records—"You and Me" on the Billy label and "Walk the Floor" on the Coop label. There was also a solo album titled *Grasshopper* (Jet LP #10) by Carradine released in the United Kingdom. None of these became hits, but David's half-brother Keith Carradine scored a Top Twenty hit titled "I'm Easy" (ABC #12117) in 1976. A new, updated syndicated version of the series, *Kung Fu: The Legend Continues,* ran from 1992 to 1996 and consisted of 88 episodes. Carradine was the only carry over from the original series. Carradine was married five times and also had a relationship with actress Barbara Hershey, but they were never wed. While shooting a film to be called *Stretch,* Carradine was found dead on June 4, 2009, in his Bangkok hotel, hanging naked by a rope in the room's closet. An autopsy showed the cause of death to be accidental autoerotic asphyxiation.

LYNDA CARTER

Most Famous TV Role: Diana Prince on *Wonder Woman*; **Networks:** ABC, CBS; **Years:** 1976–1979; **Hit Recording:** none; **Label:** Epic; **Release Year:** 1978; **Matrix:** "Toto" (Epic #50569), "All Night Song" (Epic #50624); **Chart:** none

Lynda Jean Cordova Carter was born July 24, 1951, in Phoenix, Arizona. It was obvious very early on that she'd be a performer, and by the age of five she appeared on a local TV talent show. She opted to drop out of Arizona State College to pursue a musical career. She also represented Arizona in the Miss World USA beauty pageant and won. In the international competition, she reached the semifinals. She starred as Bobbie Jo Baker in the 1976 motion picture titled *Bobbie Jo and the Outlaw* and then landed the role of *Wonder Woman* on CBS, two roles that came at a very opportune time—she was almost totally broke, but the TV show's success in particular quickly changed all that. During the run of the series, Carter got to show off her vocal abilities and recorded a couple of singles for Epic Records ("Toto" backed with "Put on a Show"—Epic #50569; "All Night Song" also backed with "Put on a Show"—Epic #50624), and a solo album titled *Portrait* (Epic LP#35308). After the series was cancelled, Carter continued to find work in episodic television and films. She has been married twice, and she has two children with her second husband, James and Jessica. She's still making music, and her official website, in fact, is called LyndaCarterSings (www.lyndacartersings.com).

RALPH CARTER

Most Famous TV Role: Michael Evans on *Good Times*; **Network:** CBS; **Years:** 1974–1979; **Hit Recordings:** "When You're Young and in Love," "Extra, Extra (Read All about It)"; **Label:** Mercury; **Release Years:** 1975–1976; **Matrix:** Mercury #73695, Mercury #73746, respectively; **Chart:** #37, #59, respectively, *Billboard* R&B

Ralph Carter was born in New York City on May 30, 1961. A role on Broadway in *Raisin*, based on Lorraine Hansberry's *A Raisin in the Sun*, got him noticed and earned him an audition for the Norman Lear *Maude* spinoff called *Good Times* on CBS. Set in a Chicago ghetto apartment, Ralph was cast as Michael Evans, the youngest member of the Evans household. It's more than a coincidence that his character was named Michael Evans—that was the name of one of the writers on the program. Indeed, this is the same Mike Evans who portrayed Lionel Jefferson on both *All in the Family* and *The Jeffersons*. Evans saw a lot of himself in the series and drew on his life experiences in his scripts. This venture utilized most of Mike Evans's time, and he opted to briefly give up his role as Lionel (actor Damon Evans portrayed Lionel in the interim).

Since Ralph Carter had been on Broadway, it was considered a good idea to release a few records by him to cash in on his popularity on TV. The result was two chart singles—"When You're Young and in Love" and "Extra, Extra (Read All about It)" for the Mercury label. "When You're

Young and in Love" was a Top Forty R&B hit, and Carter got to perform the song on an episode of TV's legendary *Soul Train* in 1975. He also got to sing on six episodes of his own show. *Good Times'* two stars, Esther Rolle and John Amos, left during the program's run, but Ralph Carter appeared in all 133 episodes. Carter made very few appearances after *Good Times* was cancelled in 1979. Rumors that he had died of AIDS in the 1980s were later debunked.

ANGELA CARTWRIGHT

Most Famous TV Roles: Linda Williams on *The Danny Thomas Show*, Penny Robinson on *Lost in Space*; **Network:** CBS; **Years:** 1957–1964, 1965–1968, respectively; **Hit Recording:** none; **Label:** Encore, Star-Bright, Ting a Ling; **Release Year:** 1959; **Matrix:** "My First Romance" (Encore #1051), "Merry Go Round" (Ting a Ling #100), *Angela Cartwright Sings* (Star-Bright LP #103); **Chart:** none

Angela Margaret Cartwright was born September 9, 1952, in Cheshire, England. What a way to start a career—her first role was as Paul Newman's daughter in *Somebody Up There Likes Me* in 1956. Her older sister, Veronica, also amassed many credits, but young Angela was seemingly never out of work. For seven seasons she portrayed Danny Thomas's stepdaughter, Linda, on *The Danny Thomas Show* (very often called *Make Room for Daddy* in syndication). After that series ran its course, she was cast as Brigitta von Trapp in the motion picture version of *The Sound of Music*. From there, she jumped into the role of Penny Robinson on the sci-fi adventure series *Lost in Space*—a show that began on a rather serious tone, but morphed into more of a sitcom in seasons 2 and 3. While on *The Danny Thomas Show*, both Angela and her older half-brother on the show, Rusty, had the opportunity to make records (see the entry for Rusty Hamer). Angela got the opportunity to sing on her sitcom, and this led to a single on the small Encore Records label ("My First Romance" backed with "I'm Not Ready") followed by one on the Ting a Ling label ("Merry Go Round" backed with "Mr. Jumbo," the latter inspired by an episode of the sitcom from 1959 titled "Linda's Giant"). There was also an album of songs appropriately titled *Angela Cartwright Sings* on the Star-Bright label. None of these became hits, but if there were a chart for cuteness, they would all have made that Top Ten. Just as *Lost in Space* was winding down, Cartwright again found work in a new updated version of *The Danny Thomas Show* in 1970 called *Make Room for Granddaddy* on ABC. This time around, however, the show only lasted a single season. Cartwright married in 1976 and has two children. She has pursued her passion for photography for over three decades and has her own website: www .angela-cartwright.com.

DAVID CASSIDY

Most Famous TV Role: Keith Partridge on *The Partridge Family*; **Network:** ABC; **Years:** 1970–1974; **Hit Recording:** "Cherish"; **Label:** Bell; **Release Year:** 1971; **Matrix:** Bell #150; **Chart:** #9 *Billboard* Hot 100

David Bruce Cassidy was born April 12, 1950, in New York City. He is the son of the late Jack Cassidy and actress Evelyn Ward. They were divorced for several years before telling David (they were often on the road and were able to hide that fact very well). In 1956, Jack married Shirley Jones, and they had three sons together, Shaun, Patrick, and Ryan—half brothers to David. In his teen years, Cassidy decided to pursue a show business career and in 1969 was cast in the extremely short-lived Broadway show called *The Fig Leaves Are Falling*. The only good thing to come from that disaster was a Hollywood screen test for Cassidy. After guest starring roles on episodic TV shows such as *Adam-12* and *Ironside*, Cassidy was groomed for stardom in a series with his stepmom to be called *The Partridge Family*. Screen Gems, drawing on their experience with *The Monkees*, knew the formula for simultaneous TV and musical success. Jones and Cassidy were the only Partridges who actually sang on the records, and they hit immediately with the number 1 hook-laden smash titled "I Think I Love You." Two more Top Ten singles followed in short order— "Doesn't Somebody Want to be Wanted?" (Bell #963) and "I'll Meet You Halfway" (Bell #996). There were also four Top Ten Partridge Family LPs—*The Partridge Family Album* (Bell #6050), *Up to Date* (Bell #6059), *The Partridge Family Sound Magazine* (Bell #6064), and *A Partridge Family Christmas Card* (Bell #6066), the latter containing a removable Christmas card from the show's cast. While these records were zooming up the charts, Cassidy also tried to make a go of it as a solo artist and scored one Top Ten gold single—a remake of the Association's "Cherish" (Bell #150) in 1971. The program ran in prime time for four seasons and a total of 96 episodes.

After the show was cancelled, Cassidy tried to establish himself as both a serious actor and a credible vocalist, but the show's taint put the kibosh on that. He did get another chance at a series, *David Cassidy: Man Undercover* on NBC in 1978–1979, but it failed to find an audience (although its premise was to influence *21 Jump Street* years later). Attempts to resurrect his recording career also fell flat. He did, however, make a small comeback when he got to sing the theme song for *The John Larroquette Show* on NBC (1993–1996). A couple of DUI arrests in 2010 and 2013, and unflattering mug shots that made the rounds on the Internet, did little for his career. In 1994, Cassidy published his autobiography titled *C'mon, Get Happy: Fear and Loathing on the Partridge Family Bus*. (See the entry for The Partridge Family.)

SHAUN CASSIDY

Most Famous TV Role: Joe Hardy on *The Hardy Boys Mysteries*; **Network:** ABC; **Years:** 1977–1979; **#1 Hit Recording:** "Da Doo Ron Ron"; **Label:** Warner Bros./Curb; **Release Year:** 1977; **Matrix:** Warner Bros./Curb #8365; **Chart:** #1 *Billboard* Hot 100

Shaun Paul Cassidy was born September 27, 1958, in Los Angeles, California. He is the son of Jack Cassidy and Shirley Jones, and the half brother of David Cassidy (see the entry under his name). Following in David's footsteps, Shaun was starring in a hit television program—*The Hardy Boys Mysteries*, with costars Parker Stevenson and Edmund Gilbert—when his recording career caught fire. His *Shaun Cassidy* album (Warner Bros./Curb #3067) had already been issued overseas, but was held back in the United States until the TV series had established itself. It became his first of three platinum LPs, including *Born Late* (Warner Bros./Curb #3126) and *Under Wraps* (Warner Bros./Curb #3222). Singer/songwriter Eric Carmen penned two of Shaun's three Top Ten singles—"That's Rock 'N' Roll" (Warner Bros./Curb #8423) and "Hey, Deanie" (Warner Bros./Curb #8488). Shaun's teen idol status, however, faded rather quickly, but luckily he was able to reinvent himself as an actor, writer, and producer. He appeared on Broadway in the popular *Blood Brothers* in 1993, and wrote and/or produced numerous TV shows with the most famous being *American Gothic* in 1995. He has been married twice and has seven children.

TED CASSIDY

Most Famous TV Role: Lurch on *The Addams Family*; **Network:** ABC; **Years:** 1964–1966; **Hit Recording:** none; **Label:** Capitol; **Release Year:** 1965; **Matrix:** "The Lurch" (Capitol #5503); **Chart:** none

Written and produced by the prolific Gary Paxton, *The Addams Family*'s Ted Cassidy attempted to start a dance craze called "The Lurch," but it wasn't a "monster" hit.

Theodore Crawford Cassidy was born in Pittsburgh, Pennsylvania, on July 31, 1932. A gifted scholar, he attended high school at the age of 11. In college (Stetson University in Florida), he majored in speech and drama, and aided by his considerable height (six feet, nine inches), was on the basketball team. His height and booming voice tended to get him typecast as out-of-the-ordinary characters such as Tarzan, and of course Lurch the butler on *The Addams Family*. His dialogue usually consisted of "You rang?" and numerous grunts and growls. While the *Addams Family* was still first run in prime time, Capitol Records had Cassidy attempt to create a new dance craze called "The Lurch." Similar in texture to "The Jerk" by the Larks (Money #106), this 1965 release had a very soulful feel to it. The vocal group in the background is not credited on the label, but Cassidy doesn't sing on the cut (he merely makes Lurch noises and utters an occasional "You rang?"). The record was not a hit, but it did get a nice push from Capitol, and Cassidy made the rounds of the teen music shows (including *Shindig* and *Shivaree*) on which he lip-synched the song. To be honest, Cassidy's contributions to the single are more of a distraction than an asset. It would have been a much better record with only the vocal group, but he had star power at the time and made the record very novel. The record itself is somewhat rare, but having a well-preserved copy of the picture sleeve that accompanied it greatly enhances its value. The flip side, "Wesley," is a narrated story featuring Cassidy's powerfully deep tones. Cassidy was so good at growls and roars that he later supplied said noises for the early seasons of TV's *The Incredible Hulk*. During that show's run, Cassidy's height began to have deleterious effects on his health, and he died on January 16, 1979, at the age of 46 after open heart surgery.

RICHARD CHAMBERLAIN

Most Famous TV Role: Dr. James Kildare on *Dr. Kildare*; **Network:** NBC; **Years:** 1961–1966; **Hit Recording:** "The Theme from *Dr. Kildare* (Three Stars Will Shine Tonight)"; **Label:** MGM; **Release Year:** 1962; **Matrix:** MGM #13075; **Chart:** #10 *Billboard* Hot 100

George Richard Chamberlain was born March 31, 1934. He was born in the right place to seek stardom—Beverly Hills, California. He attended Beverly Hills High School and Pomona College before attempting to make his mark in show business. He found some work in episodic TV on *Alfred Hitchcock Presents*, *Gunsmoke*, and *Mr. Lucky* in 1959 and 1960. He was not the first choice to portray Dr. James Kildare on TV—actor Roger Perry was, but Perry was already contracted to star in a Desilu sitcom called *Harrigan and Son* with Pat O'Brien, and Chamberlain got the nod. Perry's series only lasted a single season, while Chamberlain enjoyed a run of 191 episodes of *Dr. Kildare*. He garnered a Golden Globe award for his portrayal of the good doctor on the program, and to take advantage of his and the program's popularity, Chamberlain also released a series of albums and singles for MGM Records (*Dr. Kildare* was an MGM show). Eight singles reached the Hot 100, but only one, "The Theme from *Dr. Kildare* (Three Stars Will Shine Tonight)," reached Top Ten. His follow-up release, a remake of the Everly Brothers' "All I Have to Do Is Dream" (MGM #13121), narrowly missed the Top Ten, and a new version of Elvis

Presley's "Love Me Tender" (MGM #13097) almost penetrated the Top Twenty. His *Richard Chamberlain Sings* album (MGM # 4088) reached the Top Five.

After the show's demise in 1966, Chamberlain began to concentrate on making films for both the silver screen and the small screen. He found his true calling beginning in the late 1970s as "the king of the miniseries," and found juicy roles in *Centennial* (as Alexander McKeag), *Shogun* (as pilot Major John Blackthorne), *The Thorn Birds* (as Ralph de Bricassart), *The Bourne Identity* (as Jason Bourne), and *Dream West* (as John Fremont). He nabbed two more Golden Globes for his roles in *Shogun* and *The Thorn Birds*. He also joined the cast of a couple of prime-time series—*Island Son* and *Brothers and Sisters*—but neither equaled the popularity of *Dr. Kildare*. After many years of hints and allegations, Chamberlain confirmed that he is gay in his autobiography titled *Shattered Love* from Harper Collins Publishing.

CHARO

Most Famous TV Role: Aunt Charo on *Chico and the Man;* **Network:** NBC; **Years:** 1976–1978; **Hit Recording:** "Dance a Little Bit Closer"; **Label:** Salsoul; **Release Year:** 1978; **Matrix:** Salsoul #2048; **Chart:** #104 *Billboard* Bubbling Under

Charo was born Maria del Rosario Mercedes Pilar Martinez Molina Baeza (imagine that on a driver's license) on January 15, 1951, in Murcia, Spain. She studied music in her youth and became a rather proficient flamenco guitar player in her teens. There has always been conjecture about her actual age because she was made to appear older when she married bandleader Xavier Cugat in the late 1960s (Cugat was more than 40 years her senior). Some sources list her birth year as 1945. Charo was Cugat's fifth wife, and they divorced in 1977. She became a regular visitor to variety, talk, and game shows in the 1970s, and in 1976, she joined the cast of NBC's *Chico and the Man* in the recurring role of Aunt Charo. While with the series, Charo released a few records that managed to make the charts, albeit very low. Her album, backed by the famous Salsoul Orchestra, was named for her most famous phrase, *Cuchi-Cuchi* (Salsoul #5519). The 1977 album spawned one mildly popular single titled "Dance a Little Bit Closer" early in 1978. An attempt to set her up with her own sitcom, called *Charo and the Sergeant* for ABC, never got off the ground, and the pilot went unsold. Charo remarried in 1978 to Kjell Rasten, and they have one son together. In the 1980s, Charo sightings became fewer and farther between as she opted to move to Hawaii, start a dinner theater, and spend more time with her family. She continues to record on occasion, and when she does perform, it's usually in Las Vegas or Branson.

DAVID CHARVET

Most Famous TV Role: Matt Brody on *Baywatch*; **Network:** syndicated; **Years:** 1992–1995; **Hit Recording:** none; **Labels:** Mercury, RCA; **Release Year:** 1997; **Matrix:** "Should I Leave?" (RCA #74321–460832); **Chart:** none

David Franck Guez Charvet was born in Lyon, France, on May 15, 1972. Even though he was born in France, his father was Tunisian and his mother was Jewish. After achieving some success as a model, he turned his attention to acting. His big TV break came in 1992 when he was cast in the role of Matt Brody on *Baywatch*, and enjoyed three seasons of heartthrob status. Charvet left *Baywatch* in 1995, only to surface as Craig Field on *Melrose Place* on the Fox TV Network in 1996. He stayed with the program for two seasons, and while there attempted to kick-start his recording career. Even with a push from RCA Records, his 1997 single titled "Should I Leave?" and his *David Charvet* album (RCA #74321 485532 and RCA #74321 479301, respectively) failed to catch on. After being dropped by RCA, he opted to leap to Mercury Records in 2002 and released the *Leap of Faith* album (Mercury #5889092) only in Europe. It did fairly well in France and the United Kingdom. His recording career never did take off in the United States as he'd hoped, and Charvet returned to acting part time. He also designs and builds high-end homes. He's quite the handyman and even has his own website dedicated to his craftwork—www.davidcharvet.com.

CHUNKY A (ARSENIO HALL)

Most Famous TV Role: host of *The Arsenio Hall Show*; **Network:** syndicated; **Years:** 1989–1994, 2013–2014; **Hit Recording:** "Owwww!"; **Label:** MCA; **Release Year:** 1989; **Matrix:** MCA #53736; **Chart:** #77 *Billboard* Hot 100

Arsenio Hall was born in Cleveland, Ohio, on February 12, 1956. He had a fascination with magic as a child, and enjoyed performing in front of people. After studying at Ohio State University and Kent State, he moved to Chicago where he pursued his love of comedy. His first break in television was as the announcer for Alan Thicke's short-lived late-night talk show called *Thicke of the Night*. After serving as one of the fill-in hosts after Joan Rivers's Fox TV talk show went south, Arsenio was given his own syndicated late-night show—the original *Arsenio Hall Show* that ran from 1989 to 1994 and scored big with the younger demos. The fist pump became his trademark. During the program's run, Arsenio released a record under the alias of Chunky A—an overweight rapper—and had a minor hit record with a song called "Owwww!" in 1989. It reached number 77 on the Hot 100. Chunky A's album titled *Large and in Charge* (MCA #6354) also made the charts, reaching number 71. Hall costarred in several popular motion pictures, including *Coming to America* and *Harlem Nights*. After roles in several short-lived series (*Martial Law* and his eponymous *Arsenio* sitcom), Hall took some time off to raise his son, Arsenio Jr. His attempt at recapturing the magic of his first *Arsenio Hall Show* in 2013 lasted only one season.

DICK CLARK

Most Famous TV Role: host of *American Bandstand*; **Network:** ABC; **Years:** 1957–1987; **Hit Recording:** none; **Labels:** Buddah, Dunhill, Liberty; **Release Years:** 1967–1973; **Matrix:** "An Open Letter to the Older Generation" (Dunhill #4112), "The Day the Children Died" (Liberty #56145), "Inside Stories" (Buddah cardboard picture disc—no number); **Chart:** none

Richard Wagstaff Clark was born in Mount Vernon, New York, on November 30, 1929. His only sibling, Bradley Clark, was killed in the Battle of the Bulge in World War II. Even before his teens, Clark knew that he wanted to pursue a career in radio broadcasting. After attending Syracuse University, he started at a country radio station there and expanded his horizons as host of a local country music TV program. His move to Philadelphia and radio station WFIL led to his eventual hosting duties on *American Bandstand* in 1956, replacing the original host Bob Horn. Initially, it was a local Philadelphia program, but when it went national on ABC, Clark went with it and remained as host for over 30 years. During the show's run, he also hosted several game shows (including *The Object Is*, *Missing Links*, and *The $10,000 Pyramid*). He snagged roles in a couple of motion pictures—*Jamboree* in 1957 and *Because They're Young* in 1960.

Everything Clark touched seemed to turn to gold, with the possible exception of his recording career. His first single came in 1967 and was called "Open Letter to the Older Generation." It was more of a poem set to music than a song, and Clark merely recited the lyrics. These lyrics had a message telling parents to listen to what their kids had to say because their opinions matter. Released on ABC's own Dunhill Records label, the single failed to catch on with either parents or the younger generation. Clark's other two singles—"The Day the Children Died" for Liberty Records (a creepy song title for an icon to so many teenagers) and "Inside Stories" for Buddah Records suffered a similar fate. It's interesting that the man who played so many hit records on his own TV shows was unable to have a hit of his own. Clark didn't mind that his singles didn't sell well—he had bigger fish to fry with his Dick Clark Productions (which spawned *The American Music Awards*, *New Year's Rockin' Eve*, and *TV Bloopers and Practical Jokes*). In 2004, likely as a result of type 2 diabetes, Clark suffered a stroke that greatly impaired his speech. At this point in his career, he greatly curtailed his TV exposure but did still participate in his *New Year's Rockin' Eve* specials. A heart attack suffered after prostate surgery on April 18, 2012, ended the life of America's "oldest living teenager."

GARY CLARKE

Most Famous TV Roles: Dick Hamilton on *Michael Shayne*, Steve on *The Virginian*; **Network:** NBC; **Years:** 1960–1961, 1962–1964, respectively; **Hit Recording:** none; **Labels:** Decca, RCA; **Release Years:** 1962–1964; **Matrix:** "The Virginian" (Decca #31511), "Tomorrow May Never Come" (RCA #7982); **Chart:** none

Clarke Frederic Lamoreaux was born in Los Angeles, California, on August 16, 1933 (although some sources say 1936). He began his acting career in the 1950s in episodic TV and in a few forgettable low-budget motion pictures such as 1958's *Missile to the Moon* and 1960's *Date Bait*. His first regular series was the crime drama *Michael Shayne* on NBC in 1960. Alongside Richard Denning, Herb Rudley, and Jerry Paris, Gary Clarke portrayed Dick Hamilton—the younger brother of Shayne's girlfriend, Lucy. *Michael Shayne* lasted only a single season, but the following year Clarke was cast as Steve Hill in a weekly 90-minute NBC western called *The Virginian* (in 45 episodes). This series was a ratings hit, but had a huge amount of cast turnover (must not have been a very happy set). Only Doug McClure (Trampas) and James Drury (the Virginian) stayed for the entire nine-season run.

While enjoying visibility on TV, Clarke attempted success on vinyl as well as film. While on *Michael Shayne* he released one single for RCA Victor Records—"Tomorrow May Never Come" (written by Jackie DeShannon) backed with "One Way Ticket." A couple of years later, he released his take on "The Theme from *The Virginian*" for the Decca Records label, backed with "One Summer in a Million." His final regular series was the short-lived 1967 ABC western called *Hondo*, on which Clarke portrayed Captain Richards. Under his real name, he penned several *Get Smart* scripts several years later. Clarke was briefly wed to Pat Woodell—the original Bobbie Jo on *Petticoat Junction* (see the entry for her). He has three grown sons from a previous marriage, and he occasionally pops up at Hollywood autograph shows with other members of *The Virginian*'s cast.

CLAY COLE

Most Famous TV Role: host of the teen music show *The Clay Cole Show*; **Network:** syndicated; **Years:** 1959–1968; **Hit Recording:** none; **Labels:** Imperial, Roulette; **Release Years:** 1960–1961; **Matrix:** "Skip Skip" (Roulette #4280), "Happy Times" (Imperial #5771), "Twist around the Clock" (Imperial #5804); **Chart:** none

Clay Cole was born as Albert Rucker in Youngstown, Ohio, on New Year's Day of 1938. He was hosting teen music shows on local TV while still in his teens, and later did the same in the New York City market. There he hosted concerts at the legendary Apollo Theater and a long-running local teen TV show called *The Clay Cole Show* on WNTA-TV and then on WPIX-TV. He also portrayed himself in the 1961 rock and roll motion picture *Twist around the Clock*.

As much as he enjoyed hosting his own TV show and playing hits made by others, he very badly wanted to have his own hit single and tried for success on that avenue of show business numerous times, but met with little success. His first single was called "Here, There and Everywhere" backed with "Skip Skip" (Roulette #4280) in 1959. Even though the song was written and produced by the prolific Teddy Vann, it failed to reach the charts. In the early 1960s, he released two singles for Southern California's Imperial Records label—"Happy Times" and the title cut from his motion picture *Twist around the Clock*—but neither one caught on with his young fan base. He gave it the old college try, however, and even sang along with many of his guest performers. After almost a decade as host of *The Clay Cole Show*, he switched gears and became a successful

TV producer, and garnered a few Emmy Awards for his work. Cole died of a massive heart attack on December 18, 2010, only two weeks before his 73rd birthday. Sadly, no complete episodes of *The Clay Cole Show* are known to exist—only a few very rare clips.

BUD COLLYER

Most Famous TV Role: host of *Beat the Clock, Number Please,* and *To Tell the Truth*; **Network:** ABC, CBS; **Years:** 1950–1968; **Hit Recording:** none; **Label:** RCA Victor; **Release Year:** 1952; **Matrix:** "The Clock Game" (RCA Victor #WBY-97), *Humpty Dumpty's Album for Little Children* (RCA Victor # LBY-1015); **Chart:** none

Bud Collyer was born June 18, 1908, as Clayton Johnson Heermance Jr. in New York City. He had designs on a law career, but when he found out that radio broadcasting (at least at that time in history) paid more, he switched gears. After a prolific career on programs such as *Terry and the Pirates* and *The Adventures of Superman* (along with lucrative announcing jobs on *The Guiding Light* and *The Goldbergs*), he made a very smooth transition to television and was the emcee for two incredibly long-running game shows—*Beat the Clock* and *To Tell the Truth*. That original *Beat the Clock* ran from 1950 to 1961, and early in its run, Collyer recorded a few records for the RCA Victor label geared for children. Appropriately, to tie in to *Beat the Clock*, a single titled "The Clock Game" was released in 1952. It was a cut from his RCA Victor LP titled *Humpty Dumpty's Album for Little Children* in that same year. Collyer's picture, with his trademark bowtie, was emblazoned on the album cover, but neither the single nor the album were hugely successful.

During the run of *To Tell the Truth* in 1966, Collyer was yet again entertaining children while reprising his role as Superman in the animated Filmation series titled *The New Adventures of Superman*. After its network run, *To Tell the Truth* was to enter into syndication and Collyer was again tapped as host, but he turned down the offer because of failing health, and Garry Moore was selected in his stead. Collyer declined rapidly and died of a circulatory ailment, likely the result of a lifetime of smoking, on September 8. 1969—coincidentally, the same day the new syndicated *To Tell the Truth* made its bow on TV. Collyer's older sister, June, was the wife and costar of Stu Erwin, whose *Stu Erwin Show/The Trouble with Father* enjoyed a five-season run on ABC in television's infancy. Both *Beat the Clock* and *To Tell the Truth* have been revived numerous times, but have never attained the same level of success of Bud Collyer's original versions. Collyer was married twice, and had three children with his second wife, Marian Shockley.

JEFF CONAWAY

Most Famous TV Role: Bobby Wheeler on *Taxi*; **Networks:** ABC, NBC; **Years:** 1978–1983; **Hit Recording:** none; **Label:** Columbia; **Release Year:** 1979; **Matrix:** "City Boy" (Columbia #11192), *Jeff Conaway* (Columbia #36111); **Chart:** none

Jeffrey Conaway was born in New York City on October 5, 1950. His mother, Mary Ann, and father, Charles, were actors, and by the age of 10 Jeff was appearing on Broadway in *All the Way Home*. After years of modeling and TV commercial work, Conaway landed his first movie role in *Jennifer on My Mind* in 1971. His big break came in *Grease*—both the Broadway and movie versions. This led to his being cast as the struggling actor/taxi driver Bobby Wheeler on the much-lauded TV sitcom *Taxi* that ran on ABC from 1978 to 1982 and then on NBC from 1982 to 1983. Conaway had been part of the *Grease* soundtrack album, but his popularity on the TV sitcom led to a contract with Columbia records, an eponymous album, and a single called "City Boy" backed with "Fever in the Blood." Both sides of the single were included on the album along with eight other cuts. Bruce Springsteen's manager, Mike Appel had a lot of faith in Conaway's talent and produced the album, but it failed to catch on and Conaway's recording career was quickly aborted. (He is not to be confused with the drummer named Jeff Conaway who recorded with the Psychic Paramount, the Sabers, and the Panel Donor.)

Conaway was married three times, most notably to Olivia Newton-John's older sister, Rona. Sadly, when *Taxi* came to an end, Conaway had a hard time finding work and developed a substance abuse problem (and was in and out of rehab). In fact, in later years he appeared on Dr. Drew Pinsky's *Celebrity Rehab* TV program. Conaway never did kick the habit, and his drug abuse led to failure to recognize the symptoms of pneumonia, and he died on May 27, 2011, at the age of 60 in Encino, California. During the run of *Taxi*, he was nominated for a Best Supporting Actor Emmy Award twice, but did not win.

CHUCK CONNORS

Most Famous TV Role: Lucas McCain on *The Rifleman*; **Network:** ABC; **Years:** 1958–1963; **Hit Recording:** none; **Label:** Decca; **Release Year:** 1960; **Matrix:** "Somebody Bigger Than You and I" (Decca #31120); **Chart:** none

Kevin Joseph Connors was born on April 10, 1921, in Brooklyn, New York. He attended Seton Hall University in South Orange, New Jersey (which is also my alma mater). He found success in three different ventures—professional basketball, professional baseball, and acting. During World War II he was stationed in the army at Fort Knox, Kentucky. His six-foot-five-inch frame made him a natural for basketball, and he briefly played for the Boston Celtics after his discharge from the army in 1946. I said briefly because he left to join the Brooklyn Dodgers' spring training and after spending some time in the minor leagues, he played one game with "dem bums." He did get more than just "a cup of coffee" with the Chicago Cubs, and played 66 games with them. It's not well known, but he was also drafted by the Chicago Bears, but never did get into an NFL game.

Connors's sports career never really jelled, but as luck would have it, he was discovered by an MGM talent scout who cast him in the 1952 Spencer Tracy and Katherine Hepburn classic *Pat and Mike*. After several other films, Connors made the transition to the small screen, where he created his most famous role, Lucas McCain on the long-running ABC western titled *The Rifleman*. During the show's run, he recorded one single for the Decca label in 1960—"Somebody Bigger Than You and I" backed with "Seventy Times Seven." The record went nowhere, and much like his career in sports, Connors put making records behind him.

After *The Rifleman* enjoyed a five-season, 168-episode run, Connors moved on to *Arrest and Trial* with Ben Gazzara on ABC, followed by another western titled *Branded* on NBC and *Cowboy in Africa* on ABC. Even though all of these programs kept Connors in the public eye for most of the 1960s, none of them attained the same level of success of *The Rifleman*. After *Cowboy in Africa* he remained very busy in episodic TV, TV movies, motion pictures, and miniseries. He attempted success in a few other short-lived TV series in the 1980s—*The Yellow Rose, Werewolf,* and *Paradise*. The latter was his final series, and only two years afterward, the longtime smoker died of lung cancer and pneumonia on November 10, 1992.

Warner Bros.' *Hawaiian Eye* star Robert (Bob) Conrad recorded numerous singles for the Warner Bros. label.

ROBERT CONRAD

Most Famous TV Roles: Tom Lopaka on *Hawaiian Eye*, Jim West on *The Wild Wild West*; **Networks:** ABC, CBS; **Years:** 1959–1963, 1965–1969, respectively; **Hit Recording:** "Bye Bye Baby"; **Label:** Warner Bros.; **Release Years:** 1960–1962; **Matrix:** Warner Bros. #5242; **Chart:** #113 *Billboard* Bubbling Under

Konrad Robert Falkowski (shortened to Falk) was born March 1, 1935, in Chicago, Illinois. He attended Northwestern University and supported himself by singing in Chicago nightclubs. After numerous movie bit parts,

Warner Bros. cast him as Tom Lopaka in *Hawaiian Eye* with lovely Connie Stevens (see the entry under her name). At the time, Warner Bros. had a penchant for pressuring its TV stars into recording for its record label. Conrad had some prior singing experience, so he looked like a shoo-in for success and several singles were recorded and released during *Hawaiian Eye's* heyday. He started with "I Want You Pretty Baby" backed with "Ballin' the Jack" (Warner Bros. #5211); then came his biggest hit, "Bye Bye Baby" backed with "Love You" (Warner Bros. #5242), "Noah's Ark" backed with "Keep It Up" (Warner Bros. #5267), "The Great Magician" backed with "Just Gotta Have You" (Warner Bros. #5306), and "Cindy Is Gone" backed with the old standard "Again" (Warner Bros. #5317). All of these were recorded with the teen audience in mind and weren't very different from the kind of material that Paul Petersen and James Darren were recording. The difference was, Petersen and Darren had several big chart hits, but Conrad was never able to conquer the Hot 100. He also took part in Warner Bros.' *We Wish You a Merry Christmas* album (Warner Bros. #1337)—a compilation LP featuring the biggest Warner Bros. TV names of the day.

After the cancellation of *Hawaiian Eye* in 1963, Conrad attempted to leap into another series and was up for the role of Major Anthony Nelson for an upcoming show to be called *I Dream of Jeannie*, but the role went to Larry Hagman instead. Conrad wasn't out of work for long—he soon landed likely his most famous role as Jim West on CBS's *The Wild Wild West*. Like *Hawaiian Eye*, it lasted for four seasons. Conrad did most of his own stunts on that program—a TV rarity. In the 1970s, he portrayed Pappy Boyington in *Baa Baa Black Sheep*, later retitled *Black Sheep Squadron*. Around this same time, Conrad filmed a popular series of Eveready Battery commercials. Seen shirtless, Conrad had the battery on his shoulder and dared the viewer to knock it off. He sold a lot more batteries than phonograph records. He has been married twice and has a total of eight children.

TIM CONSIDINE

Most Famous TV Role: Mike Douglas on *My Three Sons*; **Network:** ABC; **Years:** 1960–1965; **Hit Recording:** none; **Labels:** Del-Fi, Disneyland; **Release Years:** 1958–1964; **Matrix:** "Take It from a Guy Who Knows" (Del-Fi #4212), "Who's the Lucky Guy?" (Del-Fi #4244), "The Triple R Song" (Disneyland #58); **Chart:** none

Timothy Considine was born in Los Angeles on New Year's Eve 1940. His parents were in show business, and his maternal grandfather was Alexander Pantages, for whom the legendary Pantages Theatre is named.

Grandson Tim scored two memorable roles on TV in his youth—first as Spin Evans of *Spin and Marty* fame (in all three incarnations of *Spin and Marty*) and then as Frank Hardy on *The Hardy Boys: The Mystery of The Applegate Treasure* and *The Hardy Boys: The Mystery of The Ghost Farm* on *The Mickey Mouse Club*. He was then cast as the eldest Douglas son, Mike, on the ABC version of *My Three Sons*. During each series Considine released 45 rpm records. While on *The Mickey Mouse Club* he released "The Triple R Song" geared toward kids, appropriately on the Disneyland Records label. While on *My Three Sons*, he released two singles aimed at the teen record-buying public. He got to record for the same label as fellow TV star Johnny Crawford (see the entry under his name), Del-Fi Records. Considine, however, did not attain the same level of success as Crawford. One of Considine's 45s for the label, "Take It from the Guy Who Knows," was written by the prolific Ellie Greenwich ("Leader of the Pack," "Hanky Panky," "Chapel of Love").

After five seasons, Considine opted to leave *My Three Sons* in 1965 thinking it had run its course. It was, however, picked up by CBS for a sixth season beginning in September of that year, but Considine wanted to spread his wings, and his character was never mentioned again. Much like McLean Stevenson's decision to leave *M*A*S*H* and Shelley Long's choice to leave *Cheers*, Considine's exit from *My Three Sons* proved not to be a great idea, as the series flourished on CBS, lasting for seven more seasons. Considine explored new avenues and had some modest success as a TV writer and director, but his on-screen star fizzled. Without Considine, *My Three Sons* with only two sons made little sense, so Stanley Livingston's (Chip's) real-life brother, Barry, was added to the cast as the adopted and all-important third son, Ernie. In recent years, Considine has appeared with remaining cast members at *My Three Sons* reunions and autograph shows. He has been married twice and has one child.

JACKIE COOPER

Most Famous TV Roles: Sock Miller on *The People's Choice*, Dr. Hennesey on *Hennesey*; **Networks:** CBS, NBC; **Years:** 1955–1958, 1959–1962, respectively; **Hit Recording:** none; **Label:** Dot; **Release Years:** 1957–1958; **Matrix:** "Midnight Train" (Dot #15793), "A Doodlin' Song" (Dot #15834); **Chart:** none

Jackie Cooper was born into a show business family in Los Angeles, California, on September 15, 1922. By the age of three, he was appearing in films. By the age of seven, he joined Hal Roach's *Our Gang* comedies. In

1931, he was loaned out to Paramount Studios to appear in *Skippy*, a role for which he was nominated for an Oscar. Then came success at MGM as Wallace Beery's frequent costar. Once an adult, movie roles were few and far between, and Cooper made the transition to television. The result was two hit sitcoms—*The People's Choice* on NBC (on which we could hear the funny thoughts of his pet basset hound, Cleo), and then *Hennesey* on CBS (for which his stint in the navy came in handy as he portrayed a navy doctor). During the final season of *The People's Choice*, Cooper released a couple of singles for the Dot Records label—"When My Sugar Walks down the Street" backed with "Midnight Train" and "A Doodlin' Song" backed with "Last Night on the Back Porch." Neither single made the charts, but that didn't stop Cooper—he was known to sing and play piano on his next series, *Hennesey*, with costars Abby Dalton and James Komack. He also served as the orchestra conductor on the *Hennesey* album (Signature #1049) in 1960.

After *Hennesey* was cancelled in 1962, Cooper opted to work mostly behind the scenes. He was involved in program development for Columbia's Screen Gems division from 1964 to 1970. After this, he became a prolific TV director, and garnered Emmy Awards for his work on *M*A*S*H* and *The White Shadow*. He also made a triumphant return to the silver screen as Perry White in the Christopher Reeve *Superman* films. Cooper was married three times and his 1982 autobiography is called *Please Don't Shoot My Dog*. Cooper died on May 3, 2011, in Santa Monica, California, at the age of 88. His costar on *The People's Choice*, Pat Breslin, died later that same year.

MARC COPAGE

Most Famous TV Role: Corey Baker on *Julia*; **Network:** NBC; **Years:** 1968–1971; **Hit Recording:** none; **Labels:** Avco, Metromedia; **Release Year:** 1971; **Matrix:** "Will It Be Me?" (Avco #4576), "Popi" (Metromedia #134); **Chart:** none

Marc Diego Copage was born in Los Angeles, California, on June 21, 1962. At the age of six, Copage was cast in the groundbreaking NBC dramedy called *Julia*, starring Diahann Carroll. Copage portrayed Julia's son, Corey Baker. An internal problem on the show cropped up because Copage had lost his mother in real life and began to see Carroll as his real mom, causing a rift with Carroll's real daughter, Suzanne. In the program's third and

Marc Copage, also known as Corey Baker on *Julia*, performs the theme from the popular motion picture *Popi*.

final season, Copage was signed to the Avco Records label, and one single titled "Will It Be Me?" was released as a single. He also released a version of the theme song from the United Artists motion picture *Popi* (Metromedia #134), but his young, untrained vocal efforts did not translate to sales, and aspirations of a recording career were quickly quelled. When *Julia* disappeared from the prime-time schedule, Copage persistently sought other acting roles, but opportunities were extremely few and far between. His most recent credit was as Lawyer Jim in the 2000 Bruce Willis motion picture titled *The Kid*. Copage still has designs on having a hit record and often posts his newest tunes on YouTube.

Bachelor Father bachelorette Noreen Corcoran sings about the "Love of Mike."

NOREEN CORCORAN

Most Famous TV Role: Kelly Gregg on *Bachelor Father*; **Networks:** ABC, CBS, NBC; **Years:** 1957–1962; **Hit Recording:** none; **Labels:** Carlton, Vee Jay; **Release Years:** 1959–1963; **Matrix:** "If You Would Only Be Mine" (Carlton #532), "Love Kitten" (Vee Jay #555), "Love of Mike" (Vee Jay #590); **Chart:** none

Noreen Corcoran was born in Quincy, Massachusetts, on October 20, 1943. She and her seven siblings were moved to Santa Monica, California, in 1947 where Noreen's father got a job at MGM. The Corcoran children were groomed for show business and appeared on television and in the movies. Corcoran got her big TV break in 1957 when she costarred with John Forsythe in an episode of *General Electric Theater* titled "New Girl in His Life." That popular installment of the anthology series served as the pilot for what, later that year, became a new CBS series titled *Bachelor Father*. John Forsythe had to raise his niece, Kelly, after the untimely death of her parents, the Greens. Kelly Green was then adopted by her bachelor uncle (a wealthy Beverly Hills lawyer and playboy) and she became Kelly Gregg. The program has the distinction of being cancelled twice, but then being picked up by another network. Over a five-year span, it ran first on CBS, then NBC, and finally ABC (and took on a new theme song with each network change). During the show's run, Noreen and her sister Donna Corcoran recorded a duet for New York's Carlton Records label— "If You Would Only Be Mine" backed with "Lonely Fool." It was not a hit, but Noreen got another opportunity a couple of years later as a solo performer for Vee Jay Records. With a doo-wop feel to the songs, Noreen released "Love of Mike" backed with "A Guy Is a Guy" and "Why Can't a Boy and Girl Stay in Love?" backed with "Love Kitten." None of these became big hits—"Love Kitten" was the best seller on Vee Jay.

After *Bachelor Father* came to an end in 1962, Corcoran found work in teen films such as *Gidget Goes to Rome* and *The Girls on the Beach*. By 1966, Corcoran opted to leave acting and pursue her passion for dancing, and worked with the Lewitzky Dance Company. Coincidentally, much like the title of her most famous TV show, *Bachelor Father*, Corcoran never married. She is retired and living in Chatsworth, California. She and Forsythe stayed in touch until his passing on April Fools' Day of 2010. As of this writing, *Bachelor Father* reruns were shown most recently on the Antenna TV Network.

BILL COSBY

Most Famous TV Role: Cliff Huxtable on *The Cosby Show*; **Network:** NBC; **Years:** 1984–1992; **Hit Recording:** "Little Ole Man"; **Label:** Warner Bros.; **Release Year:** 1967; **Matrix:** Warner Bros. #7072; **Chart:** #4 *Billboard* Hot 100

William Cosby was born in Philadelphia, Pennsylvania, on July 12, 1937. He was very athletic in his youth, and as one would expect, he was the class clown. During his high school years, he discovered a unique ability to make people laugh and decided to actively pursue that. Cosby honed his skills in nightclubs and eventually had the opportunity to record comedy albums. His comedy albums got him guest shots on variety and talk shows, and his star rose rapidly. His popularity earned him a groundbreaking role as Alexander Scott on NBC's *I Spy* alongside Robert Culp as Kelly Robinson. The adventure series ran for three seasons, and during that period Cosby released several singles for Warner Bros. records, and one of them became a huge Top Five hit—"Little Ole Man" in 1967. Basically, it was "Uptight (Everything's Alright)" by Stevie Wonder with new lyrics. Both Wonder and Cosby got writing credits on the label. Cosby's comedy albums sold very well, but "Little Ole Man" became his only hit single. Several of the comedy albums garnered Grammy Awards. Cosby solidified his place in TV history with several other successful programs—*The Bill Cosby Show* on NBC from 1969 to 1971, *Cosby, Cos, You Bet Your Life, The Cosby Mysteries,* and his biggest success, *The Cosby Show,* which ran from 1984 to 1992 and was very often number 1 in the Nielsen ratings. He also enjoyed a long run providing voices for the *Fat Albert and the Cosby Kids* series. Early in that show's run, in 1973, Cosby released an album for MCA (LP #333) titled *Bill Cosby—Fat Albert.* It contained mostly comedy bits about the calorically challenged Albert, his family, and his car. During his storied career, Mr. Cosby has garnered four Emmys and nine Grammys. He has a star on the Hollywood Walk of Fame, received a Kennedy Center Honor in 1998, and was inducted into the Television Hall of Fame in 1991. He has also written numerous best-selling books. Plans for a 2015 sitcom were scrapped after numerous women came forward with allegations of sexual misconduct.

WALLY COX

Most Famous TV Roles: Robinson J. Peepers on *Mister Peepers,* the voice of *Underdog,* occupied the upper left square on *The Hollywood Squares;* **Network:** NBC; **Years:** 1952–1955, 1964–1966, 1965–1973, respectively; **Hit Recording:** none; **Label:** RCA Victor, Waldorf; **Release Years:** 1953–1955; **Matrix:** "What a Crazy Guy" (RCA Victor #5278), "The Pushcart Serenade" (Waldorf Music Hall #218); **Chart:** none

Wallace Bernard Cox was born in Detroit, Michigan, on December 6, 1924. Upon moving to Evanston, Illinois, at the age of 10, he befriended Marlon Brando, who also lived in the neighborhood. They both became big stars and even roomed together in New York City when each of them was trying to break into show business. After performing comedy routines on numerous TV shows, Cox was approached for the lead role in a live NBC sitcom to be called *Peepers.* When the pilot sold, it was retitled *Mister Peepers,* and it enjoyed a four-season run. During its run, a couple of Cox's routines—"What a Crazy Guy" backed with "There Is a Tavern

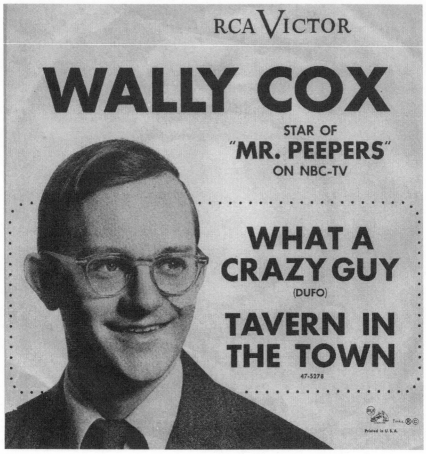

A waxing from Wally, the star of the live NBC sitcom *Mister Peepers*.

in the Town"—were recorded and released on the RCA Victor label in 1953. The program was still running in 1955 when Cox got to release yet another single called "The Pushcart Serenade" backed with "Sam, the Whistle Man." Cox also starred in another series for NBC in 1956, *The Adventures of Hiram Holliday*—a filmed sitcom. This program only lasted a single season. Cox found success in the 1960s as the voice of *Underdog* and as the upper left-hand square on *The Hollywood Squares*. While his acting career was in a serious lull, Cox died at the age of only 49, on February 15, 1973, of a heart attack. His ashes were allegedly housed at the home of his longtime friend, Marlon Brando.

BOB CRANE

Most Famous TV Role: Colonel Robert E. Hogan on *Hogan's Heroes*; **Network:** CBS; **Years:** 1965–1971; **Hit Recording:** none; **Label:** Epic; **Release Year:** 1966; **Matrix:** *Bob Crane, His Drums and Orchestra Play the Funny Side of TV* (Epic LP #24224); **Chart:** none

Bob Crane was born in Waterbury, Connecticut, on July 13, 1928. He began his career as a disc jockey, first in the Nutmeg State, and then in Los Angeles. His very innovative and popular radio broadcasts aided in his next move to television. He portrayed Dr. Dave Kelsey on the last three seasons of the long-running *Donna Reed Show* on ABC before starring in his own sitcom called *Hogan's Heroes*. Somehow, this bizarre series about having fun while in a Nazi POW camp during World War II enjoyed a six-season run on CBS, and made Bob Crane a big star as Colonel Robert Hogan. While the series was at its peak, Crane released an Epic label record album titled *Bob Crane, His Drums and Orchestra Play the Funny Side of TV*. The LP is a collection of TV theme songs, including those from *Get Smart*, *My Three Sons*, *F Troop*, *The Andy Griffith Show*, and of course, *Hogan's Heroes*. Voices on this unique album include that of Crane and actress Iris Adrian. It wasn't a big hit but did feature his costars Werner Klemperer and John Banner on the cover. Crane's career slowed after *Hogan's Heroes* was canceled in 1971, and he gravitated toward performing in dinner theaters. An attempted comeback for MTM Productions in 1975 called *The Bob Crane Show* only lasted for 13 weeks on NBC. The show's premise sounded like a winner—a hugely successful middle-aged businessman leaves his hectic job to return to college to pursue his dream of becoming a doctor, but said premise never really jelled and the program failed to find an audience. While all of this was going on, Crane was leading a double life that involved videotaping sexual encounters with a countless array of women—a sordid secret existence that likely led to his murder in an Arizona hotel room on June 29, 1978. A 2002 biopic called *Auto Focus* starred Greg Kinnear. Crane was married twice and had four children.

JOHNNY CRAWFORD

Most Famous TV Role: Mark McCain on *The Rifleman*; **Network:** ABC; **Years:** 1958–1963; **Hit Recording:** "Cindy's Birthday"; **Label:** Del-Fi; **Release Year:** 1962; **Matrix:** Del-Fi #4178; **Chart:** #8 *Billboard* Hot 100

The son of *The Rifleman*, Johnny Crawford, took a "shot" at a recording career and hit the target with three Top Twenty hits.

Johnny Crawford was born into a musical family on March 26, 1946, in Los Angeles, California. His grandfather was a song plugger around the turn of the century. Johnny inherited a love of big band music and old standards, as well as a large music collection from him. With the advent of television, he used to comb through the *TV Guide* each week and would circle the musicals (and the westerns) so he'd remember to watch them.

Crawford conquered two entertainment venues—TV and recording. He was one of the original Mouseketeers on *The Mickey Mouse Club* in 1955—always a singer. Coincidentally, his older brother Bobby portrayed Andy on the *Laramie* western TV series on NBC at the same time Johnny was portraying Mark McCain on *The Rifleman* alongside Chuck Connors on ABC. He was nominated for an Emmy Award during *The Rifleman*'s run. A friend of his parents was a good friend of Bob Keane, who owned Del-Fi Records—the label for which Ritchie Valens had recorded. Because *The Rifleman* was current, Keane thought it would be a good idea to sign Crawford to the label in 1961. In fact, Johnny made one record with his brother Bobby as the Crawford Brothers on Del-Fi. As a solo artist, Crawford was presented with some really good material from the Brill Building songwriters of the day. The only song he wasn't very fond of was one called "Patti Ann" (Del-Fi #4172). His favorite is the biggest hit, "Cindy's Birthday." He loved the song from the first time he heard it. Johnny had a string of successful singles for the label—"Rumors" (Del-Fi #4188), "Your Nose Is Gonna Grow" (Del-Fi #4181), and "Proud" (Del-Fi #4193). The latter is a very powerful song with a lot of intensity, similar to the type of material Roy Orbison was recording. Crawford was not a big rock and roll fan—he loved the music of the 1920s and '30s. However, when the Beatles and Bob Dylan came along, he greatly appreciated their music and also became a big fan of the folk singers of the day.

Crawford enjoyed that time in his life, but it was very hectic. He'd be on the set of *The Rifleman* all day, and then have recording sessions for Del-Fi at night. Plus, he was doing a lot of record hops to promote his hit singles. He lip-synched on *American Bandstand* four times. Some of the teen fans at the record hops and live performances were a bit intimidating, and he tired of that after a while. He even got to sing on *The Rifleman* on the very last episode of the series. He performed "Greensleeves" and the flip side of "Cindy's Birthday" called "Something Special."

As of this writing, *The Rifleman* is enjoying a successful run on the MeTV cable channel. Crawford has cut some promotional material for the channel and also has a new CD titled *Sweeping the Clouds Away*, on which he performs the music closest to his heart—the standards. The CD is on his own record label and is available through his website—www.crawfordmusic.com.

BRANDON CRUZ. *See* BILL BIXBY.

BILLY CRYSTAL

Most Famous TV Roles: Jodie Dallas on *Soap*, cast member on *Saturday Night Live*; **Networks:** ABC, NBC; **Years:** 1977–1981, 1984–1985, respectively; **Hit Recording:** "You Look Marvelous"; **Label:** A&M; **Release Year:** 1985; **Matrix:** A&M #2764; **Chart:** #58 *Billboard* Hot 100

William Edward Crystal was born on March 14, 1948, in New York City. His parents owned a music store, and also worked for the Commodore Records label (a jazz label). Influenced by Sid Caesar, Bob Newhart, and Rich Little, Crystal was a regular performer in comedy clubs in the early 1970s, and earned some guest spots on TV variety and talk shows. This led to his costarring role as TV's first regular gay character, Jodie Dallas, on the ABC sitcom *Soap* and enjoyed a four-season run. In 1982 he hosted his own short-lived TV variety series called *The Billy Crystal Comedy Hour* on NBC. When he joined the cast of *Saturday Night Live* for the 1984–1985 season, he also scored a moderately popular hit single. Titled "You Look Marvelous," it was based upon his popular *Saturday Night Live* impersonation of the late Fernando Lamas and was cowritten by Paul Shaffer. The record reached number 58 on the Hot 100 and remained on the chart for a dozen weeks. Crystal's biggest successes on the silver screen were still to come—*When Harry Met Sally*, *City Slickers*, *Analyze This*, *Toy Story*, and a made-for-TV movie called *61*. Crystal has also hosted the Academy Awards to much acclaim nine times, has garnered numerous Emmy Awards, and has a star on the Hollywood Walk of Fame. Crystal and his wife, Janice, have been married since 1970 and have two grown daughters.

KEN CURTIS

Most Famous TV Role: Deputy Festus Haggen on *Gunsmoke*; **Network:** CBS; **Years:** 1964–1975; **Hit Recording:** none; **Labels:** Capitol, Dot; **Release Years:** 1966–1968; **Matrix:** *Gunsmoke's Festus* (Capitol #2418), *Gunsmoke's Festus Haggen* (Dot #25859); **Chart:** none

Ken Curtis was born July 2, 1916, in Lamar, Colorado. His father was the county sheriff. Ken was on the high school football team and then served in the U.S. Army. He began his show business career as a singer and released a few recordings in the 1940s and 1950s, but none of them caught on. Curtis's father-in-law was director John Ford, and this connection was very helpful early in his acting career. After numerous motion picture roles, Curtis earned his first recurring TV role—Jim Buckley on the syndicated *Ripcord* series from 1961 to 1963 (now available on DVD). He then joined the cast of *Gunsmoke* as the cranky and unkempt jail custodian named Festus for 11 of the program's 20 seasons on CBS. During those years, Curtis released a couple of albums connected to the program— *Gunsmoke's Festus* and *Gunsmoke's Festus Haggen*. These LPs contained both vocals and spoken word cuts. Neither one was a whopping success. He remained with the show until it ended in 1975. His final series was *The Yellow Rose* on NBC from 1983 to 1984. Curtis portrayed Hoyt Coryell on the series. Curtis died in his sleep on April 28, 1991, at the age of 74. He had been living in Clovis, California, where a statue was erected in his honor. He was married twice.

D

MICHAEL DAMIAN

Most Famous TV Role: Danny Romalotti on *The Young and the Restless;*
Network: CBS; **Years:** 1984–2013; **#1 Hit Recording:** "Rock On"; **Label:**
Cypress; **Release Year:** 1989; **Matrix:** Cypress #1420; **Chart:** #1 *Billboard*
Hot 100

Michael Damian Weir was born in Bonsall, California, on April 26, 1962.
He performed as a member of the Weir family and was urged to pursue
his own career separate from them. He was a total unknown when he
first appeared on *American Bandstand* at the age of 19 in 1981 with his first
single titled "She Did It" (Leg #007). It was not a major hit, but when Damian landed the role of struggling singer Danny Romalotti on CBS's *The
Young and the Restless,* he was given another opportunity to record. This
time around he was hugely successful and scored a number 1 hit remake
of David Essex's "Rock On" in 1989. It earned Damian a gold record and
was included in the soundtrack for the Corey Feldman motion picture
Dream a Little Dream. Damian reached the Top Forty twice more with
"Cover of Love" (Cypress #1430) and "Was It Nothing at All?" (Cypress
#1451) in that same year. The latter did reach the Top Ten on the Adult
Contemporary charts. Damian left the daytime soap opera for a while
when an opportunity in *Joseph and the Amazing Technicolor Dreamcoat*
came up in the hit Minskoff Theatre revival beginning in 1993. It ran for
231 performances. Damian did revisit *The Young and the Restless* for the
program's 35th anniversary celebration in 2008. He has been married to
Janeen Damian since 1998.

BILL DANA. *See* JOSÉ JIMÉNEZ.

TOM D'ANDREA

Most Famous TV Roles: Jim Gillis on *The Life of Riley*, Tom on *The Soldiers;* **Network:** NBC; **Years:** 1953–1958; **Hit Recording:** none; **Label:** Coral; **Release Year:** 1955; **Matrix:** "Goin' on a Hike" (Coral #61466); **Chart:** none

Tom D'Andrea was born in Chicago, Illinois, on May 15, 1909. He began his career doing comedic stage routines, and teamed with actor/game show host Hal March for a popular sketch called "The Soldiers." D'Andrea and March performed the skit numerous times on NBC's *Colgate Comedy Hour*. Around the same time, NBC was reviving *The Life of Riley*, which had failed to catch on in its original TV incarnation with a young, skinny Jackie Gleason in the title role in 1949. This new version of the old chestnut starred William Bendix, who had portrayed the lovable and naive Chester A. Riley on radio. This version worked, and D'Andrea portrayed Riley's best friend, Jim Gillis. In the meantime, Hal March was portraying Joe on the live CBS sitcom *My Friend Irma*, and was then hosting the popular progressive game show *The $64,000 Question* on CBS. However, NBC wanted to capitalize on their popular soldiers sketch and gave them their own live weekly sitcom on Saturday nights during the summer of 1955. The skit as a regular series just didn't work, and it was gone after 13 weeks. However, Coral Records also thought the skit was a viable commodity and released two of the pair's skits on a 78 and 45 rpm record—"Goin' on a Hike" backed with "Goin' Overseas" in 1955. It failed to chart and Tom D'Andrea once again focused on his *Life of Riley* role. March, however, continued to make records (see the entry under his name).

The Life of Riley ended its run in 1958, and D'Andrea surfaced in a recurring role a couple of years later alongside Howard Duff in the light-hearted NBC adventure series about a gambling casino titled *Dante*. D'Andrea portrayed Biff on that single-season program. He stayed active guest starring on episodic TV shows into the 1970s, and eventually retired to Florida, where he died on May 14, 1998, one day before his 89th birthday. He left behind three sons and numerous grandchildren.

GAIL DAVIS

Most Famous TV Role: the title role on *Annie Oakley;* **Network:** syndicated; **Years:** 1953–1957; **Hit Recording:** none; **Label:** RCA Victor; **Release Year:** 1956; **Matrix:** "Why Not Save Sunshine?" (RCA #7043), "Come Back to Me" (RCA #7902), "Are You Ready?" (RCA #7484), "Annie Oakley Theme" (RCA #WBY-88), "Shake Me I Rattle" (RCA #WBY-99); **Chart:** none

Gail Davis was born as Betty Jean Grayson on October 5, 1925, in Little Rock, Arkansas. She was dancing and singing since childhood and was destined for show business. She married young, and she and her husband moved to Hollywood to pursue careers in motion pictures. Because of actress Kathryn Grayson, she was urged to change her name and became Gail Davis. Davis scored quickly and was cast in a series of films, all westerns. Her biggest break came when she was cast in the lead role on the syndicated TV western called *Annie Oakley*. The program was produced by Gene Autry's Flying A Productions, and Shelley Fabares appeared in a few episodes (see the entry under her name). Eighty-one episodes were produced, and during the show's run, Davis recorded several single records for RCA Victor. Some of the singles were geared for children— "Annie Oakley" backed with "Blue Tail the Red Fox" and "Shake Me I Rattle" backed with "Pierre and Bernadette." Several others were aimed at a more adult crowd—"Why Not Save Sunshine?" backed with "Poor Little Heart," "Come Back to Me" backed with "Into the Eyes of Texas," and "Are You Ready?" backed with "The Wabash Cannonball." Even with two different musical avenues, none of the records caught on with the public. Davis did very little on TV after the series was cancelled, with the exception of a guest shot on a 1961 episode of *The Andy Griffith Show* titled "The Perfect Female." She toured with Gene Autry's rodeos for a while and later got into the management end of the business before retiring. She was married twice and has a star on the Hollywood Walk of Fame. Davis died of cancer on March 15, 1997.

RUFE DAVIS AND SMILEY BURNETTE

Most Famous TV Role: Floyd Smoot and Charlie Pratt, respectively, on *Petticoat Junction* and *Green Acres;* **Network:** CBS; **Years:** 1963–1970; **Hit Recording:** "Steam, Cinders and Smoke"; **Label:** Rancho; **Release Year:** 1964; **Matrix:** Rancho #1001; **Chart:** none

Rufe Davis was born Rufus Davidson in Vinson, Oklahoma, on December 2, 1908. He was one of 12 children and lived on a farm. Attempting to escape his impoverished youth, he sought work in show business and by the age of 20 was with a touring company. His specialty was imitating sounds. In the 1930s he worked in radio, and by the late 1930s he began his western film career. There is a huge gap of some 15 years between his final movie credit and his first TV credits. Although I have not been able to unearth said information, I would not be surprised if the gap was caused by blacklisting.

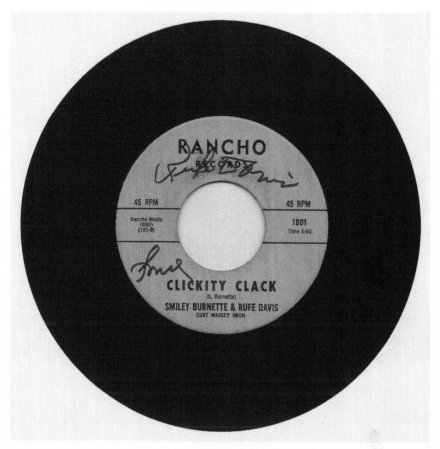

An autographed copy of "Clickety Clack" by Smiley Burnette and Rufe Davis of *Petticoat Junction*.

Davis portrayed Fred Smoot the conductor of the Cannonball mostly on *Petticoat Junction*, but also select episodes of *Green Acres*. He and his cohort on the show, Smiley Burnette, who played Charlie Pratt, released a single titled "Steam, Cinders and Smoke" backed with "Clickity Clack" in 1964. They were recorded for Burnette's Rancho Records at 12517 Hortense Street in Studio City, California. Both sides were "train tracks" relating to their TV sitcom, and Smiley Burnette's son, Stephen shared, "I played tambourine on the record, but was told by my dad I had no rhythm. Rufe Davis and my dad played all the instruments on the record, and the train sounds in the song were made by Rufe himself. He was really good at sound imitations. We didn't use any sound effect records, we didn't have to." About the Rancho label, Stephen added, "It dates back to 1947 with

Smiley Burnette and Rufe Davis as Charlie Pratt and Floyd Smoot, respectively, moving kind of slow at the junction.

over three hundred releases. We resurrected it in 1964 for this particular record." The "Steam, Cinders and Smoke" side was played on a 1970 episode of *Petticoat Junction* titled "Last Train to Pixley."

Burnette was born Lester Alvin Burnett (with no *e*—that was added later) and worked extensively with Gene Autry in the movies and on his television show. Burnette wrote a countless array of country songs, but sadly passed on at the young age of 55 during the show's run on February 16, 1967. Stephen was surprised when I told him that my own copy of the Rancho 45, found at a flea market, was signed by both Davis and Burnette, and said, "That's quite a collector's item. They only did one brief publicity tour with the record. We pressed up about one thousand copies and very few were signed."

Davis was married twice and had two children. He died at the age of 66 on December 13, 1974, in Torrance, California. Several other *Petticoat Junction* cast members made records—Edgar Buchanan, Gunilla Hutton, Meredith MacRae, and Mike Minor (see the entries for each).

RICHARD DAWSON

Most Famous TV Role: Corporal Peter Newkirk on *Hogan's Heroes*, host of the original *Family Feud*; **Networks:** ABC, CBS; **Years:** 1965–1971, 1976–1985, respectively; **Hit Recording:** none; **Label:** Carnation; **Release Year:** 1967; **Matrix:** "The Children's Parade" (Carnation #20020); **Chart:** none

Richard Dawson was born Colin Lionel Emm in Gosport, Hampshire, England, on November 20, 1932. He originally wanted to be a boxer, but instead pursued a career in comedy. After a few guest shots on episodic TV shows such as *The Jack Benny Program* and *The Dick Van Dyke Show*, he was cast as Corporal Peter Newkirk on *Hogan's Heroes* alongside Bob Crane and Werner Klemperer. The show ran for six seasons, and during its run, Dawson got to record a song called "The Children's Parade" backed with "Apples and Oranges" on the Carnation label in 1967. Dawson wasn't much of a singer and the record was not a hit. He also took part in an album titled *Hogan's Heroes Sing the Best of World War II* (Sunset #1137). After the series ended, Dawson found work as a regular on *The New Dick Van Dyke Show* and *The Match Game* (bottom center). He also hosted a couple of game shows—*Masquerade Party* and the wildly successful *Family Feud*. He also portrayed an evil game show host in the motion picture *Running Man* in 1987. Dawson died June 2, 2012, from esophageal cancer. He was married twice and had a total of three children. His first wife was actress Diana Dors.

LEO DE LYON

Most Famous TV Role: voice of Spook and Brain on *Top Cat*; **Network:** ABC; **Years:** 1961–1962; **Hit Recording:** none; **Labels:** Coral, Decca, London, MGM, Musicor; **Release Years:** 1952–1961; **Matrix:** "And the Band Played On" (MGM #11680), "For Me and My Gal" (Coral #61596), "Sick Manny's Gym" (Musicor #1001), *Like . . . Leo's Here* (London LP #2264); **Chart:** none

Leo De Lyon was born on April 25, 1926, as Irving Levin, and pursued a career in show business, propelled by a voice that possessed unlimited potential. He performed on stage with countless performers, including Judy Garland, Sandler and Young, Rosemary Clooney, Phil Silvers, Tommy Dorsey, and Buddy Rich. About the latter, De Lyon recalled, "Because of traffic in New York City, I was once late for Buddy Rich's show on the Josephine Baker tour, and I ran the last two blocks. I didn't even have time to change my clothes, and I hurriedly entered the theater to see Buddy Rich, the world-famous drummer, tap dancing brilliantly to fill time for my regular spot. Few people realize what an amazing singer he was, too."

Speaking of amazing singers, De Lyon got to sing and dance with Dorothy Loudon and Bob Haymes on a live, short-lived 1952 TV sitcom on the DuMont Network titled *It's a Business?* which focused upon song pluggers at the turn of the century (sadly, no episodes or kinescopes are known to exist). De Lyon is best known for his voice work—especially that of Spook and Brain in Hanna-Barbera's *Top Cat* series, and also the jazz swinging monkeys in Walt Disney's *The Jungle Book*. He made quite a few phonograph records. De Lyon recalled,

My first release was for MGM [#11680]. It was called "And the Band Played On," done with an oom-pa-pa feel to it, and I supplied all of the instrument sounds, using my voice. "Say It Isn't So" was on the flip side, and this recording led to a release for Coral Records [#61596] called "For Me and My Gal" backed with "Lonesome and Disgusted"—the B-side composed by Dave Lambert of jazz trio Lambert, Hendricks and Ross, inspired by an Al Capp comic strip. On the A-side, the label reads, "All vocal and instrumental sounds created by Leo De Lyon." The only instrument on the B-side is a piano in the middle of a funny operatic vocal. For the drum part, I used drum brushes, played on an empty shoebox while vocalizing the bass string part. Steve Allen told me he wore out two copies of the record playing it for his friends. It wasn't a big hit, but the A-side got a lot of airplay.

About his album, De Lyon shared,

In 1959, I got the chance to play at the club called Ciro's in Johannesburg, South Africa. I was booked there by someone who had seen me perform my act at the London Palladium. It turned out to be quite a wonderful experience—I was so well received there. I was, admittedly, a bit leery at first, but as in *The Godfather*, they made me an offer I couldn't refuse. My act was a cross between that of Victor Borge and Don Rickles with a bit of Jonathan Winters sprinkled in. I performed there every night for three weeks and was treated like royalty. I became very close with the kitchen help during my stay and would perform special private shows for them. I was backed up by a great orchestra, and the quintet's leader was affiliated with British Decca Records. He invited me to a recording studio, and if memory serves, we recorded an entire album in about four hours. The last cut on the album, "Leo in Africa," was completely ad-lib and that became the title for this album, initially released only in South Africa. Around my birthday in April of 1960, I got a call from London Records with interest in re-releasing the LP in the U.S. They had a big promotional tour lined up for me as well in all of the cities that were important for breaking a record, and the album was now called *Like . . . Leo's Here* with the picture of a real lion in a circus walking toward you on two tightropes on the cover [London #2264]. Some cuts we performed straight, but many were funny and very novel. Bob Crane—a top D. J. before becoming a TV actor—loved my version of "Unchained Melody," performed as if by a Japanese singer, and he played it until he wore it out. The album did OK, but it wasn't the success London had anticipated. Imagine my surprise over 30 years later when my son found a blog entry in *Dana's Downloadable Album of the Month* for July 2004 singing the praises of the album and my singing, impressions, and offbeat sense of humor. It said that the album was one of the unsung gems that had fallen through the cracks.

Dana's blog goes on to say, "He does some incredible imitations—not so much of people, but of musical instruments. Can't say I've ever heard Rich Little do a good trumpet, trombone or French horn!"

About a 1961 single for the Musicor Record label (#1001), De Lyon shared,

> At the time, there was a chain of gymnasiums called Vic Tanny's—a precursor to the Gold's Gyms of today. Well, a young Al Kooper—yes, indeed, the same one who would later help form Blood, Sweat and Tears—wrote a parody of Vic Tanny's and called it "Sick Manny's Gym." It was Kooper's introduction to the music industry. The artist listed on the label was Leo De Lyon and the Musclemen, and on the flip side was a song called "Plunkin'." Kooper wrote about it and about me in his autobiography, *Backstage Passes and Backstabbing Bastards: Memoirs of a Rock and Roll Survivor*.

De Lyon has also provided voices for *The Flintstones* and *The Smurfs* (to name but a few), and has made guest appearances on popular prime time series such as *Bewitched, My Mother the Car, The New Phil Silvers Show, Arrest and Trial*, and *The Incredible Hulk*. Retired as of this writing, De Lyon now resides in North Hollywood, California, maintains a lifelong affinity for jazz music, and loves to reminisce.

GEORGE DEWITT

Most Famous TV Role: host of *Name That Tune*; **Network:** CBS; **Years:** 1955–1959; **Hit Recording:** none; **Label:** MGM, RCA/Camden; **Release Years:** 1956–1957; **Matrix:** "Do You?" (MGM #12238), "Bye Bye Love" (RCA/Camden EP #403); **Chart:** none

George DeWitt was born George Florentine in Atlantic City, New Jersey, on December 30, 1922. He scored a job as a singing waiter and suddenly knew show business was in his blood. After a stint in the U.S. Army Air

Corps during World War II, DeWitt got to open for the Rat Pack as a
stand-up comic. Before too long, he was hosting his own CBS game show,
Name That Tune. During the run of that popular game show, he released
a few singles including "Do You" backed with "Fountain of the Bell" in
1956, and an EP (extended play) 45 including "Bye Bye Love," "A White
Sports Coat," "Young Love," and "Love Letters in the Sand" in 1957. He
was also part of a couple of LPs based upon his game show—*Name That
Tune* (RKO #145) and *Sing That Tune* (Epic #3562). He hosted another
short-lived TV series called *Be Our Guest* on CBS in 1960 and appeared
in *A Hole in the Head* with Frank Sinatra. After struggling to find work,
DeWitt retired in 1970, but continued to write material for other comics.
DeWitt suffered a heart attack and died July 14, 1979, leaving behind one
son named Jay.

CLIFF DEYOUNG

Most Famous TV Role: Sam Hayden on *Sunshine*; **Network:** NBC; **Year:**
1975; **Hit Recording:** "My Sweet Lady"; **Label:** MCA; **Release Years:** 1974–
1975; **Matrix:** "My Sweet Lady" backed with "Sunshine on My Shoulders"
(MCA #40156); **Chart:** #17 *Billboard* Hot 100

Clifford Tobin DeYoung was born in Los Angeles, California, on Abraham
Lincoln's birthday, on February 12, 1945. He attended California State
University. He had a band in the 1960s called Clear Light but left them
when he was cast in the Broadway musical *Hair*. He returned to California
to star in a TV movie called *Sunshine* in 1973. It was the story of a young
mother dying of cancer, and how her musician husband coped with the
loss. It featured several songs by John Denver, including "Sunshine on
My Shoulder," thus the title *Sunshine*. A Denver-penned song, "My Sweet
Lady," performed by DeYoung, was released as a single and became a big
Top Twenty hit early in 1974. The TV movie did so well that it was eventually made into a 1975 weekly half-hour dramedy series on NBC. *Sunshine*
costarred former child star Billy Mumy as Weaver, but the series was not
a ratings bonanza and lasted only 13 weeks. DeYoung continued to record,
and numerous follow-up singles were released on the MCA label, but
none of them charted. Some of those other cuts were "She Bent Me Straight
Again" (MCA #40239), "Lives" (MCA #40294), and "If I Could Put You
into My Song" (MCA #40388). DeYoung then opted to concentrate on his
acting career and found roles in two more short-lived series—*Centennial*
on NBC and *Master of the Game* on CBS. He also snagged small parts on
the silver screen in such films as *Harry and Tonto* and *Shock Treatment*. De-
Young has been married to the same woman, Gypsi, since 1970.

DONNA DOUGLAS

Most Famous TV Role: Elly May Clampett on *The Beverly Hillbillies*; **Network:** CBS; **Years:** 1962–1971; **Hit Recording:** none; **Labels:** Miracle, Oak; **Release Years:** early 1970s; **Matrix:** "Never Ending Song of Love" (Oak—no number on label), "At the End of the Rainbow" (Miracle #1002); **Chart:** none

Donna Douglas was born Doris Smith on September 26, 1933, in Louisiana. She was quite the athlete in high school, playing softball and basketball. She was crowned Miss Baton Rouge and Miss New Orleans in the 1950s. Her success in those pageants led her to New York City to seek a modeling career and got her a lot of work in print advertisements. An appearance on *The Ed Sullivan Show* led to her being cast in the Hal Wallis motion picture *Career*, and indeed, her career was now in high gear. Douglas added, "Hal Wallis picked my name, Donna Douglas, in early 1958. I liked it—I felt like a Donna Douglas."

Among her most famous TV roles is one as the misfit in the classic *Twilight Zone* episode titled "Eye of the Beholder." Douglas shared, "I'm amazed at the longevity and popularity of that episode. At a recent Monster Bash Convention in Butler, Pennsylvania, they showed that episode and the fan response was something else. I enjoyed making that episode very much—one of my few dramatic shows. That was prior to my becoming Elly May."

Speaking of Elly May, Douglas's biggest break came in 1962 when she was cast in the immensely popular nine-season sitcom classic called *The Beverly Hillbillies* alongside Buddy Ebsen, Irene Ryan, and Max Baer Jr. The program was number 1 for several of those seasons. Douglas remembered,

We were very close as a cast. I worked the most with Buddy Ebsen [Jed]—we had the most scenes together and he was a very sweet man. Irene Ryan [Granny] was a lovely, lovely lady. I miss her to this day. Max Baer Jr. [Jethro] and I recently did a large autograph show in Los Angeles. Over the three days of the event, the turnout was truly amazing—lines a mile long and nonstop. That was such a fun time with Max. The entire cast of the show released a record album in the middle 1960s. I hear that copies of the album frequently pop up for sale on eBay. I'm often asked to sign copies at autograph conventions.

She is often thought to be the vocalist on a 1962 recording titled "He's So Near" on the Arlen Records label. The artist on the label is listed as Donna Douglas, but Douglas responded, "No, that's not me. That's the

U.K. singer named Donna Douglas. I didn't release a 45 rpm record until the early 1970s on the Oak Records label—'Never Ending Song of Love' backed with 'You Make My Heart Wanna Sing.'" Douglas also recorded a 45 for the Miracle label (#1002) titled "At the End of a Rainbow." About her gospel albums, Douglas said, "They were fun to record—two albums, now on CD. I still offer them at autograph shows and sell a lot of them."

When asked for a fun anecdote about the many wild "critters" used on *The Beverly Hillbillies* Douglas said, "We were using a mountain lion in one episode, and as sure as I know my name, I knew that mountain lion was gonna bite me. It did, on my arm. I wasn't seriously hurt, but that event really sticks out in my mind."

What's she up to nowadays? Douglas answered, "I have my children's book, a children's coloring book, a cookbook (with a lot of Hollywood stories), and a new CD all available at my website—www.donnadoug lasofficialwebsite.com." On January 1, 2015, Douglas passed away.

MIKE DOUGLAS

Most Famous TV Role: host of *The Mike Douglas Show*; **Network:** syndicated; **Years:** 1963–1882; **Hit Recording:** "The Men in My Little Girl's Life"; **Label:** Epic; **Release Year:** 1965; **Matrix:** Epic #9876; **Chart:** #6 *Billboard* Hot 100

Mike Douglas was born as Michael Dowd Jr. in Chicago, Illinois, on August 11, 1920. He began singing in the choir and then on local radio. He briefly worked with Kay Kyser's big band. A decade later, while hosting a local talk show that was gaining in popularity, he was given the opportunity of a lifetime—national syndication. In 1963, *The Mike Douglas Show*, with its trademark asterisks decorating the set, began an almost 20-year run. Douglas, who got to sing on most episodes of the show, got to parlay his on-screen success into a hit record in 1965—"The Men in My Little Girl's Life"—for Epic Records. The record was rather novel and zoomed up and down the charts very quickly—peaking at number 6 but spending only nine weeks in the Hot 100. The record sparked an answer record from children's TV hostess Fran Allison, called "The Girls in My Little Boy's Life" (RCA Victor #8767), but it failed to make the charts (see the entry under her name). His program garnered one Emmy Award for Individual Achievement in Daytime Television, and had the unique feature of week-long guest hosts, including John Lennon and Yoko Ono, Tony Bennett, and Richard Pryor. One of his most memorable guests was Tiger Woods as a child, golfing with Jimmy Stewart and Bob Hope. After many years based in Philadelphia, the show moved to Los Angeles in 1978 and attempted to modernize itself with a traveling roadshow format, and came to an end in 1982. Douglas wrote two memoirs years apart—*My Story* in 1979 and *I'll Be Right Back: Memories of TV's Greatest Talk Show* in 1999. After beating prostate cancer in the 1990s, he died very suddenly on his 86th birthday in 2006, leaving behind a wife, Genevieve, and three daughters, Kelly, Michele, and Christine. Mike Douglas is not to be confused with actor Michael Douglas.

HUGH DOWNS

Most Famous TV Roles: host of *Concentration*, Jack Paar's sidekick on *The Tonight Show*, cohost of *The Today Show*, cohost of *20/20*; **Networks:** ABC, NBC; **Years:** 1958–1969, 1957–1962, 1962–1971, 1978–1999, respectively; **Hit Recording:** none; **Label:** Epic; **Release Year:** 1959; **Matrix:** *An Evening with Hugh Downs* (Epic LP #3597); **Chart:** none

Hugh Malcolm Downs was born in Akron, Ohio, on February 14, 1921. He started as a radio announcer in Lima, Ohio, and with the advent of television began a storied career. For a time, he clocked the most hours on-screen of anybody in the business. The highlights of his long career are as Jack Paar's sidekick on *The Tonight Show*, cohost of *The Today Show*, longtime host of NBC's classic game show *Concentration*, and the Emmy-winning cohost of *20/20* with Barbara Walters. In 1959, Downs attempted success at yet another avenue of show business—playing guitar and singing. This venture spawned one album for Epic Records in 1959 titled *An Evening with Hugh Downs*. Said album consisted of mostly folk, country songs and standards such as "Scarlet Ribbons" and "Drink to Me Only with Thine Eyes." It was not a success, but luckily he kept his many day jobs. Downs has been married to the same woman, Ruth Sheehan, since 1944 and they have two children. He was one of the first inductees into the Game Show Hall of Fame.

PATTY DUKE

Most Famous TV Role: Patty and Cathy Lane on *The Patty Duke Show*; **Network:** ABC; **Years:** 1963–1966; **Hit Recording:** "Don't Just Stand There"; **Label:** United Artists; **Release Year:** 1965; **Matrix:** United Artists #875; **Chart:** #8 *Billboard* Hot 100

HER VERY FIRST RECORD!!!

PATTY DUKE   UA 875

SINGS

DON'T JUST STAND THERE

B/W EVERYTHING BUT LOVE

UNITED ARTISTS RECORDS

She loved to rock and roll and a hot dog made her lose control. Patty Duke reached Top Ten with "Don't Just Stand There," aided by *The Patty Duke Show*.

Anna Maria Duke was born December 14, 1946, in Elmhurst, New York. Duke came from a broken home, and when her parents split up, she went to live with family friends, the Ross family (John and Ethel) and they also became her managers. She was renamed Patty Duke to mirror child star Patty McCormack of *The Bad Seed*. Duke appeared on the soap opera *The Brighter Day* in the late 1950s, and also appeared in numerous anthology drama series on TV. She was then cast in a lead role in Broadway's *The Miracle Worker*. When the play became a motion picture, Duke reprised her role and garnered an Oscar for her portrayal. Despite all of her experience in dramatic roles, Duke was cast in two roles in a 1963 situation comedy called *The Patty Duke Show* on ABC, on which she portrayed both Patty and identical cousin Cathy Lane. The program was filmed for United Artists, and the studio thought she might also appeal to the teen record-buying public. They were right. Even though Duke wasn't much of a singer, she did manage to place one ballad in the Top Ten in 1965—"Don't Just Stand There." It was released with a picture sleeve. Of course, Duke performed the song on her sitcom. She also had a Top Thirty follow-up titled "Say Something Funny" (United Artists #915), but for all intents and purposes, her recording career was over as fast as it had begun. One of her final singles was an answer to Bobby Goldsboro's "Whenever He Holds You" titled "Whenever She Holds You" (United Artists #978).

The Patty Duke Show ran for three seasons, and by the time it was cancelled in 1966, Duke was 20 and ready for more grown-up roles, such as Neely O'Hara in *The Valley of the Dolls*. While married to fellow sitcom star John Astin, she was known as Patty Duke Astin (1972–1985). She remained extremely active in episodic TV programming, TV miniseries, and TV movies. Speaking of TV movies, she won her only Emmy for her role in the 1970 TV movie titled *My Sweet Charlie*. Duke was unable to find success in another regular series of her own. She gave it the old college try, however, and starred in *It Takes Two* with Richard Crenna in 1982, *Hail to the Chief* in 1985, *Karen's Song* in 1987, and *Amazing Grace* in 1995. None of these made it past the first season.

In her memoirs, *Call Me Anna*, Duke revealed that the Rosses had treated her poorly and squandered almost all of her money. She was under their thumb, however, until the age of 18. She also divulged her newly diagnosed bipolar disorder, and the struggles of her teen years. She has a star on the Hollywood Walk of Fame. *The Patty Duke Show* is running in syndication (as of this writing) on the Antenna cable channel, and all three seasons of the sitcom are available on DVD.

SANDY DUNCAN

Most Famous TV Role: Sandy Hogan on *The Hogan Family*; **Network:** CBS, NBC; **Years:** 1987–1991; **Hit Recording:** none; **Label:** Decca; **Release Year:** 1971; **Matrix:** "I Am a Woman in a Man's World" (Decca #32728); **Chart:** none

Sandra Kay Duncan was born in Henderson, Texas, on February 20, 1946. She was earning a living as an actress by the age of 12 in a local Tyler, Texas, production of *The King and I*. Her breaks on TV came in the 1960s in commercials and in a brief stint on the soap opera *Search for Tomorrow*.

Her film debuts came in the very early 1970s in *The Million Dollar Duck* and Neil Simon's *Star-Spangled Girl*. She snagged her own series on CBS in 1971 called *Funny Face*, and also released a 45 rpm single for Decca Records. The recording was very pro–women's lib, and Duncan, backed by a group called Hope for the Future, performed "I Am a Woman in a Man's World," backed with "Liberation Now," but it was not a good seller. After filming 13 episodes of her sitcom, production was cut short when Duncan had to undergo immediate surgery to remove a benign tumor behind one of her eyes. She lost sight in that eye and also lost the TV show, despite very decent ratings.

After her recovery, the program was retooled and recast, now as *The Sandy Duncan Show* in 1972. The theme song and the baby pictures in the opening credits were the same, and she still portrayed Sandy Stockton, but had a totally different job, apartment, and friends. The latter show was also different in that it was filmed before a live audience, unlike *Funny Face*, which had been filmed single camera style with a laugh track. Placed on Sunday nights, the show failed to find an audience and was gone before 1973 began. Her biggest triumphs came with her much lauded performance as *Peter Pan* on Broadway in the late 1970s and as Sandy Hogan in *The Hogan Family* from 1987 to 1991, first on NBC and then CBS. Sandy replaced Valerie Harper as the matriarch on the sitcom after Harper's much publicized salary dispute and ultimate firing. The program was initially called *Valerie*, but eventually evolved into *The Hogan Family*. Duncan also became a familiar presence in a long series of commercials for Wheat Thins snack crackers. The most used word to describe her is *perky*. Duncan has been married three times and has two grown sons, Jeffrey and Michael.

DON DURANT

Most Famous TV Role: Johnny Ringo on *Johnny Ringo*; **Network:** CBS; **Years:** 1959–1960; **Hit Recording:** none; **Label:** RCA Victor; **Release Year:** 1960; **Matrix:** "Johnny Ringo Theme" (RCA Victor #7760); **Chart:** none

Don Durant was born Donald Allison Durae in Long Beach, California, on November 20, 1932. He never met his father, who was killed in a traffic accident before Don's birth. Durant had his own tragedy at the age of 11 when he was on a bicycle that was struck by a cement truck. He recovered fully and played football in high school, and entertained the troops while in the U.S. Navy. He got some bit parts on episodic TV shows in

Don Durant wrote and performed the theme song for his Four Star Studios TV series called *Johnny Ringo*.

the 1950s and often sang anonymously on *The Jack Benny Program* and in DeSoto commercials. In 1958, Durant was cast in a pilot by an up-and-coming producer named Aaron Spelling. That Four Star Studios program was a western called *Johnny Ringo*, and it was picked up by CBS for the 1959–1960 TV season. Durant played the lead role, and also composed, performed, and released the "Johnny Ringo Theme" on an RCA Victor single backed with "The Whistling Wind." The record was not a big hit. Durant also released a single on a country music label called Fabor Records—"Seal Rock" backed with "Love Me Baby" (Fabor #4040). Even though the ratings for the TV program were decent, CBS cancelled the series in 1960 in favor of adding a sitcom to the lineup. Durant continued with guest shots on other western such as *Laramie, The Virginian, Wagon Train,* and *Wide Country,* but never had another series of his own. By the middle 1960s, Durant called it a career and retired from show business. After a long battle with lymphoma, Durant died on March 15, 2005, leaving behind his wife, Trudy, and two children, Jeffrey and Heidi.

E

BOBBIE EAKES

Most Famous TV Roles: Macy Alexander Sharpe on *The Bold and the Beautiful,* Krystal Carey on *All My Children;* **Networks:** ABC, CBS; **Years:** 1988–2003, 2003–2011, respectively; **Hit Recording:** "Crazy World"; **Label:** Epic; **Release Year:** 1988; **Matrix:** Epic #07432; **Chart:** #71 *Billboard* Hot 100

Bobbie Eakes was born in Georgia on July 25, 1961. From a family of five girls, she gravitated toward the performing arts at a very early age and formed her first band at age 16. In 1982, she was Miss Georgia in the Miss America Pageant. In 1987–1988, at just about the same time she began to accrue an enviable list of TV credits with guest-starring roles on *Matlock, The Wonder Years, Cheers,* and *Falcon Crest,* she landed a recording contract with the Epic label. Eakes elaborates, "That was a girl band called Big Trouble. Julia Farey played bass, Suzy Zarow played drums, and Rebecca Ryan played keyboards—I sang lead. We weren't a huge hit, but we had a lot of fun. We sang on *American Bandstand* and played the Montreux Pop Fest." The group's biggest single was titled "Crazy World" (Epic #07432), which was included on the eponymous *Big Trouble* LP (Epic #40850).

Eakes really hit her stride on TV soap operas, with long runs on *The Bold and the Beautiful* (1988–2003) as Macy Alexander Sharpe and *One Life to Live* (2004–2005) as Krystal Carey—a role she then carried over to *All My Children* (2005–2011). Eakes added, "I also recorded several soap opera albums. I had a double-platinum CD in Europe called *Bold and Beautiful Duets.* It was huge. We sold out two nights at a 10,000-seat arena in Rotterdam in 1995. I also recorded a duet with country music star Collin Raye titled 'Tired of Loving this Way.'"

Eakes's current (as of this writing) touring show, called *Turn the Page,* is a must see.

Hope this will "make your day"—one of several attempts at success on vinyl by *Rawhide* star Clint Eastwood.

CLINT EASTWOOD

Most Famous TV Role: Rowdy Yates on *Rawhide*; **Network:** CBS; **Years:** 1959–1966; **Hit Recording:** none; **Labels:** Cameo, Certron, GNP, Gothic, Paramount, Warner Bros.; **Release Years:** 1961–1970; **Matrix:** "Unknown Girl of My Dreams" (Gothic #005), "Rowdy" (Cameo #240), "Get Yourself Another Fool" (GNP #177), "Burning Bridges" (Certron #10010); **Chart:** none

Clinton Eastwood Jr. was born in San Francisco, California, on May 31, 1930. He allegedly weighed over 11 pounds at birth. He was urged in high school to take part in stage plays. While serving at Fort Ord in California, he was discovered by Universal Studios. After appearing in a few films, Eastwood was then cast in CBS's *Rawhide* series as Rowdy Yates. The series enjoyed a seven-year run. During its run, Eastwood also released a few records. He recorded for a myriad of record labels, beginning with Gothic Records in 1961 ("Unknown Girl of My Dreams"). Follow-up releases for the Cameo, GNP Crescendo, and Certron labels also failed to chart. Surprisingly, Eastwood was a fair vocalist, but failed to find the right song to propel him to vinyl stardom. He more than made up for it in motion pictures as an actor (*The Good, the Bad and the Ugly; Dirty Harry; Play Misty for Me; A Fistful of Dollars*) and eventually an Oscar-winning director for *The Unforgiven* and *Million Dollar Baby*.

Eastwood became the target of many late-night talk show jokes after his ill-fated chat with an empty chair at the Republican National Convention in 2012. His most recent work, as of this writing, was the disappointing movie adaptation of Broadway's *The Jersey Boys*, about the life and music of Frankie Valli and the Four Seasons. He has been married and divorced twice.

BUDDY EBSEN

Most Famous TV Roles: Jed Clampett on *The Beverly Hillbillies*, Barnaby Jones on *Barnaby Jones*; **Network:** CBS; **Years:** 1962–1971, 1973–1980, respectively; **Hit Recording:** none; **Label:** MGM, Reprise; **Release Years:** 1964–1965; **Matrix:** "Ballad of Jed Clampett" (MGM #13210), "Howdy" (Reprise #389), *Howdy* (Reprise LP #6174); **Chart:** none

Christian "Buddy" Ebsen Jr. was born in Belleville, Illinois, on April 2, 1908. A short time after his 10th birthday, his family relocated to Florida, where Buddy honed his dancing skills. Times were hard in the 1920s, and Ebsen and his sister Vilma moved to New York to try their luck as dancers. They got a contract with MGM, but only Buddy found success in the movies. He danced with Shirley Temple in *Captain January* and with Judy Garland in *Broadway Melody of 1938*. He was cast as the Tin Man in *The Wizard of Oz*, but was allergic to the silver makeup and had to bow out of the project.

Even with that unfortunate missed opportunity, Ebsen more than made up for it with his whopping success in television. He first appeared as

George Russell on Walt Disney's *Davy Crockett* series (as well as Sheriff Brady on Disney's *Corky and White Shadow* serial), and then as Sergeant Hunk Marriner on the short-lived NBC series *Northwest Passage*. Then in 1962, he was cast as Jed Clampett on *The Beverly Hillbillies*. He earned the role after being "discovered" in his memorable role as Doc Golightly in *Breakfast at Tiffany's* in 1961. Somehow *The Beverly Hillbillies'* writers were able to stretch the simple fish-out-of-water premise into a very highly rated nine-season run. During the series' ratings reign, Ebsen had the opportunity to release a couple of 45 rpm records. In 1964, he recorded his own version of "The Ballad of Jed Clampett," made famous by Flatt and Scruggs in the opening credits of the sitcom. Ebsen's version on MGM Records was not a big hit, but he got to try again for Reprise Records in 1965 with both a single and an album titled *Howdy*. Ebsen's records didn't chart, but are highly prized today by TV memorabilia collectors.

Ebsen had the great fortune of jumping from one hit show right into another—*Barnaby Jones* in 1973. This show costarred Lee Meriwether as his daughter-in-law and partner in fighting crime. It took a while to catch on, but eventually settled in for a seven-year run, once again on CBS. One of the few highlights of the silver screen version of *The Beverly Hillbillies* was the surprise cameo by Ebsen—not as Jed Clampett, but rather as Barnaby Jones. Ebsen has a star on the Hollywood Walk of Fame. He was married three times and was an avid numismatist. He died after a bout with pneumonia at the age of 95 on July 6, 2003.

BARBARA EDEN

Most Famous TV Role: the genie on *I Dream of Jeannie*; **Network:** NBC; **Years:** 1965–1970; **Hit Recording:** none; **Label:** Dot; **Release Year:** 1967; **Matrix:** "I Wouldn't Be a Fool" (Dot #16999), "Rebel" (Dot #17022), "Pledge of Love" (Dot #17032), *Miss Barbara Eden* (Dot LP #3795); **Chart:** none

Barbara Eden was born Barbara Jean Morehead in Tucson, Arizona, on August 31, 1931. Her parents divorced when she was very young. Her mother loved to sing around the house, and that musical influence sparked young Barbara's interest in the performing arts. She was selected as Miss San Francisco in 1951, but then lost out when she entered the Miss California contest. Despite the loss, she became active in episodic TV in the 1950s and appeared, most notably, on *I Love Lucy*, *Bachelor Father*, and *Perry Mason*. On her own first series, Eden portrayed nearsighted Loco Jones on *How to Marry a Millionaire*. The series ran in syndication for two seasons. After that show was cancelled, Eden found work as Elvis Pre-

BARBARA
EDEN

I WOULDN'T
BE A FOOL
B/W
BEND IT!

PRODUCED BY
RANDY WOOD
ARRANGED AND CONDUCTED BY
BILL JUSTIS

SEE REVERSE SIDE FOR
INSTRUCTIONS — HOW TO DO
"THE BEND"

Barbara Eden's Jeannie dreamed of success as a singer, but to no avail.

sley's costar in *Flaming Star*. She landed in another sitcom beginning in 1965 as a genie found in a bottle by an astronaut on a desert island. She got to wear an outfit with a bare midriff on the show with the understanding that her navel was always to be covered. That role in *I Dream of Jeannie* came to both define and pigeonhole her. The series lasted for five seasons and 139 episodes. During its run, Eden attempted to make the most of the musical influence from her mother, and recorded several singles and an album for the Dot Records label in 1967. Eden wasn't exactly the best singer in the world, and her vocals were buried in echo to belie that fact. The singles and the album failed to make the charts, and Eden soon returned her focus to her hit sitcom.

A few years after the show's cancellation, Eden earned a role in the movie called *Harper Valley P.T.A.* based upon the hit Jeannie C. Riley song. The movie role led to her being cast in the TV sitcom version that ran from 1981 to 1982. At the turn of the century, Eden played Florence Unger in the touring version of *The Female Odd Couple* opposite Olive Madison portrayed by Rita MacKenzie. Her memoirs are titled *Jeannie Out of the Bottle*. She received a star on the Hollywood Walk of Fame in 1988. She has been married three times, including to *Broken Arrow* star Michael Ansara.

VINCE EDWARDS

Most Famous TV Role: Dr. Ben Casey on *Ben Casey*; **Network:** ABC; **Years:** 1961–1966; **Hit Recordings:** "Why Did You Leave Me?" "Don't Worry 'bout Me," "No, Not Much"; **Labels:** Colpix, Decca, Kama Sutra, Remember, Russ-Fi; **Release Years:** 1962–1967; **Matrix:** "Why Did You Leave Me?" (Russ-Fi #7001), "Don't Worry 'bout Me" (Decca #31413), "No, Not Much" (Colpix #771); **Chart:** #68, #72, respectively, *Billboard* Hot 100, and #108 Bubbling Under

Vince Edwards was born Vincent Edward Zoino in Brooklyn, New York, on July 9, 1928. He and a twin brother, Anthony, were the youngest of seven children. He was on the swim team in school, and studied acting at the American Academy of Dramatic Arts. He scored a few film roles in the 1950s, but became a star in the early 1960s when he nabbed the role that defined his career, *Ben Casey*. He also directed a few episodes. While enjoying the ride on a hit series, Edwards also released several records on numerous labels. Even though Edwards was a decent singer, his TV fame didn't quite translate into hit single recordings. However, his *Vincent Edwards Sings* album (Decca LP #4311) did reach the Top Five. A few of his singles scraped the bottom of the Hot 100, but none of them clicked in a big way. The biggest sellers were "Why Did You Leave Me?" on the Russ-Fi label, "Don't Worry 'bout Me" on the Decca label, and "No, Not Much" for Colpix Records. Other far less successful singles included "Say It Isn't So" (Decca #31426), "You'll Still Have Me" (Decca #31460), "Looking for Someone" (Decca #31534), "Per Te Per Me" (Decca #31563), "Unchained Melody" (Decca #34074), "To Be with You" (Kama Sutra #221), and "I've Got the Whole World to Hold Me Up" (Remember #7773). During the run of *Ben Casey*, Edwards and *Dr. Kildare*'s Richard Chamberlain (see the entry under his name) developed a rivalry, culminating in a heated confrontation in Central Park in 1964.

After *Ben Casey* was cancelled, Edwards returned to the silver screen, but hits were few and far between. *Devil's Brigade* from 1968 was likely

While watching his patients' charts, *Ben Casey* star Vince Edwards tried to scale the music charts.

his biggest success. A starring role in a new 1970 ABC series called *Matt Lincoln* lasted only 13 weeks. On the program, Edwards portrayed a hip young psychiatrist. While making his last film, *The Fear* in 1995, he was diagnosed with prostate cancer and died on March 16 the following year.

BILL ENGVALL

Most Famous TV Role: star of *The Bill Engvall Show*; **Network:** TBS; **Years:** 2007–2009; **Hit Recording:** "Here's Your Sign (Get the Picture)"; **Label:** Warner; **Release Year:** 1997; **Matrix:** Warner #17491; **Chart:** #43 *Billboard* Hot 100

William Ray Engvall Jr. was born in Galveston, Texas, on July 27, 1957. He started his comedy career at open mic nights at Dallas area nightclubs. His first TV break came on the short-lived Delta Burke sitcom called *Delta*. He then scored the recurring role of Bill Pelton on *The Jeff Foxworthy Show* between 1995 and 1997, and during this time scored a Top Fifty single (with the help of Travis Tritt) called "Here's Your Sign (Get the Picture)." "Here's your sign" is Engvall's most famous routine (especially on the Blue Collar Comedy Tour). Engvall didn't sing on the record—he left those duties to Tritt. The song earned Engvall a gold record. In the new millennium, he starred in his own eponymous sitcom on TBS, and as of this writing is the host of the long-running game show *Lingo* on GSN. Engvall has been married to Gail since 1982, and they have two children. Family members are often used as fodder for his stand-up routines.

BOB EUBANKS

Most Famous TV Role: host of *The Newlywed Game*; **Network:** ABC; **Years:** 1966–1974; **Hit Recording:** none; **Labels:** Goliath, Tracy; **Release Year:** 1963; **Matrix:** "Smoke That Cigarette" (Goliath #1354), "Heaven of the Stars" (Tracy #6101); **Chart:** none

Robert Leland Eubanks was born in Flint, Michigan, on January 8, 1938. The family moved to Pasadena, California, while he was very young, and he grew up with a passion for music. After spending several years as a child model, he found work as a disc jockey beginning in the 1950s. He had a great voice for radio and became very popular. During that time, Eubanks also released a couple of 45s on small Southern California record labels. First came a version of the old country standard "Smoke, Smoke, Smoke That Cigarette" on the Goliath label, and that was followed by "Heavens of the Stars" on the Tracy label. The latter was similar to "The Three Stars" by Tommy Dee, and Eubanks recited the names of rock and roll stars who had passed on. He also produced numerous rock and roll concerts in the 1960s and had his own chain of nightclubs called the Cinnamon Cinder, accompanied by a local television program, *The Cinnamon Cinder Show*, which originated in those clubs. There was even a hit record about the nightclubs, "The Cinnamon Cinder" by both the Pastel Six and the Cinders.

That TV show ran from 1963 to 1965, and one year after its cancellation, Eubanks experienced his biggest break in show business when he was named host of a new Chuck Barris game show called *The Newlywed Game*. The unpredictable and provocative answers and comments from

Before hosting game shows, Bob Eubanks (backed by the Highbrows) was "game" for a hit record, but never did reach the bonus round.

the couples rendered the show a whopping success and it ran until 1974 in its original form, including a weekly prime-time version on ABC. It has been brought back successfully numerous times with Eubanks as host, and as of this writing new episodes were still being produced with host Sherri Shepherd on the GSN cable channel. Eubanks also hosted several other less famous quiz programs such as *Rhyme and Reason*, *Card Sharks*, *Dream House*, and *All-Star Secrets*. Eubanks has had a long run as one of the hosts of the yearly *Tournament of Roses Parade* on New Year's Day. He published his autobiography, *It's in the Book, Bob*, in 2004. He has been married twice and has four children.

CHAD EVERETT

Most Famous TV Role: Dr. Gannon on *Medical Center*; **Network:** CBS; **Years:** 1969–1976; **Hit Recording:** none; **Labels:** Calliope, Marina, MGM; **Release Years:** 1971–1976; **Matrix:** "Leave It to Love" (Calliope #8001), "I Got Love for You, Ruby" (Calliope #8006), "All Strung Out" (Marina #503), "You're My Soul and Inspiration" (Marina #508), *All Strung Out* (MGM LP #2501), *Chad* (Calliope LP #7001); **Chart:** none

Raymon Lee Cramton was born in South Bend, Indiana, on June 11, 1937. His family moved to Dearborn, Michigan, in his childhood years. It was there that he played football in high school, and also took roles in stage plays. Beginning in the early 1960s he earned guest-starring roles on episodic TV shows such as *Surfside 6*, and his first recurring role came about on the short-lived ABC western adventures series *The Dakotas* (he played Deputy Del Stark) in 1963. His big break came in 1969 when he was cast in CBS's *Medical Center* as Dr. Joe Gannon. The series ran for seven seasons, and during its run, there were several attempts to make a recording star out of Everett. He wasn't much of a singer, but he made the ladies swoon and he recorded several singles for the Calliope and Marina labels, an EP 45 for MGM, and an album simply titled *Chad* for Calliope. He performed a few of the songs from his album on variety and talk shows, but none of his releases caught on. After years of alcohol addiction, he found religion and conquered his demons. He starred in another series in 1994, the short-lived *McKenna* on ABC. He has a star on Hollywood's Walk of Fame and was married to Shelby Grant for 45 years until her death in 2011. Everett died the following year of lung cancer on July 24, 2012, at the age of 75.

TOM EWELL

Most Famous TV Role: Tom Potter on *The Tom Ewell Show*, Billy Truman on *Baretta*; **Network:** ABC; **Years:** 1975–1978; **Hit Recording:** none; **Label:** Dot; **Release Year:** 1961; **Matrix:** "More Than Just a Friend" (Dot #16353); **Chart:** none

Tom Ewell was born Samuel Yewell Tompkins in Owensboro, Kentucky, on April 29, 1909. He disobeyed his family's wishes that he become a lawyer and instead pursued acting. He made his Broadway debut while still in his 20s and his movie debut in his early 30s. He often appeared much older on-screen than his actual age. In the 1950s, he had the opportunity to costar with two of Hollywood's most beautiful ladies—Marilyn Monroe in *The Seven Year Itch* and Jayne Mansfield in the rock and roll motion picture *The Girl Can't Help It*. In 1960, he got to star in his own sitcom, *The Tom Ewell Show* on CBS. The show had a promising premise as Ewell portrayed Tom Potter—the only male in a house full of women (his wife, his three daughters, his mother-in-law, and even female pets). It lasted only one season, but during its run Ewell made a record for the Dot label—"More Than Just a Friend" backed with "Never Say No to a Man." Both songs were taken from the early 1960s remake of the musical *State Fair*, in which Ewell costarred. The single was not a big hit. Ewell later snagged his most famous TV role as Billy Truman on the Robert Blake crime drama titled *Baretta*. Ewell was nominated for an Emmy Award for his portrayal of Truman, the retired cop, but did not win. Ewell gave series TV one more shot in 1981 as Doc Jerome Kullens on the very funny but short-lived western spoof ABC sitcom *Best of the West*. Ewell was married twice but had only one child, Taylor. Ewell died in Los Angeles at the age of 85 on September 12, 1994. His mother lived to be 109.

F

SHELLEY FABARES

Most Famous TV Role: Mary Stone on *The Donna Reed Show*, Christine Armstrong Fox on *Coach*; **Network:** ABC; **Years:** 1958–1965, 1989–1997, respectively; **#1 Hit Recording:** "Johnny Angel"; **Label:** Colpix; **Release Year:** 1962; **Matrix:** Colpix #621; **Chart:** #1 *Billboard* Hot 100

Shelley Fabares was born as Michele Marie Fabares in Santa Monica, California, on January 19, 1944. She began acting at the age of 3 and by 10 was appearing on episodic TV. Her first credited role came on an episode of the long-running *Loretta Young Show*, and her first recurring role came on the syndicated *Annie Oakley* series. In 1958, she was cast in a new Screen Gems sitcom starring movie star Donna Reed. Fabares, the niece of performer Nanette Fabray (yes, they spell their surnames differently), was cast as Mary Stone, the teenaged boy-crazy daughter of Donna and her doctor husband, Alex Stone (portrayed by Carl Betz). Most often sponsored by Campbell's Soup, the program ran for eight seasons, and Fabares stayed for a majority of the show's run.

Screen Gems was an imprint of Columbia Pictures, as was the Colpix Records label, and the powers-that-be thought it would be a great idea if their popular young costars on the show made records. Fabares was against the idea, as she wasn't much of a singer, but a Screen Gems mandate brought her into the recording studio. The first song she was given, "Johnny Angel," had been recorded twice before, unsuccessfully by both Laurie Loman and Georgia Lee, but when Fabares's version was included in an episode of the series titled "Donna's Prima Donna," it caught the attention of the record-buying public and was propelled to the coveted number 1 spot on the Hot 100. The actor who portrayed her younger brother, Jeff, on the program also recorded for Colpix and he had two hits in the Top Twenty (see the entry for Paul Petersen). "Johnny Angel" was followed up with "Johnny Loves Me," but it failed to crack the Top Twenty and Fabares's recording career was over as quickly as it

SHELLEY FABARES

OF THE DONNA REED SHOW
Produced by Tony Owen
Distributed by SCREEN GEMS, INC.

sings

JOHNNY LOVES ME

Record Arr. & Prod.
by STU PHILLIPS

Colpix Records
A Division of Columbia Pictures Corp. • Printed in U.S.A.

CP 636

B/W   I'M GROWING UP

Assisted by exposure on *The Donna Reed Show*, Shelley Fabares became a reluctant recording star, albeit briefly.

had begun, although she did continue to record for Vee Jay (#632—"Lost Summer Love" backed with "I Know You'll be There") and ABC/Dunhill Records (#4001—"My Prayer" backed with "Pretty Please"; #4041—"See You 'Round the Rebound" backed with "Pretty Please") into the middle 1960s.

After leaving the show, Fabares surfaced in three Elvis Presley movies—*Clambake*, *Spinout*, and *Girl Happy*. Then came a long string of sitcom work and recurring roles in *The Little People/The Brian Keith Show*, *The Practice* (with Danny Thomas), *One Day at a Time* (with her aunt Nanette), *Highcliffe Manor*, and yet another sitcom that lasted for eight seasons, *Coach* with Craig T. Nelson and Jerry Van Dyke. She was nominated for an Emmy Award twice for her role on *Coach*, but did not win. She was married to record producer Lou Adler from 1964 to 1980, and has been wed to *M*A*S*H*'s Mike Farrell since 1984. In 2000, Fabares underwent successful liver transplant surgery. Since providing character voices for the animated *Superman* series of the late 1990s, she has made very few appearances on TV.

BARBARA FELDON

Most Famous TV Role: Agent 99 on *Get Smart*; **Networks:** CBS, NBC; **Years:** 1965–1970; **Hit Recording:** none; **Label:** RCA Victor; **Release Year:** 1965; **Matrix:** "99" (RCA Victor #8954); **Chart:** none

Barbara Feldon attempted to crack the Hot 100 with "99" (and the flip side called "Max"), inspired by her hit sitcom *Get Smart*.

Barbara Feldon was born as Barbara Ann Hall in Butler, Pennsylvania on March 12, 1933. She was trained in her craft at the Pittsburgh Playhouse. She began her career as a model and won the top prize on TV's *$64,000 Question* in 1957. Her category of expertise was Shakespeare. In the early 1960s, she found work in TV commercials and episodic TV—most notably, the popular *Man from U.N.C.L.E.* and *12 O'Clock High.* She performed extensively on stage, but it was a TV sitcom that defined her when, in 1965, she was cast in the Mel Brooks spy spoof called *Get Smart.* She portrayed "Agent 99" for five seasons on the program (four on NBC and one on CBS). During the show's run, she and Maxwell Smart got married and had kids.

In 1966 while the show was a hot commodity, Feldon sang (in reality, recited) a novelty song for RCA Victor Records about her role on the series, simply titled "99" and backed with "Max." It didn't come out as good as they had expected, and it failed to make the charts. There were no follow-up singles. Even though she was married to Smart on the series, in real life, she was married to Lucien Verdoux Feldon and later *Get Smart's* producer Burt Nodella (both marriages ended in divorce). She was twice nominated for an Emmy Award during *Get Smart's* prime-time years, but did not win. She did reprise her role for the 1989 reunion film called *Get Smart Again.* She does an occasional guest spot, but today prefers writing.

SALLY FIELD

Most Famous TV Roles: Gidget on *Gidget,* Sister Bertrille on *The Flying Nun;* **Network:** ABC; **Years:** 1965–1966, 1967–1970, respectively; **Hit Recording:** "Felicidad"; **Label:** Colgems; **Release Year:** 1967; **Matrix:** Colgems #1008; **Chart:** #94 *Billboard* Hot 100

Sally Field was born in Pasadena, California, on November 6, 1946. Actor and stuntman Jock Mahoney was her stepfather. Sally followed in his footsteps and pursued acting. With very little experience except for natural talent, she was cast in the lead on the TV sitcom version of *Gidget.* It wasn't a hit and was cancelled after only one season, but has had a strong afterlife in reruns. After a recurring role on NBC's *Hey, Landlord* as Woody's sister Bonnie, she earned another starring role—this time as Sister Bertrille, *The Flying Nun.* During the program's first season, once again good old Screen Gems attempted to make their TV star into a recording star. One of the show's early episodes featured Field singing a song titled "Felicidad," and it was released as a single on Columbia/ Screen Gems' Colgems Records label. Even though Field wasn't much of a singer, the show's popularity helped "Felicidad" crack the Hot 100. Two less successful singles followed—"You're a Grand Old Flag" backed with "Golden Days" (Colgems #1014) and "Months of the Year" backed with "Gonna Build Me a Mountain" (this cut was a duet with series co-star Marge Redmond, who portrayed Sister Jacqueline). Her *Flying Nun* album (Colgems LP #106) peaked at number 172.

The series enjoyed a three-season run, and Field attempted to jump into another comedy with a gimmick, but this time around (as a new bride with ESP), *The Girl with Something Extra* became a single-season sitcom. Ratings were mediocre, and originally NBC had thoughts of bringing that show back for a second season, but because Field and costar John Davidson didn't get along very well, that idea was tabled. Field then sought meatier roles in motion pictures—a move that garnered her two Academy Awards (we like her; we really like her) for *Norma Rae* and *Places in the Heart*. She also won an Emmy for her portrayal of a young lady named *Sybil* with a dissociative identity disorder that led to her having 16 different and distinct personalities. Among her other films are *Smokey and the Bandit*, *Murphy's Romance*, *Forrest Gump*, *Soapdish*, and *Mrs. Doubtfire*. Sally wasn't yet done with television, and her new series in 2006, *Brothers and Sisters*, earned her another Emmy for her portrayal of Nora Walker. Most recently, she was seen in a series of TV commercials for the osteoporosis drug called Boniva. We like her; we still really like her.

KIM FIELDS

Most Famous TV Role: Tootie Ramsey on *The Facts of Life*; **Network:** NBC; **Years:** 1979–1988; **Hit Recording:** none; **Labels:** Critique; **Release Year:** 1984; **Matrix:** "He Loves Me, He Loves Me Not" (Critique 12-inch single), "Dear Michael" (Critique #705); **Chart:** none

Kim Fields was born in New York City on May 12, 1969. Her mother, Laverne "Chip" Fields, was an actress, and young Kim followed suit. By 1978, Kim had her first regular role in a TV series when she portrayed Angie Ellis on the short-lived *Baby, I'm Back* on CBS. The cancellation of that series proved to be beneficial to Fields because she was cast in another series, *The Facts of Life*, the following year. She then settled in for a nine-season run as Dorothy "Tootie" Ramsey on the NBC sitcom. During the show's long run, Fields signed with Critique Records and released a seven-inch single called "Dear Michael" and a 12-inch single titled "He Loves Me, He Loves Me Not." Neither release made the charts. After her "Tootie" days came to an end in 1988, Fields went back to school to get

A tune from Tootie. *The Facts of Life* costar Kim Fields attempted to cash in on her TV popularity.

her degree, but returned to acting in 1993 for yet another popular Fox series, *Living Single*, as Regine Hunter. During the run of the show she became known professionally as Kim Fields Freeman after marrying Jonathan Freeman. That marriage lasted from 1995 to 2001. She married again in 2007, and as of this writing is still with husband number 2, Christopher Morgan. They have two children. In recent years, Fields has changed her focus to directing.

EDDIE FONTAINE

Most Famous TV Role: PFC Pete D'Angelo on *The Gallant Men;* **Network:** ABC; **Years:** 1962–1963; **Hit Recording:** "Nothin' Shakin'"; **Labels:** Argo, Sunbeam; **Release Years:** 1958–1963; **Matrix:** Argo #5309 and Sunbeam #105; **Chart:** #64 *Billboard* Hot 100

Eddie Fontaine was born as Eddie Reardon in Jersey City, New Jersey, on March 6, 1934. After serving in the U.S. Army, he sought work as a singer and an actor. The singing came first, and he scored a minor hit with "Rock Love" for RCA Victor's X Records label (#0096) in 1955. The following year, he scored a role in the color rock and roll motion picture titled *The Girl Can't Help It.* Fontaine's biggest hit single came in 1958 with "Nothin' Shakin'" released first on the Sunbeam label and then Argo when it began selling fairly well. Fontaine's next conquest was television, and he earned a costarring role on the Warner Bros. wartime action drama called *The Gallant Men.* Fontaine played PFC Pete D'Angelo alongside Robert McQueeney as Conley Wright, William Reynolds as Captain Jim Benedict, and Richard X. Slattery as First Sergeant John McKenna. The hour-long drama aired on ABC from October of 1962 until September of 1963.

Warner Bros. at this time in history was famous for urging its TV stars to record for its label. Fontaine was no exception, and in 1962 he released "My Heart Belongs to You" (Warner Bros. #5313) and "Sin" (Warner Bros. #5345). Sadly, neither the records nor the TV show were big hits. After *The Gallant Men* was cancelled, he never had another regular role in a series but did guest star on *Baretta, Starsky and Hutch, Medical Center, The Rockford Files, Quincy,* and *Happy Days.* He did some prison time in the 1980s after being convicted in a murder-for-hire case. After his release, Fontaine attempted to get his career back on track. His comeback never happened, and he succumbed to throat cancer on April 13, 1992.

FRANK FONTAINE

Most Famous TV Role: Crazy Guggenheim on *American Scene Magazine* and *The Jackie Gleason Show;* **Network:** CBS; **Years:** 1962–1967; **#1 Hit Recording:** *Songs I Sing on "The Jackie Gleason Show";* **Label:** ABC Paramount; **Release Years:** 1962–1966; **Matrix:** "Easter Parade" (ABC Paramount #10430), "Oh, How I Miss You Tonight" (ABC Paramount #10491), "Alouette" (ABC Paramount #10517), "Any Man Who Loves His Mother" (ABC Paramount #10574), "I'm Counting on You" (ABC Paramount #10618), "Someday" (ABC Paramount #10662), *Songs I Sing on "The Jackie Gleason Show"* (ABC Paramount LP #442); **Chart:** #1 *Billboard* Top Pop Albums

A museum piece from Crazy Guggenheim (Frank Fontaine) of *American Scene Magazine* and *The Jackie Gleason Show*. Like Jim Nabors, his character voice and his singing voice didn't match.

Frank Fontaine was born in Cambridge, Massachusetts, on April 19, 1920. He had minor roles in several motion pictures in the 1950s, but made a name for himself in the 1960s thanks to exposure on Jackie Gleason's programs *The American Scene Magazine* and *The Jackie Gleason Show*. His most famous character was a learning-challenged man named Crazy Guggenheim—an act that certainly would never fly in the modern PC climate. He usually appeared in Gleason's "Joe the Bartender" sketch. However, on the same show (often in the same scene) he would sing a song in a totally normal voice, a la Jim Nabors. During Fontaine's run on two different Jackie Gleason series in the 1960s, he released a series of singles and albums on the ABC Paramount label. Several of his albums mentioned or alluded to Gleason—*Songs I Sing on "The Jackie Gleason Show"* (ABC Paramount #442—a number 1 hit), *More Songs I Sing on "The*

Jackie Gleason Show" (ABC Paramount #490), and *How Sweet It Is* (ABC Paramount #514). Despite his popularity on Gleason's programs, none of his 45s made the charts. The Warner Bros. cartoon character Peter Puma was patterned after Crazy Guggenheim. Fontaine always appeared older than his actual years, and he died of a heart attack in Spokane, Washington, on August 4, 1978, at the age of only 58.

JAMES FRANCISCUS

Most Famous TV Role: John Novak on *Mr. Novak;* **Network:** NBC; **Years:** 1963–1965; **Hit Recording:** none; **Label:** MGM; **Release Year:** 1965; **Matrix:** "Droppity Drop Outs" (MGM #13319); **Chart:** none

James Franciscus was born in Clayton, Missouri, on January 31, 1934. He graduated magna cum laude from Yale University with a degree in English and theater arts. He began his career guest starring on episodic TV programs before securing his first recurring role as Detective Jim Halloran on the much-lauded ABC TV drama titled *Naked City* in the 1958–1959 season. Next came a short-lived role as Russ Andrews on the CBS detective drama set on the east side of Manhattan called *The Investigators* in 1961. His next TV role as a teacher is probably his most memorable. For two seasons on NBC (1963–1965), he portrayed Mr. Novak on the MGM drama series of the same name. Coincidentally, he went undercover as a teacher in one episode of *Naked City.* During *Mr. Novak's* run, he conveniently released a school-related song on the MGM label (of course). It was called "Droppity Drop Out" backed with "Oh, Friday Day," and it was released during the program's second season. The show was popular with teenagers, and there was even a novelty record released by Jackie and Gayle in 1965 (Capitol #5325) titled "Why Can't My Teacher Look like Mr. Novak." Franciscus's second most famous TV role came in 1971 when he portrayed Mike Longstreet, a blind New Orleans insurance investigator on ABC's *Longstreet.* The program started strong, but was not able to maintain the quality of the early scripts and lasted only one season. He also appeared in numerous motion pictures including *Beneath the Planet of the Apes* and supplied the voice for *Jonathan Livingston Seagull.* He was married twice and had four children from his first. He died on July 8, 1991, of emphysema at the age of only 57.

WILLIAM FRAWLEY

Most Famous TV Role: Fred Mertz on *I Love Lucy*, Bub O'Casey on *My Three Sons*; **Networks:** ABC, CBS; **Years:** 1951–1960, 1960–1965, respectively; **Hit Recording:** none; **Label:** Dot; **Release Year:** 1958; **Matrix:** *William Frawley Sings the Old Ones* (Dot LP # 3061); **Chart:** none

William Frawley was born in Burlington, Iowa, on February 26, 1887. Against his religious parents' wishes, he wanted to be an actor. He eventually found steady work in Vaudeville. He both danced and sang, and is credited with being the first to sing "My Melancholy Baby." Upon Vaudeville's demise, he found steady work as a character actor both on Broadway and in motion pictures.

With the advent of television, he attempted to make the transition, although he was already in his 60s. Frawley found out about Lucille Ball and Desi Arnaz's new series and called them to see if they'd consider casting him. Ball and Arnaz were very eager to use Frawley, but CBS was hesitant because of a reputation for drinking and absenteeism. There were no problems with Frawley, and he remained for the show's long and historic run. He did have one clause in his contract—he wouldn't have to work when the New York Yankees were playing in the postseason (he was quite the baseball fan). The program ran for six seasons initially in a half-hour format from 1951 to 1957, and then as a reinvented series of hour-long specials from 1957 to 1960 called *Westinghouse Desilu Playhouse* initially and then *The Lucy Desi Comedy Hour* in syndication. He sang fairly often on the sitcom, and it was during the show's latter period that Frawley was tapped to record his old Vaudeville numbers on an album called *William Frawley Sings the Old Ones* for Dot Records. Among the classic old songs—"Moonlight Bay," "Cuddle Up a Little Closer," "By the Light of the Silvery Moon," "Carolina in the Morning," and his signature tune "My Melancholy Baby." Trying to compete against rock and roll in 1958 was a real uphill battle, and the album failed to become a hit. Frawley didn't get another opportunity for any other solo albums (although he was a participant in several soundtrack albums).

Just as Lucy's hour-long series was winding down, there was talk of a Vivian Vance and William Frawley spinoff, but he and Vance had a contentious relationship and she put the kibosh on the idea. Frawley immediately found steady work in another legendary sitcom, *My Three Sons*. He portrayed Bub O'Casey on the show's ABC run from 1960 to 1965. When the program jumped to CBS in 1965, Frawley jumped ship because of failing health and was replaced by William Demarest as Uncle Charlie. His final TV appearance came in a cameo on *The Lucy Show* in October of 1965 as a horse trainer. A short time later, he suffered a massive heart attack and died on March 3, 1966. He was married only once, had no children, and has a star on the Hollywood Walk of Fame.

JONATHAN FRID

Most Famous TV Role: Barnabas Collins on *Dark Shadows;* **Network:** ABC; **Years:** 1966–1971; **Hit Recording:** *Dark Shadows;* **Label:** Philips; **Release Year:** 1969; **Matrix:** Philips LP #314; **Chart:** #18 *Billboard* Top Pop Albums

John Herbert Frid was born in Ontario, Canada, on December 2, 1924. During World War II he served in the Royal Canadian Navy. He earned a degree in directing at Yale University School of Drama, and his Broadway debut came in 1964 as an understudy in *Roar like a Dove*. His earliest TV work was for the CBC (Canadian Broadcasting Company), but beyond a "shadow" of a doubt, his most famous role came in the ABC daytime drama called *Dark Shadows*. It ran from 1966 to 1971 and amassed a huge cult following. Frid agreed to take part in the show—as Barnabas Collins, a 200-year-old vampire—only because he needed cash, and was assured it wouldn't last very long. He settled in for a five-year run and became a household name, especially with the younger generation. Its popularity led to a big screen version called *House of Dark Shadows* in 1970.

During the show's run, Frid released one 45 rpm record for the Philips label (distributed by Mercury Records, and indeed the same Philips Company that nowadays makes TV sets and light bulbs)—a song called "I'll Be with You Always" (Philips #40633) that was performed on the show. It was not a big hit, but the *Dark Shadows* album (Philips LP #314) peaked at number 18 in 1969. After the program was cancelled in 1971, Frid returned to Broadway. Years later, he came to embrace the popularity of his role on *Dark Shadows*, and began making appearances at TV autograph shows and *Dark Shadows* fan conventions. Coincidentally, Frid filmed a cameo appearance in Tim Burton's 2012 motion picture remake of *Dark Shadows*, and it became his last. A short time later, after suffering a fall, Frid died of complications from pneumonia on April 14, 2012, at the age of 87.

ROBERT FULLER

Most Famous TV Role: Dr. Kelly Brackett on *Emergency!*; **Network:** NBC; **Years:** 1972–1977; **Hit Recording:** none; **Labels:** Ace-Hi, Challenge; **Release Year:** 1964; **Matrix:** "I Remember Asking Grandma" (Ace-Hi #0158), "What Is a Quail Hunter?" (Challenge #59250); **Chart:** none

Robert Fuller was born as Buddy Lee in Troy, New York (an only child), on July 29, 1933. His mother was a dance instructor, and young Buddy took acting and dancing lessons. His first job in show business was as a stunt man. At this time, he changed his name to Robert Fuller. Just as he was getting started and beginning to gain some traction in the industry, he was drafted into the U.S. Army. After his discharge, he picked up where he left off, and found small roles in numerous motion pictures. He also found work in episodic TV, and eventually landed the regular role of Jess Harper on *Laramie* on NBC. After a five-year run on that show, Fuller immediately jumped over to another long-running western, *Wagon Train* on ABC. He portrayed Cooper Smith from 1963 to 1965, and while there he got to record a couple of 45 rpm records. First came "I Remember Asking Grandma" for the Ace-Hi Records label. The record bombed, and Fuller then jumped over to a larger label—Gene Autry's Challenge Records. This single was titled "What Is a Quail Hunter?" but it, too, failed to make much of a splash. He tried one more time and recorded an album in German in 1967. It was released only overseas and details about the album are sketchy.

Fuller left *Wagon Train* in 1965, and for the next several years added numerous movie and episodic TV roles to his résumé. In 1972, he snagged his biggest role—that of Dr. Kelly Brackett on the NBC drama series called *Emergency!* The program ran for six seasons and has enjoyed a nice long run in syndication. After several guest appearances on CBS's *Walker, Texas Ranger*, Fuller opted to retire. As of this writing, he is living on a farm in Texas with his second wife, Jennifer. He has three children from his first marriage.

ANNETTE FUNICELLO

Most Famous TV Role: one of the original Mouseketeers on *The Mickey Mouse Club*; **Network:** ABC; **Years:** 1955–1957; **Top Ten Recordings:** "Tall Paul," "O Dio Mio"; **Labels:** Buena Vista, Disneyland; **Release Dates:** 1959–1960; **Matrix:** "Tall Paul" (Disneyland #118), "O Dio Mio" (Buena Vista #354); **Chart:** #7, #10, respectively, *Billboard* Hot 100

The object of many schoolboy crushes, Annette Funicello of *The Mickey Mouse Club* scored four Top Twenty hits, including "Pineapple Princess."

Annette Funicello was born in Utica, New York, on October 22, 1942. The family moved to Los Angeles where she was discovered in a performance of *Swan Lake*, and was instantly cast as one of the original Mouseketeers on ABC's *The Mickey Mouse Club*. She matured quickly, and teenage boys began to make up the show's biggest demographic. Beginning in 1957, Funicello participated in several other Disney TV projects. In 1959, Walt Disney branched out into popular music and Funicello was placed on the Disneyland and Buena Vista Records labels. She covered a song called "Tall Paul" that was originated by Judy Harriet (Surf #5027), and it became an instant Top Ten hit in 1959. Three other Top Twenty singles followed—"First Name Initial" (Buena Vista #339), "Pineapple Princess" (Buena Vista #362), and "O Dio Mio" (Buena Vista #354). Simultaneously, Funicello joined *The Danny Thomas Show* as Gina Minelli—a live-in exchange student. The adult Funicello then moved on to the silver screen and a series of beach movies with costar Frankie Avalon (*Beach Party, Muscle Beach Party, Bikini Beach, Beach Blanket Bingo,* and *How to Stuff a Wild Bikini).* She and Avalon reunited in 1987 for *Back to the Beach.* She was featured in a long series of Skippy Peanut Butter commercials, and got her star on the Hollywood Walk of Fame in 1993. At the same time, she was diagnosed as having multiple sclerosis, which eventually claimed her life on April 8, 2013, at the age of 70, leaving behind her second husband, Glenn Holt, and three children—Gina, Jack, and Jason.

ALLEN FUNT

Most Famous TV Role: host of *Candid Camera;* **Network:** CBS, syndicated; **Years:** 1948–present; **Hit Recording:** none; **Label:** Cameo; **Release Year:** 1964; **Matrix:** "Cee Cee's Theme" (Cameo #294); **Chart:** none

Allen Albert Funt was born in Brooklyn, New York, on September 16, 1914. After studying at Pratt Institute and Cornell University, his interests turned to fun, gentle pranks that exhibited patently human foibles. His mischief began in 1946 on ABC Radio as *Candid Microphone.* The advent of television and the visual image of average people being "punked" before our very eyes only enhanced the popularity of his concept, and *Candid Camera* was born—enjoying a long, storied run on CBS, and then in syndication. The phrase "Smile, you're on *Candid Camera*" became a big part of the American lexicon. One might consider *Candid Camera* to be the nucleus for the glut of reality programming that began to flourish near the end of the 20th century.

Funt also released two filmed hidden-camera documentary motion pictures—*What Do You Say to a Naked Lady?* and *Money Talks.* The creation has outlived its creator—Funt died on September 5, 1999, just days short of his 85th birthday. His son Peter Funt carried the torch and the hosting duties into the 21st century. Another of Allen's sons, Bill Funt, recalled an unusual 45 rpm record with his dad's name on it. He shared,

The name of the artist was Allen Funt and Orchestra (Cameo #294) from 1964. My dad really had nothing to do with this instrumental record, but as I recall he did use the "Cee Cee's Theme" side of the 45 on the show. "Cee Cee" was short for *Candid Camera.* The B-side of the record is a complete mystery to me. It's called "Theme from the Young Ones." That does not ring any

A theme to make you "smile"—the *Cee Cee* in "Cee Cee's Theme" stands for *Candid Camera*.

bells. Perhaps it was also used on the program, but I can't be certain. I gave it a listen on YouTube, and on there it is credited to Dave Appell. My guess is that, being Cameo labelmates, they were put out as one single.

A DVD box set of many of the program's finest moments was made available in 2005, titled *Candid Camera: Five Decades of Smiles*, and can still be purchased online as of this writing. A new version of the series debuted on TV Land in 2014 with Mayim Bialik as host.

G

DAVE GARROWAY

Most Famous TV Role: host of the original *Today Show*; **Network:** NBC; **Years:** 1952–1961; **Hit Recording:** none; **Label:** Cameo; **Release Year:** 1958; **Matrix:** "Danny Boy" (Cameo #148); **Chart:** none

David Cunningham Garroway was born in Schenectady, New York, on July 13, 1913. His family moved around a lot in his youth, and eventually landed in St. Louis, Missouri. After a profound lack of success in various jobs, he attempted to find his niche in radio. His career started at the legendary KDKA in Pittsburgh, Pennsylvania, in the late 1930s. It was there he earned the nickname "the Roving Announcer." After a few years, he jumped to a larger market—Chicago. Then duty called, and he enlisted in the U.S. Navy during World War II, only to pick up where he left off, as a jazz disc jockey in the Windy City. Then came television, and in 1949, an experiment called *Garroway at Large*, originating from Chicago. Truly one of the pioneers of TV talk, Garroway was selected by Pat Weaver as host of a new NBC TV morning program to be called simply *The Today Show*. It debuted on January 14, 1952, and its success is obvious in the fact that the program is still running today. During his nine-year stay, Garroway recorded "Danny Boy" backed with "Dance, Everyone, Dance" for Philadelphia's Cameo Records label (Cameo #148) as the Dave Garroway Orchestra in 1958. It wasn't a hit, and was a bit out of place in 1958—a year laden with rock and roll hits.

Even though his TV show was very successful, Garroway remained a presence on radio. He was a very busy man, but suffered from depression. He allegedly became very difficult to work with in his final years on *The Today Show*, and eventually resigned on June 16, 1961. He then returned his focus to radio on WCBS-AM in New York City. He jumped around from radio market to radio market and tried several times to rekindle his TV career, but his many attempts failed to attain the success of his original *Today Show*. Other than returning for several *Today*

127

reunion programs and writing a couple of books, Garroway seemingly disappeared from the public eye. He was married three times and had three children. After heart surgery, his depression got the best of him in 1982, and Garroway, one of TV's pioneers, died of a self-inflicted gunshot wound on July 21 of that year.

KATHY GARVER

Most Famous TV Role: Cissy Davis on *Family Affair*; **Network:** CBS; **Years:** 1966–1971; **Hit Recording:** none; **Label:** Aquarian; **Release Year:** 1967; **Matrix:** "Lem, the Orphan Reindeer" (Aquarian #381); **Chart:** none

Uncle Bill, Uncle Bill, Cissy made a record. It's "Lem, the Orphan Reindeer" by *Family Affair*'s Kathy Garver.

Kathleen Marie Garver was born in Long Beach, California, on December 13, 1945. One of her first roles was as a slave the 1956 motion picture *The Ten Commandments*. Then came television. She auditioned for the lead role in a syndicated Desilu sitcom in 1958 called *This Is Alice*. That role went to Patty Ann Gerrity, but Garver was cast as one of Alice's best friends, Sally. That series only lasted a single season, and Garver then found guest star work on episodic TV shows such as *Father Knows Best*, *The Rifleman*, and *The Bing Crosby Show*.

While attending UCLA for a degree in speech and drama, Garver snagged the role of a lifetime—Cissy Davis, the elder sibling of Buffy and Jody on the CBS sitcom *Family Affair*. During that show's five-season run, Garver also attempted success as a recording artist. She recorded a holiday song called "Lem, the Orphan Reindeer"—written by prolific songwriters Tommy Boyce and Bobby Hart—for the Aquarian Records label, an imprint of Columbia Records. It wasn't a hit, and Garver abandoned the pursuit of a recording career.

After *Family Affair* was cancelled in 1971, Garver became a successful voice actor, providing cartoon voices for programs such as *The Fonz and the Happy Days Gang*, *Spider Man and His Amazing Friends*, *Chuck Norris: Karate Kommandos*, and *The New Yogi Bear Show*. In 2011 she published *The Family Affair Cookbook*, and at last word was working on her autobiography titled *Surviving Cissy: My Family Affair of Life in Hollywood*. Her husband's name is David, and they have one son, Reid.

HENRY GIBSON

Most Famous TV Role: costar on *Rowan and Martin's Laugh-In*; **Network:** NBC; **Years:** 1968–1971; **Hit Recording:** none; **Labels:** A&M; **Release Years:** 1968–1969; **Matrix:** "Unborn Children" (A&M #1190); **Chart:** none

Henry Gibson was born as James Bateman in Germantown, Pennsylvania, on September 21, 1935. He was the president of the drama club in school. After college, he served as an intelligence officer in the U.S. Air Force. His stage name intentionally sounds like that of dramatist Henrik Ibsen, author of *A Doll's House* and *Hedda Gabler*. He began performing as a child, and as an adult began reading his humorous poems on *The Tonight Show with Jack Paar*. After guest-starring roles on *The Joey Bishop Show*, *The Dick Van Dyke Show*, and *The Beverly Hillbillies*; a single season as Insigna on the sitcom version of *Mister Roberts*; and a role in Jerry Lewis's *The Nutty Professor*, he became a hot commodity and was given a regular role on

NBC's *Rowan and Martin's Laugh-In*. Gibson appeared on the program weekly from 1968 to 1971. His most common segments on the program were his poems (always read while holding a large flower), and his appearances as a priest during the cocktail party scenes. During the show's run he released one single on the A&M label titled "Unborn Children" backed with "The Population Song." It wasn't a hit by any stretch of the imagination. A few years later, he played the leader of the Illinois Nazis in *The Blues Brothers Movie* and also became a very prolific voice actor for animation—*Aaahh! Real Monsters*, *Rugrats*, *Hey Arnold*, *Rocket Power*, *King of the Hill*, and *The Grim Adventures of Billy and Mandy*. His final recurring TV role was as Judge Clark Brown on *Boston Legal*. Gibson and his wife, Lois, had three children. She preceded him in death by two years. Gibson died of cancer on September 14, 2009.

KATHIE LEE GIFFORD

Most Famous TV Role: cohost of *Live with Regis and Kathie Lee* and *The Today Show*; **Networks:** ABC, NBC; **Years:** 1988–2000, 2008–present, respectively; **Hit Recording:** none; **Label:** Warner Bros.; **Release Year:** 1993–1995; **Matrix:** *Christmas Carols* (Warner Bros. CD #4155), *Sentimental* (Warner Bros. CD #7897155), *It's Christmas Time* (Warner Bros. CD #8389085); **Chart:** none

Kathie Lee Epstein was born in Paris, France, on August 16, 1953. Her father, Aaron was stationed in France at the time, but Kathie Lee was raised in Bowie, Maryland. Her first stage name, Kathie Lee Johnson, was a result of her first marriage to composer Paul Johnson. Her first big TV break came as the singer on the game show *Name That Tune* from 1974 to 1978. She was then cast in a short-lived *Hee Haw* sitcom spinoff called *Hee Haw Honeys* in 1978. She and Paul Johnson divorced in 1983. In 1986, she married a sports figure many years her senior, Frank Gifford. Her biggest claim to fame came beginning in 1988 as Kathie Lee Gifford when she was cast as the cohost on *Live with Regis and Kathie Lee*. While with the program, she released several CDs for Warner Bros. (including two Christmas CDs). None of them made the charts, but were decent sellers among her most devoted fan base. She remained with the hit ABC show until 2000, and after a break surfaced on the daily fourth hour of *The Today Show*, this time teamed with Hoda Kotb. In the new millennium, Gifford has released a few more CDs for small independent labels such as LML and On the Lamb.

JOHNNY GILBERT

Most Famous TV Role: announcer on *Jeopardy;* **Network:** syndicated; **Years:** 1984–present; **Hit Recording:** none; **Labels:** Golden Crest, Janel; **Release Year:** 1958; **Matrix:** *Johnny Gilbert Magic Melodies from Music Bingo* (Golden Crest LP), *Johnny Gilbert Sings for You* (Janel EP #19307); **Chart:** none

John L. Gilbert III was born on July 13, 1924, in Newport News, Virginia. He began as a choir boy and wanted to become a professional singer, and received vocal training. Singing, however, is not how Gilbert made his mark. He did sing with a band in his native Virginia, but that led to a job as an emcee and the eventual opportunity to host a 1958 TV game show called *Music Bingo.* Gilbert also got to sing on the program and during its run released a record album called *Johnny Gilbert Magic Melodies from Music Bingo* using the *Music Bingo* set as a backdrop on the cover. There was also *Johnny Gilbert Sings for You* a while later—an EP consisting of six cuts. This EP may not have been commercially available, as it contains the words *souvenir album* on the cover. Neither was a whopping success, but both albums have recently been remastered and reissued.

After *Music Bingo* was cancelled, Gilbert hosted several other game shows including *Camouflage, Fast Draw, Words and Music,* and *Beat the Odds.* He was also the announcer for *Yours for a Song* with Bert Parks, and *The Price Is Right* with Bill Cullen. Announcing proved to be his bailiwick, and among his credits are *The Joker's Wild, Tic Tac Dough, Dream House,* and *$25,000 Pyramid.* However, the gig he landed in 1984 proved to be the most enduring. Gilbert was named the announcer for the new syndicated version of *Jeopardy* hosted by Alex Trebek, and more than 30 years hence, now a nonagenarian, Gilbert is still saying, "This Is *Jeopardy*" on a daily basis (as of this writing).

DARLENE GILLESPIE

Most Famous TV Role: a Mouseketeer on *The Mickey Mouse Club;* **Network:** ABC; **Years:** 1955–1958; **Hit Recording:** none; **Labels:** Coral, Disneyland; **Release Years:** 1956–1960; **Matrix:** "I Loved I Laughed I Cried" (Coral #62178), "Sittin' on the Balcony" (Disneyland #50), "Butterfly" (Disneyland #51), "Rock-a-Billy" (Disneyland #52), "Break of Day" (Disneyland #60), "Together Time" (Disneyland #61), "The Unbirthday Song" (Disneyland #715), "Alice in Wonderland" (Disneyland #4015); *Darlene of the Teens* (Disneyland LP #3010); **Chart:** none

Darlene Gillespie was born in Montreal, Canada, on April 8, 1941. Before her teen years, Darlene took dancing and singing lessons and they served her well. In 1955, she auditioned for a role on *The Mickey Mouse Club* and got the gig. She performed on the program for three seasons and took part in the *Corky and White Shadow* and *Spin and Marty* segments. The Walt Disney Company attempted to make a recording star of Gillespie, but unlike Annette Funicello, Gillespie failed to chart any singles. However, it wasn't for a lack of trying. She released a litany of 45s and even a few 78s for the Disneyland Records label (including numerous *Corky and White Shadow* singles), and several in the Mouskemusicals, Mouskethoughts, and Mousketunes series. There was also an album titled *Darlene of the Teens* in 1957. This LP was later reissued as *Darlene Gillespie Sings Top Tunes of The 50s* (Disneyland LP #3010). Even a switch to the Coral label in 1959 failed to generate sales.

Likely because of her longtime presence on *The Mickey Mouse Club*, she was not taken seriously after the original version of the program came to an end, and she quickly faded from public view. She attempted a comeback as a country artist in the 1970s under the pseudonym of Darlene Valentine and recorded "April Is the Month for Love" for the Alva Records label (#111), but success was not in the cards. She returned to the spotlight in 1998, but not in a good way—she and her third husband were convicted of fraud, and she served three months of a two-year prison sentence. More legal problems arose in 2005 when she and her husband were indicted in yet another case of fraud. Somewhere, Cubby is weeping.

JACKIE GLEASON

Most Famous TV Role: Ralph Kramden on *The Honeymooners*; **Network:** CBS, DuMont; **Years:** 1952–1970; **Hit Recording:** "Autumn Leaves"; **Label:** Capitol; **Release Year:** 1955; **Matrix:** Capitol #3223; **Chart:** #50 *Billboard* Hot 100

John Herbert "Jackie" Gleason was born in Brooklyn, New York, on February 26, 1916. Much like his *Honeymooners* character Ralph Kramden, he lived on Chauncey Street. When Jackie was only nine, his father abandoned the family and left them to fend for themselves. A brother named Clemence died in his early teens, and Jackie became an only child and his mom became the breadwinner for the family; like Ralph, she worked for Manhattan Transit. Gleason helped out with money earned working as a carnival barker, emcee, comedian, and actor. In his early 20s he began scoring bit parts in motion pictures. He was not a huge success on the silver screen and jumped over to the burgeoning new television industry in the late 1940s. He was cast as TV's first Chester A. Riley on *The Life of Riley* in 1949. Even though the filmed series won an Emmy, it was not a ratings success and was cancelled after one season. Gleason then found his niche in TV variety, first on the tiny DuMont Television Network on a live program called *Cavalcade of Stars*, and then on *The Jackie Gleason Show*. A sketch on those shows titled "The Honeymooners" became legendary, and was even spun off into a filmed CBS sitcom.

Gleason was a man of many talents and also recorded a bevy of record albums and cowrote the theme songs for his programs. Most were instrumentals, but he did release a vocal 45 in 1964—"Casey at the Bat" backed with "I Had but 50 Cents" (Capitol #5420). The single was released while Jackie's weekly program was called *American Scene Magazine*. The vocal single wasn't a hit, but Gleason's mood music albums were hugely successful, many reaching Top Ten—*Music for Lovers Only* (Capitol #475), *Music to Remember Her* (Capitol #570), *Romantic Jazz* (Capitol #568), *Music to Change Her Mind* (Capitol #632), *Night Winds* (Capitol #717), and the number 1 *Lonesome Echo* (Capitol #627). Gleason didn't sing on any of these cuts, but he did conduct the orchestra and also penned many of the tunes.

When "The Honeymooners" sketch was resurrected for the color *Jackie Gleason Show* episodes of the late 1960s, both Gleason and Art Carney did a lot of singing. These hour-long episodes, nowadays referred to as *The Color Honeymooners*, resembled Broadway shows. In these episodes, Alice is portrayed by Sheila MacRae instead of Audrey Meadows, and Trixie Norton by Jane Kean instead of Joyce Randolph. Gleason continued to release albums for Capitol through 1969. Despite his uncanny flair for comedy, Gleason was a very good and underappreciated serious actor as well, as seen in *The Hustler*, *Gigot*, and *Requiem for a Heavyweight*.

Gleason was married three times and had two children with wife number 1, Genevieve Halford. His final film role came in a costarring role with Tom Hanks in *Nothing in Common* in 1986. He died of colon cancer on June 24, 1987.

GEORGE GOBEL

Most Famous TV Role: host of *The George Gobel Show*; **Network:** CBS, NBC; **Years:** 1954–1960; **Hit Recording:** none; **Labels:** RCA Victor, Souncot; **Release Years:** 1954–1957; **Matrix:** "Bright Red Convertible" (RCA Victor #6483), "Old Sam" (Souncot #1140), "Big Gold Cadillac" (Souncot #1144); **Chart:** none

George Gobel was born in Chicago, Illinois, on May 20, 1919. He was an only child. Early in his career, he had designs on becoming a country singer. Luckily for us, he switched his focus to comedy after his World War II army hitch came to an end. His low-key, unique delivery was very endearing, and he was quickly given his own variety program on NBC beginning in the fall of 1954. His production company, Gomalco, is best known for *Leave It to Beaver*. Sponsored by Dial Soap, *The George Gobel Show* ran for six seasons—five on NBC and one on CBS. He was called "Lonesome George," even though his wife, "Spooky Old Alice" (portrayed by a couple of different actresses), appeared in or at least was alluded to on most episodes.

Gobel attempted to sing in many episodes, but was invariably interrupted. He did, however, release several 45s during his TV reign—"Bright Red Convertible" backed with "Birds and the Bees," "Old Sam" backed with "Are You a Turtle?" and "Big Gold Cadillac" backed with "In the Jungle." He wasn't the greatest singer in the world, but he held his own. After the cancellation of his variety series in 1960, he made one more attempt at a hit record—"Scarlet Ribbons" backed with "Soon I'll Wed My Love" (Decca #31594). Gobel also got to sing in the Broadway musical called *Let It Ride*, which enjoyed a very short ride on the Great White Way. After success in Las Vegas in the 1960s, Gobel became a regular on *The Hollywood Squares*, replacing Charley Weaver. At this same time, he also found a considerable amount of work in motion pictures. Gobel died in 1991 after suffering complications from heart surgery.

THE GOLDDIGGERS

Most Famous TV Role: semiregulars on *Dean Martin Presents the Golddiggers*, semiregulars on *The Dean Martin Show*, hosts of *The Golddiggers Show*; **Network:** NBC; **Years:** 1968–1970, 1970–1971, 1971, respectively; **Hit Recordings:** none; **Labels:** Metromedia, RCA Victor; **Release Year:** 1971; **Matrix:** *The Golddiggers* (Metromedia LP #1009), *We Need a Little Christmas* (Metromedia LP #1012), *The Golddiggers Today* (RCA Victor LP #4643); **Chart:** none

The Golddiggers, a female troupe of comely young dancers and singers, performed very much in the style of a Las Vegas show. Their biggest career boost came with the help of Dean Martin. The Golddiggers were semiregulars on his *Dean Martin Show* as well as *Dean Martin Presents the Golddiggers* before hosting their very own short-lived *The Golddiggers Show* in 1971. They released three albums—*The Golddiggers*, and *We Need a Little Christmas* in 1969 for Metromedia Records and *The Golddiggers Today* for

RCA Victor Records in 1971—but the troupe proved to be a much more popular visual act than audio act, and the albums failed to chart. The RCA album was also available in the eight-track format. The troupe, sometimes consisting of as many as 13 girls, continues to perform today. Dozens upon dozens of nubile young women have come and gone, but the Gold-diggers name lives on.

FRANK GORSHIN

Most Famous TV Role: the Riddler on *Batman*; **Network:** ABC; **Years:** 1966–1968; **Hit Recording:** none; **Label:** A&M; **Release Year:** 1966; **Matrix:** "The Riddler" (A&M #804); **Chart:** none

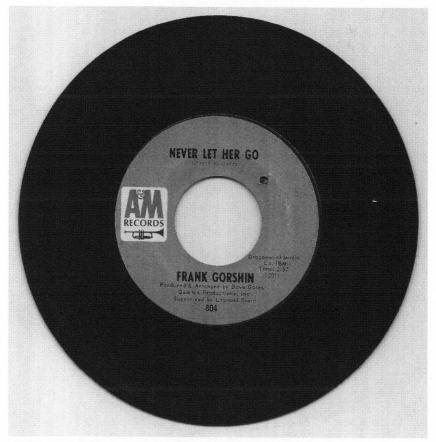

While enjoying success with a recurring role on *Batman* as the Riddler, Frank Gorshin attempted success on vinyl with "Never Let Her Go" written by future Bread member David Gates, backed with "The Riddler" written by Mel Torme.

Frank Gorshin was born in Pittsburgh, Pennsylvania, on April 5, 1933. After his army hitch was up in the middle 1950s, he began finding work in episodic TV programs such as *Mr. Lucky*, *Frontier Doctor*, and *Hennesey*, while performing stand-up and impressions on variety shows such as *The Ed Sullivan Show*. He also snagged roles in numerous B movies of the 1950s such as *Hot Rod Girl* and *Invasion of the Saucer Men*. He is most fondly remembered as the Riddler on ABC's immensely popular live action *Batman* series from 1966 to 1968.

During the show's run, he released a single, produced by David Gates (later of Bread) on Herb Alpert and Jerry Moss's A&M label. One side of the single was a novelty cut titled "The Riddler" (written by Mel Torme) on which Gorshin recites a long list of riddles. However, on the flip side is a ballad written by David Gates called "Never Let Her Go." The single showcased Gorshin's versatility, and he was hoping that one of the two sides would catch on with the record-buying public. The record was released with a picture sleeve with Gorshin in his Riddler attire on one side, and in a suit with a lit cigarette in hand on the other. It was not a big hit and no other singles by Gorshin were released for A&M. He tried again a few years later with a remake of "Turn Around, Look at Me" for the King Records label (#6336), but it too failed to catch the public ear.

At this time, he found fairly steady work on Broadway in *Guys and Dolls* and *Jimmy*. He remained a very popular Las Vegas performer for decades and was often part of *The Dean Martin Celebrity Roasts*. Coincidentally, his final TV appearance was as himself on an episode of *CSI* titled "Grave Danger." Gorshin died of lung cancer on May 17, 2005—just two days before the *CSI* episode aired. Gorshin was married only once and had one son, Mitchell.

LOU GOSSETT JR.

Most Famous TV Role: Fiddler on *Roots*; **Network:** ABC; **Year:** 1977; **Hit Recording:** none; **Label:** B. T. Puppy, Warner Bros.; **Release Years:** 1970–1971; **Matrix:** "San Francisco Bay Blues" (Warner Bros. #7201), "Tinglin'" (B. T. Puppy #560); **Chart:** none

Louis Cameron Gossett Jr. was born in Brooklyn, New York, on May 27, 1936. He was very athletic, but a sports injury led him into a few high school stage productions. He was so good that he abandoned his athletic pursuits and focused on theater when attending NYU. Gossett soon conquered Broadway, then motion pictures, and eventually television. He

Before he was Fiddler on the *Roots* miniseries, Lou Gossett Jr. fiddled around with a recording career. Even with the Tokens and Bill Cosby behind him, his records failed to catch on.

was also quite musically inclined as well, and wrote a song for Richie Havens titled "Handsome Johnny."

While starring in the single season series, *The Young Rebels* as Isak Poole from 1970 to 1971, Gossett released several 45s on the Warner Bros. and B. T. Puppy labels—"Where Have All the Flowers Gone" backed with "Just a Girl" (Warner Bros. #7078), "San Francisco Bay Blues" backed with "You're in a Bad Way" (Warner Bros. #7201), and "Tinglin'" backed with "Old Jay Gould" (B. T. Puppy #560). In 1974, he released three more unsuccessful singles for the Powertree label and afterward opted to focus only on his acting. Gossett earned recurring roles in a couple of other short-lived series—*The Lazarus Syndrome* in 1979 as Dr. MacArthur St. Clair, *The Powers of Matthew Star* in 1982 as Walt Shepherd, and in the lead role on *Gideon Oliver* in 1989, but by far his most famous TV role came with his Emmy-winning portrayal of Fiddler on the miniseries *Roots* in 1977. He also achieved great notices for his big-screen role as Gunnery Sergeant Emil Foley in 1982's *An Officer and a Gentleman*. He has been married three times, fathered one son and adopted another. He is a prostate cancer survivor.

DON GRADY

Most Famous TV Role: Robbie Douglas on *My Three Sons*; **Networks:** ABC, CBS; **Years:** 1960–1972; **Hit Recordings:** "Children of St. Monica" by the Windupwatchband, "Yellow Balloon" by Yellow Balloon, "Good Feelin' Time" by Yellow Balloon; **Label:** Canterbury; **Release Years:** 1966–1967; **Matrix:** Canterbury #501, #508, #513, respectively; **Chart:** #132 *Billboard* Bubbling Under, #25 *Billboard* Hot 100, Bubbling Under #101, respectively

Don Grady was born Don Agrati in San Diego, California, on June 8, 1944. His mother, Mary, was a talent agent and assisted her young son in becoming one of the original Mouseketeers on *The Mickey Mouse Club*. He also found work in episodic TV shows such as *The Rifleman*, *The Betty Hutton Show*, and *Wagon Train* before being cast as the middle child on a new ABC sitcom in 1960 titled *My Three Sons*. The program starred Fred MacMurray and William Frawley, and the original series ran for five seasons on ABC. After the death of William Frawley as Bub, character actor William Demarest took his place as Uncle Charley. The eldest son, Tim Considine as Mike, left the show at this time, and when it was picked up by CBS, Robbie became the senior son and a new adopted brother, Ernie (Barry Livingston), was added to maintain the *My Three Sons* premise. Few expected the program to linger for 7 more seasons on CBS, making for a total of 12, and an amazing 357 episodes. Don Grady was in every episode, and during the program's run, tried to become a pop music star. He came close a few times, beginning in 1966 with a single called "Children of St. Monica" as by Don Grady and the Windupwatchband. The song "bubbled under" the Hot 100 for a couple of weeks and then disappeared. Grady then became part of another group on the Canterbury Records label called The Yellow Balloon. "The Yellow Balloon" by The Yellow Balloon peaked at number 25 on the Hot 100 in the spring of 1967 and Grady, rather anonymously, had a fair-sized hit single on his hands. Only one other single by the band, "Good Feelin' Time" bubbled under the Hot 100, peaking at number 101 during the summer of 1967. He also attempted solo success with numerous singles released as by Don Grady for Canterbury, as well as Capitol, Challenge, and Orange Empire Records with little success.

After the cancellation of *My Three Sons*, Grady attempted to distance himself from the Robbie role and, under his real name of Don Agrati, released an album for the Elektra label titled *Don Agrati* (Elektra #75057), but it failed to achieve success. Grady also wrote numerous songs, with the theme for *The Phil Donahue Show* likely being the most famous. He kept his acting chops honed while with the touring cast of *Pippin, Damn Yankees*, and *Godspell*. Grady died of cancer at the age of 68 on June 27, 2012, and is survived by his second wife, Virginia, and two children, Tessa and Joey.

TERESA GRAVES

Most Famous TV Role: Christy Love on *Get Christy Love*; **Network:** ABC; **Years:** 1974–1975; **Hit Recording:** none; **Label:** Calendar, Kirshner; **Release Year:** 1970–1974; **Matrix:** "A Time for Us" (Calendar #5001), *Teresa Graves* (Kirshner LP #104); **Chart:** none

Teresa Graves was born in Houston, Texas, on January 10, 1948. She always wanted to be a singer and an actress, and for the most part, her dreams came true. She joined the cast of *Rowan and Martin's Laugh-In* on NBC in 1969 and stayed until 1970. At the same time, she, with the help of Don Kirshner, attempted to get a recording career underway. She released an eponymous album on the Kirshner Records label, but it failed to catch on. She got another shot a few years later when she made history by being the first African American to star in a weekly hour-long TV drama. The detective show, called *Get Christy Love*, was set in the Los Angeles Police Department. The concept began as a TV movie and did well enough in the ratings to become a series. Despite all of the buzz about the series, it lasted only one season. During its run, however, Don Kirshner released a single by Graves on his Calendar label subsidiary—"A Time for Us" backed with "We're on Our Way" (Calendar #5001). It was released with a Teresa Graves photo picture sleeve. Much like her show, the record was not a hit. In that same year, she became a Jehovah's Witness and eventually left show business to devote more time to her religion. While living in Los Angeles on October 10, 2002, her home caught fire and Graves eventually died after being found unconscious. She was only 54.

LORNE GREENE

Most Famous TV Role: Ben Cartwright on *Bonanza*; **Network:** NBC; **Years:** 1959–1973; **#1 Hit Recording:** "Ringo"; **Label:** RCA Victor; **Release Year:** 1964; **Matrix:** RCA Victor #8444; **Chart:** #1 *Billboard* Hot 100

Lorne Greene was born as Lyon Himan Green in Ottawa, Ontario, Canada, on February 12, 1915. He was a drama instructor at summer camp, and it was there he perfected his skills. He began as a radio newscaster for the CBC (Canadian Broadcasting Company). His booming voice was

In between all those Beatles records in 1964, Lorne Greene of *Bonanza* managed to sneak in a number 1 hit called "Ringo." "The Man" was a less successful follow-up.

perfect for documentary films, and eventually he parlayed that into acting in films, including 1957's *Peyton Place*. He found his greatest success on the small screen and began as a guest star on episodic programs. He got very lucky very quickly, and was cast as Ben Cartwright in a new NBC western called *Bonanza* in 1959, and settled in for almost a decade and a half on the Ponderosa.

During the program's long and successful Sunday night run, Greene also scored a number 1 hit on the Hot 100 called "Ringo." It was recited rather than performed, but the interesting story and Greene's dulcet tones made it a hit. Even though the record came in 1964, the year the Beatles hit it big in the United States, the song is not about Ringo Starr, but rather Johnny Ringo, an outlaw of the old West. It was quite a feat to reach number 1 in that year—the British Invasion groups and the up-and-coming superstars of Motown owned the charts. Greene also scored one Top Forty album, *Welcome to the Ponderosa* (RCA Victor #2843), that same year.

Greene's recording career was short-lived, and he never again reached the Top Fifty, but he didn't need to. Although not as big as Ben Cartwright on *Bonanza*, Greene's role as Commander Adama on the sci-fi drama called *Battlestar Galactica* did bring him more TV success. He also had a long run in a series of Alpo Dog Food commercials. Greene was married twice and had a total of three children. Coincidentally, he had just signed a contract for a *Bonanza* revival when he contracted pneumonia and died on September 11, 1987, in Santa Monica, California.

GREG (EVIGAN) AND PAUL (SHAFFER)

Most Famous TV Roles: B.J. McCay on *B.J. and the Bear* and Joey Harris on *My Two Dads* (Evigan), band leader on *Late Night with David Letterman* and *The Late Show with David Letterman* (Shaffer); **Networks:** CBS, NBC; **Years:** 1979–1981, 1987–1990 (Evigan), 1982–present (Shaffer); **Hit Recording:** none; **Label:** Casablanca; **Release Year:** 1977; **Matrix:** *Greg and Paul: A Year at the Top* (Casablanca LP #7068); **Chart:** none

Before each went on to bigger and better things, Greg Evigan and Paul Shaffer starred in a CBS sitcom called *A Year at the Top* in 1977 from Norman Lear Productions. Production and conceptual problems during the early stages led to numerous different pilots being filmed, and constant cast and crew changes. Don Kirshner was involved early on, but he was eventually phased out. The program focused upon struggling singer/songwriters who, after making a pact with the devil (played by a very flamboyant Gabriel Dell), enjoyed superstardom and "a year at the top."

On the umpteenth try, CBS finally greenlighted the pilot with Greg Evigan and Paul Shaffer as the pop duo Greg and Paul. All of the effort and energy employed to get this sitcom on the air was truly in vain as it lasted only five weeks on CBS's prime-time schedule. During that extremely short time span, an album by Greg and Paul was released by the red hot Casablanca Records label, featuring songs performed on the series, including the *A Year at the Top* theme song and "She's a Rebel," which was also released on a single (Casablanca #893). Both the album and the series bombed, and Evigan tried once more for musical stardom on the small Amboy label with a solo single titled "I'm Right with You" backed with "People I Know" (Amboy #116), but it wasn't meant to be. He did find TV success on *B.J. and the Bear* and *My Two Dads*, and Paul Shaffer has enjoyed a historic run on David Letterman's late-night talk shows, first on NBC and then CBS.

ROSEY GRIER

Most Famous TV Role: host of *The Rosey Grier Show*, Rosey Robbins on *Make Room for Granddaddy*; **Network:** ABC, syndicated; **Years:** 1968–1970, 1970–1971, respectively; **Hit Recording:** "People Make the World"; **Label:** Amy; **Release Year:** 1968; **Matrix:** Amy #11029; **Chart:** #126 *Billboard* Bubbling Under

Roosevelt "Rosey" Grier was born the 7th of 11 children on July 14, 1932, in Cuthbert, Georgia. After becoming a notable college football player for Penn State, he donned number 76 for the New York Giants, and then became one of the "Fearsome Foursome" for the Los Angeles Rams, along with Lamar Lundy, Merlin Olsen, and Deacon Jones. Grier shared, "I learned an awful lot in my football years by playing with and against the best. By the way, I was in five World Championship games, but only one Pro Bowl, not two, as it says on the Internet. That was a lot of fun and a great honor."

Grier tore his Achilles tendon, effectively ending his career. Grier added, "I also bit almost totally through my tongue. To this day, there is still some numbness there." None of these injuries kept Grier from the public eye. In fact, it was at this time the public got to see Grier's many other talents—writing, singing, and acting. He hosted a talk show titled *The Rosey Grier Show* and earned recurring roles on such TV series as *The White Shadow*, *Daniel Boone*, and *Make Room for Granddaddy*. Grier stated, "That was a great learning experience. I learned to speak properly; I learned how to play and develop real, believable, and convincing characters; and I grew up—I matured. I loved working with Danny Thomas because I got to act *and* make music on his show."

Speaking of music, Grier made a lot of it. He recorded for a myriad of record labels such as A&M, Amy, D-Town, Liberty, MGM, Ric, United Artists, and 20th Century Fox. Was he aware that some of his singles, such as "Pizza Pie Man" (D-Town #1058) and "In My Tenement" (Ric #112), had become valuable collector's items? Grier replied, "No, I had no idea. However, that makes sense because I recently had someone come up to me and ask about 'Pizza Pie Man,' to my surprise. My own personal favorite song is 'It's Alright to Cry' from *Free to Be You and Me* with Marlo Thomas, and I'm very proud of my current CD of gospel music called *Let the Old Man Play*." The CD, containing a new version of one of his biggest hits (composed by his good friend and former neighbor, the late Bobby Womack), "People Make the World," can be obtained at www.roseygrier .com. "People Make the World" was a song dedicated to Bobby Kennedy (Grier was present at his assassination). Which did he favor more, his NFL career or his singing career? Amazingly, Grier answered, "Singing, because even more than football, singing allows one to really express themselves, to talk to people, inspire them and connect with them. Don't get me wrong, I loved playing football, but singing brings me the most joy."

Today's NFL greats make a lot of money, and Grier's advice to them is, "Be more appreciative of how fortunate you are, play by the rules, be a good responsible role model, don't forget to give back, and most of all, smile more."

Grier's autobiography is aptly titled *The Gentle Giant*. His most memorable work, which received the most unexpected response, was *Needlepoint for Men*. He is a Christian minister, and remains a very active champion for charities such as Impact Urban America, World Impact, and the Prostate Cancer Foundation.

It should be noted that the members of the Fearsome Foursome also made one record for the Capitol label (#5482) titled "Fly in the Buttermilk" backed with "Stranded in the Jungle."

CLU GULAGER

Most Famous TV Roles: Billy the Kid on *The Tall Man*, Emmett Ryker on *The Virginian*; **Network:** NBC; **Years:** 1960–1962, 1964–1968, respectively; **Hit Recording:** none; **Labels:** Capitol, Deville; **Release Years:** 1960–1961; **Matrix:** "Billy the Kid" (Deville #116), "Chiquita Mia" (Capitol #4524); **Chart:** none

Clu Gulager was born William Gulager in Holdenville, Oklahoma, on November 16, 1928. The nickname "Clu" allegedly came from the sound made by birds called martins that were prevalent near his home. He served in the U.S. Marine Corps before turning his attention to acting. He was part Native American, had the right look for TV westerns, and found a lot of guest-starring roles before scoring a regular role as Billy the Kid on *The Tall Man* with Barry Sullivan as Pat Garrett. That show lasted for two seasons, and during that time it was thought that Gulager was a good candidate for a recording career as well. He released singles on both the Capitol and Deville Records labels with his mug emblazoned on the picture sleeve, but even that failed to make his 45s into big hits. Even the song about his TV character, "Billy the Kid," missed the Hot 100. Gulager quickly abandoned his pursuit of rock and roll stardom and was quickly absorbed into the cast of *The Virginian* as Deputy Sheriff Emmett Ryker. The grind of filming a 90-minute weekly western led to his decision to leave the still popular show in 1968 after four seasons. He then found success on the silver screen in popular films such as *The Last Picture Show*, *McQ*, *The Return of the Living Dead*, and *Winning*. Keeping it in the family, Gulager's son John is now an up-and-coming movie director. Gulager was married only once and is a widower—his wife, Miriam, died in 2003.

JASMINE GUY

Most Famous TV Role: Whitley Gilbert on *A Different World*; **Network:** NBC; **Years:** 1987–1993; **Hit Recordings:** "Another like My Lover," "Just Want to Hold You"; **Label:** Warner Bros.; **Release Year:** 1991; **Matrix:** "Another like My Lover" (Warner Bros. #19486), "Just Want to Hold You" (Warner Bros. #19330); **Chart:** #66, #34, respectively, *Billboard* Hot 100

Jasmine Guy was born in Boston, Massachusetts, on March 10, 1962, but was raised in Atlanta, Georgia. After a stint with the Alvin Ailley Dance Troupe, she got her big TV break as a dancer (a nonspeaking role) on Debbie Allen's popular *Fame* TV series on NBC, based upon the blockbuster motion picture. Then came a costarring role that turned into a leading role on a sitcom. Guy portrayed southern belle Whitley Gilbert on *The Cosby Show* spinoff, *A Different World*, beginning in 1987. The program originally starred Lisa Bonet, but when she left, it continued with Guy in the forefront.

To capitalize on the opportunity, Guy also simultaneously sought success as a recording artist. In 1991, she managed to crack the Hot 100 a couple of times with "Another like My Lover" and "Just Want to Hold

You" for the Warner Bros. label. Her *Jasmine Guy* album (Warner Bros. LP #26021) peaked at number 143 and was her only charted album. She fared a little better on the R&B charts. After the series ended in 1993, she found steady work in motion pictures and her first love, the Broadway stage. She was also a frequent guest star on TV sitcoms, and most recently earned recurring roles on *Dead like Me* and *The Vampire Diaries*. Guy's only marriage ended in divorce, and at last report, she and her daughter, Imani, are back home in Atlanta.

H

BUDDY HACKETT

Most Famous TV Role: Stanley Peck on *Stanley*; **Network:** NBC; **Years:** 1956–1957; **Hit Recording:** "Chinese Rock and Egg Roll"; **Label:** Coral; **Release Year:** 1956; **Matrix:** Coral #61594; **Chart:** #87 *Billboard* Hot 100

Buddy Hackett was born as Leonard Hacker in Brooklyn, New York, on August 31, 1924. He began his comedy career in the Catskills (a.k.a. the Borscht Belt). A three-year stint in the army briefly interrupted his pursuit of fame and fortune. Upon being discharged, Hackett found some work in nightclubs and then on Broadway in a show called *Lunatics and Lovers*. It was there that he was discovered by Max Liebman and brought over to television. After placing Buddy in a couple of TV specials, Liebman cast him in a new live NBC sitcom called *Stanley* in 1956. By 1956, most prime-time programming was prerecorded, so *Stanley* was somewhat of an anomaly. Hackett played Stanley Peck, a dreamer and schemer who ran the newsstand in a New York City hotel lobby. Carol Burnett, Dick Gautier, and Paul Lynde were also in the cast, starting their own careers. Also in 1956, Hackett released a series of half-narrated, half-sung singles for the Coral Records label, including his biggest hit—the very politically incorrect "Chinese Rock and Egg Roll" (it was also anti–rock and roll). The record got him more attention than the TV series, and *Stanley* was cancelled.

Hackett wasn't very upset when the show came to an end—his stand-up comedy star was on the rise. He was always a popular guest on variety, game, and talk shows, and he eventually landed in a few very popular motion pictures—*It's a Mad, Mad, Mad, Mad World*; *The Music Man*; and *The Love Bug*. He also continued making records and even sang on a few. His versions of "Itsy Bitsy Teenie Weenie Yellow Polka Dot Bikini" (Laurel #1014) and "Looey Looey" (Laurel #1017) in 1962 were quite unique, to say the least (but not big sellers). In later years, Hackett became active in providing voices for animation, including his stint as Crabby on the

Famous for his comedy recordings, Buddy Hackett, who was the star of NBC's *Stanley*, sings on this cover of Brian Hyland's "Itsy Bitsy Teenie Weenie Yellow Polka Dot Bikini."

popular series *The Fish Police*, and Scuttle in *The Little Mermaid* motion picture. He also recorded numerous stand-up specials for HBO. Hackett was married only once, to Sherry Cohen. Son Sandy followed in his famous father's comedy footsteps. Buddy Hackett had been battling obesity and diabetes for many years, and suffered a stroke in June of 2003. He died a week later on June 30 at the age of 78.

LARRY HAGMAN

Most Famous TV Roles: Major Anthony Nelson on *I Dream of Jeannie,* J.R. Ewing on *Dallas;* **Networks:** CBS, NBC; **Years:** 1965–1970, 1978–1991, respectively; **Hit Recording:** none; **Label:** Lorimar; **Release Year:** 1980; **Matrix:** "Ballad of the Good Luck Charm" (Lorimar #70044); **Chart:** none

Larry Hagman was born in Fort Worth, Texas, on September 21, 1931. His mother was Broadway actress Mary Martin, most famous for portraying Peter Pan. Mary and her husband, Benjamin, divorced when Larry was quite young, and he was sent to live with his grandmother. When his grandmother died, Larry moved to New York to reunite with his mother. While there, he became enamored with the stage and opted to follow in his mother's footsteps.

Hagman's career was put on hold while he enlisted in the U.S. Air Force in 1952, where he spent most of his time entertaining the troops. After being discharged, Hagman enjoyed a successful run in numerous Broadway productions and tried his luck in television beginning in the very late 1950s. After numerous guest appearances on episodic television programs, he earned the regular role of the genie's master on *I Dream of Jeannie*—a situation comedy that has enjoyed an amazing run in syndication. After five seasons, the program was cancelled and Hagman had trouble finding another hit show on TV, and starred in two short-lived sitcoms—*The Good Life* and *Here We Go Again.* A turn to TV drama proved to be an extremely wise choice, and as J.R. Ewing, Hagman struck oil and gold as the star of the long-running sensation known as *Dallas.* The program was a Lorimar production, and Lorimar also, briefly, had a record label. Hagman recorded "Ballad of the Good Luck Charm" backed with "My Favorite Sins" for the Lorimar label (#70044) in 1980. The record came with a picture sleeve featuring Hagman wearing a 10-gallon hat. It wasn't a big hit. His only other recordings were as part of cast recordings from Broadway shows in which he appeared. Hagman briefly reprised his legendary role of J.R. Ewing on the new TNT version of the show in 2012. He appeared in 17 of the episodes, but was in failing health because of acute myeloid leukemia and died on November 23, 2012. A J.R. tribute episode was aired on March 11, 2013. Hagman was married only once and had two children, Heidi and Preston. This new *Dallas* was cancelled in 2014.

ARSENIO HALL. *See* CHUNKY A.

Rusty Hamer of *The Danny Thomas Show* tried to parlay his TV fame into success on vinyl. The result—"Two of a Kind" written by Aaron Schroeder and Wally Gold, who also wrote "Good Luck Charm" for Elvis.

RUSTY HAMER

Most Famous TV Role: Rusty Williams on *The Danny Thomas Show/Make Room for Daddy, The Joey Bishop Show,* and *Make Room for Granddaddy;* **Networks:** ABC, CBS; **Years:** 1953–1964, 1964–1965, 1970–1971, respectively; **Hit Recording:** none; **Label:** Mercury; **Release Year:** 1959; **Matrix:** "Two-of-a-Kind" (Mercury #71464); **Chart:** none

Russell Hamer was born in Tenafly, New Jersey, on February 15, 1947. He practically grew up on *Make Room for Daddy* (which later became *The*

Danny Thomas Show when it moved from ABC to CBS in 1957). Hamer was only six when the show began. He and Danny Thomas are the only cast members that stayed for all 11 seasons. Hamer's freckles and wavy red hair led to his being called Rusty in real life and on the program. During the program's run, both Hamer and his stepsister on the show, Angela Cartwright, got to make vinyl recordings. He first got to sing at the age of nine in 1956 on an episode called "The Talented Kid."

Even as a 12-year-old, Rusty wasn't much of a singer, and released only one single—"Two-of-a-Kind" backed with "If My Mother Only Would Let Me." It came with a cute picture sleeve, but didn't sell well. As Hamer matured, he outgrew the cute wise-cracking kid phase, and seemed awkward and out of place on the program. After *The Danny Thomas Show* ended its long run, Hamer briefly continued playing Rusty Williams in the final season of *The Joey Bishop Show* on CBS, and then again on the sequel series in 1970 called *Make Room for Granddaddy*.

In later years, Hamer failed to find enough acting gigs to maintain a living and eventually totally left the business and worked on an oil rig and even became a short-order cook. Like many child stars who disappear from the public eye in their adulthood, Rusty grew more and more depressed and, while living in Louisiana, suffered a fatal self-inflicted gunshot wound at the age of 42 on January 18, 1990. He has a star on the Hollywood Walk of Fame.

NOEL HARRISON

Most Famous TV Role: Mark Slate on *The Girl from U.N.C.L.E.*; **Network:** NBC; **Years:** 1966–1967; **Hit Recordings:** "A Young Girl," "Suzanne"; **Labels:** London, Reprise; **Release Years:** 1965–1967; **Matrix:** "A Young Girl" (London #9795), "Suzanne" (Reprise #0615); **Chart:** #51, #56, respectively, *Billboard* Hot 100

Noel Harrison was born in London, England, on January 29, 1934. He is the son of actor Rex Harrison from his first of six marriages. For many years, Noel lived with his maternal grandparents. At the age of 15, he moved with his mother to the Swiss Alps. It was there he became an avid skier and pursued an interest in repertory theater. He also taught himself to play the guitar, and upon arriving in the United States in the 1960s, began performing in nightclubs. During his run as Mark Slate on *The Girl from U.N.C.L.E.*, he released several singles, and a couple of them made the charts—"A Young Girl," written by Charles Aznavour for London

"The first Noel." Noel Harrison, who played Mark Slate on *The Girl from U.N.C.L.E.*, utilized his "powers" and managed a couple of minor chart hits as a vocalist.

Records, and "Suzanne," written by Leonard Cohen for Reprise Records. Both of those barely missed the Top Fifty. He also released the *Noel Harrison* album (London #459) and *Collage* (Reprise #6263) in that same year. *The Girl from U.N.C.L.E.*, which starred Stephanie Powers, only lasted one season, but has enjoyed a healthy life in reruns.

After the show was cancelled, Harrison continued recording, and had a Top Ten hit in the United Kingdom with the theme from *The Thomas Crown Affair* titled "Windmills of Your Mind." In the 1970s, he was a member of the touring company of *The Fantasticks, Camelot, The Sound of Music, My Fair Lady*, and *The Man of La Mancha*. After suffering a heart attack, Harrison died on October 19, 2013, leaving behind five children—he was 79. The DVD box set for *The Girl from U.N.C.L.E.* was released by Warner Bros. in 2011.

DAVID HASSELHOFF

Most Famous TV Role: Michael Long in *Knight Rider*, Mitch Buchannon in *Baywatch*; **Networks:** NBC, syndicated; **Years:** 1982–1986, 1989–2000, respectively; **Hit Recording:** none in the United States; **Labels:** Ariola, CBS, Silver Blue, White; **Release Years:** 1984–2012; **Matrix:** *Night Rocker* (Silver Blue LP #39893), *Crazy for You* (Ariola LP #78468), *Looking for Freedom* (Ariola LP #260050), *David* (White LP #261972), *You Are Everything* (Ariola LP #74321); **Chart:** *Looking for Freedom* and *Crazy for You*—Top Ten on Austrian, German, and Switzerland music charts

David Hasselhoff was born in Baltimore, Maryland, on July 17, 1952. His family moved around a lot, and for a time he lived in Jacksonville, Florida, and Atlanta, Georgia. In school, he was very active in athletics and in school plays. Soon after studying at the California Institute for the Arts, he hit the jackpot in television. From 1975 to 1982, he portrayed Dr. William Foster Jr. on *The Young and the Restless* on CBS. From there, he jumped into the role of Michael Long in *The Knight Rider* on NBC from 1982 to 1986, and got to drive a Pontiac Trans Am with a talking computer. While on this series, he released a record album called *Night Rocker* on the Silver Blue Records label. It wasn't a hit in the United States, but became a number 1 sensation in Austria.

Hasselhoff, nicknamed "the Hoff," landed in yet another hit series beginning in 1989—the jigglefest known as *Baywatch*. Actually, the program wasn't a success when it debuted on NBC, but became a juggernaut when it moved into syndication and ran for over a decade. During the long run of this show, Hasselhoff continued have success on vinyl as well, and many of his albums reached Top Ten in Germany, Switzerland, and Austria (*David*, *Crazy for You*, *Looking for Freedom*, and *You Are Everything*). Hasselhoff's battles with alcoholism became public knowledge in 2007 because of a video showing him, inebriated and shirtless, eating a cheeseburger off of a Las Vegas hotel room floor. He's been divorced twice and has two daughters. As of this writing, Hasselhoff was seen most recently on the COZI TV network promoting the reruns of his *Knight Rider* series.

SHERMAN HEMSLEY

Most Famous TV Roles: George Jefferson on *The Jeffersons*, Deacon Ernest Frye on *Amen*; **Networks:** CBS, NBC; **Years:** 1975–1985, 1986–1991, respectively; **Hit Recording:** none; **Label:** Sutra; **Release Year:** 1990; **Matrix:** "Ain't That a Kick in the Head" (Sutra #088); **Chart:** none

Sherman Hemsley was born in South Philadelphia, Pennsylvania, on February 1, 1938. He dropped out of school to join the U.S. Air Force and served four years. After being discharged, he attended the Academy of Dramatic Arts. Upon moving to New York City, he snagged the role of Gitlow in the Broadway musical titled *Purlie*. After that came a stint in Vinnette Carroll's musical *Don't Bother Me, I Can't Cope*. Hemsley was then invited to join the cast of *All in the Family* as George Jefferson. He was hesitant to leave his Broadway role for television, but it certainly proved to be a good move. After a couple of years in the role on *All in the Family*, he starred in the CBS spinoff called *The Jeffersons* and enjoyed an 11-season run.

A short two years later, Hemsley got to star in another successful sitcom. This show was called *Amen*, and this time he portrayed a deacon on NBC, and lucked into another five-season success. In 1990, during this show's run, Hemsley recorded a song titled "Ain't That a Kick in the Head" on the Sutra label. This "Ain't That a Kick in the Head" was different from the old standard of the same name. It had a tempo and melody very similar to Janet Jackson's "What Have You Done for Me Lately?" It wasn't a hit, but Hemsley got to lip-synch it on *Soul Train* on April 28, 1990. Hemsley also got to sing on his sitcom in an episode titled "Ernie and the Sublimes" from season 5. In the episode, the deacon gets his old doo-wop group together for one final performance, and he sings lead vocals while bedecked in a green sequined tuxedo. He also voiced the character of B. D. Richfield on the ABC puppet series titled *Dinosaurs* from 1991 to 1994. He was later slated to star in a remake of *Mister Ed* in 1999, but that project never did come to fruition. After a bout with lung cancer, Hemsley died in his El Paso, Texas, home on July 24, 2012. The extremely private Hemsley never married and had no children.

DWAYNE HICKMAN

Most Famous TV Roles: Chuck on *The Bob Cummings Show*, Dobie on *The Many Loves of Dobie Gillis*; **Network:** CBS; **Years:** 1955–1959, 1959–1963, respectively; **Hit Recording:** none; **Labels:** ABC Paramount, Capitol; **Release Years:** early 1960s; **Matrix:** "School Dance" (ABC Paramount #9908), *Dobie* (Capitol LP #1441); **Chart:** none

Actor Dwayne Hickman had roles in two memorable black-and-white CBS sitcoms from television's infancy—*The Bob Cummings Show* (a.k.a. *Love That Bob*) and *The Many Loves of Dobie Gillis*. Some will recall that he also made records. Hickman shared, "I was approached because I was on

TV's *Dobie Gillis* was encouraged to "work" on a recording career, but met with only minor success. He's seen here in a treasured autographed photo in his famous "Thinker" pose.

these two popular weekly series. Everyone who was a teen on a show or in movies at the time was being approached. I was talked into the project by my manager/agent. The program's producers saw it as great publicity for the show. I would never have gone after it myself. I was pushed by my reps."

Did he get to choose his own material? Hickman stated, "Yes, I consulted with Don Costa, who was the producer on 'School Dance' [ABC-Paramount #9908], and Karl Engemann who did the *Dobie* album [Capitol #1441]. When I was recording the album I was working with top-notch studio musicians who looked so bored with me. We took a break and they cleared the room to hang out in the studio down the hall where Sinatra was recording. Then it was back to me. If they were bored with me before, they were really unimpressed when they returned. Sinatra did one take . . . I did 15. And it didn't get any better."

On *The Many Loves of Dobie Gillis*, Bob Denver's character Maynard G. Krebs was a huge jazz music fan. Hickman recalled, "He loved jazz in real life, too. Bob loved all kinds of music. Personally, I loved Elvis and country music. Johnny Cash was always a favorite. Years later, when I worked in Las Vegas booking entertainment for Howard Hughes' Landmark Hotel, I was responsible for bringing country music performers to the strip. Before that, they only performed at the downtown casinos."

Speaking of *The Many Loves of Dobie Gillis*, the four-season complete DVD box set is now available from Shout Factory.

LAWRENCE HILTON-JACOBS

Most Famous TV Role: Freddie "Boom Boom" Washington on *Welcome Back, Kotter*; **Network:** ABC; **Years:** 1975–1979; **Hit Recording:** none; **Label:** ABC, MCA; **Release Years:** 1975–1978; **Matrix:** "Fly Away to My Wonderland" (ABC #12351), "Baby, Your Eyes" (ABC #12448); *All the Way . . . Love* (MCA LP #1127), *Lawrence Hilton-Jacobs* (MCA LP #1045); **Chart:** none

Lawrence Hilton-Jacobs was born in New York City on September 4, 1953. He was the fifth (the middle child) of nine children and attended Wilkes University. He loved the theater and worked with the Negro Ensemble Company until he landed his role of a lifetime—that of Freddie "Boom Boom" Washington in a new James Komack TV sitcom for ABC called *Welcome Back, Kotter*. The program ran for four seasons and catapulted John Travolta to superstardom. During the show's run, Hilton-Jacobs tried to make a go of a musical career and released a couple of albums, including *Lawrence Hilton-Jacobs* and *All the Way . . . Love*, and a single called "Fly Away to My Wonderland" backed with "When We Can," but none of these fulfilled his dreams of chart success, and they were soon forgotten. Hilton-Jacobs tried his hand at producing an album for an R&B group called Halo, and he also sang background vocals on Rick James's *Street Songs* album from 1981. He has remained active in show business, occasionally snagging bit parts in movies or guest starring roles on TV series. His unique way of addressing Gabe Kaplan on *Welcome Back, Kotter* as "Mr. Kah-Taire" is timeless and unforgettable.

AL HODGE

Most Famous TV Role: Captain Video on *Captain Video and His Video Rangers*; **Network:** DuMont, syndicated; **Years:** 1949–1956; **Hit Recording:** none; **Label:** RCA Victor; **Release Year:** 1950; **Matrix:** "Captain Video and the Captives of Saturn" (RCA Victor #WY2009); **Chart:** none

Albert E. Hodge was born in Ravenna, Ohio, on April 18, 1912. After participating in athletics and plays in school, his first job was running a dry cleaning business. He majored in drama at Miami University. His first big break in show business was portraying *The Green Hornet* on radio from 1936 to 1943. Opportunity knocked quickly during television's infancy when Richard Coogan opted to leave the lead role in the DuMont network's *Captain Video and His Video Rangers* TV series. Hodge jumped at the chance to fill the void, and enjoyed a run on the program from 1951 to 1955. The amateurish, low-budget show was very popular with the younger generation. It and Jackie Gleason's *Cavalcade of Stars* were the only hits on that network. DuMont closed up shop in 1956, leaving only three networks—ABC, CBS, and NBC.

During the run of *Captain Video and His Video Rangers*, Al Hodge released a single on RCA Victor for kids. It was the story of "Captain Video and the Captives of Saturn." It was a popular novelty item for kids who were fans of the show, but it failed to chart. After DuMont folded in 1956, Hodge hosted a syndicated kids' show titled *Captain Video's Cartoons* for one season. After this he went the guest-star route, and appeared on episodic TV shows such as *Naked City, The Phil Silvers Show, Hawaiian Eye, M Squad,* and *Alfred Hitchcock Presents*. After 1961, he showed up extremely infrequently on TV and in movies. Hodge was married three times and had one daughter and two stepchildren. He died in a hotel room at the age of 66 on March 19, 1979.

EARL HOLLIMAN

Most Famous TV Role: Lieutenant Bill Crowley on *Police Woman*; **Network:** NBC; **Years:** 1974–1978; **Hit Recording:** none; **Labels:** Capitol, Hi-Fi, Prep; **Release Years:** 1959–1962; **Matrix:** "I'm in the Mood for Love" (Capitol #4194), "We Found Love" (Capitol #4254), "There'll Be No Teardrops Tonight" (Hi-Fi #5074); **Chart:** none

Henry Earl Holliman was born in Delhi, Louisiana, on September 11, 1928. He was put up for adoption at birth, and was taken in and named by an oil field worker named Henry Holliman. He tried to make it in Hollywood at a young age, but was unsuccessful and enlisted in the navy during World War II where he performed in a few navy productions. After his discharge, Holliman studied at the Pasadena Playhouse and began finding work in motion pictures in the 1950s. For his role in *The Rainmaker* in 1956, he garnered a Golden Globe Award for Best Supporting Actor. His first shot at television was as Sundance in a western series called *Hotel de Paree* on CBS from 1959 to 1960.

During this time, Holliman released a couple of singles on a major record label, Capitol—"I'm in the Mood for Love" backed with "Wanna Kiss You Tonight" and "We Found Love" backed with "Willingly." None of these became hits and Holliman was dropped from the Capitol Records roster. After one season on CBS on Friday nights, *Hotel de Paree* was also dropped and Holliman soon found another regular role opposite Andrew Prine on an NBC series set along the rodeo circuit called *Wide Country*. Holliman portrayed Mitch Guthrie, and while on this series got another record deal—this time with the Hi-Fi label. While there, he released "There'll Be No Teardrops Tonight" backed with "Road to Nowhere." Once again, neither the show nor the recording became successful. Holliman went the guest-starring route for a while on episodic TV shows such as *Bonanza*; *12 O'Clock High*; *The Virginian*; *The Fugitive*; *Marcus Welby, M.D.*; *Alias Smith and Jones*; *Medical Center*; *Gunsmoke*; and *Ironside*. In 1974, he landed a regular role on his first hit series, *Police Woman*, as Lieutenant Bill Crowley opposite the lovely Angie Dickinson. The program ran until 1978. In the 1990s, he was a regular on two short-lived sitcoms—*Delta* and *P.S. I Love You*. Since 2000, his only credits are in TV and video documentaries. He has a star on the Hollywood Walk of Fame, and occasionally appears at autograph shows and at San Diego's famous Comic-Con. For many years, he owned his own dinner theater in San Antonio, Texas.

ROBERT HORTON

Most Famous TV Role: Flint McCullough on *Wagon Train*, Shenandoah on *A Man Called Shenandoah*; **Network:** NBC; **Years:** 1957–1962, 1965–1966, respectively; **Hit Recording:** none; **Label:** Columbia; **Release Years:** 1964–1965; **Matrix:** "The Very Thought of You" (Columbia #78864), "King of the Road" (Columbia #43562); **Chart:** none

Robert Horton was born as Meade Howard Horton Jr. in Los Angeles, California, on July 29, 1924. He graduated from Hollywood High School in 1942, and by the early 1950s had a contract with MGM and appeared in numerous films. His early television work was mostly on anthology programs such as *Climax*, *Lux Video Theater*, *Studio 57*, *Celebrity Playhouse*, *General Electric Theater*, *Alfred Hitchcock Presents*, and *Cavalcade of America*. In 1957, he secured a lead role in the NBC western *Wagon Train* as Scout Flint McCullough, and he remained with the program only until 1962 when the program jumped to ABC.

Speaking of ABC, in 1965, Horton was cast in the lead role on a new western half-hour series titled *A Man Called Shenandoah*. On the program, he played a man with amnesia who took on the name Shenandoah. During the program's single-season run, Horton released a couple of 45s on the major Columbia Records label—"The Very Thought of You" backed with "Hey There" and "King of the Road" backed with "Julie." There was also a *The Very Thought of You* LP (Columbia #9002) and even *A Man Called Shenandoah* LP (Columbia #9208), but none of Horton's recordings made a splash. Horton also appeared on Broadway in *110 in the Shade*, which ran for over 300 performances, and was part of the original cast album (RCA Victor # 1085). After *A Man Called Shenandoah* was cancelled, Horton turned to guest starring on episodic TV drama programs. For all intents and purposes, Horton retired in the early 1990s, but has remained in touch with fans and has his own website—www.roberthorton.com. He has been married three times.

ROCK HUDSON

Most Famous TV Role: Commissioner Stewart McMillan on *McMillan and Wife*; **Network:** NBC; **Years:** 1971–1977; **Hit Recording:** none; **Labels:** Decca, Stanyan; **Release Years:** 1959, 1971; **Matrix:** "Pillow Talk" (Decca #30966), *Rock, Gently: Rock Hudson Sings the Songs of Rod McKuen* (Stanyan LP #001); **Chart:** none

Rock Hudson was born Roy Harold Scherer Jr. in Winnetka, Illinois, on November 17, 1925. He served in the U.S. Navy during World War II, and afterward moved to Los Angeles to seek work as an actor. He changed his name to Rock Hudson as suggested by a talent agent. He is best remembered in motion pictures for his romantic comedies, mostly with Doris Day as his costar. Their *Pillow Talk* in 1959 was quite popular, and Hudson even got to release the title song on a 45 on the Decca label. It wasn't a hit, but he tried again in the early 1970s, just as he was making the transition from the silver screen to the small screen in *McMillan and Wife* with costar Susan St. James on NBC. This time around, he released an entire album of Rod McKuen compositions for the tiny Stanyan Records label.

Despite the popularity of his TV series, the album titled *Rock, Gently: Rock Hudson Sings the Songs of Rod McKuen* was not a big seller. Hudson's secret double life was exposed when he contracted and died of AIDS on October 2, 1985, a short time after working on *Dynasty*. He was married briefly to Phyllis Gates from 1955 to 1958 in an early attempt to quell the rumors about his sexual preference.

THE HUDSON BROTHERS

Most Famous TV Role: hosts of *The Hudson Brothers Razzle Dazzle Show*; **Network:** CBS; **Years:** 1974–1975; **Hit Recordings:** "So You Are a Star," "Rendezvous"; **Labels:** Casablanca, Rocket; **Release Years:** 1974–1975; **Matrix:** "So You Are a Star" (Casablanca #0108), "Rendezvous" (Rocket #40417); **Chart:** #21, #26, respectively, *Billboard* Hot 100

Bill, Mark, and Brett Hudson of Portland, Oregon, began making music in the late 1960s as the New Yorkers, named for the Chrysler model (even though their name was "Hudson"). They then evolved into Everyday Hudson, and eventually the Hudson Brothers. Before having any chart success, the entertaining brothers scored their own TV series. *The Hudson Brothers Show* was a summer replacement for *The Sonny and Cher Comedy Hour*, and they did well enough in the ratings to warrant their own Saturday morning series called *The Hudson Brothers Razzle Dazzle Show* for the Tiffany Network. Their exposure on TV also aided their recording career. Previously, they'd been jumping from label to label, but when they landed at Casablanca Records in 1974 they scored their biggest hit called "So You Are a Star." The following year, they signed with Elton John's new Rocket Records label and had one more hit with a song called "Rendezvous." None of the brothers' albums ever cracked the Hot 100. After a short-lived syndicated series called *Bonkers!* they tried their luck in motion pictures, but *Hysterical* and *Zero to Sixty* did not become box office bonanzas. The elder Hudson, Bill, was married to Goldie Hawn from 1976 to 1980 and is the father of Oliver and Kate Hudson.

WARREN HULL

Most Famous TV Role: host of *Strike It Rich*; **Network:** CBS; **Years:** 1951–1958; **Hit Recording:** none; **Label:** BBS; **Release Year:** 1954; **Matrix:** "Morning Prayer" (BBS #128); **Chart:** none

John Warren Hull was born in Gasport, New York, on January 17, 1903—his parents were Quakers. Warren attended New York University with every intention of pursuing a career in business. The business he gravitated to, however, was show business and he then attended the Eastman School of Music and worked in Broadway musicals in the 1920s. From there, he lent his dulcet tones to radio and hosted the original version of *Your Hit Parade* and then graduated to motion picture musicals for Warner Bros. After his Warner Bros. contract lapsed, he signed with Columbia and made numerous serial dramas for them. His biggest claim to fame was a tear-jerking, heart-tugging game show called *Strike It Rich.* Needy people came on as contestants, and the most woeful story, as adjudicated by the audience, was deemed the winner. It started in radio, and then moved to daytime television in 1951 and ran for seven seasons on CBS. There was also a nighttime version that ran for four years on the same network concurrently. During this time, Hull attempted to have success as a recording artist and released "The Morning Prayer" for the BBS Records label of Philadelphia, Pennsylvania, in 1954. However, even though he was in numerous Broadway and motion picture musicals, he recites the words to the song. After the show was cancelled, he hosted a topical interview show called *Who in the World?* but it didn't enjoy the successful run of *Strike It Rich.* By the middle 1960s, Hull opted to retire. He was married four times and had four children. He has two stars on the Hollywood Walk of Fame (one for radio, one for television). He died of heart failure on September 14, 1974. He was 71.

TAB HUNTER

Most Famous TV Role: Paul Morgan on *The Tab Hunter Show;* **Network:** NBC; **Years:** 1960–1961; **Hit Recordings:** "Young Love," "Ninety-Nine Ways"; **Labels:** Dot, Warner Bros.; **Release Years:** 1957–1963; **Matrix:** "Young Love" (Dot #15533), "Ninety-Nine Ways" (Dot #15548); **Chart:** #1, #11, respectively, *Billboard* Hot 100

Tab Hunter was born Arthur Andrew Kelm in New York City on July 11, 1931. He seemed to excel at everything he attempted. He was adept at athletics—especially figure skating and horseback riding. His motion picture career took off quickly, with notable roles in *The Burning Hills* with Natalie Wood, *Gunman's Walk* with Van Heflin, *That Kind of Woman* with Sophia Loren, and *The Pleasure of His Company* with Debbie Reynolds. Among his most memorable motion picture moments is his turn as Joe Hardy in the musical film version of *Damn Yankees.*

After Hunter had conquered the silver screen, the *Billboard* music charts were next. Hunter recalled, "While on a movie tour in Chicago, a local DJ named Howard Miller put me in touch with Randy Wood of Dot Records to pursue a recording career. Things happened very quickly, and I cut 'Young Love' and 'Ninety-Nine Ways' and many other tunes at Ryder Sound on Santa Monica Boulevard in Hollywood. I earned a gold record for each of those songs. I'm very proud of those." It should be noted that "Young Love" reached number 1 on *Billboard*'s Hot 100.

Hunter then conquered the small screen with his own eponymous sitcom. *The Tab Hunter Show* debuted on Sunday night, September 18, 1960, at 8:30 p.m. on NBC. The sitcom featured Hunter as Paul Morgan—a handsome, young playboy with a spacious Malibu beach house, a harem of beautiful women, and a successful comic strip called *Bachelor at Large*. Thirty-two black-and-white episodes were filmed single-camera style with a laugh track, and Hunter shared, "*The Tab Hunter Show* was actually pretty lame. It started out great, but quickly went downhill from there."

Hunter's own autobiography, *Tab Hunter Confidential: The Making of a Movie Star*, is still available from Algonquin Books. He has a star on the Hollywood Walk of Fame on Hollywood Boulevard and a Golden Palm Star on the Palm Springs Walk of Stars.

GUNILLA HUTTON

Most Famous TV Role: Billie Jo Bradley on *Petticoat Junction*, cast member on *Hee Haw*; **Networks:** CBS, syndicated; **Years:** 1965–1966, 1969–1992, respectively; **Hit Recording:** none; **Labels:** Dial, Dot, Green Mountain; **Release Years:** 1972–1974; **Matrix:** "You Say the Prettiest Things" (Dial #1015), "You're Gonna Get Loved" (Dot #17525), "End of Our Love Song" (Dot #17548), "We've Got Old-Fashioned Love" (Green Mountain #415); **Chart:** none

Gunilla Hutton was born Gunilla Freeman in Sweden on May 15, 1944. Her family moved to the United States in her youth, and she attended high school in Fort Worth, Texas. While still a teenager, she became the second of three young ladies to portray Billie Jo Bradley on the sitcom *Petticoat Junction* during its seven-year run. She only stayed for the 1965–1966 season, and was replaced by Meredith MacRae. A couple of years later, Hutton surfaced on the long-running syndication juggernaut known as *Hee Haw*. She was a regular on the program for 23 years, from 1969 until 1992. Early in her stay on *Hee Haw*, Hutton released several 45 rpm records. First came "You Say the Prettiest Things" backed with "The Greatest Story Never Told," then "You're Gonna Get Loved" backed with "See the Lady Crying," "End of Our Love Song" backed with "Cody," and "We've Got Old-Fashioned Love" backed with "Chowchilla Dust." Despite the popularity of the TV program, none of these singles made much of a splash. Hutton also made numerous appearances as a guest star on game shows and on *The Love Boat*. Not much has been heard from Gunilla since *Hee Haw* shut the barn doors for good in 1992.

J

JANET JACKSON

Most Famous TV Role: Penny Woods on *Good Times*, Cleo Hewitt on *Fame*; **Networks:** ABC, CBS; **Years:** 1977–1979, 1984–1985, respectively; **Biggest Hit Recording:** "That's the Way Love Goes"; **Labels:** A&M, Elektra, Island, Virgin; **Release Years:** 1982–2010; **Matrix:** Virgin #12650; **Chart:** #1 *Billboard Hot 100*

Janet Damita Jo Jackson was born in Gary, Indiana, on May 16, 1966—the youngest of the Jacksons. As a three-year-old, she watched her brothers soar to the top of the music charts. At one time, she had designs upon becoming a jockey, but caught the show biz bug instead. At the age of 11 she was cast as Penny Woods, a neighbor of the Evans family on *Good Times*. That role lasted for two seasons. From there she jumped into a short-lived ABC sitcom called *A New Kind of Family* that only lasted a matter of weeks. She was young and resilient and earned a recurring role as Charlene DuPrey on *Diff'rent Strokes*, and then spent an entire season as Cleo Hewitt on NBC's *Fame*.

At this same time, she began following in her brothers' footsteps and got her own recording career underway. Initially, she scored a couple of Top Ten hits on the R&B charts, such as "Young Love" (A&M #2440) in 1982 and "Don't Stand Another Chance" (A&M #2660) in 1983. It was after her run on *Fame* that she crossed over and accrued a long string of Top Ten hits, such as "What Have You Done for Me Lately" (A&M #2812), "Nasty" (A&M #2830), "When I Think of You" (A&M #2855), "Control" (A&M #2877), and "Let's Wait Awhile" (A&M #2906) to name but a few. She also scored six number 1 albums—*Control* (A&M #5106), *Janet Jackson's Rhythm Nation* (A&M #3920), *Janet* (Virgin #87825), *The Velvet Rope* (Virgin #44762), *All for You* (Virgin #10144), and *Discipline* (Island #010735).

Jackson was briefly married to James DeBarge from the R&B group De-Barge, but that marriage was later annulled. She married producer Rene

Elizondo in 1991 and they divorced in 2000. She never fully got the acting bug out of her system, and secured roles in motion pictures such as *The Nutty Professor II: The Klumps, Why Did I Get Married? Why Did I Get Married Too?* and *For Colored Girls.* Janet, along with Justin Timberlake, took part in one of the most famous, or rather infamous, Super Bowl Halftime performances—Super Bowl XXXVIII on February 1, 2004, in Houston, Texas. One of Janet's breasts was exposed on live television and caused an amazing uproar. It was amusingly referred to as "Nipplegate" and more people remember that aspect of the broadcast more than the final score—New England Patriots 32, Carolina Panthers 29.

JOSÉ JIMÉNEZ (BILL DANA)

Most Famous TV Role: José Jiménez on *The Spike Jones Show, The New Steve Allen Show, The Danny Thomas Show,* and *The Bill Dana Show*; **Networks:** ABC, CBS, NBC; **Years:** 1960–1961, 1961, 1961–1963, 1963–1965, respectively; **Hit Recording:** "The Astronaut"; **Label:** Kapp; **Release Year:** 1961; **Matrix:** Kapp #409; **Chart:** #19 *Billboard* Hot 100

Bill Dana was born as William Szathmary in Quincy, Massachusetts, on October 5, 1924. He began as a page at NBC, but his obvious talent made him a very popular guest star on comedy and variety shows. His alter ego, the very politically incorrect José Jiménez, made him a star. The Jiménez character became a regular fixture on *The Spike Jones Show, The New Steve Allen Show,* and *The Danny Thomas Show* in the early 1960s. During this time, Dana even had a popular hit record titled "The Astronaut." It was a comedy routine featuring José Jiménez and his thick accent being interviewed by Don Hinckley before his adventure in outer space. It became a surprise Top Twenty hit. The *José Jiménez—the Astronaut (The First Man in Space)* album reached the Top Five (Kapp LP #1238). Dana was such a success, he eventually got his own sitcom called *The Bill Dana Show,* on which his José Jiménez character worked as a hotel bellhop. Dana's costars on the two-season NBC wonder later became famous in their own right. Jonathan Harris, later Dr. Zachary Smith on *Lost in Space,* portrayed the hot-tempered hotel manager, Mr. Phillips. Don Adams portrayed the inept hotel inspector, Byron Glick, who was, for all intents and purposes, a Maxwell Smart in training. Speaking of Don Adams, Dana's brother, Irving Szathmary, wrote the theme song for *Get Smart* as well as *I'm Dickens, He's Fenster.* As ethnic humor became less and less accepted, appearances by José Jiménez became few and far between. Dana remained busy writing comedy material for other comedians. He also wrote TV scripts, including the famous Sammy Davis, Jr. episode of *All in the Family* titled "Sammy's Visit," and he later secured the recurring role of Angelo, Sophia's brother, on *The Golden Girls*. As of this writing, Bill Dana is a nonagenarian—he turned 90 on October 5, 2014. Even after his heyday in the 1960s, he remained active in recurring roles on *St. Elsewhere, Too Close for Comfort,* and *Zorro & Son*.

DENNIS JOEL

Most Famous TV Role: Roy Strickland on *The Betty Hutton Show*; **Network:** CBS; **Years:** 1959–1960; **Hit Recording:** none; **Labels:** Tape, VMC; **Release Year:** 1959–1969; **Matrix:** "Dream of Mine" (Tape #101), "You're Good for Me" (Tape #102), "Where Were You Last Night?" (Tape #103), *Come to the Party* (VMC LP #130); **Chart:** none

Dennis Joel, born August 29, 1947, was a child actor, perhaps best known for his role as Roy Strickland on *The Betty Hutton Show*. The sitcom starred screen legend Betty Hutton as Goldie Appleby, a manicurist and former showgirl who inherited the large estate of Mr. Strickland, one of her customers, when he died suddenly and unexpectedly. She was also named the guardian of Strickland's three teenagers. They resented her at first, but grew to love her. Dennis Joel got the most face time and lines on the show, but sadly it lasted only one season. Attempts to make a recording star out of him failed. He released several singles for the small Tape Records label and years later, an LP on the VMC label. All the Tape label 45s exhibited what has become known as the "teen sound." Joel also played opposite Greer Garson in the Broadway production of *Auntie Mame*. Garson was so fond of young Dennis that she would have adopted the boy if the opportunity arose.

After the cancellation of *The Betty Hutton Show*, Joel could often be seen guest starring on episodic TV shows such as *Bachelor Father, Mr. Novak, The Farmer's Daughter, The F.B.I., Family Affair, Ironside, The Blue Knight, McKeever and the Colonel,* and *Leave It to Beaver*. There is a dearth of information about Dennis Joel, but child star John Eimen, who worked with Joel on *The Betty Hutton Show, McKeever and the Colonel,* and *Leave It to Beaver,* shared, "He lived in the San Fernando Valley, as did I, and we used to run into one another from time to time. I was at the recording studio one night while he was recording his album. We both used to hang out a lot at the Bla Bla Café, where many very good singing acts performed."

Child star Dennis Joel of *The Betty Hutton Show* attempted to make it as a recording star, but to no avail.

The 1969 album *Come to the Party* featured a psychedelic shirtless photo of Joel on the cover and was very different from the 45s released in his youth. It was issued as by Dennis Olivieri, and its sound is rather difficult to categorize. It was likely funded by Joel himself. Eimen added, "Unlike the earlier records from Dennis's youth, he wrote all the songs on his album, and they were all very personal." At that same time, he also used his real name, Dennis Olivieri, while a regular on the short-lived ABC series titled *The New People* in the fall of 1969. He portrayed Stanley Gabriel on this show, which utilized the same premise as *Lost*, but with much less success. He was a young man with a bundle of talent, but was never able to find the right vehicle to propel him to superstardom. In his final years, Joel worked as a hired clown for children's parties and loved his work. In fact, at his funeral, guests were given red clown noses to wear as a tribute. He died of cancer, a relative unknown on September 27, 2006.

ARTE JOHNSON

Most Famous TV Role: regular on *Rowan and Martin's Laugh-In*; **Network:** NBC; **Years:** 1968–1971; **Hit Recording:** none; **Label:** Reprise; **Release Year:** 1968; **Matrix:** "Very Interesting" (Reprise #0753); **Chart:** none

Arte Johnson was born as Arthur Stanton Eric Johnson in Benton Harbor, Michigan, on January 20, 1929. He attended the University of Illinois and, on a whim, auditioned for a part in the motion picture *Gentlemen Prefer Blondes* and got it. After working in a couple of off-Broadway shows, he attempted success in the new medium called television. He was then cast in a long series of unsuccessful sitcoms—*It's Always Jan, Sally, Don't Call Me Charlie,* and *Many Happy Returns.* His first successful series cast him in a dramatic role on the long-running ABC soap opera *General Hospital* in 1963.

It was obvious that his many talents would eventually launch him into a successful, memorable series, and that occurred beginning in 1968 with the surprise hit, *Rowan and Martin's Laugh-In.* Many thought the program would be gone in 13 weeks, but it caught the eye and the fancy of the viewing public and became a ratings bonanza—propelling its cast into instant stardom. Arte Johnson was among those that became household names, and his elderly masher character along with his characterization of a German soldier became his most famous. He was usually paired on-screen with Ruth Buzzi, and the two were also paired on record in 1968 (see the entry under Ruth Buzzi for more). Johnson's most famous lines on the program were, "Want a walnetto?" and "Very interesting, but stupid." The latter was used as the title for a 45 rpm record by Johnson and Buzzi, to attempt to cash in on the program's meteoric rise. However, it failed to make the charts, and no follow-ups were issued. The record didn't win any awards, but Johnson did win an Emmy while on the series. After leaving the show in 1971, he found steady work providing voices for animation, and was briefly a game show host on the short-lived NBC series called *Knockout.* He has been married to the same woman, Gisela, since 1968. He is a non-Hodgkin lymphoma survivor and an avid golfer.

DON JOHNSON

Most Famous TV Roles: Detective James "Sonny" Crockett on *Miami Vice,* Inspector Nash Bridges on *Nash Bridges*; **Networks:** CBS, NBC; **Years:** 1984–1989, 1996–2001, respectively; **Hit Recording:** "Heartbeat"; **Label:** Epic; **Release Year:** 1986; **Matrix:** Epic #06285; **Chart:** #5 *Billboard* Hot 100

Pictured in his *Miami Vice* garb, Don Johnson cashed in with "Heartbeat"—his only Top Five hit.

Donnie Wayne Johnson was born in Flat Creek, Missouri, on December 15, 1949. At the time, his parents were still in their late teens. The family moved to Wichita, Kansas, while he was still a child, and while attending high school there he became very active in theater. He then studied drama at San Francisco's American Conservatory Theatre. Coincidentally, one of his later TV series, *Nash Bridges*, was set in that city. After a lot of theater work, he landed the role of a lifetime—that of "Sonny" Crockett on the crime drama called *Miami Vice*. Not only was the NBC show a big hit, it also had a huge impact upon the fashion of the day (pastel colors and no socks).

During the show's five-year run, Johnson also mounted an attempt at a recording career and succeeded, albeit briefly. He landed a contract with Epic Records, and in 1986 reached the Top Five with a song titled "Heartbeat." It was also the title cut from a gold Top Twenty album (Epic #40366) in that same year. Unfortunately, he was never able to penetrate the Top Five again, but he did reach number 25 on a duet with Barbra Streisand called "Till I Loved You" (Columbia #08062) from the Broadway musical called *Goya*. Luckily for Johnson, he was not typecast as Crockett and emerged in 1996 with another hit series, *Nash Bridges*, and enjoyed another five-year run. Johnson has been married five times, most notably to actress Melanie Griffith. The third time, however, wasn't the charm for his next series, *Just Legal* in 2005, which was cancelled after only three episodes. He won two Golden Globe Awards for *Miami Vice*, and has a star on the Hollywood Walk of Fame.

DEAN JONES

Most Famous TV Role: Ensign O'Toole on *Ensign O'Toole*; **Network:** ABC, NBC; **Years:** 1962–1964; **Hit Recording:** none; **Label:** ABC-Paramount; **Release Year:** 1962; **Matrix:** "I've Lost Her Love" (ABC-Paramount #10283), "The Proud Don't Cry" (Liberty #55502); **Chart:** none

Dean Carroll Jones was born in Decatur, Alabama, on January 25, 1931. He caught the entertainment bug while in high school, and worked for the campus radio station. He then served in the U.S. Navy during the Korean War. Coincidentally, his first starring role on TV was in a military sitcom called *Ensign O'Toole*. At this same time, Jones received a recording contract from ABC-Paramount Records. The result was one single— "I've Lost Her Love" backed with "Old Joe Clark." It was not a hit, and he tried again for Liberty Records with "The Proud Don't Cry" backed with "What Do I Do with My New Tattoo of You?" but met with similar results. He also recorded an album for Valiant Records a short time later titled *Introducing Dean Jones* (Valiant #407), and a single from the album titled "Women" backed with "Strawberries and Wine" (Valiant #6055), but when it was released in 1964, the nation's focus was on British groups such as the Beatles and Manfred Mann. *Ensign O'Toole* wasn't a big hit, either. In fact, Jones starred in numerous unsuccessful TV shows—*The Chicago Teddy Bears, What's It All About, World?* and *Herbie, the Love Bug*. The latter was the TV version of the hit motion picture. Jones found his niche in light-hearted Disney films such as *The Love Bug, That Darn Cat,*

The Ugly Dachsund, The Million Dollar Duck, The Horse in the Gray Flannel Suit, and *The Shaggy D.A.* In 1994, he supplied the voice for a character named George Newton on the animated version of *Beethoven,* based upon the motion picture series about a St. Bernard. He has been married twice, has three children, and became a born-again Christian in 1973.

K

LANI KAI

Most Famous TV Role: Kelly on *Adventures in Paradise*; **Network:** ABC;
Years: 1959–1962; **Hit Recording:** none; **Labels:** Hana Ho, Keen; **Release
Year:** 1959–1968; **Matrix:** "Little Brown Girl" (Keen #2023), "I'm Gonna
Leave My Heart at Home" (Keen #2103), "Isle of No Aloha" (Keen #2109),
"Malia" (Hana Ho #1024); **Chart:** none

Lani Kai's real name, believe it or not, was George Clarence Dennis
James Von Ruckleman Woodd III. He was born in Honolulu, Hawaii, on
August 15, 1936. He was passionate about music—performing and com-
posing, and got his big break when he was dragged by his mother, under
protest, to an audition for a new 20th Century Fox TV series to be called
Adventures in Paradise. George sailed through the audition with flying
colors and was cast as Kelly the nightclub singer on the program, which
enjoyed a three-season run on ABC. Because he didn't look like a George
Von Ruckleman Woodd, his professional name was changed to Lani Kai.
During this period, he also snagged a role in Elvis Presley's most popular
film, *Blue Hawaii*. He got to record several singles, mostly cha chas, for
the Keen Records label (on which Sam Cooke had his first big hits). Kai
wasn't as fortunate, and "I'm Going to Leave My Heart at Home" backed
with "Batik," "Little Brown Girl" backed with "Beach Party," and "Isle of
No Aloha" backed with "Now There Are None" failed to crack the Hot
100. Years later, on the local Hana Ho label, Kai attempted success yet
again on vinyl with a song titled "Malia," but it met with very minor local success. After *Adventures in Paradise* came to an end in 1962, Kai found
himself typecast and was only able to find work on *Hawaiian Eye* and *Hawaii Five-O*. After many years out of the business, Kai died suddenly and
unexpectedly at a friend's home in Oahu on August 24, 1999, only days
after his 63rd birthday.

171

DICK KALLMAN

Most Famous TV Role: Hank Dearborn on *Hank*; **Network:** NBC; **Years:** 1965–1966; **Hit Recording:** none; **Labels:** Capitol, RCA Victor; **Release Year:** 1966; **Matrix:** *Dick Kallman Drops in as Hank* (RCA Victor LP #3485), *Hank Sings* (Capitol LP #6150); **Chart:** none

Dick Kallman was born on July 7, 1933, in Brooklyn, New York. He was an accomplished singer, comic, and actor. His brief moment in the sun occurred in 1965 when he was cast as Hank Dearborn in the NBC sitcom called *Hank* (not to be confused with the Kelsey Grammer series of the same name). Hank was a very enterprising young man who was raising his young sister after the tragic death of their parents. Hank was a jack-of-all-trades and also cleverly managed to get a college education by trickery. This program from Warner Bros. Television failed to garner ratings high enough to warrant a second season, but the writers found out about cancellation in time to film a final episode on which some of the loose ends were gathered for closure. During the program's run, Kallman released an album for RCA Victor—*Dick Kallman Drops in as Hank*. The album was not a sensation, but a couple of singles from the album were released—"Lookin' Around" backed with "You're the One" (RCA #8676) and "On a Clear Day" backed with "I Believe in You" (RCA #8762). There was also the *Hank Sings* album released for Capitol Records of Canada.

When the TV show was cancelled, Kallman guest starred in a couple of episodes of ABC's *Batman*. Kallman then utilized his vocal prowess and appeared mostly in musical stage productions. In the 1970s, he switched gears and designed a line of women's clothing. He also dabbled in antiques and art collecting. On February 22, 1980, Kallman was found murdered in his New York luxury apartment, the victim of an apparent robbery. Allegedly, none of the rare art pieces lifted from his home have ever been recovered.

GABRIEL KAPLAN

Most Famous TV Role: Gabe Kotter on *Welcome Back, Kotter*; **Network:** ABC; **Years:** 1975–1979; **Hit Recording:** "Up Your Nose"; **Label:** Elektra; **Release Year:** 1977; **Matrix:** Elektra #45369; **Chart:** #91 *Billboard* Hot 100

Gabriel Kaplan was born in Brooklyn, New York, on March 31, 1945. Like many other boys from Brooklyn at that time, he wanted to play for the Dodgers. He simply wasn't good enough to make it and sought another vocation. He found work in a hotel where many comedians performed on weekends. He became interested in stand-up comedy and honed his skills in the 1960s before making it big in the 1970s. His routines about his childhood became very popular, and he did the variety and talk show circuit, before landing his own sitcom called *Welcome Back, Kotter*, set in his native Brooklyn. The reason the show worked so well is that the character he portrayed was a Xerox copy of the real Kaplan. The program made celebrities of Robert Hegyes, Ron Palillo, Lawrence Hilton-Jacobs (see the entry under his name), and especially John Travolta (see the entry for him, too). One of the popular phrases on the show was "Up your nose with a rubber hose." This inspired a song by Kaplan called "Up Your Nose" for Elektra Records. The record cracked the Hot 100 and spent three weeks there, aided by the popularity of the program. After the cancellation of that sitcom, Kaplan tried another called *Lewis and Clark*, but this one didn't click and was gone after 13 weeks. Kaplan is a poker enthusiast and has reignited his stand-up career after many idle years. His memoirs were titled *Kotter's Back*. His wife on the program, Julie, was played by the late Marcia Strassman (see the entry for her).

KAPTAIN KOOL AND THE KONGS

Most Famous TV Role: Kaptain Kool and the Kongs on *The Krofft Supershow;* **Network:** ABC; **Years:** 1976–1978; **Hit Recording:** "And I Never Dreamed"; **Label:** Epic; **Release Year:** 1978; **Matrix:** Epic #50627; **Chart:** none

Kaptain Kool and the Kongs were the hosts of ABC's *Krofft Supershow*, a weekly 90-minute Saturday morning program for kids, consisting of regular segments titled *Electra Woman and Dynagirl, Wonderbug, Dr. Shrinker, Magic Mongo, The Lost Saucer,* and *Bigfoot and Wildboy*. Around that, Kaptain Kool (Michael Lembeck) and the Kongs (Mickey McMell as Turkey, Debbie Clinger as Superchick, and Louise Duart as Nashville) performed rock songs and introduced each of the segments. Duart recalled,

> The most memorable part of my journey would have to be meeting the network executive in charge of kidvid named Squire Rushnell. He originally saw me at Madison Square Garden in New York City doing the live version of the TV show *H.R. Pufnstuf* that the Kroffts produced. I was playing the role of Witchiepoo. Squire was doing television projects with Sid and Marty

Krofft, and they were looking for a comedian to play the part of Nashville, and Squire said, "How about hiring the girl who did Witchiepoo?" Since that suggestion came from the vice president of ABC, it carried a certain amount of weight and I was hired. I loved doing the show with Michael, Mickey, and Debbie. We had a wonderful time and a close relationship. I don't keep in touch with them as much as I'd like but they are all very special to me. Squire was with ABC for over twenty years, and later went on to become the best-selling author of the *When God Winks* books. Thirty-five years after meeting Squire, I married him. We are blissfully happy, living on Martha's Vineyard doing projects together. The part of Nashville changed my life, and I will be forever grateful to Sid and Marty Krofft for introducing me to Squire. I went on to do a lot of work for the Kroffts, including *D.C. Follies.*

During *The Krofft Supershow's* run, Kaptain Kool and The Kongs re-leased an eponymous album for Epic Records (LP #35447). A single was released from the album, "And I Never Dreamed" backed with "Sing Me a Song." The program was later revamped and moved over to NBC with the Bay City Rollers as the stars.

WILLIAM KATT

Most Famous TV Role: Ralph Hinkley on *The Greatest American Hero;* **Network:** ABC; **Years:** 1981–1983; **Hit Recording:** none; **Label:** MCA; **Release Years:** 1982–1983; **Matrix:** "A Girl like You" (MCA #52086), *Secret Smiles* (MCA LP #5346); **Chart:** none

William Theodore Katt was born in Los Angeles, California, on February 16, 1951. He is the son of two famous actors—Bill Williams (TV's star of *Adventures of Kit Carson*) and Barbara Hale (Della Street of *Perry Mason*). He followed in his parents' footsteps and pursued an acting career. He garnered a role in the original *Carrie* and was considered for the role of Luke Skywalker in *Star Wars*, but the role went to Mark Hamill. After working on the movie version of *Pippin*, Katt snagged his most famous role in 1981—that of Ralph Hinkley, *The Greatest American Hero*. His char-acter's name was briefly changed to Ralph Hanley in that same year after John Hinckley attempted to assassinate President Ronald Reagan. In the latter part of the program's three-season run, Katt attempted success as a recording artist (as Billy Katt) and released an album called *Secret Smiles*, and a single from the album titled "A Girl like You" backed with "By the Sea." It didn't prove to be "the greatest American hit," and Katt's contract with MCA records was not extended. After the program was cancelled, Katt got to work with his mother on a few of those *Perry Mason* TV movies of the 1980s as Paul Drake Jr. In recent years, Katt has gravitated toward voice acting for animation. He has been married twice and has a daughter, two sons, and one stepson. At press time, a new Fox version of *The Greatest American Hero* was being developed.

STUBBY KAYE

Most Famous TV Role: host of *Shenanigans*; **Network:** ABC; **Years:** 1964–1965; **Hit Recording:** none; **Labels:** Capitol, Decca; **Release Years:** 1959–1965; **Matrix:** "I'm Married to a Strip Tease Dancer" (Decca #31294), "The Ballad of Cat Ballou" (Capitol #5412); **Chart:** none

Stubby Kaye was born as Bernard Katzin in New York City on November 11, 1918. Music and comedy were in his blood and he began by appearing in a long series of Broadway musicals in the 1950s including *Guys and Dolls* and *Li'l Abner*. He made the transition to the burgeoning television industry and costarred in two short-lived sitcoms—*Love and Marriage* with William Demarest (1959–1960) on NBC and *My Sister Eileen* with Elaine Stritch (1960–1961) on CBS. He was a semiregular on the game show called *PDQ* and also hosted a game show geared for kids during the 1964–1965 season for ABC called *Shenanigans*. None of these were renewed for a second season, but during this time Kaye released several records. He had previously been part of a few soundtrack albums, but as a solo performer he released "I'm Married to a Strip Tease Dancer" backed with "Lydia, the Tattooed Lady" and "The Ballad of Cat Ballou" backed with "They Can't Make Her Cry" for Capitol. Speaking of *Cat Ballou*, Kaye had a role in that film starring Jane Fonda and Lee Marvin. After the cancellation of *Shenanigans* in 1965, Kaye returned to his Broadway roots. His last big film role was as Marvin Acme in 1988's *Who Framed Roger Rabbit?* Kaye was married twice and had a great sense of humor about his baldness and considerable girth. He died of lung cancer at the age of 79 on December 14, 1997.

TOM KENNEDY

Most Famous TV Role: host of *You Don't Say!*; **Network:** NBC; **Years:** 1963–1969; **Hit Recording:** none; **Label:** Tower; **Release Year:** 1968; **Matrix:** "Phantom 309" (Tower #410); **Chart:** none

Tom Kennedy was born in Louisville, Kentucky, as James Edward Narz on February 26, 1927. He's the younger brother of fellow game show host Jack Narz, and Jack was the brother-in-law of yet another game show emcee, Bill Cullen. Brother Jack kept the Narz surname, but James opted to become Tom Kennedy (although he did use the name Jim Narz from 1948 to 1957 on radio). Kennedy was the announcer for *Dr. I.Q.*, the Betty White sitcom *A Date with the Angels*, and the local Los Angeles panel show *Words about Music* hosted by Frank DeVol. About the latter, Kennedy recalled, "I'd almost forgotten about that show. Yes, Frank DeVol was a great talent. The highlight of working on that show was getting to meet the amazing Louis Armstrong. That was unforgettable."

Kennedy's first gig hosting his own game show came in 1958 with the short-lived *Big Game*—a show that might be frowned upon by PETA (People for the Ethical Treatment of Animals) were it to air today because of its big game–hunting motif. His first big hit show—*You Don't Say!*—aired on NBC from 1963 to 1969 and even spawned a nighttime version. While on that program, Tom got to record for the Capitol Records label subsidiary called Tower. Kennedy shared,

> I don't remember a lot about the record. It was something my agent set up for me. My brother, Jack Narz, and his brother-in-law, Bill Cullen, also made records during that period. The B-side of my record, "The Last Goodbye," was a cover of a famous song by country singer Red Sovine. I'm pretty certain that "Phantom 309" was the A-side. We didn't record it at the Capitol studios, but rather at a studio on Ventura Boulevard in Studio City. There was a very famous blind pianist on the record, a friend of George Shearing, but I have forgotten his name.

After *You Don't Say!* was cancelled in 1969, Kennedy tried something different and briefly hosted a syndicated talk program titled *The Real Tom Kennedy Show*. After this, he returned to game shows and hosted a bevy of them, with *Split Second, Body Language, Name That Tune, To Say the Least, Password Plus, Whew!* and *Break the Bank* being the highlights. For the most part, he retired in 1989. Kennedy was married only once, to Betty—a marriage that lasted 58 years until his wife died in 2011. He has four children.

SAJID KHAN

Most Famous TV Role: Raji on *Maya*; **Network:** NBC; **Years:** 1967–1968; **Hit Recording:** none; **Label:** Colgems; **Release Year:** 1968; **Matrix:** "Getting to Know You" (Colgems #1026), "Dream" (Colgems #1034), *Sajid* (Colgems LP #114); **Chart:** "Getting to Know You" #108, "Dream" #119 *Billboard* Bubbling Under

Sajid Khan was born in India on December 28, 1951. He was adopted by Indian film producer Mehboob Khan, who had his own Mehboob film studio. He appeared in a few of his father's films and eventually attempted to become a success in the United States. His most famous TV role was as Raji, costar and friend of Jay North on the MGM single-season series titled *Maya* in 1967. The program aired on NBC, and Jay North tried to make a TV comeback and distance himself from his previous *Dennis the Menace* days by donning dark brown hair on the program. During the latter part of the show's run in 1968, the same record label that made stars of the Monkees sought to repeat that success by recording Khan. Colgems Records released several singles by him—"Getting to Know You" backed with "Ha Kam," and "Dream" backed with "Someday," along with his eponymous *Sajid* album. His singles got some attention and some airplay and both bubbled under the *Billboard* Hot 100. The album did not chart. After *Maya* was cancelled, Khan found work in some British films, but was never again a regular on a U.S. TV series. He eventually changed his vocation and opened his own costume jewelry company in his native India. He has been married only once and has one son named Sameer.

THE KIDS FROM C.A.P.E.R.

Most Famous TV Role: The cast of *The Kids from C.A.P.E.R.*; **Network:** NBC; **Years:** 1976–1977; **Hit Recording:** none; **Label:** Kirshner; **Release Year:** 1976; **Matrix:** *The Kids from C.A.P.E.R.* (Kirshner LP #34347); **Chart:** none

The Kids from C.A.P.E.R. was a Saturday morning musical sitcom for kids from Alan Landsburg/Don Kirshner Productions. The program revolved around a group of youngsters who, through the 927th Police Precinct in North South Weston, formed a group known as C.A.P.E.R. (the Civilian Authority for the Protection of Everybody Regardless). The program starred Steve Bonino as P.T., Cosie Costa as Bugs, Biff Warren as Doomsday, and John Lansing as Doc. Each C.A.P.E.R. member had one special quality for solving crimes and mysteries—a keen sense of smell (P.T.), superhuman strength (Bugs), the ability to communicate with the animal world (Doomsday), and brain power (Doc). Between sleuthing duties, the group also found time to sing and recorded one album for Don Kirshner's eponymous record label in 1976—an album that contained songs performed on the show, such as "Say It" and "Lullabye Girl." The program's theme song was written by the prolific Ron Dante of the Archies.

DURWARD KIRBY

Most Famous TV Role: cohost of *Candid Camera*, regular cast member on *The Garry Moore Show*; **Network:** CBS; **Years:** 1958–1967; **Hit Recording:** none; **Label:** Davis; **Release Year:** 1958; **Matrix:** "Crime Doesn't Pay!" (Davis #999); **Chart:** none

Homer Durward Kirby was born in Covington, Kentucky, on August 24, 1911. He studied engineering in college, but was distracted by a passion for radio announcing. After serving in the navy during World War II, he got serious about his career choice and worked in radio and then on television with Garry Moore. Kirby was well over six feet tall and had a pleasant, deep, booming voice, and work as an announcer came easily. His easy-going persona also made him the ideal second banana/straight man, and he had long runs in that capacity on both *The Garry Moore Show* and *Candid Camera*. On the latter, he was Allen Funt's costar. In the early days of *The Garry Moore Show*, Kirby lent his dulcet tones to a 45 rpm record for Joe Davis's small Davis Records label of New York. The song was titled "Crime Doesn't Pay!" and the label said, "Descriptive recitation by Durward Kirby. Musical Accompaniment by the Patriots." The record was issued with a picture sleeve but sold poorly, and Kirby's recording career came to a screeching halt. Kirby was often parodied on *The Rocky and Bullwinkle Show* as Kirward Derby. Kirby wrote several books, including *Bits and Pieces of This and That* and *My Life—Those Wonderful Years*. He was also a regular fixture in TV commercials for Ivory liquid dish detergent and Polaroid. Kirby was married only once and had two sons. He died of congestive heart failure on the Ides of March 2000.

JACK KLUGMAN. *See* THE ODD COUPLE.

TED KNIGHT

Most Famous TV Role: Ted Baxter on *The Mary Tyler Moore Show*, Henry Rush on *Too Close for Comfort*; **Networks:** ABC, CBS, syndicated; **Years:** 1970–1977, 1980–1986, respectively; **Hit Recording:** none; **Label:** Ranwood; **Release Year:** 1976; **Matrix:** "The Man Who Used to Be" (Ranwood #1045), *Hi, Guys* (Ranwood LP #8149); **Chart:** none

Tadeusz Wladyslaw Konopka was born in Terryville, Connecticut, on December 7, 1923. He was a high school dropout and enlisted in the army during World War II. After the war, he studied theater and acting in Hartford. He also developed an affinity for ventriloquism. In television's infancy, he landed a local Rhode Island kid's show and got to employ his ventriloquism skills. He also found a lot of work doing voice-over announcements and commercials. This evolved into small roles in motion pictures and episodic television shows. He finally earned his day in the sun when he was cast as the pompous and naive Twin Cities newscaster Ted Baxter on *The Mary Tyler Moore Show*—a role for which two Emmys were bestowed. Near the end of this memorable and lovable ensemble sitcom's run, Knight released an album titled *Hi, Guys* (named for a line he often uttered when entering a room on the show). The album contained a goodly amount of remakes of earlier pop music classics such as "Itsy Bitsy Teenie Weenie Yellow Polka Dot Bikini," "Who Put the Bomp?" "Blueberry Hill," "Mr. Custer," "The Cover of the Rolling Stone," and "Chick-a-Boom." A couple of songs from the album were released as a Ranwood single in that same year—"The Man Who Used to Be" backed with "May the Bird of Paradise Fly up Your Nose." None of these became hits, but made for quite a fun novelty item.

After *The Mary Tyler Moore Show* came to an end after seven seasons, Knight jumped right into another show—a short-lived sitcom with an unusual premise. On *The Ted Knight Show* on CBS, Knight portrayed Mr. Dennis who ran an escort service in New York City. The series came to an end after only six episodes and was a spinoff of another short-lived series from Paramount called *Busting Loose*. Knight hit pay dirt yet again in 1980 with his portrayal of Judge Smails in the hit motion picture *Caddyshack*, and on ABC in *Too Close for Comfort*, which ran for three seasons in prime time and then continued in a slightly altered syndicated format. At this time *The Ted Knight Show* title was utilized yet again, but more successfully this go 'round. Sadly, during the run of this syndicated version, Knight took ill and succumbed to cancer at the age of 62 on August 26, 1986.

KRISTY AND JIMMY MCNICHOL

Most Famous TV Roles: "Buddy" Lawrence on *Family* (Kristy) and Jack Fitzpatrick on *The Fitzpatricks* (Jimmy); **Networks:** ABC (*Family*), CBS (*The Fitzpatricks*); **Years:** 1976–1980; **Hit Recording:** "He's So Fine"; **Label:** RCA Victor; **Release Year:** 1978; **Matrix:** RCA #11271; **Chart:** #70 *Billboard* Hot 100

Christina Ann McNichol was born in Los Angeles, California, on September 11, 1962. Her slightly older brother, Jimmy, was born July 2 of the previous year. Brother and sister appeared in dozens of TV commercials in the latter part of the 1960s and then branched out into guest-starring roles on episodic TV shows. Christina (a.k.a. Kristy) earned her first regular series role on the short-lived 1974 series called *Apple's Way*—a program similar to *The Waltons* in its tone. Her next series, *Family*, was much more successful and ran for four seasons on ABC. At this same time, Jimmy McNichol landed in two short-lived series—*The Fitzpatricks* and *California Fever*. Brother and sister McNichol performed the theme song for the latter and also recorded an album titled *Kristy and Jimmy McNichol* (RCA Victor #2875) produced by former members of the Tokens of "The Lion Sleeps Tonight" fame, Mitch and Phil Margo. The album spawned one moderately popular single, a remake of the Chiffons' "He's So Fine" in 1978. In the 1980s, Jimmy landed the role of Josh Clayton on ABC's *General Hospital*, and Kristy surfaced in the popular *Golden Girls* spinoff titled *Empty Nest* as Barbara Weston from 1988 to 1992. She later found work voicing characters for animated TV shows. Both have retired from show business. Jimmy has worked in the construction field for several years, and Kristy stays busy with charity work. (Also see the entry for Christopher Atkins.)

LISA KUDROW. *See* PHOEBE BUFFAY AND THE HAIRBALLS.

L

CHERYL LADD

Most Famous TV Role: Kris Munroe on *Charlie's Angels;* **Network:** ABC; **Years:** 1977–1981; **Hit Recording:** "Think It Over"; **Label:** Capitol; **Release Year:** 1978; **Matrix:** Capitol #4599; **Chart:** #34 *Billboard* Hot 100

Cheryl Ladd was born Cheryl Ann Stoppelmoor in Huron, South Dakota, on July 12, 1951. Her first Hollywood aspirations were as a singer under the name of Cherie Moor. She got a job as one of the singing voices for the animated *Josie and the Pussycats* series. She is credited on the *Josie and the Pussycats* album (Capitol LP #665) as Cheryl Ann Stoppelmoor. Songs on the album included the Jackson Five's "I'll Be There" and Bread's "It Don't Matter to Me." Because she was also very photogenic, Ladd also got offers for nonsinging guest-starring roles on popular episodic TV shows such as *Happy Days, The Partridge Family,* and *The Rookies.* Her husband at the time was David Ladd, son of screen legend Alan Ladd. Cherie Moor then became Cheryl Ladd, and she soared quickly in the business.

Opportunity knocked in 1977 when Farrah Fawcett-Majors opted to leave the hit Aaron Spelling series *Charlie's Angels,* and Ladd was tapped to portray her younger sister, Kris. Ladd became a celebrity overnight and thought this sudden fame might get her recording career on the right track. She got to quickly release an album for Capitol Records called *Cheryl Ladd* (Capitol #11808). The LP only reached number 129 on the Albums chart, but a single from the album, "Think It Over" (not to be confused with the Buddy Holly song of same name), became a moderately popular Top Forty hit. A follow-up album titled *Dance Forever* (Capitol #11927) only got to number 179. Ladd's recording career was not quite the splash she anticipated, and she never reached the charts again in the United States, but did release a couple of moderately popular albums in Japan in the early 1980s. She briefly had the lead role in a revival of *Annie Get Your Gun* on Broadway, and for a time became the queen of made-for-TV movies. She then landed in two other less successful TV series—*One*

West Waikiki, on which she portrayed a medical examiner named Dr. Holliday, and *Las Vegas* as Jill Deline. In recent years, she has written children's books and painted several lithographs. Both are available on her official website, www.cherylladd.com.

JACK LALANNE

Most Famous TV Role: host of *The Jack LaLanne Show*; **Network:** syndicated; **Years:** 1951–1985; **Hit Recording:** none; **Label:** J. L. L.; **Release Year:** 1959; **Matrix:** "Climb Every Mountain" (J. L. L. #1); **Chart:** none

Francois Henri "Jack" LaLanne was born in San Francisco, California, on February 26, 1914. The family moved to Bakersfield and then Berkeley, California. When his dad died of heart disease at the age of 58, Lalanne dedicated himself to health and exercise. He opened one of the first health and fitness spas in 1936 in Oakland, California, and eventually brought his health and exercise regimens to television in its infancy. His syndicated program inspired many and ran, in one form or another, for over three decades (beginning in black and white). He encouraged viewers to get off the couch and mimic his moves. In 1959, he and big band singer Connie Haines released an inspiring two-sided song titled "Climb Every Mountain" backed with "Prosperity." It was released on LaLanne's own Jack LaLanne Records label and made available to TV viewers. There was also an instructional album (no singing, no label name) called *Glamour Stretcher Time*—it accompanied an elastic cord used for exercising. In later years he had his own line of vitamins and juicers. Jack had a chain of exercise spas that years later were bought up by the Bally Company. He definitely did something right—he lived to be 96 and remained very active almost until the end. He was married twice and had three children. He died of respiratory failure after contracting pneumonia. He refused to see a doctor and is alleged to have worked out the day before his passing.

LORENZO LAMAS

Most Famous TV Role: Lance Cumson on *Falcon Crest*; **Network:** CBS; **Years:** 1981–1990; **Hit Recording:** "Fools like Me"; **Label:** Scotti Brothers; **Release Year:** 1984; **Matrix:** Scotti Brothers #04686; **Chart:** #85 *Billboard* Hot 100

Lorenzo Lamas-Craig was born in Santa Monica, California, on January 20, 1958. He is the son of actress Arlene Dahl and actor Fernando Lamas. In his early teens the family moved to New York City. Lorenzo longed to be an actor like his parents and studied at a film actor's workshop. A short while later, he landed in *Grease* on Broadway, and then became a frequent guest star on prime-time series such as *Switch*, *Hotel*, *Fantasy Island*, and *The Love Boat*. His first regular role on a series became his most famous—Lance Cumson (yes, it was spelled that way) on *Falcon Crest* from 1981 to 1990. It was thought that Lamas might also find success in the recording industry early in the show's run, and he took part in an album titled *TV Stars on Record* (CBS #40506) in 1983. He then got to release a single for Scotti Brothers Records—a ballad called "Fools like Me" backed with "Smooth Talker" in 1984. It hovered near the very bottom of the Hot 100 for five weeks, and the idea of big success as a singer was quickly dashed.

After almost a decade on CBS, *Falcon Crest* was cancelled and Lamas readied for his next series—a syndicated show called *Renegade*. Lamas played Reno Raines on this popular syndicated series that ran from 1992 to 1997. Lamas sported shoulder-length hair and rode a motorcycle on the show, portraying a man on the run after exposing corruption in the police department. In the new millennium he served as a panelist on the short-lived reality show titled *Are You Hot?* and enjoyed a three-year run as Hector Ramirez on *The Bold and the Beautiful* (2004–2007). Lamas has been married five times, and, coincidentally, two of his brides were named Shawna (what are the odds?).

DAVID L. LANDER. *See* LENNY AND THE SQUIGTONES.

AUDREY LANDERS

Most Famous TV Role: Afton Cooper on *Dallas*; **Network:** CBS; **Years:** 1981–1989; **Hit Recording:** none; **Labels:** Curb, Epic; **Release Years:** 1981–1984; **Matrix:** "Happy Endings" (Curb #52339), "The Apple Don't Fall Far from the Tree" (Epic #50615), "You Thrill Me" (Epic #50781); **Chart:** none

Audrey Landers was born as Audrey Hamburg in Philadelphia, Pennsylvania, on July 18, 1956. Performing was in her blood and she was doing community theater by the age of nine. By the 1970s, she earned recurring roles on such soap operas as *The Secret Storm* on CBS and *Somerset* on NBC. She was one of the stars of a spooky and extremely short-lived NBC sitcom from 1979 (lasted four episodes) called *Highcliffe Manor* with Shelley Fabares. Her big break came when she landed the role of Afton Cooper on CBS's *Dallas* beginning in 1981.

Landers always had a passion for singing, and it was thought that her newly found fame on TV could greatly aid her recording career. She released a couple of singles for Epic Records—"The Apple Don't Fall Far from the Tree" backed with "How Would You Like Someone to Love You?" and "You Thrill Me" backed with "What's It Gonna Be Like Tomorrow?" Neither of these caught on in the United States, and she then jumped to Curb Records for two more singles—"Happy Endings" backed with "Manuel, Goodbye" and "Hurricane Man" backed with "Boy"—but once again there was little reaction in the United States. However, much like David Hasselhoff's musical career, Landers's music became very popular in Germany, and a long string of singles for both the Ariola and WEA labels kept her on the German music charts for much of the middle to late 1980s. Landers has remained busy on numerous soap operas, the syndicated series *Burn Notice*, and the recent *Dallas* remake on TNT. She also has her own website, www.audreylanders.com, on which her line of jewelry can be purchased. She is the sister of actress Judy Landers, and together they briefly recorded as Rock Candy. Audrey has been married only once and has two children.

MICHAEL LANDON

Most Famous TV Roles: Little Joe Cartwright on *Bonanza*, Charles Ingalls on *Little House on the Prairie*; **Network:** NBC; **Years:** 1959–1973, 1974–1982, respectively; **Hit Recording:** none; **Labels:** Candlelight, Fono Graf, RCA Victor; **Release Years:** 1959–1964; **Matrix:** "Gimme a Little Kiss (Will Ya, Huh?)" (Candlelight #1017, Fono Graf #1240), "Linda Is Lonesome" (RCA Victor #8330); **Chart:** none

Michael Landon was born into a show business family as Eugene Orowitz in Queens, New York, on October 31, 1936. In his youth, the family moved to the Cherry Hill, New Jersey, area. He was very athletic as a young man and was most adept at track and javelin throwing. He gravitated toward the theater, inspired by his parents, and found work very quickly. One of his first roles was in the forgettable motion picture *I Was a Teenage Werewolf*. During the movie's short run in theaters, Landon released a 45 rpm record for the small Candlelight label—"Gimme a Little Kiss (Will Ya, Huh?)" backed with "Be Patient with Me." It wasn't a big hit and singing was not his forte. He also accrued quite a résumé of guest-starring roles on television on programs such as *The Rifleman* and *Wanted: Dead or Alive*. When he landed a regular role on the NBC western *Bonanza*, the Candlelight record was rereleased on the Fono Graf label (with a picture sleeve) to cash in on his newfound popularity. *Bonanza* ran for 14 seasons, from

Bonanza's Little Joe made a little record called "Gimme a Little Kiss (Will Ya, Huh?)" but wisely stayed on the Ponderosa.

1959 to 1973. In 1964 when costar Lorne Greene had success with a recording called "Ringo" for RCA Victor Records, the label signed Landon as well, but he met with much less success. Landon released one single for the label—"Linda Is Lonesome" backed with "Without You." He also participated in two cast albums from the TV show—*Bonanza: Ponderosa Party Time* (RCA LP #2583) and *Christmas on the Ponderosa* (RCA LP #2757).

Landon's recording career may have been a bust, but he was a consistent presence on television. After the cancellation of *Bonanza* in 1973, Landon settled in for an eight-year run on *Little House on the Prairie*, from 1974 to 1982. He then lucked into yet another hit NBC series—*Highway to Heaven*—from 1984 to 1988. Landon starred as Jonathan Smith, an angel sent back to earth to aid people. If he hadn't taken ill and been diagnosed with pancreatic cancer, he would have had yet another series called *Us*. Because of the ailment, the project never became a series. Landon died on July 1, 1991, at the age of 54. He was married three times and had a total of nine children. He has a star on the Hollywood Walk of Fame.

JOI LANSING

Most Famous TV Role: Shirley Swanson on *The Bob Cummings Show/Love That Bob*; **Network:** CBS; **Years:** 1956–1959; **Hit Recording:** none; **Label:** REO; **Release Year:** 1958; **Matrix:** "Love Me" (REO #1007); **Chart:** none

Joi Lansing was born as Joy Brown in Salt Lake City, Utah, on April 6, 1928. Just as her teen years were beginning, the family moved to Los Angeles, California. A very short time later, she began a modeling career and then an acting career. She was schooled on the MGM lot. She was a devout Mormon, didn't drink or smoke, and allegedly never posed nude. The blond bombshell did however often wear very revealing costumes and bikinis. She landed a lot of movie and TV work, but was usually type-cast in the same kind of cheesecake roles. She guest starred on popular TV programs such as *I Love Lucy*, *The People's Choice*, *Bat Masterson*, *Petticoat Junction*, *The Beverly Hillbillies*, *The Adventures of Ozzie and Harriet*, and *Sugarfoot*. She scored a recurring role on *The Bob Cummings Show* (a.k.a. *Love That Bob*) as a regular model in Bob's photography studio, but never had more than a few lines per show.

During the program's run, Lansing had the opportunity to release a 45 rpm record to cash in on her modest amount of fame. The record was released on the REO label in 1957 and was titled "Love Me" backed with "What's It Gonna Be?" The record received very little airplay and failed to chart. Lansing wasn't given the chance to release a follow-up single, and the idea of a recording career was tabled for the time being. She guest starred as Sergeant Helen J. O'Hara in the memorable episode of *The Adventures of Superman* titled "Superman's Wife," and then earned a recurring role in another series in 1960 called *Klondike* with costars Ralph Taeger and James Coburn. The NBC adventure series failed to find an audience and was cancelled after only four months. Lansing attempted to resurrect her recording career in the middle 1960s, and she got to perform in Las Vegas with Red Buttons. In the early 1970s Lansing was diagnosed with breast cancer. Her surgery was unsuccessful, and she died at the age of 44 on August 7, 1972.

LAVERNE AND SHIRLEY (PENNY MARSHALL AND CINDY WILLIAMS)

Most Famous TV Role: Laverne (Penny Marshall) and Shirley (Cindy Williams) on *Laverne and Shirley*; **Network:** ABC; **Years:** 1976–1983; **Hit Recording:** "Sixteen Reasons"; **Label:** Atlantic; **Release Year:** 1976; **Matrix:** Atlantic #3367; **Chart:** #65 *Billboard* Hot 100

Penny Marshall was born as Carole Penny Marshall on October 15, 1943, in New York City, New York, and Cindy Williams was born as Cynthia Jane Williams in Van Nuys, California, on August 22, 1947. They first appeared on *Happy Days* on November 11, 1975, in an episode titled "A Date with Fonzie." They were portrayed in the episode as "easy," but when they earned their own Paramount Studios spinoff series on ABC called *Laverne and Shirley* on January 27, 1976, that aspect of their personalities was toned down and they became anything but promiscuous. The program debuted at number 1 in the Nielsen ratings, and the girls were propelled into instant stardom. To cash in on that popularity, the girls released an album in that same year called *Laverne and Shirley Sing* (Atlantic LP #18203). The album didn't chart, but a single from the album, a remake of Connie Stevens's "Sixteen Reasons," cracked the Hot 100 and reached number 65. It was their only chart single and was backed with "Chapel of Love," the old Dixie Cups' classic. Kenny Loggins was one of the musicians on the album.

Despite a tempestuous and tumultuous history behind the scenes, the series lasted until May 10, 1983. It was initially set in Milwaukee where the girls worked at the same bottle-capping job in Shotz Brewery, but eventually moved to Burbank in 1980. Cindy Williams left the show in 1982 (she was pregnant in real life), and it was said that her character married an army medic named Walter Meany. Garry Marshall loved rhymes, and her married name became Shirley Feeney-Meany. The program was never the same after she left, and by May of 1983, the show left the prime-time ABC lineup. Penny Marshall then followed in her famous brother Garry's footsteps and became a successful director. Cindy Williams enjoyed a two-year run in another sitcom, *Getting By*, from 1993 to 1994. (See the entry for Lenny and the Squigtones.)

PETER LAWFORD

Most Famous TV Role: Nick Charles on *The Thin Man;* **Network:** NBC; **Years:** 1957–1959; **Hit Recording:** none; **Labels:** Bravo, Decca, Harlequin, Verve; **Release Years:** 1954–1969; **Matrix:** "Comfortable" (Bravo #1302), "Swinging with Rhythm and Blues" (Decca #29581), "Frightfully Nice" (Harlequin #401), "Kickapoo Kick" (Verve #10034); **Chart:** none

Peter Lawford was born in London as Peter Sydney Ernest Aylen on September 7, 1923. His parents divorced while he was still a baby, and he was raised mostly in France where he was homeschooled. By the time he was seven, he was appearing in British films. In the 1940s he was signed by MGM Studios, and one of his early films placed him opposite Mickey Rooney in *A Yank at Eton.* The movie was quite a success, and Lawford was soon in demand. Because of a serious arm injury, he was exempt from participating in World War II.

In television's infancy, he starred in a single-season sitcom called *Dear Phoebe* as an advice columnist. During the show's short run (1954–1955), he released his first phonograph record, "Swinging with Rhythm and Blues" backed with "I Love You" for Decca Records. It was not a big hit, but more were on the way. When Lawford landed his next series, the much more successful *The Thin Man* in 1957 (based upon the movie series), he also released "Kickapoo Kick" backed with "I Don't Want to Be a Gentleman" for Verve Records and "Frightfully Nice" backed with "Two Ladies in the Shade of the Banana Tree" for Harlequin Records. He was also part of a soundtrack album from the TV musical titled *The Ruggles of Red Gap* (Verve #15000). In the late 1950s, Lawford became part of the famous Rat Pack that consisted of Frank Sinatra, Sammy Davis Jr., Dean Martin, and Joey Bishop. All five appeared in the 1960 original version of *Oceans 11.* Lawford's first wife was Patricia Helen Kennedy, sister of the future president. Lawford was married four times and in three of the four relationships he was many years their senior. He appeared in many more films. He was also a frequent guest on talk, variety, and game shows. Lawford died of cardiac arrest on Christmas Eve 1984 at the age of only 61. He has a star on the Hollywood Walk of Fame.

JOEY LAWRENCE

Most Famous TV Role: Joey Russo on *Blossom;* **Network:** NBC; **Years:** 1991–1995; **Hit Recording:** "Nothing My Love Can't Fix"; **Label:** Impact/ MCA; **Release Year:** 1993; **Matrix:** Impact/MCA #54562; **Chart:** #19 *Billboard* Hot 100

Joey Lawrence was born as Joseph Lawrence Mignogna Jr. in Montgomery, Pennsylvania, on April 20, 1976. He has two younger brothers—Matthew and Andrew. After a lot of commercial work as a child, Joey attended USC. His first recurring role was that of Joey Donovan on NBC's *Gimme a Break* from 1983 to 1987. He then landed probably his most famous role—that of Joey Russo on *Blossom,* again on NBC. During the run of this show, Lawrence attempted success as a recording star and fared pretty well, albeit briefly. Singing was nothing new for Lawrence— he'd performed on *The Tonight Show with Johnny Carson* at the age of five. In 1993 he reached number 19 on the Hot 100 with "Nothing My Love Can't Fix" and is listed as one of the cowriters of the song. A follow-up single, "Stay Forever" (Impact/MCA #54653), just missed the Top Fifty. His eponymous *Joey Lawrence* album peaked at number 74 on the Top Pop Albums chart, on which it stayed for 22 weeks. Lawrence remained very busy after *Blossom* wilted, and earned recurring roles on *Brotherly Love, American Dreams, Run of the House,* and *Half and Half,* and a costarring role on *Melissa and Joey.* He has also become quite the fitness devotee and has worked as one of the Chippendale Dancers on occasion. He has been married twice and has two children. Lawrence continues to record on occasion, and his music is available online.

VICKI LAWRENCE

Most Famous TV Roles: costar on *The Carol Burnett Show,* star of *Mama's Family;* **Network:** CBS, NBC, syndicated; **Years:** 1967–1978, 1983–1990, respectively; **#1 Hit Recording:** "The Night the Lights Went Out in Georgia"; **Label:** Bell; **Release Year:** 1973; **Matrix:** Bell #303; **Chart:** #1 *Billboard* Hot 100

Vicki Lawrence was born Vicki Ann Axelrad in Inglewood, California, on March 26, 1949. She took an early interest in singing and dancing, and was a cheerleader in school. While still a teenager, she appeared in the documentary film *The Young Americans* in the middle 1960s. She wrote a note to Carol Burnett, noting their resemblance, and her timing was impeccable. Burnett just happened to be looking for someone to play her younger sister on her up-and-coming variety show, and the rest is history. She spent 11 happy years as a regular on CBS's *The Carol Burnett Show*, from 1967 to 1978.

While the show was at its peak popularity, Lawrence had the opportunity to showcase another of her many talents—singing. A song released on the Bell Records label called "The Night the Lights Went out in Georgia," written by prolific songwriter Bobby Russell (Lawrence's husband at the time), zoomed to number 1 on the charts and earned Lawrence a gold record, presented to her on *The Carol Burnett Show*. The song was also the title cut on her album, which just missed the Top Fifty. She placed a couple of other songs, "He Did with Me" (Bell #362) and "The Other Woman" (Private Stock #036), near the bottom of the Hot 100, but never again came near the Top Fifty.

After the demise of *The Carol Burnett Show* in 1978, Lawrence stayed busy on the small screen with her own talk show called *Vicki!* a game show titled *Win, Lose or Draw*; and most notably, a spinoff of *The Carol Burnett Show* called *Mama's Family*. The spinoff ran from 1983 to 1990, first on NBC and then in syndication. From 2001 to 2005 she portrayed Greg's mother Natalie Warner on CBS's *Yes, Dear*. She most recently had a recurring role as Mamaw Stewart on Disney's *Hannah Montana* series. Lawrence has been married to the same man, Al Schulz, since 1974. They have two grown children. Lawrence won an Emmy for her work on Burnett's show.

MEADOWLARK LEMON

Most Famous TV Role: Meadowlark Lemon on *Hello, Larry*; **Network:** NBC; **Years:** 1979–1980; **Hit Recording:** none; **Label:** Casablanca; **Release Year:** 1979; **Matrix:** "My Kids" (Casablanca #969), "Sweet Georgia Brown" (Casablanca #2210), *My Kids* (Casablanca LP #7132); **Chart:** none

Meadowlark Lemon was born as Meadow Lemon III in Wilmington, North Carolina, on April 25, 1932. As a child, he dreamed of being a member of the Harlem Globetrotters, and in 1955 his dream came true. He stayed with the team for over 20 years and was dubbed "the Clown Prince." He made his first attempt at recording in 1966 on the small RSVP Records label. The song was called "Personally," and it was not a hit. He didn't try again until the late 1970s when he plunged into acting. He starred in a popular Burger King TV commercial in 1978 that featured a huge stack of hamburgers, assembled "your way." He was a cast member of McLean Stevenson's NBC sitcom called *Hello, Larry* in 1979–1980, and at that time released an album and a couple of singles for the Casablanca Records label. His album was called *My Kids*. "My Kids" was also a cut from the album released on 45. Another of the album cuts, "Po Folk's Disco," is significant because disco was all the rage at the time, and Casablanca Records was one of the most successful disco labels. The album and the singles didn't fare very well, and a while after *Hello, Larry* was cancelled, Lemon became an ordained minister. He is extremely proud of the day he was enshrined in the Naismith Memorial Basketball Hall of Fame. He is married to Dr. Cynthia Lemon and has 10 children.

LENNY AND THE SQUIGTONES (MICHAEL MCKEAN AND DAVID L. LANDER)

Most Famous TV Role: Lenny (Michael McKean) and Squiggy (David L. Lander) on *Laverne and Shirley*; **Network:** ABC; **Years:** 1976–1983; **Hit Recording:** *Lenny and Squiggy Present Lenny and the Squigtones*; **Label:** Casablanca; **Release Year:** 1979; **Matrix:** Casablanca LP #7149; **Chart:** #205 *Billboard* Top Pop Albums

Lenny Kosnowski and Andrew Squiggman were bizarre characters portrayed by Michael McKean and David L. Lander, respectively, on the period sitcom called *Laverne and Shirley* from 1976 to 1983. They were not the sharpest tools in the shed, but had impeccable timing to walk into the girls' apartment at the most inopportune moment. During the show's historically tumultuous run, Laverne and Shirley released phonograph records, as did Lenny and Squiggy—as Lenny and the Squigtones. Their *Lenny and Squiggy Present Lenny and the Squigtones* album spent five weeks near the bottom of the *Billboard* Albums chart. It was reportedly recorded live at the Roxy Theatre, and perhaps the most popular cut on the album is "Star Crossed" (performed on the series in an episode titled "From Suds to Stardom"). Michael McKean wrote the song. The album has garnered interest in recent years because Christopher Guest, later Nigel Tufnel of Spinal Tap, plays guitar. McKean portrayed David St. Hubbins in that film, *This Is Spinal Tap*. Some of the 1950s-style tunes on the Casablanca album have bizarre titles such as "Creature without a Head" and "So's Your Old Testament." Other songs from the album—"Night after Night" and "If Only I'd've Listened to Mama" were performed in the "Annual Shotz Talent Show" episodes. The duo performed two other songs from the album—"King of the Cars" and "Love Is a Terrible Thing"—on a July 9, 1979, episode of *American Bandstand*. Both McKean and Lander have become extremely prolific voice actors for animation.

ROBERT Q. LEWIS

Most Famous TV Role: host of *The Robert Q. Lewis Show* and *The Name's the Same*; **Networks:** CBS, NBC; **Years:** 1950–1956; **Hit Recording:** "Where's a Your House?"; **Labels:** Columbia, Coral, MGM; **Release Year:** 1951; **Matrix:** MGM #11056; **Chart:** none

Robert Q. Lewis was born as Robert Goldberg in New York City on April 5, 1921. By the age of 10, he knew he wanted to be a radio performer. He began performing on the radio the following year, and was a radio operator for the Signal Corps of the U.S. Army during World War II. After the war, he jumped right back into broadcasting without missing a beat. Lewis also became quite a proficient actor in motion pictures and television, but is most fondly recalled for his work as a game show host, panelist, and raconteur. Always seen wearing black-rimmed glasses, Lewis hosted his own eponymous *Robert Q. Lewis Show* on CBS in the early 1950s while also hosting a variety series titled *The Show Goes On* on the very same network. He also released several phonograph records during this period—all for major record labels such as Columbia, Coral, and MGM—but none of them made the charts. Let's just say that he didn't record serious love songs for these labels. Most of his material was humorous, or in the case of "Where's a Your House?" an answer/parody on the MGM label to the Rosemary Clooney Columbia original titled "Come On-a My House." Even though it didn't chart, it became Lewis's most famous recording. Perhaps Lewis's most famous hosting duties came from 1952 to 1954 with the TV game show *The Name's the Same*, on which the panel had to figure out with which famous person the contestant shared a name. During the run of this show, Lewis released "Hard-Hearted Hannah" for the Coral label (#61292). A few years later, in 1958 he also hosted the original version of the game show *Make Me Laugh* on ABC. He attempted one more recording, an album for Atco Records in the late 1960s titled *I'm Just Wild about Vaudeville* (Atco #212), but it was sadly out of place among all of the rock and psychedelic music of the era. Lewis was always seen smoking cigarettes on-screen in television's infancy, and after accruing a long resume of TV guest appearances, he developed emphysema and died on December 11, 1991, at the age of 65. Lewis never married and had no immediate family.

SHARI LEWIS

Most Famous TV Role: host of *Shariland* and *The Shari Lewis Show*; **Network:** NBC, PBS, syndicated; **Years:** 1956–1958, 1960–1963, respectively; **Hit Recording:** none; **Label:** RCA Victor; **Release Years:** 1958–1964; **Matrix:** *Fun in Shariland* (RCA Victor LP #1006), *Jack and the Beanstalk and Other Stories* (RCA Victor LP #1052); **Chart:** none

Shari Lewis was born Sonia Phyllis Hurwitz in the Bronx, New York, on January 17, 1933. Her father was a magician and he taught her his craft in her youth. Within a very short amount of time, she learned every aspect of the performing arts—acting, dancing, acrobatics, juggling, violin, piano, ballet, baton twirling, and ice skating. However, it was her adeptness at ventriloquism that garnered the most attention. Shortly after her ventriloquism helped her win first prize on *Arthur Godfrey's Talent Scouts*, she was approached to host her own show. It began as a local kids' program and went under numerous titles, including *Hi, Mom*, for which Lewis won a Peabody Award. Her puppets, such as Lamb Chop and Charlie Horse, became so popular that RCA Victor gave her the opportunity to make a record called *Fun in Shariland*. In 1960, NBC gave her a network show airing on Saturday mornings, and this really established Lewis and her skills. RCA gave her another opportunity to record in the early 1960s with *Jack and the Beanstalk and Other Stories*.

Over the years, Lewis and her puppets appeared in numerous shows, including a long run on PBS on *Lamb Chop's Play-Along* and then *Charlie Horse's Music Pizza*. Sadly, the latter was her last project, and after being diagnosed with uterine cancer, she died on August 2, 1998, at the age of 65. She won 12 Emmy Awards during her career and was a true overachiever, writing several books, hosting dozens of TV specials, conducting symphonies here and abroad, and making numerous videos. She was married twice and is survived by a daughter, Mallory.

GEORGE LINDSEY

Most Famous TV Role: Goober Pyle on *The Andy Griffith Show, Mayberry R.F.D.*, and *Hee Haw*; **Network:** CBS; **Years:** 1964–1968, 1968–1971, 1972–1992, respectively; **Hit Recording:** none; **Label:** Capitol; **Release Year:** 1969; **Matrix:** "96 Miles to Bakersfield" (Capitol #2450); **Chart:** none

George Lindsey was born in Fairfield, Alabama, on December 17, 1928. He was raised in Jasper, Alabama, and later attended North Alabama University and was the football team's quarterback. After serving in the U.S. Air Force, he developed an interest in theater and attended the American Theatre Wing in New York City. He then moved to Los Angeles and found work in small roles on episodic TV shows. He didn't join the cast of *The Andy Griffith Show* as Goober Pyle (Gomer's cousin) until 1964 (it had already been on the air for four years). Griffith left the show while it was number 1 in the ratings in 1968, and the program was reinvented as *Mayberry R.F.D.* and Goober's role was expanded. This "new" series lasted for three seasons on CBS, and during this period, Lindsey attempted success as a recording artist. Even with a major label, Capitol Records behind him, and two former members of Buddy Holly's Crickets' (Sonny Curtis and Jerry Allison's) material, Lindsey failed to have a hit with "96 Miles to Bakersfield." The flip side was "It's Such a Pretty World Today." Both songs were also included on Capitol LP #230 titled *96 Miles to Bakersfield*. Two other albums by Lindsey, *Goober Sings* (Capitol #2965) and *George Goober Lindsey Goes to Town* (MCA #5353), also failed to make the charts.

After the cancellation of *Mayberry R.F.D.* as part of CBS's decision to cancel all of its rural sitcoms (including *The Beverly Hillbillies* and *Green Acres*), Lindsey got to portray Goober Pyle yet again on the syndicated version of *Hee Haw* from 1972 to 1992. Despite his longevity and success as Goober, Lindsey was not fond of reminiscing with fans at autograph conventions about his TV years (although he attended many). He has a highway named for him near his childhood home in Jasper, Alabama. His autobiography, *Goober in a Nutshell*, was published in 1995. Lindsey took ill in 2012 and died a short time later on May 6 of that year. His only marriage ended in divorce. He is survived by two children, Camden and George Jr.

ART LINKLETTER

Most Famous TV Role: host of *People Are Funny* and *House Party*; **Network:** CBS, NBC; **Years:** 1952–1969; **Hit Recording:** "We Love You, Call Collect"; **Label:** Capitol; **Release Year:** 1969; **Matrix:** Capitol #2678; **Chart:** #42 *Billboard* Hot 100

Gordon Arthur Kelly was born in Moose Jaw, Saskatchewan, Canada, on July 17, 1912. He was abandoned by his natural parents while only weeks old, and was adopted by Mary and Fulton John Linkletter. A short while later his new family moved to San Diego, California, where he remained through his college years at San Diego State University. His degree was in teaching, but his interest in broadcasting soon usurped his studies. After working at radio stations in San Diego and San Francisco, Art Linkletter was ready for the big time and began hosting the original *People Are Funny* on the radio in Hollywood. He also appeared in a motion picture titled *People Are Funny* in 1946, and eventually the program was adapted for television where it ran from 1954 to 1961 on NBC. He also made several very wise investments in the hula hoop, in Milton Bradley's game of Life, and in Disneyland's film and photo concession. His *House Party* show on CBS's daytime schedule ran from 1952 to 1969, and one of the daily highlights was the segment with the kids and their spontaneous, unfiltered, often embarrassing answers to Linkletter's questions. This popular segment eventually evolved into several *Kids Say the Darndest Things* books and even a syndicated TV series with that title.

Despite all of the successes in Linkletter's life, including a marriage that lasted almost 75 years, there was also some sorrow. He released a recitation on 45 rpm about his daughter and the new permissive society for Capitol Records titled "We Love You, Call Collect." The heartfelt single was recorded shortly before Linkletter's daughter, Diane (who answered the recitation on the flip side with "Dear Mom and Dad"), committed suicide on October 4, 1969. The record surprisingly caught on with the public and just missed the Top Forty on *Billboard*'s Hot 100. It won a Grammy Award in 1970 for Best Spoken Word Recording. It was Linkletter's only chart single. He lived to be 97, and when he died on May 26, 2010, he left behind his wife, Lois; four children; seven grandchildren; and 15 great-grandchildren.

PEGGY LIPTON

Most Famous TV Role: Julie Barnes on *The Mod Squad*; **Network:** ABC; **Years:** 1968–1973; **Hit Recording:** none; **Label:** Ode; **Release Years:** 1968–1970; **Matrix:** "Stoney End" (Ode #114), "Lu" (Ode #124), "Wear Your Love like Heaven" (Ode #66001); **Chart:** #121, #102, #108, respectively, *Billboard* Bubbling Under

Margaret Ann Lipton was born in New York City on August 30, 1946. She was rather withdrawn and shy as a child, but found a way out of her shell through modeling, music, and acting. She made her TV debut on the short-lived NBC sitcom called *The John Forsythe Show* in 1965. After numerous guest-starring roles, she was ready for a recurring role and hit pay dirt in 1968 on ABC's very popular *The Mod Squad* alongside Michael

Cole, Clarence Williams III, and Tige Andrews. Lipton also became a fashion icon with her long hair, miniskirts, and love beads. She won a Golden Globe Award for her portrayal of Julie Barnes on the program in 1971.

Lipton's attempts at simultaneous success on the music charts had disappointing results. She released numerous singles for the Ode Records label between 1968 and 1970 (during the TV show's run), but her efforts took her to the Bubbling Under charts three times. She is, perhaps, best known for releasing a version of the Laura Nyro composition titled "Stoney End" before Barbra Streisand made it a Top Ten hit. She also recorded Nyro's "Lu" in 1970, and released a cover version of Donovan's "Wear Your Love like Heaven," but it just wasn't meant to be, although she shares composing credits on Frank Sinatra's 1984 hit "L.A. Is My Lady." Lipton was married to music producer Quincy Jones for over a decade and had two children. After taking many years off to raise said children, she returned to acting and had a run on TV's *Twin Peaks* in the early 1990s. Lipton is a colon cancer survivor since 2004.

RICH LITTLE

Most Famous TV Roles: Stan Parker on *Love on a Rooftop*, regular on *The Kopykats (The ABC Comedy Hour)*; **Network:** ABC; **Years:** 1966–1967, 1972, respectively; **Hit Recording:** none; **Labels:** Colgems, Sound Stage 7; **Release Years:** 1966–1968; **Matrix:** "That's Life" (Colgems #1013), "One Bo-Dillion Dollars" (Sound Stage 7 #2567); **Chart:** none

Richard Little was born in Ottawa, Ontario, Canada, on November 26, 1938. His father was a doctor, but Little didn't follow in his father's footsteps. He and an impressionist partner named Geoff Scott developed an act in the 1950s, and before he was even of legal age, Little was performing with Scott in nightclubs in Canada, mimicking local political figures. His first work in the theater was as an usher, but he would soon be on that stage. His first regular role on television was on the much ballyhooed but short-lived *Judy Garland Show*. A couple of years later, he worked with another Judy—Judy Carne—on the Screen Gems sitcom *Love on a Rooftop* as the neighbor Stan Parker, the inventor, who was always borrowing things and never returning them. Little did release several comedy albums, but he did sing on a single released during *Love on a Rooftop*'s single-season run—"That's Life" backed with "Did I Ever Really Live?" for Colgems (a division of Screen Gems). It wasn't a big hit and neither was "One Bo-Dillion Dollars" backed with "I Catch Myself Crying" for the Sound Stage

7 label. Little later became a regular on a memorable but unsuccessful program called *The Kopykats* for ABC in 1972. He also, briefly, hosted his own *Rich Little Show* in 1976 on NBC. However, he was best in nightclubs and as a talk, game, and variety show guest. His 1982 album titled *The First Family Rides Again* (Boardwalk LP #33248) reached the Top Thirty. He was also a popular regular fixture on the *Dean Martin Celebrity Roasts*. He has been married four times and has one child.

STANLEY LIVINGSTON

Most Famous TV Role: Chip Douglas on *My Three Sons*; **Networks:** ABC, CBS; **Years:** 1960–1972; **Hit Recording:** none; **Label:** Marilyn; **Release Year:** 1962; **Matrix:** "Hairspray" (Marilyn #03); **Chart:** none

Stanley Livingston was born in Los Angeles, California, on November 24, 1950. His first TV appearance was on *You Asked for It* as one of the "water babies," an underwater swim group. He was still a toddler at the time. This appearance led to articles in popular magazines such as *Vogue* and *McCall's*. Livingston was suddenly in demand and earned a recurring role in a few dozen episodes of *The Adventures of Ozzie and Harriet* as Stanley, the neighbor boy. His biggest break came in 1960 when he was cast as the original youngest son, Chip Douglas, on *My Three Sons*. The show debuted on ABC, where it ran for five seasons. It then jumped to CBS for seven more, but with changes. William Demarest replaced William Frawley, and Tim Considine (see the entry under his name) left the show, and Stanley Livingston's younger brother, Barry, then became the youngest—the adopted third son, Ernie.

Early in the show's long run, Livingston released a pop single for the Southern California label called Marilyn Records. "Hairspray" is the A-side and "Pen Pal" is the B-Side. The release was obviously from early in the show's run, as Livingston sounded quite young. Livingston recalled,

A singer and producer named Bobby Please approached me and my parents about making a record. It was a period when a lot of young actors on regular TV shows were making records. The label was called Marilyn, and was probably named for Bobby Please's wife, Marilyn. Coincidentally, it was also my mom's name. Bobby "Boris" Pickett of "Monster Mash" fame played on the record, and disc jockey Art Laboe and his Original Sound Company helped with distribution. I actually liked the B-side, "Pen Pal," better, but "Hairspray" was chosen as the A-side. The "Hairspray" side features an aerosol sound effect in the beginning, and we did a lot of takes until we got just the

A "Chip" shot. *My Three Sons* costar Stanley Livingston recorded a minor hit called "Hairspray" early in the show's run. Notice Gary Paxton's first name on the label misspelled as *Garry*.

right aerosol sound using a can of Raid, of all things. This was probably late 1961 or early 1962. It did get quite a bit of airplay in California, and to our surprise, "Hairspray" became a number 1 hit in Stockton, California. This led to a memorable concert there. They flew us in for the event, and I was on the bill with Shelley Fabares, Eddie Hodges, and Duane Eddy.

It was his only recording. Additionally, Livingston said, "I was only eleven at the time. Had I been just a few years older, the record would probably have become more popular with teenage girls."

After a dozen years on the sitcom, Stanley guest starred in numerous episodic TV programs, but eventually turned most of his interest to prolifically writing, producing, and directing programs for PBS. Livingston has the distinction of having a recurring role on two of TV's longest-running sitcoms—*The Adventures of Ozzie and Harriet* and *My Three Sons*. About his character on *My Three Sons*, Chip Douglas, Livingston shared, "It was very flattering years later when Jim Carrey's character in *The Cable Guy* was named Chip Douglas. That was very cool." With tongue in cheek, Livingston's brother, Barry, has a recurring role on *Anger Management* as a therapist named Stanley. He added, "And Barry's son, Spencer, is the real musician of the family. He's currently quite a success in two different groups—the Alternates and Alex and the Constellation. They work almost nonstop in Southern California." Stanley's production company is called First Team Productions, and his website, www.stanleylivingston .com, is chock-full of *My Three Sons* photographs and memories.

GLORIA LORING

Most Famous TV Role: Liz Chandler on *Days of Our Lives*; **Network:** NBC; **Years:** 1981–1986; **Hit Recording:** "Friends and Lovers"; **Label:** Carrerre; **Release Year:** 1986; **Matrix:** Carrerre #06122; **Chart:** #2 *Billboard* Hot 100

Gloria Loring was born Gloria Jean Goff on December 10, 1946, in Hell's Kitchen on New York City's west side. Loring said,

> I come from at least five generations of musicians. We always had big band music around the house—my dad played trumpet for Tommy and Jimmy Dorsey, and my mom was a big band singer. The first albums I bought were by the great Ella Fitzgerald, and singer Eddie Fisher was a friend of the family and my babysitter. However, growing up in the 1950s, I also had an affinity for rock and roll. In the early 1960s, I became a fan of the folk music scene. I had long blonde hair at the time, like Mary Travers of Peter, Paul and Mary, and I was asked by three guys with a folk band to join them, and we became known as Those Four. I was still in my teens at the time, and we played hootenannies in the local folk scene for a year or so. After I graduated high school, I opted to go on as a solo. My career really got going in 1968 with one hundred appearances on *The Merv Griffin Show* and an LP titled *Today* for MGM Records. The engineer on that album, Brooks Arthur, has kept in touch after all these years. He is currently the supervisor for the music in Adam Sandler's motion pictures.

In the 1970s, she recorded under the alias Cody Jameson, and had a hit country crossover single titled "Brooklyn" for Atco Records (#7073). Loring shared, "I don't recall the origin of the name Cody Jameson, but that was done because I had become associated with pop music, and 'Brooklyn' had a real country feel to it. It became a Top Forty hit on the country charts, and even crossed over. It was just a 'one off' release—I never made another under that name."

She and then husband Alan Thicke cowrote the theme songs for the popular NBC sitcoms *Diff'rent Strokes* and *The Facts of Life*. Loring recalled, "That was more of Alan's thing, as he had written special material songs for the CBC. I'm very appreciative that he brought me in on those projects. I was pretty new to writing at that time, and it was a great learning experience. Most people don't know it, but that's my voice on *The Facts of Life* theme. I'm still getting royalty checks."

A short time later, she began a long run on *Days of Our Lives* as Liz Chandler. Loring stated,

> Being on that show opened me up to a whole new audience. I had previously done countless variety and talk shows, but this was all brand-new territory. I was really nervous and tentative—it was my first acting job. That season, the program added eleven new characters, and a year later only two remained, and I was one of the two. I was constantly in fear of being fired—I was so green at the time. However, eventually they let my character, Liz, sing at Doug's Place. As the Liz character gained confidence singing on the show, so did I.
>
> About three years into my run as Liz, I was sulking about never having had a hit record to *Days* associate producer Beth Milstein. She and I decided I needed a great song that I could sing on the show, with the hope of it catching on with the public. Talk about the Law of Attraction! The very next day I was presented with the song "Friends and Lovers." I knew instantly it was a hit song. However, every record label turned it down. Undaunted, I hung in there and eventually got the song released on CBS/Sony's Carrerre label [#06122], where my duet partner on the tune, Carl Anderson, was already recording. Wouldn't you know, I was right—it zoomed up the charts very fast, reaching number one in many cities and number two nationally.

Several years later, Loring and Anderson recorded a new version of their big hit, and Loring added, "I realized that I didn't own a version of 'Friends and Lovers' I had recorded with Carl, so I called and asked him to do that with me. I'm so glad I called when I did, because a year later, Carl was diagnosed with leukemia and left us within a few months."

About the *Days of Our Lives Celebrity Cookbook*, Loring remembered, "I did that for my four-year-old son with diabetes. The proceeds of more than a million dollars went to the Juvenile Diabetes Research Foundation to help find a cure. In recent years, Halle Berry, the Jonas Brothers, and many other celebrities have continued helping JDRF."

After leaving *Days of Our Lives*, Loring continued to amass a long list of credits for guest appearances on episodic TV programs, and garnered a recurring role on the syndicated series *Renegade* as Melissa Dixon. She also got to guest star on several other Stephen J. Cannell programs.

Musical talent continues in the family—Loring is the proud mother of the immensely popular Robin Thicke, and shared, "It's very interesting that we both had our biggest hit records in our thirties. In fact, my latest CD titled *The Playlist* contains a duet ('The Prayer') with Robin."

Loring remains very busy with a new book and CD in the works. Her autobiography, inspired by a quote from Albert Einstein, is called *Coincidence Is God's Way of Remaining Anonymous*. Why was that title chosen? Loring replied, "Because so much of my life and success has been prompted by wondrous coincidences." The book and *The Playlist* CD are both available at her website, www.glorialoring.com.

ALLEN LUDDEN

Most Famous TV Role: host of *Password*; **Networks:** ABC, CBS, NBC; **Years:** 1961–1969, 1971–1975, 1979–1982; 1984–1989; **Hit Recording:** none; **Label:** RCA Victor; **Release Year:** 1964; **Matrix:** *Allen Ludden Sings His Favorite Songs* (RCA Victor LP #2934); **Chart:** none

Allen Ellsworth was born in Mineral Point, Wisconsin, on October 5, 1917. Allen's father died from the flu epidemic when Allen was very young, and his mother remarried a physician named Homer Ludden Jr. Allen was a drama and English major at the University of Texas. After serving in the U.S. Army, he pursued a career in radio. He eventually parlayed his success there into television and hosted the *G.E. College Bowl*, and eventually the program that made him rich and famous—*Password*. It was on this program that Ludden met his future bride, Betty White. It was his second marriage and her third. In 1972, the couple appeared together on the most popular episode of *The Odd Couple* titled "Password." Beginning on CBS in 1961, *Password* eventually played on all three major networks and its title was later expanded to *Password Plus* and *Super Password*.

Ludden was also active in stage productions, and during the run of the original *Password* he released an album titled *Allen Ludden Sings His Favorite Songs* for RCA Victor in 1964. It consisted of old standards such as "Where or When?" "Call Me Irresponsible," "Me and My Shadow," and "The Very Thought of You." It wasn't a big hit, but Ludden had his day job on which to fall back. In between the different incarnations of *Password*, the affable Ludden hosted a few other game shows such as *Stumpers, The Liar's Club*, and *Win with the Stars*. He had to bow out of his *Password* duties for a time in 1979 when he was diagnosed with stomach cancer and underwent chemotherapy treatments that rendered him too weak to host the program. Ludden returned to the program for a time, but so did the cancer and he died on June 9, 1981, only a handful of days before his 18th anniversary. His widow, Betty White, never remarried.

M

PATRICK MACNEE. *See* HONOR BLACKMAN.

MEREDITH MACRAE

Most Famous TV Role: Billie Jo Bradley on *Petticoat Junction*; **Network:** CBS; **Years:** 1966–1970; **Hit Recording:** none; **Labels:** Canjo, Capitol; **Release Years:** 1964–1967; **Matrix:** "Image of Love" (Canjo #103), "Who Needs Memories of Him?" (Capitol #2000); **Chart:** none

Meredith MacRae was born in Houston, Texas, on May 30, 1944. She is the daughter of celebrities Gordon and Sheila MacRae. Meredith credited her parents with instilling in her a work ethic and humility. Her first recurring role on TV was on *My Three Sons* as Sally Ann Morrison, Mike's girlfriend (1963–1965). During her time on the program, MacRae recorded a single for the small Canjo Records label—"Image of Love" backed with "Time Stands Still." It wasn't a big hit, but she'd get another opportunity to record in the future. When Mike (Tim Considine) left the show in 1965, MacRae's role was written out of the show. She was then free to pursue other career possibilities, and was cast as the third and final Billie Jo Bradley on CBS's *Petticoat Junction* beginning in 1966. She had numerous attempts to sing on the program, and landed at a major record label this time around—Capitol. However, she released "Who Needs Memories of Him?" backed with "Goodbye Love" for the label, and not much happened. She was also part of two singles released as by "The Girls from *Petticoat Junction*" in 1968 (along with Linda Kaye Henning and Lori Saunders)—"If You Could Only Be Me" backed with "I'm So Glad That You Found Me" (Imperial #66329) and "Thirty Days Hath September" backed with "Wheeling, West Virginia" (Imperial #66346). No other singles followed. She remained on *Petticoat Junction* until its cancellation in 1970, at which point she made guest appearances on dozens of game shows. She also worked tirelessly for numerous charities. She was married three times, the second of which was to actor Greg Mullavey—costar of *Mary Hartman, Mary Hartman*. Sadly, in 1999, after experiencing dizziness and headaches, MacRae was diagnosed with brain cancer. She died the following year on July 14, 2000, at the age of 56, leaving behind one child.

SHEILA MACRAE

Most Famous TV Role: Alice Kramden on *The Jackie Gleason Show*; **Network:** CBS; **Years:** 1966–1970; **Hit Recording:** none; **Label:** ABC; **Release Year:** 1966; **Matrix:** "I'm Counting on You" (ABC #10963), *How Sweet She Is* (ABC LP #611); **Chart:** none

Sheila MacRae was born as Sheila Margaret Stephens in London, England, on September 24, 1921. She and her parents left the United Kingdom right before the onset of World War II. She married actor/singer Gordon MacRae in 1941 and both appeared together on stage often. They had four children together—two boys and two girls—the most famous of which was Meredith (see the entry for her). MacRae's first recurring role was as Madelyn Richmond on the soap opera *General Hospital* in 1963. Beginning in 1966, she stepped into some pretty big shoes and took over the role of Alice Kramden on *The Jackie Gleason Show*. These are the episodes now referred to as *The Color Honeymooners*. These episodes were much more like a Broadway musical than the original—there was a lot of singing and dancing. Speaking of singing, while portraying Alice Kramden, Sheila released a single and an album for ABC Records. The single was "I'm Counting on You" backed with "You Always Hurt the One You Love." The album was titled *How Sweet She Is*. Both were released in 1966, but neither made much of an impact. After many years out of the public eye, MacRae surfaced on an NBC dramedy from 1990 called *Parenthood* and portrayed Marilyn Buckman. However, her comeback was short-lived and the series only lasted 13 weeks (not to be confused with the later more successful program with that title). MacRae lived to be 92 and died suddenly on March 6, 2014.

GEORGE MAHARIS

Most Famous TV Role: Buz Murdock on *Route 66*; **Network:** CBS; **Years:** 1960–1963; **Hit Recording:** "Teach Me Tonight"; **Label:** Epic; **Release Year:** 1962; **Matrix:** Epic #9504; **Chart:** #25 *Billboard* Hot 100

George Maharis
DON'T FENCE ME IN
and ALRIGHT, OKAY, YOU WIN

EPIC
OUTSTANDING HIGH FIDELITY THROUGH RADIAL SOUND
A PRODUCT OF CBS
5-9569

Route 66 star George Maharis caused a "Buz" with a few moderately popular singles during the show's run.

George Maharis was born in Astoria, New York, on September 1, 1928. He was one of seven children born to Greek immigrants who owned a restaurant. He had designs upon becoming a singer, but held off on that dream until his acting career gained traction. His studies took place at the Actors Studio, and he then got his feet wet in a few off-Broadway productions and guest starred in numerous TV drama programs, such as *Naked City, Studio One,* and *Search for Tomorrow.* His biggest break came in 1960 when he earned the role of Buz Murdock on the original *Route 66* on CBS. He and costar Martin Milner (as Tod Stiles) traveled the country in a hot Corvette convertible in search of adventure. In 1962, Maharis got a chance to realize his dreams of becoming a popular singer when he kicked off a long relationship with Epic Records. The result was one Top Thirty single, a new version of the old standard "Teach Me Tonight." Surprisingly, his follow-up single—a vocal version of the *"Route 66* Theme" (Epic #2227)— failed to chart. His *George Maharis Sings* album (Epic LP #26001) reached the Top Ten. Apparently, Epic had a lot of faith in Maharis's vocal abilities, and 13 more singles and seven albums were released. Maharis left *Route 66* during the third season. Some say he left because of complications from hepatitis, while others aver that he wanted to pursue a motion picture career. He then amassed a list of modestly popular movie roles in films such as *The Happening* and *Quick! Before It Melts*. He returned to series television in 1970 in the short-lived detective show called *The Most Deadly Game* on ABC. He also appeared nude in *Playgirl* magazine in 1973. Countless TV guest-starring roles and frequent stage work followed. Nowadays he pursues another passion—painting.

JOCK MAHONEY

Most Famous TV Role: star of *Yancy Derringer;* **Network:** CBS; **Years:** 1958–1959; **Hit Recording:** none; **Label:** Decca; **Release Year:** 1958; **Matrix:** "Cowboy" (Decca #30437); **Chart:** none

Jock Mahoney was born Jacques O'Mahoney in Chicago, Illinois, on February 7, 1919. He was raised in Davenport, Iowa, and served in the U.S. Marine Corps during World War II. He started his show business career as a stuntman, and eventually earned two western TV series. The first one, the syndicated *Range Rider,* came in television's infancy and ran for two seasons. It was produced for Gene Autry's Flying A Productions. Mahoney then got a shot at a CBS network series in 1958. It was called *Yancy Derringer* and was set in the Civil War era. During the show's run, Mahoney released a single for a major label, Decca Records, titled "Cowboy" backed with "Gold." Not much happened with the record, and the idea of making a recording star out of him was abandoned.

After *Yancy Derringer* was cancelled in 1959, Mahoney got to play Tarzan. He lost out to Lex Barker for the role in 1948, replacing Johnny Weismuller, but got his chance in the 1960s in the films *Tarzan Goes to India* and *Tarzan's Three Challenges.* Because he was already in his 40s, the producers of the franchise then opted to go younger, and these were his only two shots at his dream role. He was married three times, and one of his stepchildren, Sally Field, became very famous (you like her, you really like her). Mahoney suffered a stroke a short time after an automobile accident and died on December 15, 1989, at the age of 70.

LEE MAJORS

Most Famous TV Roles: Heath Barkley on *The Big Valley*, Colonel Steve Austin on *The Six Million Dollar Man*, Colt Seavers on *The Fall Guy*; **Network:** ABC; **Years:** 1965–1969, 1974–1978, 1981–1986, respectively; **Hit Recording:** none; **Label:** Scotti Brothers; **Release Year:** 1982; **Matrix:** "The Unknown Stuntman" (Scotti Brothers #03170); **Chart:** none

Lee Majors was born as Harvey Lee Yeary in Wyandotte, Michigan, on April 23, 1939. He was raised by an aunt and uncle after his natural parents were killed when he was a baby. He attended college in Kentucky and, after being injured playing football, gravitated toward the performing arts. After a year of acting school, he found a few small roles on episodic TV programs such as *Gunsmoke* and *Alfred Hitchcock Presents*. His big break came when he was cast as Heath Barkley in *The Big Valley* alongside Barbara Stanwyck. Majors could seemingly do no wrong, and jumped from successful series to successful series. After *The Big Valley* came *Owen Marshall, Counselor at Law* (as Jess Brandon), *The Six Million Dollar Man* (as Steve Austin), and *The Fall Guy* (as Colt Seavers). *The Fall Guy* theme song, titled "The Unknown Stuntman" (backed with "Lust in a Lady's Eye"), performed by Majors, was released on a 45 on the Scotti Brothers label, but failed to make the charts. Majors's wife at the time, Farrah Fawcett, is mentioned in the lyrics. He has been married four times, and in 2003 had heart bypass surgery. Yes, despite what you remember about *The Six Million Dollar Man*, he does not have bionic parts; thus the surgery.

HOWIE MANDEL

Most Famous TV Role: Dr. Wayne Fiscus on *St. Elsewhere*, host of *Deal or No Deal*; **Network:** NBC; **Years:** 1982–1988, 2005–2009, respectively; **Hit Recording:** none; **Label:** Warner Bros.; **Release Year:** 1985; **Matrix:** "I Do the Watusi" (Warner Bros. #28696); **Chart:** none

Howard Michael Mandel was born in Toronto, Ontario, Canada, on November 29, 1955. He was frequently in trouble during high school for being a class clown and a prankster. His original career choice was to open his own carpeting business, but that was quickly swept under the rug and somehow his life made a sharp left turn for stand-up comedy. His wild on-stage antics got a lot of attention, and before long, he was cast as a regular (Dr. Wayne Fiscus) on the NBC series titled *St. Elsewhere*. The program enjoyed a six-year run. While on *St. Elsewhere*, Mandel also embarked on a stand-up comedy schedule called "The Watusi Tour" and even released a single and video directed by Jerry Kramer titled "I Do the Watusi." The title was the answer to bizarre questions within the lyrics such as, "What do you do when your dog has been glued to your head?" and "What do you do when a guy puts mayonnaise on your shoulder?" The record may not have become a huge hit, but Mandel had other successes up his sleeve. He is the creator of the long-running animated series called *Bobby's World*. He hosted an eponymous syndicated talk show in 1998. He also earned parts in popular motion pictures, including *Gremlins* and *A Fine Mess*.

A new, very different-looking Mandel emerged in the new millennium. Now with a shaved head, Mandel was named as host of the new U.S. version of the game show *Deal or No Deal*. The program became immensely popular and was aired several times a week on NBC. A daytime version was then added, but this proved to be too much of a good thing, and the program's popularity began to dwindle because of overexposure. It was revealed that Mandel had a condition called mysophobia, a potent fear of coming in contact with germs (he will not shake hands without latex gloves). Coincidentally, his most successful album is called *Fits like a Glove* (Warner Bros. LP #25327). He has only been married once, has three children, and has a star on the Hollywood Walk of Fame.

JOHNNY MANN

Most Famous TV Roles: bandleader on *The Joey Bishop Show*, host of *Johnny Mann's Stand Up and Cheer*; **Networks:** ABC, syndicated; **Years:** 1967–1969, 1971–1974, respectively; **Hit Recording:** "Up, Up and Away"; **Label:** Liberty; **Release Year:** 1967; **Matrix:** Liberty #55972; **Chart:** #91 *Billboard* Hot 100

Johnny Mann was born John R. Mann on August 30, 1928, in Baltimore, Maryland. He very quickly became a popular and prolific arranger, composer, entertainer, conductor, and recording artist. Mann worked with some of the great early names in rock and roll, and shared, "It was great fun working with Eddie Cochran, the Crickets, Johnny Burnette, and Bobby Vee at Liberty Records. We were all just getting started and it was very exciting."

Mann seamlessly made the transition to television and worked on *The Alvin Show* (Dave Seville and the Chipmunks were also on Liberty Records) and *The Danny Kaye Show*. He is fondly remembered as the music director on *The Joey Bishop Show* (his ABC late-night talk show), and Mann said, "All of those memories of working with Joey and Regis Philbin are in my own self-published soft-cover book titled *The Music Mann: My Life in Song*, available at my own official website, www.johnnymannsingers .com."

Mann has recorded over 40 albums, and his biggest hit single was a version of the Jimmy Webb composition "Up, Up and Away." Mann said, "That song was even bigger in the U.K. It was number one there. I won a Grammy for it. Actually, I won two Grammys during my career, but during an earthquake one of them was broken."

From 1971 to 1974, Mann hosted *Johnny Mann's Stand Up and Cheer* series. Mann recorded 84 episodes of the very patriotic show, and stated, "I wish I could get the series back on television—Me-TV or TV Land. I need to find a sponsor to get that done." Mann debunked a long-standing belief that comedienne Vicki Lawrence was a member of the Johnny Mann Singers, and Mann said, "That is just not true. She was never in the group."

The very familiar and famous music radio jingles recorded by the Johnny Mann Singers are still used by many radio stations across the United States. Mann got a Golden Palm Star on the Palm Springs Walk of Stars in 1998. From 2005 to 2014, Mann and his wife, Betty, resided in Anderson, South Carolina, and loved that new location. Mann wrote Anderson University's new Centennial Alma Mater, "Sounds of Anderson." The university also presented him with an honorary doctorate in humanities. Sadly, on June 18, 2014, Mann died suddenly at the age of 85, shortly after he was interviewed for this book. Surely this was among his final interviews, and one I will long treasure.

HAL MARCH

Most Famous TV Role: host of *The $64,000 Question*; **Network:** CBS; **Years:** 1955–1958; **Hit Recording:** none; **Labels:** Columbia, Coral, Dot; **Release Years:** 1955–1958; **Matrix:** "Goin' on a Hike" (Coral #61466), "Love Is *The $64,000 Question*" (Columbia #40684), "Hear Me Good" (Dot #15655); **Chart:** none

Hal March was born Harold Mendelson in San Francisco, California, on April 22, 1920. He began his career in radio as part of a comedy team paired with actor Bob Sweeney. With the advent of television, he formed a new partnership with Tom D'Andrea. They conjured up a popular skit called "The Soldiers," and they performed it often on *The Colgate Comedy Hour* on NBC. That skit became a live weekly sitcom called *The Soldiers* in 1955, but it only lasted 13 weeks. The duo also released a record for the Coral label, in character—"Goin' on a Hike" backed with "Goin' Overseas" (Coral #61466)—but like the series, it wasn't a big success. Tom D'Andrea's biggest claim to fame came as Jim Gillis, the sidekick on the sitcom called *The Life of Riley*. March also found success on his own, as host of the immensely popular *$64,000 Question*. During the show's run, March released a couple of records for major labels—"Love Is *The $64,000 Question*" backed with "Do It Yourself" for Columbia Records and "Hear Me Good" backed with "One Dozen Roses" for Dot. None of these were wildly successful, and March experienced a reversal of fortune when the quiz show scandals hit, and *The $64,000 Question* was alleged to be among the culprits. The scandal put the kibosh on his career for several years. He returned to game shows about a decade later and briefly hosted a syndicated show called *It's Your Bet*, but took ill a couple of months later. He was diagnosed with lung cancer and had to bow out of the series. March, a longtime smoker, died at the age of only 49 on January 19, 1970. He left behind a wife, three children, and two stepchildren.

ANDREA MARCOVICCI

Most Famous TV Role: Dr. Betsy Chernak Taylor on *Love Is a Many Splendored Thing*, Fran Brennan Gates on *Trapper John, M.D.*; **Network:** CBS; **Years:** 1970–1973, 1984–1986, respectively; **Hit Recording:** none; **Labels:** Bell, Private Stock; **Release Years:** 1970–present; **Matrix:** "In Our Time" (Bell #852), "What Is a Friend?" (Bell #894), "I'm Dreaming" (Private Stock #45198); **Chart:** none

Actress and singer Andrea Marcovicci was born in New York City on November 18, 1948. When asked about using her birthdate, Marcovicci responded, "Oh, yes, please do. I recently had a big 65th birthday celebration at Joe's Pub in Manhattan. I'm very proud of my age." Even though her surname sounds very Italian, Marcovicci said, "My father was Romanian. The original name was Marcovici, but an extra *c* was added to the end to help with pronunciation."

About her musical influences, Marcovicci recalled,

> My biggest influence was my mother—a great torch singer, but I would add Edith Piaf, Billie Holiday, Judy Collins, Joni Mitchell, and Joan Baez. In my

late teens, I became active in the folk music scene, and sang on open mic nights at the Gold Bug and the Bitter End. However, I hadn't yet mustered up a lot of confidence about performing in public, and I was very nervous doing it. Luckily, a short time later I got the recurring role of Dr. Betsy Chernak Taylor on the daytime soap opera called *Love Is a Many Splendored Thing*. I had the opportunity to sing on the show numerous times, and this greatly boosted my confidence.

At this same time, Marcovicci recorded a few singles for the Bell Record label—"In Our Time" (#852) and "What Is a Friend?" (#894). She added, "A few years later, Ron Dante of the Archies and Cuff Links worked on some songs with me for Private Stock Records in the style of Barry Manilow, but because I was involved in so many diverse projects at the time—performing Shakespeare, working in television, and moonlighting in nightclubs—the label abandoned the project and only released one single, 'I'm Dreaming.'"

Despite the disappointment at Private Stock, Marcovicci was racking up a very impressive list of TV credits as Gloria Berrenger on *The Berrengers*, as Cynthia Chase on *Hill Street Blues*, and as Dr. Fran Brennan Gates on *Trapper John, M.D.* Marcovicci has very fond memories of the latter, and stated,

> I got to work with the amazingly handsome Gregory Harrison on that show, and all of those wonderful animals. I played a veterinarian, and I grew very fond of the spider monkey and even the snake—a huge python who was completely wrapped around me in one episode. I wasn't afraid of the snake at all. However, on a motion picture project with John Gielgud, I had to have a tarantula crawl all over my body. I was petrified, but realized that I had to do it—it was my job to do it and do it well. I harnessed my fear, confronted it, and persevered through the many takes I had to do until it was just right. Yes, it was horrible, but I did it and I would gladly do it again.

Speaking of movies, Marcovicci added, "My very first film was Woody Allen's *The Front* directed by Martin Ritt. Woody was so kind, and I learned so much about comedy from him on that project. I was even nominated for a Golden Globe in that film. I also loved doing *Irene in Time* because of all the improvisation (which is a lot harder than memorizing a script). What an amazing learning experience."

Marcovicci really found her musical niche in the 1980s, and has been dubbed "the Cabaret Goddess" and "the Queen of Cabaret." She enjoyed a long run performing at New York's legendary Algonquin, famous for Dorothy Parker and the round table. Marcovicci holds the record—an unprecedented 25 seasons at the Algonquin's Oak Room. She was the final performer ever to play the room. "They still have a Marcovicci Suite there—my name is still on the door."

When asked about her favorite musical project, Marcovicci replied, "An out-of-print CD titled *What Is Love?* However, so many other CDs come in a close second, and are all available at my website, www.marcovicci.com." Those CDs include *My Christmas Song for You, December Songs, As Time Goes By: The Best of Andrea Marcovicci*, and the new one simply titled *Smile*.

When asked whether she preferred singing or acting, Marcovicci pondered a long time before answering and stated, "I would have to say singing because the response from the audience is instantaneous. There is no better feeling than putting a smile on someone's face with your song. Don't get me wrong, I love to act, and on stage, you get an immediate reaction, but with movies and television it sometimes takes a very long time to get that audience reaction, and a lot depends upon how the project is edited."

About her wishes for the future, Marcovicci shared, "I would love to be a regular on a program like *Criminal Minds*. I'm based in California nowadays, and going to the studio every day and working on that kind of show is my dream. That would be a simply delicious experience."

STUART MARGOLIN

Most Famous TV Role: Angel on *The Rockford Files*; **Network:** NBC; **Years:** 1974–1980; **Hit Recording:** none; **Label:** Warner Bros.; **Release Year:** 1980; **Matrix:** *And the Angel Sings* (Warner Bros. LP #3439); **Chart:** none

Stuart Margolin was born in Davenport, Iowa, on January 31, 1940. Margolin is truly a jack-of-all-trades in show business and, although not a household name, has an awesome résumé consisting of writing, directing, composing, and acting. He wrote a few songs for the pop vocal group known as the Parade. The group was best known for the Top Twenty hit titled "Sunshine Girl" (A&M #841), but Margolin did not compose that one. He was a regular on *Love, American Style* and was seen in most of the short skits in between the long segments. He then got to costar with James Garner on two different TV series—*Nichols* in 1972 and *The Rockford Files* from 1974 to 1980. He portrayed Angel on the latter and garnered two Emmy Awards for the role. Near the end of *The Rockford Files* run, he released an album titled *And the Angel Sings* for Warner Bros. Records, but its success did not match that of the TV series. He reprised his role for the Rockford TV movies that ran in the middle 1990s. As of this writing, Margolin's most recent credits include a role in the Richard Gere motion picture *Arbitrage* and the hit TV series *NCIS*. He is the brother of writer/director/producer Arnold Margolin.

Funny man and sitcom second banana Guy Marks wrote and recorded a ripe old 45 called "Loving You Has Made Me Bananas."

GUY MARKS

Most Famous TV Role: Freddie on *The Joey Bishop Show*; **Network:** NBC; **Year:** 1962; **Hit Recording:** "Loving You Has Made Me Bananas"; **Label:** ABC; **Release Year:** 1966; **Matrix:** ABC #11055; **Chart:** #51 *Billboard* Hot 100

Guy Marks was born as Mario Scarpa in Philadelphia, Pennsylvania, on October 31, 1923, the youngest of 11 children. Mario's father was an accomplished clarinet player, and each of his 11 children were given names of opera characters. Mario's name came from *La Tosca*. During his school years, he became quite adept at doing impressions of his teachers and celebrities. After a stint in the military, he was egged on by friends to perform his countless imitations on stage. Up until that time, he had been working odd jobs, but he soon abandoned those in favor of performing. He changed his name to Guy Marks and was a winner on *Arthur Godfrey's Talent Scouts*. This uniquely and brilliantly funny man imitated not only celebrities, but also animals, insects, and inanimate objects very adeptly. He soon made the talk and variety show circuit. He then landed a regular role as Freddie on an NBC sitcom called *The Joey Bishop Show*. His stay on the series was truncated, allegedly because he was just too funny (and he was), stealing everyone else's thunder. After appearing in more than half of the episodes from the 1962–1963 season, Marks was replaced with Corbett Monica.

After several guest appearances on *The Dick Van Dyke Show*, *My Favorite Martian*, and *The Danny Thomas Show*, Marks surfaced as the second banana on the single-season sitcom called *The John Forsythe Show*. The program ran during the 1965–1966 season, but Marks's talents were wasted in that unfunny series, set in an all-girls school. His next sitcom venture, the western comedy titled *Rango*, starred Tim Conway. This series was a much better fit for Marks's abilities and employed a lot of slapstick. Marks portrayed a Native American named Pink Cloud. During *Rango*'s run on ABC in 1967, Marks released a moderately popular record titled "Loving You Has Made Me Bananas" backed with "Forgive Me, My Love." The A-side just missed the Top Fifty and did sell enough to warrant the release of the *Loving You Has Made Me Bananas* album (ABC #648). The album consisted of funny versions of old standards. Several other singles—such as "Meet Me Tonight by the Postage Machine" backed with "This Is Forever" (ABC #11099) and "How the West Was Really Won" (years later, a popular skit on *The Dean Martin Celebrity Roasts*) backed with "This Is Forever" (ABC #11148)—failed to make the charts. He then returned to the talk and variety show circuit and was a frequent visitor to *The Merv Griffin Show*. One of his most memorable guest-starring roles came as "Igor" on a popular episode of the TV version of *The Odd Couple* called "The Odd Candidate." Speaking of *The Odd Couple*, Marks's last recurring TV role came on Jack Klugman's short-lived NBC sitcom *You, Again?* in 1986. Marks portrayed a character named Harry. Marks was married three times and died of cancer at the age of 64 on November 28, 1987. He should have become a much bigger star, but never did quite find the perfect TV role.

PENNY MARSHALL. *See* LAVERNE AND SHIRLEY.

PETER MARSHALL

Most Famous TV Role: host of *The Hollywood Squares*; **Network:** NBC, syndicated; **Years:** 1966–1981; **Hit Recording:** none; **Labels:** Decca, Dot, Melba; **Release Years:** 1967–1969; **Matrix:** "The Gift" (Decca 32228), *For the Love of Pete* (Dot LP #25930); **Chart:** none

Peter Marshall was born as Pierre LaCock in Huntington, West Virginia, on March 30, 1926. His elder sister, actress Joanne Dru, starred in movies such as *All the King's Men*, *Red River*, and *She Wore a Yellow Ribbon*. She also starred in a single season sitcom called *Guestward Ho* in 1960 on ABC. Her younger brother wisely changed his given name to Peter Marshall, and was in the cast for a live 1949 variety series called *Let There Be Stars*. The program lasted only seven weeks on ABC, and at least one kinescope of the program (that includes an embarrassing minstrel show segment) exists in the Paley Center for Media in Beverly Hills, California.

Marshall struggled to find work throughout the 1950s, and even attempted a borderline rock and roll record in 1956 titled "My Lovely Love" backed with "Nice and Cozy" for New York City's Melba Records label. It was not a hit, and for a time it looked as though things would not ever break in his favor. That is, until 1966 when Marshall's friend Morey Amsterdam recommended him for hosting duties on an up-and-coming NBC game show to be called *The Hollywood Squares*. Bert Parks had emceed the pilot, but Marshall got the gig and finally found his niche. The program became a sensation and garnered Marshall an Emmy Award. The program resurrected the careers of regulars Charley Weaver, Wally Cox, Rose Marie, and Paul Lynde.

During the show's early years, Marshall tried for recording success again, and released a single for Decca Records called "The Gift" backed with "When I Look in Your Eyes." He also released the cleverly titled *For the Love of Pete* album for Dot Records in 1969. It included a version of the "Theme from *The Hollywood Squares*" with lyrics. The records didn't sell well, but Marshall had his day job on which to fall back. There was also a nighttime version of *The Hollywood Squares* with bigger money and prizes at stake. After 15 years, the show left the air. Marshall then found a lot of work on Broadway and hosted several other much less successful game shows such as *Yahtzee* and *All-Star Blitz*. He has been married three times, and one of his sons, Pete LaCock, is a retired major league baseball player, having played for the Chicago Cubs and Kansas City Royals (thus, he saw little or no postseason action). Nowadays, Marshall lives in Palm Springs, California.

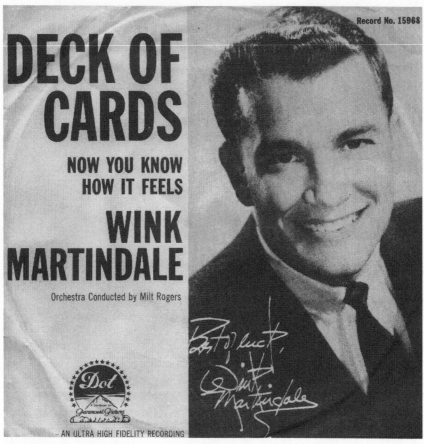

Coincidentally, the man who would later deal out cards on *Gambit* had a Top Ten hit with the clever "Deck of Cards."

WINK MARTINDALE

Most Famous TV Role: host of *Gambit* and *Tic Tac Dough*; **Network:** CBS, NBC, syndicated; **Years:** 1972–1986; **Hit Recording:** "Deck of Cards"; **Labels:** Dot, Ranwood; **Release Years:** 1959–1973; **Matrix:** Dot #15968; **Chart:** #7 *Billboard* Hot 100

Winston Conrad Martindale was born in Jackson, Tennessee, on December 4, 1933. He began his broadcasting career as a teenager on a local Jackson radio station. He was then hired by WHBQ in Memphis—the radio station that played the first Elvis record, "That's All Right, Mama." He was one of the stars of a low-budget black-and-white rock and roll film in 1958 called *Let's Rock*. Martindale performed (lip-synched) "All Love Broke Loose" in the film. It was released on a single (Dot #15728) but was not a big hit. However, the following year, Wink scored a Top Ten spoken word hit called "Deck of Cards" about a soldier who used a deck of cards for his prayer book and Bible. Coincidentally, Wink's most famous game show, *Gambit*, featured a gigantic deck of cards. During the run of *Gambit*, he attempted to resurrect his recording career and signed with the Ranwood label and, tying in to his hit TV show, released a remake of "Deck of Cards" (Ranwood #963). It was not a hit the second time around, and he tried once more with "America: An Affirmation" backed with "The People" (Ranwood #1005), but after this single failed to catch on, he was released from his recording contract. On his very first game show, *What's This Song?* on NBC (it began as a local Los Angeles game show called *What's the Name of this Song?*), he used the name *Win* Martindale, but later reverted back to *Wink*. He hosted several other game shows—*How's Your Mother-in-Law? Words and Music, Las Vegas Gambit, Can You Top This?* and one of his biggest successes, the syndicated remake of *Tic Tac Dough*. He was among the first to be inducted into the Game Show Hall of Fame in Las Vegas in 2007. He was the inspiration for the talking toy called *Mr. Game Show* from the Galoob Company. He has been married twice and had four children with his first wife.

TONY MARTINEZ

Most Famous TV Role: Pepino, the hired hand on *The Real McCoys*; **Network:** ABC, CBS; **Years:** 1957–1963; **Hit Recording:** none; **Labels:** Del-Fi, Kip, RCA Victor; **Release Years:** 1957–1959; **Matrix:** "Mantilla" (RCA Victor #6548), "The Waiting Game" (Kip #220), *The Many Sides of Pepino* (Del-Fi LP #1205); **Chart:** none

Tony Martinez was born in San Juan, Puerto Rico, on January 27, 1920. He moved to New York City to attend the Juilliard School of Music. He was, in fact, a very accomplished musician (he played five instruments) and singer and appeared in small roles in motion pictures, including *Rock around the Clock* in 1956. He was discovered playing in a Hollywood nightclub in 1957 and was instantly cast as Pepino, the hired farmhand for a new ABC sitcom to be called *The Real McCoys*. He is best remembered for referring to Walter Brennan's character on the program as "Señor Grandpa." Even though the role was extremely stereotypical, Martinez was grateful for the six seasons of steady work. Despite the stereotype, Martinez's license plates read "Pepino," and he was proud of his success.

During this period, Martinez also attempted to show the world his vast musical talents and bandleader abilities with "Mantilla" backed with "Campus Merengue" for RCA Victor Records, "The Waiting Game" backed with "You Can't Save Your Love" for Kip Records, and *The Many Sides of Pepino* album for Del-Fi Records. The latter was the same label for which Ritchie Valens recorded, with much more success. After the sitcom was cancelled by CBS in 1963, Martinez ventured into something very special—a nearly 40-year run in *Man of La Mancha* on Broadway and in touring troupes. His last TV appearance came at the age of 80 in 2000 on the defunct Nashville Network. Said cable channel was airing reruns of the sitcom at that time, and aired a reunion of surviving cast members. He died in Las Vegas two years later on September 16, leaving behind five children.

GROUCHO MARX

Most Famous TV Role: host of *You Bet Your Life*; **Network:** NBC; **Years:** 1950–1961; **Hit Recording:** none; **Label:** Decca; **Release Year:** 1952; **Matrix:** "Hooray for Captain Spaulding" (Decca #28158), "Go West Young Man" (Decca #28160); **Chart:** none

Groucho Marx was born Julius Henry Marx in New York City on October 2, 1890. He and his brilliant brothers made 13 popular comedic motion pictures together. Groucho was known for his lack of good posture, mustache, eyebrows, glasses, cigar, and quick wit. After his successes in film he found instant meteoric fame in the new medium of television, beginning in 1950 with a comedy show masked as a quiz show called *You Bet Your Life*. The program began on radio and translated well to the new audience. His famous line, "Say the secret woid and win a hundred dollars," carried through the program's 11-year run. The program's theme song was an instrumental version of "Hooray for Captain Spaulding" from the Marx Brothers' film *Animal Crackers*. Because of the popularity of the TV series, Groucho released a version of the song on the Decca label in 1952, backed with "Omaha, Nebraska." There was also a *Hooray for Captain Spaulding* 10-inch album (Decca #5405). This was followed by "Go West, Young Man" backed with "Show Me a Rose." None of these made a big splash. After the cancellation of *You Bet Your Life*, Marx attempted a similar series on CBS titled *Tell It to Groucho*, but it failed to become a ratings winner and was short-lived. However, his influence upon comedians who followed is immeasurable. He was married three times, each ending in divorce. He had three children from his first two. Marx grew very frail in his 80s, and after contracting pneumonia died on August 19, 1977. His death occurred three days after that of Elvis Presley and, thus, didn't receive the proper attention. He has a star on the Hollywood Walk of Fame.

MARY-KATE AND ASHLEY OLSEN

Most Famous TV Role: Michele Tanner (Mary-Kate and Ashley Olsen, alternating) on *Full House;* **Network:** ABC; **Years:** 1987–1995; **Hit Recording:** none; **Label:** Zoom Express; **Release Years:** 1992–1993; **Matrix:** *Brother for Sale* (Zoom Express LP #35016), *I Am the Cute One* (Zoom Express LP #35038); **Chart:** none

Mary-Kate and Ashley Olsen, the Olsen Twins, were born in Sherman Oaks, California, on June 13, 1986. Contrary to popular belief, they are not identical twins, but did alternate portraying the same character, Michele Tanner, on *Full House* beginning at nine months of age. Because of child labor laws, the twins were used to comply with the number of hours a child could work. They grew up on the show and stayed for the entire run. During the program's long run, the Olsen Twins released a couple of albums for the Zoom Express label. They were six when they released *Brother for Sale* in which they offered their mischievous brother for 50 cents and seven when they released *I Am the Cute One* in which they competed for the title of the cutest. Each had an accompanying video. After *Full House* came to an end in 1995 the girls sought other opportunities, which included a feature film titled *It Takes Two* and another series—the short-lived *Two of a Kind* in 1998 on ABC. There was some very astute marketing behind the twins as well, and this led to a line of clothing, accessories, toys, games, magazines, posters, fragrances, makeup, dolls, and countless other items under the company name of Dualstar. They are among the wealthiest women in show business.

WAYNE MASSEY

Most Famous TV Role: Johnny Drummond on *One Life to Live;* **Network:** ABC; **Years:** 1980–1984; **Hit Recordings:** "With Just One Look in Your Eyes," "You Are My Music, You Are My Song," "When It's Down to Me and You"; **Labels:** Epic, MCA, Polydor; **Release Years:** 1980–1986; **Matrix:** "With Just One Look in Your Eyes" (Epic #05398), "You Are My Music, You Are My Song" (Epic #05693), "When It's Down to Me and You" (Epic #05842); **Chart:** #5, #10, #17, respectively, *Billboard* Country

Wayne Massey was born Donald Wayne Massey in Glendale, California. He is a graduate of Brigham Young University. He got extremely lucky, was discovered, and beginning in 1980, was cast as Johnny Drummond in the long-running soap opera *One Life to Live*. At the same time, he attempted success as a recording star, but initially achieved only very marginal success as a solo performer for the Polydor and MCA Records labels. His first release for Polydor, "The Theme from *One Life to Live*," scraped the very bottom of the charts. He also recorded a *One Life to Live* album (Polydor LP #6309). Massey released eight singles while a member of the show's cast, but didn't make much headway in the recording industry. That is, until he began recording with his third wife, country singer Charly McClain. His biggest successes on the charts came after he decided to leave the soap opera. The duet scored three Top Twenty country hits and toured the country circuit, but Massey quickly tired of the politics of show business and by 1990 had completely removed himself from it. He never looked back.

JERRY MATHERS

Most Famous TV Role: Theodore "Beaver" Cleaver on *Leave It to Beaver*; **Networks:** ABC, CBS; **Years:** 1957–1963; **Hit Recording:** none; **Labels:** Atlantic, White Cliffs; **Years:** 1963–1966; **Matrix:** "Wind-Up Toy" (Atlantic #2156), "Happiness Is Havin'" (White Cliffs #236); **Chart:** none

As the child star of the iconic black-and-white TV sitcom *Leave It to Beaver* for six hilarious seasons, Jerry Mathers effectively captured the wonder and mystery of childhood and the oft confusing adult world surrounding it. Enjoying a seemingly unceasing run in syndication, the Cleaver clan is still warmly welcomed into tens of thousands of homes on a daily basis, including mine.

You might not know, however, that the program's young star also made a few records. Did he record them against his will? Jerry Mathers shared,

> No, I really did want to make the records and I had a lot of fun doing it. Nino Tempo from the duo April and Nino scored the music. Their big hit, of course, was "Deep Purple." Mine was called "Wind-Up Toy" backed with "Doncha Cry" for the legendary Atlantic label in 1963, written by Arthur Resnick and Jeff Barry. I don't recall what recording studio we used, but I do remember we had a large orchestra. "Wind-Up Toy" got a lot of airplay, although it didn't make Top Fifty. We used it as a promotional tool to do appearances at amusement parks and county fairs. The label founders Neshui

Leave It to Beaver star Jerry Mathers with author Bob Leszczak. Mathers recorded "Wind Up Toy" for Atlantic Records during his sitcom's six-year run.

and Ahmet Ertegun came to my house to hear me sing. Afterwards, my father and the Ertegun brothers played Ping-Pong in our backyard while they negotiated the terms for the contract and I listened.

The record's number on the Atlantic label is 2156, and the artist is listed as "Beaver" Jerry Mathers.

Who were some of his favorite recording acts of the 1960s? Mathers replied, "My favorite groups are Cream, Jefferson Airplane, and the Rolling Stones." His love for that sound is apparent in another Mathers recording from 1966 on the White Cliffs label (#236) titled "Happiness Is Havin'" backed with "In Misery." This time around, the artist on the label was listed as Beaver and the Trappers, and Mathers shared, "The Trappers were high school friends of mine. You may know Richard Correll, the drummer. He played my friend Richard Rickover on *Leave It to Beaver*, and went on to become a successful TV sitcom director. Ron Cacabe was on guitar and Jim Seward played bass. I do not remember where that was recorded, although I do recall it was a professional studio."

Few celebrities have copies of their own 45s, but Mathers stated, "I do have copies of the records, and I am always surprised by the number of people that bring one or both of the 45s for me to autograph when I do personal appearances all over the country. I am still very interested in music and play with an old-time music folk group for fun. No, we don't have any plans to record, but I do love to sing and play guitar."

By the way, the record by Beaver and the Trappers is sought after by fans of "garage rock" and often fetches well over a hundred dollars.

DAVID MCCALLUM

Most Famous TV Roles: Illya Kuryakin on *The Man from U.N.C.L.E.*, Dr. Donald "Ducky" Mallard on *NCIS*; **Networks:** CBS, NBC; **Years:** 1964–1968, 2003–present, respectively; **Hit Recording:** "Communication"; **Label:** Capitol; **Release Year:** 1966; **Matrix:** Capitol #5571; **Chart:** #117 *Billboard* Bubbling Under

David McCallum Jr. was born in Glasgow, Scotland, on September 19, 1933. His mother was an accomplished cellist, and his father, David McCallum Sr., was an orchestra leader. David Jr. played the oboe and his life was being geared toward music, that is, until he switched gears and opted to pursue acting. In his teen years, he acted on radio for the BBC. After a series of small roles on television and in motion pictures, McCallum was cast as a Russian agent (at the height of the Cold War) named Illya Kuryakin on NBC's new spy series titled *The Man from U.N.C.L.E.* Robert Vaughn as Napoleon Solo was listed as the star of the program, but McCallum and his Beatle-esque hair style on the show became a phenomenon, with tons of mail received each week from female admirers. During the show's four-season run, McCallum attempted to cash in on his musical roots with a song titled "Communication" for Capitol Records. It featured an all-girl chorus used as backup for McCallum's narration and motorcycle sound effects. The record wasn't a major sensation, but it did spend five weeks on *Billboard*'s Bubbling Under chart. It fared even better in the United Kingdom, peaking at number 32. It was McCallum's only chart single, but he did also have two albums that charted—*Music: A Part of Me* (Capitol LP #2432) and *Music: A Bit More of Me* (Capitol LP #2498). Still bigger things were in the future for him. He had the great fortune to be cast as the medical examiner nicknamed "Ducky" on the original *NCIS* beginning in 2003, and settled in for a historic run of well over a decade. McCallum has been married twice—to actress Jill Ireland from 1956 to 1967 and to Katherine Carpenter since 1967.

DOUG MCCLURE

Most Famous TV Role: Trampas on *The Virginian;* **Network:** NBC; **Years:** 1962–1971; **Hit Recording:** none; **Label:** Polydor; **Release Year:** 1972; **Matrix:** "Use What You Got" (Polydor #14058), "Mr. and Mrs. Untrue" (Polydor #14068); **Chart:** none

Douglas McClure was born in Glendale, California, on May 11, 1935. In his early 20s, he began accruing a long list of TV credits on westerns such as *Death Valley Days, Maverick,* and *The Adventures of Jim Bowie.* Before long, he was cast in his first of many regular TV roles as Frank Flippen on *The Overland Trail* in 1960 on NBC. Said program starred *The Life of Riley's* William Bendix and only lasted a matter of months. McClure immediately jumped into a much more successful show—*Checkmate* on CBS. McClure was seemingly never out of work, and after *Checkmate's* two-season run, he quickly landed his most famous role as Trampas on *The Virginian* and enjoyed a nine-year run. He got to play Trampas again years later on a special episode of *The Fall Guy* with Lee Majors. In 1972 he was cast as Grover on *Search* with Hugh O'Brian and Tony Franciosa.

During the run of this series, McClure branched out and tried for a concurrent career in music. This resulted in a couple of singles for the Polydor label—"Use What You Got" backed with "The Old Messiah" and "Mr. and Mrs. Untrue" backed with "Lighthouse." He wasn't much of a singer, and that fact was quickly exposed in live performances on variety and talk shows. Neither of his singles caught on, but McClure didn't care because he was soon cast in yet another series, *Barbary Coast* with costar William Shatner. This series, set in the 1870s, lasted only a matter of months. After a long string of westerns and dramas, McClure landed a role as Mayor Applegate in a syndicated sitcom called *Out of This World.* Sadly, McClure worked in an era of television in which smoking was considered the norm. Only a short time after his star on the Hollywood Walk of Fame was unveiled, he died of lung cancer on February 5, 1995, at the age of 59. He was married five times.

MICHAEL MCKEAN. *See* LENNY AND THE SQUIGTONES.

Hi-Yo. Game show host and *Tonight Show* announcer Ed McMahon was on his own *Star Search* with the release of this 45.

ED MCMAHON

Most Famous TV Role: announcer/sidekick on *The Tonight Show with Johnny Carson*; **Network:** NBC; **Years:** 1962–1992; **Hit Recording:** none; **Labels:** Cameo, Capitol; **Release Years:** 1967–1971; **Matrix:** "Beautiful Girl" (Cameo #474), "Those Beautiful Girls" (Capitol #3213), *And Me, I'm Ed McMahon* (Cameo LP #2009); **Chart:** none

Ed McMahon was born in Detroit, Michigan, on March 6, 1923, but was raised in Lowell, Massachusetts. He started his announcing career as a bingo caller in Maine. He moved quickly in broadcasting. He began as a radio announcer in Massachusetts and rapidly ascended to WCAU-TV in

Philadelphia, Pennsylvania. He abandoned his career during World War II, in which he was a Marine Corps flight instructor. He was later recalled for duty during the Korean War. His first national broadcast came in 1957 as the announcer for a game show called *Two for the Money* hosted by humorist Sam Levenson. A short time later, he was teamed with Johnny Carson the first time around as the announcer on a game show first called *Do You Trust Your Wife?* and later retitled *Who Do You Trust?* That program ran for five years until Carson was tapped to take the reins of *The Tonight Show* from Jack Paar in October of 1962. McMahon was once again called upon to be Carson's announcer and second banana in this new venture. Said venture led to a historic 30-year run on NBC. McMahon never stood still, and during this time hosted a couple of daytime game shows—*Missing Links* and *Snap Judgment.* Sadly, no episodes of either of his NBC game shows are known to have survived.

While hosting *Snap Judgment*, McMahon also dabbled in recording. He connected with Philadelphia's Cameo Records label and released an album called *And Me, I'm Ed McMahon* and a single titled "Beautiful Girl" backed with "The Loving Heart." However, this came near the end of Cameo Records. The company was experiencing serious cash flow problems at this time, and couldn't actively promote its new releases and folded a short while later after many successful business years. A few years later, McMahon tried yet again, this time with the much more solvent Capitol Records label and recorded a song with a title similar to the A-side of his 45 on Cameo. This one was called "Those Beautiful Girls" backed with "Why Don't You Love Me Blues?" but the result was similar—it was not a hit. McMahon wisely stayed with television and eventually hosted the successful *Star Search* program, was a regular fixture on the yearly *Jerry Lewis MDA Telethon*, worked with Dick Clark on his *Bloopers* specials, and was seen regularly in those commercials for Publishers Clearing House contests. He uttered his final "Here's Johnny" on May 22, 1992, when Carson walked away from *The Tonight Show* and was very rarely seen again. McMahon, however, remained busy after Carson left and did numerous guest-star appearances on episodic TV shows. He severely injured his neck after a fall in 2007 and was never quite the same. He died on June 23, 2009, and was honored posthumously by the Philadelphia Broadcasters Hall of Fame in 2010.

EDDIE MEKKA

Most Famous TV Role: Carmine Ragusa on *Laverne and Shirley*; **Network:** ABC; **Years:** 1976–1983; **Hit Recording:** none; **Label:** American General; **Release Year:** 1979; **Matrix:** "Big Boss Man" (American General #100); **Chart:** none

Rudolph Edward Mekjian was born in Worcester, Massachusetts, on June 14, 1952. After a stint on Broadway in *The Lieutenant*, as Eddie Mekka he auditioned for and won the role of Carmine Ragusa (a.k.a. "the Big Ragoo") on Paramount's *Laverne and Shirley*. He is of Armenian heritage, but portrayed an Italian American singer and dancer on the program from 1976 to 1983. Even though the sitcom was set in the 1950s, Mekka released a disco record in 1979 for the American General Records label. The song was called "Big Boss Man" and was included in the soundtrack for a very forgettable 1980 motion picture titled *Mafia on the Bounty*. Neither the movie nor the record caught on. Since the cancellation of *Laverne and Shirley* in 1983, Mekka has amassed an impressive list of guest starring roles on episodic TV shows such as *Moonlighting, Crossing Jordan*, and *24*, and has reunited with Cindy Williams on a couple of projects. He has been married twice and has one child.

BURGESS MEREDITH

Most Famous TV Role: the Penguin on *Batman*; **Network:** ABC; **Years:** 1966–1968; **Hit Recording:** none; **Label:** ABC, Colpix; **Release Year:** 1964–1966; **Matrix:** "No Goodbye" (Colpix #690), "The Escape" (ABC #10798); **Chart:** none

Oliver Burgess Meredith was born in Cleveland, Ohio, on November 16, 1907. He graduated from Amherst College and appeared on Broadway and film beginning in 1930. He interrupted his show business career to serve in the air force during World War II. After resuming his acting career, and with the advent of television, he found steady work on countless anthology drama shows such as *Robert Montgomery Presents, Celanese Theatre, Omnibus*, and *The United States Steel Hour*. He also starred in four memorable episodes of *The Twilight Zone*, including the famous "Time Enough at Last" episode in 1959. He was cast as Principal Woodridge on the James Franciscus series *Mr. Novak* from 1964 to 1965. During that time, Meredith released a single for the Capitol label—"No Goodbye" backed with "Home in the Meadow." The record was not a hit and there were no follow-ups for Capitol. However, years later when Meredith earned a recurring role as The Penguin on TV's *Batman* series on ABC, he released a show-related record titled "The Capture" backed with "The Escape." The novelty record came with a black-and-white picture sleeve and has become somewhat of a collector's item. It's credited as "an original narration by Burgess Meredith" and is chock-full of the Penguin's famous "quacking" sounds from the program.

In the 1970s, Meredith was cast as a regular in the short-lived *Search* on NBC and in the 1980s on the *All in the Family* spinoff titled *Gloria* on CBS. His greatest successes came as Mickey Goldmill in the *Rocky* series of motion pictures. One of his last roles, Grandpa, came in 1996 in the Jack Lemmon/Walter Matthau motion picture sequel titled *Grumpier Old Men*. Meredith died on September 9, 1997, at the age of 89 from melanoma. He was married four times, and his autobiography was titled *So Far, So Good* in 1994. He is remembered as one of the finest actors of the century.

DON MEREDITH

Most Famous TV Role: color commentator for *NFL Monday Night Football*; **Network:** ABC; **Years:** 1970–1984; **Hit Recording:** none; **Label:** Dot; **Release Year:** 1973; **Matrix:** "Travelin' Man" (Dot #17489); **Chart:** none

Joseph Don Meredith was born in Mount Vernon, Texas, on April 10, 1938. He was very adept at football and basketball in high school, but also performed in many school plays. He played college football at Southern Methodist University. He was taken by the upstart Dallas Cowboys in 1960 and was the backup quarterback until getting the starting job in 1963. He stayed with the team until his early retirement in 1969. He was NFL Player of the Year in 1966 and was named to the Pro Bowl three consecutive years. He made the quick transition to color commentator for the new *NFL Monday Night Football* program on ABC beginning the following year. His nickname was Dandy Don and in 1973 tried to parlay his TV success into success on the record charts. For the Dot label, he released one single—"Travelin' Man" backed with "Them That Ain't Got It Can't Lose." He did, however, broaden his horizons with a series of Lipton Tea commercials. He was married three times and had three children. He died suddenly after suffering a brain hemorrhage on December 5, 2010, at the age of 72. In 2007 he was the recipient of the Pro Football Hall of Fame's Pete Rozelle Radio-Television Award.

ALYSSA MILANO

Most Famous TV Role: Samantha Micelli on *Who's the Boss?* Phoebe Halliwell on *Charmed*; **Network:** ABC, WB; **Years:** 1984–1992, 1998–2006, respectively; **Hit Recording:** *Alyssa*; **Label:** Canyon International; **Release Year:** 1989; **Matrix:** Canyon International LP #00026; **Chart:** #15 Oricon Charts, Japan

Alyssa Milano was born in Brooklyn, New York, on December 19, 1972. Because of crime in their neighborhood, the family moved to Staten Island when Alyssa was quite young. After several off-Broadway productions, she earned the role of Samantha on ABC's *Who's the Boss?* Suddenly, the East Coast accent Alyssa had been trained to lose was needed for the part. Once it was obvious that the program was a hit, the family moved from Staten Island to Hollywood. Her look and mannerisms on the show were said to be the inspiration for the animated Ariel in *The Little Mermaid*. During the sitcom's eight-season run, Milano attempted a successful recording career, and beginning in 1989 released numerous albums that were very successful in Japan, but not in the United States. Among the highlights are the *Alyssa* (Canyon International #00026) and *Locked inside a Dream* albums (Canyon International #00204). She also participated in the 1991 "Voices That Care" single (Giant #19350) released as a morale booster for U.S. troops involved in Desert Storm. Milano was a member of the choir on that single, in effect, her only chart hit in the states. She was also a cast member on two other hit shows, *Melrose Place* and *Charmed*. She has been married twice and has two children.

MIKE MINOR

Most Famous TV Role: Steve Elliott on *Petticoat Junction;* **Network:** CBS; **Years:** 1966–1970; **Hit Recording:** none; **Label:** Dot; **Release Years:** 1966–1973; **Matrix:** *This Is Mike Minor* (Dot LP #25750); **Chart:** none

Not to be confused with the professional baseball pitcher, Mike Minor the actor and singer was born Michael Fedderson, the son of Don Fedderson, producer of *My Three Sons* and *Family Affair*. Mike was born in San Francisco, California, on December 7, 1940, exactly one year before "the day that will live in infamy." He was performing as a singer beginning in his early teens. His character, a pilot named Steve Elliott, crashed his plane in Hooterville and was cared for by Betty Jo Bradley, played by Linda Kaye Henning, on *Petticoat Junction* and became a regular. After his recovery, Steve and Betty Jo became an item and were married both on- and offscreen. Minor was a regular on the sitcom from 1966 to 1970 and often sang on the show. He also made numerous records for the Dot label during this period. He released an album called *This Is Mike Minor* in 1966, and also a few singles for Dot, including "Room Full of Roses" backed with "Thank You, Love" (Dot #17044). Despite the show's popularity, none of his records clicked. After *Petticoat Junction* came to an end in 1970, Minor made the rounds of the daytime soap operas—*As the World Turns,*

Petticoat Junction costar Mike Minor sang often on the sitcom, but failed to have even a "minor" hit single.

The Edge of Night, All My Children, and *Another World.* Sandwiched around his five-year marriage to Linda Kaye Henning, Minor was married twice more and has one child from his first marriage. His other claim to semi-fame is singing the first season theme ("Primrose Lane") for ABC's *The Smith Family* starring Henry Fonda. He is passionate about the game of golf and, as of this writing, still plays with a celebrity group known as the Hollywood Hackers.

THE MONKEES

Most Famous TV Role: stars of their own musical sitcom, *The Monkees*; **Network:** NBC; **Years:** 1966–1968; **#1 Hit Recordings:** "Daydream Believer," "I'm a Believer," "Last Train to Clarksville"; **Label:** Colgems; **Release Years:** 1966–1968; **Matrix:** "Daydream Believer" (Colgems #1012), "I'm a Believer" (Colgems #1002), "Last Train to Clarksville" (Colgems #1001); **Chart:** #1 *Billboard* Hot 100 (all three songs)

The Monkees TV series was inspired by the Beatles' antics in their first motion picture, *A Hard Day's Night*. The group was assembled for the TV series. Several big name performers, such as Stephen Stills, Danny Hutton, Harry Nilsson, and Paul Williams auditioned for the show, but were not cast. The final four were Peter Tork, Mike Nesmith, Micky Dolenz, and Davy Jones. They did have musical experience—Nesmith had written a song titled "Different Drum"; Dolenz had recorded, unsuccessfully, for the Challenge Records label; Davy Jones had recorded for the Colgems subsidiary Colpix Records; and Peter Tork was a fairly accomplished guitar player. Dolenz had the most TV experience, having starred in the 1950s series *Circus Boy* under the name Mickey Braddock.

The manic *Monkees* sitcom, set at 1334 North Beechwood Drive, was an immediate hit, especially with young girls, and the Monkees became an instant presence on the record charts, too. They had some legendary people behind the scenes—Don Kirshner and songwriters such as Tommy Boyce and Bobby Hart, Neil Sedaka, Carole King and Gerry Goffin, and Neil Diamond. The group scored three number 1 singles (and several others that reached Top Ten) and four number 1 albums—*The Monkees* (Colgems #101), *More of the Monkees* (Colgems #102), *Headquarters* (Colgems #103), and *Pisces, Aquarius, Capricorn & Jones, Ltd.* (Colgems #104). All four albums went multiplatinum for the Colgems label—an imprint of the Columbia/Screen Gems Company. Initially, because of the show's frantic filming schedule, the guys didn't play their own instruments, but later insisted upon it. They also, eventually, got to wrangle control of the material and releases, but were not as successful once that transition occurred. The program's first season garnered a coveted Emmy Award for Outstanding Comedy Series. Despite the sitcom's popularity, it didn't finish in the Top Thirty in either of its two seasons. After the show ended its two-season run, the Monkees appeared in a motion picture titled *Head*, but it was not quite the success it was expected to be. The soundtrack album failed to reach the Top Forty (Colgems #5008). The guys officially broke up in 1970. *The Monkees* sitcom has enjoyed a long run in syndication reruns. A 1986 reunion tour was immensely successful and included another platinum album—*Then and Now: The Best of the Monkees* (Arista #8432). Just as another was being organized in 2012, Davy Jones died suddenly on Leap Day at the age of 66.

CANDY MOORE

Most Famous TV Role: Chris Carmichael on *The Lucy Show*; **Network:** CBS; **Years:** 1962–1965; **Hit Recording:** none; **Label:** Sable; **Release Year:** 1962; **Matrix:** "It's Your Turn Now" (Sable #101); **Chart:** none

The tiny Sable label was unable to get *The Lucy Show*'s Candy Moore a hit single. Moore did get her picture on the record label, however.

Candy Moore was born as Candace Lee Klaasen in Maplewood, New Jersey, on August 26, 1947. She guest starred on a number of episodic programs such as *One Step Beyond, Leave It to Beaver, My Three Sons, Rawhide, The Loretta Young Show,* and *Wagon Train.* She then starred in an unsold pilot titled *Time Out for Ginger*—a pilot that costarred Margaret Hamilton of *The Wizard of Oz.* Moore's biggest break was being cast as Lucille Ball's daughter in Ball's second sitcom (and first without Desi) called *The Lucy Show* in 1962. She played Lucy's eldest of two children, Chris Carmichael, famous for always saying, "Motherrrrrrrr" in disgust when house rules or curfews were enforced. She had a younger brother named Jerry on the program, played by Jimmy Garrett. Divorcee Vivian Bagley (Vance) lived there, too, with her son, Sherman Bagley, played by Ralph Hart. During the program's first season, Candy Moore also cut a record for the Sable Records label, issued with a now rare picture sleeve. The record was called "It's Your Turn, Now" backed with "Living Stone," and despite the popularity of Lucy's new series, the record bombed and no follow-ups were issued.

In 1965, *The Lucy Show* was retooled as Vivian Vance announced her retirement, and suddenly Lucy Carmichael was childless and living in California, and her best friend was Mary Jane (Mary Jane Croft). The only carryover from the other format was Lucy's boss at the bank, Theodore J. Mooney (Gale Gordon), who, inexplicably, also moved to California. Candy Moore was never a regular in a series again (although she did guest star on *The Donna Reed Show* several times with different character names). Over a decade later, in 1980, she earned the small role of Linda in Martin Scorsese's *Raging Bull,* but for the most part disappeared from the public eye. She was briefly married to character actor Paul Gleason—they have one daughter. She is alleged to have been the model for the album cover for the Cars on their *Candy-O* album from 1979 (Elektra #507). Today she lives in Beverly Hills and is a journalist and author.

GARRY MOORE

Most Famous TV Roles: host of *The Garry Moore Show* and *I've Got a Secret;* **Network:** CBS; **Years:** 1952–1964; **Hit Recording:** none; **Labels:** Columbia, Warner Bros.; **Release Year:** 1958–1959; **Matrix:** "Them There Eyes" (Warner Bros. #5061), *My Kind of Music* (Columbia LP #717), *Garry Moore Presents That Wonderful Year 1930* (Warner Bros. LP #1283); **Chart:** none

Garry Moore was born Thomas Garrison Morfit III in Baltimore, Maryland, on January 31, 1915. Dropping out of college was not detrimental to

The Garry Moore Show's popular "That Wonderful Year" segment led to the release of "Them There Eyes." However, the eyes didn't have it.

his career. In fact, he dropped out to pursue work in radio and became a success. He became Garry Moore as the result of a radio contest aimed at shortening his birth name—the winner earned $100. With the advent of television, he briefly hosted a couple of half-hour variety shows for CBS in 1950 and 1951. He was then named as host of a new game show/panel show called *I've Got a Secret* in 1952—a show he hosted until 1964. In 1958, he took on double duty on CBS with an eponymous variety series with costar and lifelong friend Durward Kirby. The program also costarred some very funny ladies—Marion Lorne, Dorothy Loudon, and Carol Burnett. During the run of this variety series, Moore released record albums for both Columbia Records and Warner Bros. Records. The latter was inspired by an ongoing feature on his TV show called "That Wonder-

ful Year." The album, *Garry Moore Presents That Wonderful Year 1930*, included music from that year. "Them There Eyes," a cut on the album, was
released as a single. It may have been a popular feature on the TV show,
but that didn't translate to a flurry of record sales and no other albums in
the series were released.

Moore decided to retire in 1964 when *The Garry Moore Show* was cancelled. He also surrendered hosting duties on *I've Got a Secret* at the same
time and went on a trip around the world. His retirement, however, was
short-lived and he attempted a TV comeback with a new variety series in
1966, again called *The Garry Moore Show*, but this version only lasted 13
weeks. A few years later he hosted the syndicated version of *To Tell the
Truth* until being diagnosed with throat cancer (a long-time smoker, always seen with a cigarette on camera), at which point Joe Garagiola took
the reins. Moore survived for many years after successful throat surgery,
but eventually succumbed to emphysema on November 28, 1993, at the
age of 78. He is not to be confused with Gary Moore of the rock band
called Thin Lizzy.

ROGER MOORE

Most Famous TV Role: Simon Templar on *The Saint*; **Network:** NBC; **Years:**
1962–1969; **Hit Recording:** none; **Label:** Warner Bros.; **Release Year:** 1959;
Matrix: *We Wish You a Merry Christmas* (Warner Bros. LP #1337), "Where
Does Love Go?" (CBS #2014); **Chart:** none

Roger Moore was born in Stockwell, London, England, on October 14,
1927. He served in the military shortly after World War II, and became a
captain. After serving, he turned his attention to acting and started as a
model for print advertising. His first film contract came in 1954 for MGM
and was a disaster—none of his films became hits. He was let out of his
contract early and turned to television. In his first series, he portrayed the
title character *Ivanhoe* in 1958, and then Silky Harris in *The Alaskans* for
Warner Bros. in 1959. At this time, Warner Bros. gathered most of their TV
stars for a seasonal album on their own Warner Bros. label. Roger Moore's
contribution to the album is a recited cut titled "Once in David's Royal
City." The album was released in 1959 as *We Wish You a Merry Christmas:
15 Christmas Favorites by Warner Bros. Stars.* From there, he costarred for
a single season on *Maverick* as cousin Beau Maverick from 1960 to 1961,
again for Warner Bros., and then he almost instantly found work as Simon
Templar in *The Saint*. The first seasons of the program were syndicated
by ITC and filmed in England. Because of its popularity, it then became a
regular prime-time NBC series for two seasons on NBC from 1967 to 1969.

Sometime during the period of 1965–1967, Moore released a 45 rpm record for CBS Records called "Where Does Love Go?" backed with "Tomorrow after Tomorrow" in the United Kingdom. It came with a picture sleeve, and once again featured the dulcet tones of Moore in recitation form. It wasn't a hit, but he had bigger and better things on his plate. Beginning with *Live and Let Die* in 1973 and ending with *A View to a Kill* in 1985, Moore portrayed Bond, James Bond, in seven motion pictures. He would actually have started much earlier than 1973 had he not been contractually obligated to TV. He has been married four times and has long been involved in charity work for UNICEF. He got a star on the Hollywood Walk of Fame in 2007. He has written several books about the Bond experience, the most recent of which, *Bond on Bond*, was issued in 2012 to tie into the 50th anniversary of the first Bond film.

GARRETT MORRIS

Most Famous TV Roles: regular on *Saturday Night Live*, Earl on *Two Broke Girls*; **Networks:** CBS, NBC; **Years:** 1975–1980, 2011–present, respectively; **Hit Recording:** none; **Labels:** MCA; **Release Year:** 1979; **Matrix:** "I Wanna Be a Cowboy but I'm Too Short" (MCA #41243), *Saturday Night Sweet* (MCA LP #51198); **Chart:** none

Garrett Morris was born in New Orleans, Louisiana, on February 1, 1937. He studied at the Juilliard School of Music and was a soloist with the Harry Belafonte Singers for a time. He also performed in the Broadway musical *Hallelujah, Baby*, among others before becoming one of the original cast members on *Saturday Night Live* in 1975. Likely his most famous character on that program was sports figure Chico Escuela, who, in broken English, uttered the phrase, "Baseball has been berry, berry good to me." He was also known for his many celebrity impressions on the program, including Louis Armstrong, James Brown, and Sammy Davis Jr. Near the end of his stay on *SNL*, Morris released an album titled *Saturday Night Sweet* for MCA Records. One of the album cuts, a disco song titled "I Wanna Be a Cowboy but I'm Too Short in the Saddle" was released as a single in 1979, but didn't rustle up a huge amount of sales. After several years of guest-starring roles, Morris was cast as Martin Lawrence's first boss on *Martin*, but when Morris was shot in a robbery attempt he had to bow out of the role to recuperate. After recovering totally, he surfaced in a regular role as Uncle Junior on *The Jamie Foxx Show*, and most recently earned the recurring role of Earl on CBS's *Two Broke Girls*.

GREG MORRIS

Most Famous TV Role: Barney Collier on *Mission: Impossible;* **Network:** CBS; **Years:** 1966–1973; **Hit Recording:** none; **Label:** Dot; **Release Year:** 1968; **Matrix:** "Come Rain or Come Shine" (Dot #22948), *For You* (Dot LP #25851); **Chart:** none

Francis Gregory Morris was born in Cleveland, Ohio, on September 27, 1933. He attended the University of Iowa where he worked on the college radio station and also participated in school plays. He secured a few guest-starring roles on episodic TV shows such as *The Twilight Zone*, as well as a couple of episodes of *The Dick Van Dyke Show*, including the popular "That's My Boy" episode in which Rob believes that when Laura gave birth, the baby was switched in the hospital. Morris's biggest break came when he was cast as Barney Collier on CBS's spy thriller, *Mission: Impossible*. Morris remained with the program from 1966 to 1973. His next regular role was as Lieutenant David Nelson on Robert Urich's ABC drama series *Vegas*. He made a few guest appearances on the new, short-lived version of *Mission: Impossible* on which his son, Phil Morris, had a regular role. Greg Morris was diagnosed with brain cancer in the 1990s and died young, at the age of only 62, on August 27, 1996. He left behind his only bride, Leona, and three children. He is alleged to have seen the Tom Cruise movie version of the series shortly before his death, and was not at all pleased.

HOWARD MORRIS. *See* THE THREE HAIRCUTS.

DONNY MOST

Most Famous TV Role: Ralph Malph on *Happy Days;* **Network:** ABC; **Years:** 1974–1983; **Hit Recording:** none; **Label:** Casablanca, United Artists; **Release Year:** 1977–1980; **Matrix:** "I Only Want What's Mine" (Casablanca #2248), "All Roads Lead Back to You" (United Artists #871), *Donny Most* (United Artists LP #696); **Chart:** none

Donny Most was born in Brooklyn, New York, on August 8, 1953. While attending Lehigh University, he dropped out before graduating to pursue a show business career. Most's first TV work came in guest-starring roles on episodic TV shows such as *Emergency!* and *Police Story*. In 1974, he earned a regular role on a new sitcom called *Happy Days*. His character in this period piece was called Ralph Malph, a red-headed teenager whose favorite phrase was "Hot-cha-cha." His best friends were Richie and Potsie, and he was often teased by Fonzie. During the run of the show, he also attempted a recording career. He released an album called *Donny Most* and a couple of singles—"All Roads Lead Back to You" backed with "Better to Forget Him" and "One of These Days" backed with "Early Morning"—for the United Artists label in 1976. These singles went absolutely nowhere. He tried again a few years later with a single titled "I Only Want What's Mine" backed with "Sharing Our Love" (Casablanca #2248), but had the same result. Most stayed with the sitcom through 1983 and then decided to move on. He then found a lot of voice work for animated programs such as *Teen Wolf* and *Dungeons and Dragons*. In recent years he changed his professional name to *Don* Most. He is married to Morgan Most and they have two children.

MR. T.

Most Famous TV Role: Sergeant Bosco B. A. Baracus on *The A Team*; **Network:** NBC; **Years:** 1983–1987; **Hit Recording:** none; **Label:** Columbia, MCA, RCA Victor; **Release Years:** 1984–1988; **Matrix:** "The Ten Commandments of Love" (Columbia #04589), "Don't Talk to Strangers" (Columbia #04701), "Treat Your Mother Right" (MCA #53481); **Chart:** none

Laurence Tureaud was born in Chicago, Illinois, on May 21, 1952. He is the youngest of 12 children. He studied martial arts and was quite proficient in wrestling and football. In fact, he went to college on a football scholarship but didn't finish. After a stint in the army, he tried out for the Green Bay Packers, but a bad knee put the kibosh on his being selected. He then found work as a bouncer and a bodyguard. He got to take part in an NBC TV show called *America's Toughest Bouncer*, and came to the attention of Sylvester Stallone, who selected him for *Rocky III*. As Clubber Lang, Mr. T uttered his famous "I pity the fool" line. His sudden popularity led to his most famous role—that of B. A. Baracus on NBC's long-running series *The A Team*. On the program, he portrayed an ex-army commando on the run with three others. During his five-season run on the series, he also made a few records. He wasn't much of a singer and performed his songs somewhere between singing, reciting, and grunting. Most of his songs had a message aimed at kids—"Don't Talk to Strangers" and "Treat Your Mother Right" being prime examples. None of these became big hits even though kids were a huge part of his fan base. After

The A Team ended in 1987, Mr. T. quickly found another show—*T and T,* on which he portrayed T. S. Turner. That program ran from 1988 to 1990. He briefly hosted a show for the TV Land network called *I Pity the Fool* in 2006, and he was inducted into the WWE Hall of Fame in 2014.

MARTIN MULL

Most Famous TV Role: Barth Gimble, host of *Fernwood Tonight* and *America 2-Night;* **Network:** syndicated; **Years:** 1977–1978; **Hit Recording:** none; **Label:** ABC, Capricorn, Elektra; **Release Years:** 1977–1979; **Matrix:** "Santafly" (Capricorn #282), "Bombed Away" (ABC #12251), "Get Up, Get Down" (ABC #12304), "The Fruit Song" (Elektra #46056), "Bernie Don't Disco" (Elektra #46057), *Sex and Violins* (ABC LP #1064); **Chart:** none

Martin Mull was born in Chicago, Illinois, on August 18, 1943. He studied painting in school, but gravitated to the performing arts instead. He portrayed both Barth and Garth Gimble on *Mary Hartman, Mary Hartman*. His Barth character earned the spinoff series called *Fernwood Tonight* and later *America 2-Night* with cohost Fred Willard. During this period, Mull released an album titled *Sex and Violins* and numerous singles such as "Bombed Away" backed with "Boogie Man" and "Get Up, Get Down" backed with "The Humming Song" for ABC Records. There was also "Santafly" (a holiday parody of "Superfly") backed with "Santa Doesn't Cop Out on Dope" for the Capricorn label and "The Fruit Song" backed with "Pig in a Blanket" as well as "Bernie Don't Disco" backed with "Run and Run" for the Elektra label. Prior to his success on TV, Mull did make the music charts with a takeoff on "Dueling Banjos" from *Deliverance* called "Dueling Tubas" (Capricorn #19) in 1972. It reached number 92 on the Hot 100. After the cancellation of *America 2-Night*, Mull jumped from short-lived series to short-lived series, including *Domestic Life, His & Hers, The Jackie Thomas Show,* and the animated *Family Dog*. After getting these flops under his belt, he fared much better with recurring roles on *Roseanne, Sabrina the Teenage Witch, 'Til Death,* and *Two and a Half Men*. He also appeared in several popular films, including *Mr. Mom, Mrs. Doubtfire, Jingle All the Way,* and *Clue*. Mull's been married three times and he has one daughter.

EDDIE MURPHY

Most Famous TV Role: regular on *Saturday Night Live;* **Network:** NBC; **Years:** 1980–1985; **Hit Recording:** "Party All the Time"; **Label:** Columbia; **Release Year:** 1985; **Matrix:** Columbia #05609; **Chart:** #2 *Billboard* Hot 100

Edward Regan Murphy was born in Brooklyn, New York, on April 3, 1961. His dad died when he was very young, and when his mom took ill, he was put into foster care. His time in foster care influenced much of his comedy, and he was writing and performing his own routines while a teenager. He earned a stint on *Saturday Night Live* from 1980 to 1985 and developed characters such as Buckwheat, Gumby, and Mr. Robinson. During his time on the show, he released a marginally successful single titled "Boogie in Your Butt" backed with "Enough Is Enough" (Columbia #03209). After that one, he recorded a song written by funk superstar Rick James called "Party All the Time." It became a huge platinum single and just missed number 1 on the Hot 100. His only other chart single, "Put Your Mouth on Me" (Columbia #68897), was cowritten by Eddie and Narada Michael Walden. It reached the Top Thirty. Murphy also released two popular stand-up comedy specials—*Delirious* and *Raw*. He is as famous for his hit movies (*Beverly Hills Cop, Coming to America, 48 Hours, Trading Places*) as his bombs (*The Adventures of Pluto Nash, Holy Man, I Spy, Metro, Norbit*). He more than redeemed himself for those missteps with his brilliant voice work in the *Shrek* series, and was nominated for an Academy Award for his role as James "Thunder" Early in *Dreamgirls*. Eddie has a star on the Hollywood Walk of Fame and has five children from his marriage to Nicole Mitchell. He has several other children from three other relationships. As of this writing, a *Beverly Hills Cop 4* is slated for 2016 release, and Murphy was the recipient of the 2015 Mark Twain Prize for American Humor.

JAN MURRAY

Most Famous TV Role: host of *Treasure Hunt;* **Network:** ABC, NBC; **Years:** 1956–1959; **Hit Recording:** none; **Label:** MGM; **Release Year:** 1958; **Matrix:** "Treasure Hunt" (MGM #12715); **Chart:** none

Jan Murray was born as Murray Janofsky, in the Bronx, New York, on October 4, 1916. He took an interest in comedy routines as a small boy and was soon performing his own. He worked on the Vaudeville stage and then the Borscht Belt in the Catskill Mountains. He was there in television's infancy with a series of game shows such as *Go Lucky, Meet Your Match,* and *Dollar a Second* before his successful stint as the original host of *Treasure Hunt.* While emceeing that program, he released a 45 rpm single for the MGM label appropriately titled "Treasure Hunt" (it was backed with "So Long, Au Revoir"). Murray wasn't much of a singer, but he gave it the old college try. The TV show was a hit but not the single, and no follow-up singles were released. After *Treasure Hunt* ended its run, Murray continued his stand-up comedy work in nightclubs and on countless variety shows. He was also a celebrity guest on countless game shows and hosted a few more of his own—*Jan Murray's Charge Account* (sometimes called *The Jan Murray Show*) and *Chain Letter*. He also showed off his acting chops in numerous motion pictures (*Thunder Alley; A Man Called Dagger; History of the World, Part I; Tarzan and the Great River*) and episodic TV shows (*Car 54, Where Are You? Dr. Kildare; The Lucy Show; Love American Style; The Joey Bishop Show; Fantasy Island; The Practice*; and *The Fall Guy*). He was married twice and had four children. Murray was passionate about the game of golf, but had to give up it and performing because of severe asthma. Murray died at the age of 89 on July 2, 2006. He has a star on the Palm Springs Walk of Stars.

LORENZO MUSIC

Most Famous TV Role: Carlton the doorman on *Rhoda*; **Network:** CBS; **Years:** 1974–1978; **Hit Recording:** none; **Label:** United Artists; **Release Year:** 1977; **Matrix:** "The Girl in 510" (United Artists #64); **Chart:** none

Lorenzo Music was born as Gerald David Music in Brooklyn, New York (but raised in Duluth, Minnesota), on May 2, 1937. At the University of Duluth, he met Henrietta, the future Mrs. Music. They formed a comedy act and worked as Gerald and His Hen. He later changed his name to Lorenzo Music and found periodic work on *The Smothers Brothers Comedy Hour*. He was also a talented writer and penned scripts for *Love American Style, The Mary Tyler Moore Show, The Bob Newhart Show*, and *Rhoda*. He played a very funny recurring character on *Rhoda*—Carlton the doorman. He was never seen on camera, but had many of the funniest lines on the show, heard only on the intercom in Rhoda's New York apartment. While working on this program, Music released a single (as Carlton, the door-man) titled "The Girl in 510" backed with "Who Is It?" The record wasn't a hit but was funny nonetheless. His distinctive voice was also utilized for the animated *Garfield* TV specials and the *Garfield and Friends* series. Music and his wife briefly hosted a syndicated nightly series titled *The Lorenzo and Henrietta Music Show*. Music died at the young age of 64 on August 4, 2001, from cancer.

N

JIM NABORS

Most Famous TV Role: Gomer Pyle on *The Andy Griffith Show* and *Gomer Pyle, U.S.M.C.*; **Network:** CBS; **Years:** 1962–1969; **#1 Hit Recording:** *Jim Nabors Christmas Album*; **Label:** Columbia; **Release Year:** 1967; **Matrix:** Columbia LP #9531; **Chart:** #1 *Billboard* Top Pop Albums

James Thurston Nabors was born in Sylacauga, Alabama, on June 12, 1930. He attended the University of Alabama. He briefly lived in New York City and worked for the United Nations, but his asthma caused him to move to the drier air in Southern California. There, he was a film editor for NBC by day and a club performer by night. He was discovered there by Bill Dana and brought over to the struggling *Steve Allen Show*, but only appeared a few times before the series was cancelled. Luckily Andy Griffith caught his act at the same nightclub and that was the big boost Nabors's career needed. He portrayed the goodhearted hayseed Gomer Pyle on *The Andy Griffith Show*, and was so popular he earned his own CBS spinoff titled *Gomer Pyle, U.S.M.C.* Nabors's nightclub act consisted of speaking like Gomer, but singing in a rich, powerful baritone voice. During the five-year run of his spinoff sitcom, Nabors released numerous albums for Columbia Records, and earned three gold records—*Jim Nabors Sings Love Me with All Your Heart* (Columbia #9358), *The Lord's Prayer and Other Sacred Songs* (Columbia #9716), and the number 1 smash called *Jim Nabors' Christmas Album* (a hit every Christmas from 1967–73). As Gomer, he also recorded a song titled "Gomer Says Hey" on his *Shazam* album (Columbia LP #2368). After *Gomer Pyle, U.S.M.C.* ended in 1969, Nabors jumped to a variety series called *The Jim Nabors Hour*, also on CBS. A couple of the regulars from his sitcom followed him to the variety show (Ronnie Schell, Frank Sutton). During the two-season run of this show, Nabors scored yet another Top Forty album titled *The Jim Nabors Hour* (Columbia #30129) and a sequel called *For the Good Times/The Jim Nabors Hour* (Columbia #30449) that peaked at number 75.

After his variety series was cancelled, he grew weary of prime-time television and opted to mostly perform in stage productions and concerts, although he was persuaded into regular work on a couple of Sid and Marty Krofft shows—*The Krofft Supershow* and *The Lost Saucer*. He did, however, come back year after year to the debut episode of each season's *Carol Burnett Show* kickoff (Burnett considered him her good luck charm). He agreed to appear in the reunion special *Return to Mayberry* in 1986, but did very little else for the small screen. In 1994, he contracted hepatitis B, and it resulted in liver failure necessitating a transplant. Said transplant was hugely successful and Nabors was extremely grateful for this new lease on life. He got a star on the Hollywood Walk of Fame in 1991, and in 2013, immediately after same-sex marriage became legal in the state of Washington, Nabors married his longtime partner, Stan Cadwallader.

JACK NARZ

Most Famous TV Role: host of *Dotto, Now You See It,* and *Seven Keys;* **Network:** ABC, CBS, NBC; **Years:** 1958, 1961–1964, 1974–1975; **Hit Recording:** none; **Label:** Dot; **Release Year:** 1958; **Matrix:** *Sing the Folk Hits with Jack Narz* (Dot LP #25244); **Chart:** none

---

John Lawrence "Jack" Narz Jr. was born November 13, 1922, in Louisville, Kentucky. He and his younger brother, Jim, both sought a similar calling in the entertainment industry. Jack's son, David Narz, recalled,

> My dad, after gaining some momentum in the business, urged his brother, Jim, to come out and give it a try. After a short time, both brothers, Jack and Jim, had the same agent. However, in early TV, if one program was sponsored by Ford and another by Chevrolet, having two guys with the same last name pledging their allegiance to competing automobile manufacturers appeared as a conflict. After a lunch meeting with their agent at the legendary Brown Derby, they emerged as Jack Narz and Tom Kennedy. They did consider the name Jim Kennedy for a while, but thought there might be confusion with an up-and-coming politician named Kennedy. Jim was dropped and they went with Tom. He did use the name Jim Narz on *Dr. IQ* and *Words about Music*, and my dad was Johnny Narz briefly on *Place the Face* when the host was Jack Smith (they couldn't have a pair of Jacks). However, when Bill Cullen took over the hosting duties on that show, it was no longer an issue. Cullen became a great friend and eventually a brother-in-law.

Narz's other early credits include being the announcer for the kids' show *Space Patrol*, and the on-screen announcer for Betty White's first TV sitcom, the long-running *Life with Elizabeth*. The program was divided into three segments each week, and Narz would set the scene for each of the short comedy vignettes. Jack's son, David, recalled,

> One of the biggest breaks for my dad was *The Bob Crosby Show*. Occasionally Bob wouldn't make it in, and my dad would take the reins, and he would frequently sing. I think that exposure led to my dad getting to record an album titled *Sing the Folk Hits with Jack Narz* for Dot Records (#25244). He is pictured on the cover with a piece of straw between his teeth. At the time, he was hosting probably the most popular game show on TV called *Dotto*. He thought it would be a no-brainer—*Dot* Records and a show called *Dotto*—a great tie-in. Unfortunately, a short time later the quiz show scandals hit, and *Dotto* disappeared quickly.

Songs on the album include "On Top of Old Smokey," "Tom Dooley," "Skip to My Lou," and "Goodnight, Irene." Mirroring his success, brother Tom Kennedy also amassed an impressive list of game show hosting gigs, and also made a vinyl recording—a spoken word single for Tower Records (#410) titled "Phantom 309" (see the entry for him).

Narz's popular game show being taken from him must have been devastating, but he rebounded very quickly with a long list of very memorable game show successes such as *Seven Keys*, *Video Village*, *I'll Bet*, *It's Your Bet*, *Concentration*, *Beat the Clock*, and *Now You See It*. He also portrayed, appropriately, an emcee on a 1966 episode of the ABC sitcom *The Farmer's Daughter* called "My Papa, the Politician."

In 2005, Jack Narz and his brother were honored with the Bill Cullen Award for Lifetime Achievement from the Game Show Congress. After a long illness, Narz died on October 15, 2008.

DAVID NAUGHTON

Most Famous TV Roles: Billy Manucci on *Makin' It*, Jack Kincaid on *My Sister Sam*; **Networks:** ABC, CBS; **Years:** 1979, 1986–1988, respectively; **Hit Recording:** "Makin' It"; **Label:** RSO; **Release Year:** 1979; **Matrix:** RSO #916; **Chart:** #5 *Billboard* Hot 100

David Walsh Naughton was born in Hartford, Connecticut, on February 13, 1951. He's the younger brother of actor James Naughton. Musical talent ran in the family, and James Naughton had musical success on Broadway in *City of Angels*, *Chicago*, and *I Love My Wife*. David attended the London Academy of Music and Dramatic Arts. Coincidentally, he was later the star of a popular motion picture titled *An American Werewolf in*

London. He first came to our attention in those "I'm a Pepper" commercials for Dr. Pepper soda pop. Because of the popularity of those ads, he got his own TV series in 1979 at the height of the disco era on ABC called *Makin' It*. That sitcom, from Mark Rothman and Lowell Ganz (who had previously worked on *The Odd Couple, Happy Days,* and *Laverne and Shirley*), was the brainchild of Michael Eisner—the head of Paramount at the time. It only lasted for nine episodes before being cancelled. One of the biggest problems was that the show aired on Friday nights, and young people wanted to *be* at a disco, not home watching a show *about* a disco. After the program was gone from the prime-time schedule, the theme song performed by David Naughton began to catch on. Released as a single, the disco single zoomed into the Top Five and earned a gold record for selling over a million copies. It was Naughton's only hit single. He surfaced in 1986 in yet another TV sitcom—*My Sister Sam* starring Pam Dawber. This program had more legs than his previous effort, and lasted for two seasons. Naughton portrayed Jack Kincaid, a photojournalist who lived across the hall from Sam. He also made the rounds on episodic TV shows such as *MacGyver; Murder, She Wrote; JAG; Seinfeld;* and *Melrose Place*. Naughton has been married three times, each ending in divorce.

RICKY NELSON

Most Famous TV Role: himself on *The Adventures of Ozzie and Harriet;* **Network:** ABC; **Years:** 1952–1966; **#1 Hit Recordings:** "Poor Little Fool," "Travelin' Man"; **Labels:** Decca, Imperial, Verve; **Years:** 1957–1973; **Matrix:** "Poor Little Fool" (Imperial #5528), "Travelin' Man" (Imperial #5741); **Chart:** both #1 *Billboard* Hot 100

Eric Hilliard Nelson was born in Teaneck, New Jersey, on May 8, 1940. The Nelsons remained in New Jersey a short time, and then moved to the Hollywood area when Rick and his older brother David were quite young in 1942. Their father, Ozzie, was on tour with his band, and had some steady work in radio on *The Raleigh Cigarette Hour* with Red Skelton. Opportunity knocked when Skelton was drafted, and the program became *The Adventures of Ozzie and Harriet* beginning in 1944. Other actors played the sons on radio. In 1952, they tested the TV waters and settled in for a 14-year run on ABC, now with their real sons in the cast. The show was never a blockbuster hit, never finishing in the Top Thirty for any of its 14 years, but it did well enough and sold enough of the sponsors' products to last for 435 episodes. In the early days of TV, they made 39 episodes each season. Except for a select few color episodes in the final season,

Two teen idols—*Ozzie and Harriet*'s Rick Nelson with author Bob Leszczak. Nelson scored 27 Top Twenty hits, two of which reached number 1.

most of the 435 were black and white. It all started with a theatrical film called *Here Come the Nelsons*, which served as a kind of TV pilot episode. It did so well, it paved the way for a shot at the new medium of television.

Meanwhile, Ricky played football at Hollywood High School and dabbled in clarinet and drums. He took a liking to rock and roll in his teen years and tried to impress a girl by telling her that he had a recording contract. He didn't at the time, but his musical dad helped him secure one with Verve Records. Nelson got to perform the record, a cover of Fats Domino's "I'm Walkin'" on an episode of the show called "Ricky, the Drummer" on April 10, 1957. The record sold like hotcakes. In fact, both sides of the Verve single, "I'm Walkin'" and "A Teenager's Romance" (Verve #10047), reached the Top Ten. A follow-up called "You're My One and Only Love" (Verve #10070) featured Nelson on one side only, and it just missed Top Ten, peaking at number 14. Nelson then signed with Imperial Records, most famous for Fats Domino, and amassed an amazing string of 27 Top Twenty hits. Nelson performed at least one song (usually the newest one) on most episodes of the program (at the end). Many of his 45s became two-sided hits because the public just couldn't get enough of Ricky Nelson. To avoid overexposure, Ozzie suggested that Ricky decline offers to appear on *American Bandstand*. He did find some success in motion pictures, however (*Rio Bravo, Wackiest Ship in the Army*).

After his biggest hit, "Travelin' Man" backed with "Hello, Mary Lou," Ricky grew up, and from then on was known as *Rick* Nelson on all of his recordings. He switched over to the Decca label in 1963 and had two more hits, "Fools Rush In" and "For You" (Decca #31533 and #31574, respectively), before the British Invasion did a number on his chart success. After "For You" in 1964, Nelson didn't make the Top Ten again until "Garden Party" (Decca #32980) in 1972. His comeback was short-lived, and soon Nelson was performing on the oldies circuit. While heading to a New Year's Eve performance on the final day of 1985, his private plane went down over DeKalb, Texas. There were no survivors. He was inducted into the Rock and Roll Hall of Fame in 1987, and has stars on both the Hollywood Walk of Fame and the Palm Springs Walk of Stars.

NICHELLE NICHOLS

Most Famous TV Role: Uhura on *Star Trek*; **Network:** NBC; **Years:** 1966–1969; **Hit Recording:** none; **Label:** Epic; **Release Year:** 1968; **Matrix:** "Know What I Mean?" (Epic #10131), *Down to Earth* (Epic LP #26351); **Chart:** none

Nichelle Nichols was born as Grace Dell Nichols in Robbins, Illinois, on December 28, 1932. She studied the performance arts in Chicago and was soon cast in shows such as *Carmen Jones* in Chicago and *Porgy and Bess* in New York City. Her first experience with producer Gene Roddenberry came in the 1963 NBC drama series *The Lieutenant*. The series starred Gary Lockwood and Nichols guest starred in the episode titled "To Set It Right." After doing some modeling work, she was cast as Uhura, a regular in Roddenberry's most famous TV venture beginning in 1966—*Star Trek*. After the first season, she thought about leaving to pursue success on Broadway, but wisely stayed. The kiss she shared with William Shatner on-screen is likely television's first interracial kiss, at least in the United States.

During the show's three-season run, Nichols earned a recording contract with the Epic label. She had performed previously in musicals on stage, and occasionally toured with Duke Ellington and Lionel Hampton as a vocalist, but was now on vinyl. Her album for the label was cleverly called *Down to Earth*, and her single was "Know What I Mean?" backed with "Why Don't You Do Right?" Neither was a whopping success, but she did get to try again a decade later for the R-Way label and released "Uhura's Theme" backed with "Beyond Antares" (R-Way 1001), but met with the same result. After the original *Star Trek* series left the prime time schedule, she provided the voice of Uhura again for *Star Trek: The Animated Series* and appeared in six *Star Trek* motion pictures. A true lover of space travel, she has donated her time to several NASA projects over the years. Her autobiography, released in 1994, is called *Beyond Uhura: Star Trek and Other Memories*. An asteroid has been named in her honor.

LEONARD NIMOY

Most Famous TV Role: Mr. Spock on *Star Trek;* **Network:** NBC; **Years:** 1966–1969; **Hit Recording:** *Mr. Spock's Music from Outer Space, 2 Sides of Leonard Nimoy;* **Label:** Dot; **Release Years:** 1968–1970; **Matrix:** *Mr. Spock's Music from Outer Space* (Dot LP #25794), *2 Sides of Leonard Nimoy* (Dot LP #25835); **Chart:** #83, #97, respectively, *Billboard* Top Pop Albums

Leonard Nimoy was born in Boston, Massachusetts, on March 26, 1931. He wanted to be an actor, but his parents wanted him to pursue a more stable career. His grandfather urged him to follow his heart. His grandfather won, and Leonard was appearing in local productions before his 10th birthday. His film career began in the early 1950s, but was briefly interrupted by a stint in the U.S. Army. Upon his return, he found small

The very "enterprising" Leonard Nimoy's "star trek" included making phonograph records. His LPs sold much better than his singles.

roles in countless B movies and also secured some guest starring work on episodic TV series such as *Dragnet, The Untouchables, Rawhide, Bonanza, The Outer Limits,* and *Perry Mason.* Nimoy and future costar William Shatner first appeared together in an episode of *The Man from U.N.C.L.E.* called "The Project Strigas Affair." Nimoy then had a decision to make. He had an offer to become a cast member on *Peyton Place* as well as an offer to portray a Vulcan named Mr. Spock on a new sci-fi program for NBC to be called *Star Trek.* He chose correctly. The program was never a major hit in prime time and only lasted three seasons.

During the original run on NBC, Nimoy got to record several albums and singles for the Dot Records label. Singing wasn't his forte, but he did have some success. His albums for Dot were *Mr. Spock's Music from Outer Space, A Touch of Leonard Nimoy* (Dot #25910), *2 Sides of Leonard Nimoy,* and *The Way I Feel* (Dot #25883). Two of them charted, albeit near the bottom of said chart. His singles included "Cotton Candy" backed with "The Ballad of Bilbo Baggins" (Dot #17028), "Theme from *Star Trek*" backed with "Visit to a Sad Planet" (Dot #17038), "I'd Love Making Love to You" backed with "Please Don't Try to Change My Mind" (Dot #17125), "Here We Go 'Round Again" backed with "Consilium" (Dot #17175), and "Time to Get It Together" backed with "The Sun Will Rise" (Dot #17330).

After the original series was cancelled, Nimoy provided the voice for Mr. Spock on *Star Trek: The Animated Series,* and many forget that he joined the cast of *Mission: Impossible* in seasons 4 and 5, replacing Martin Landau. He appeared in many of the *Star Trek* motion pictures and directed two. He also hosted a syndicated series titled *In Search of* which explored the paranormal. He narrated a show called *Ancient Mysteries* for the A&E Network from 1994 to 1997. After an amazing run, Nimoy surrendered the role of Spock to actor Zachary Quinto. He has written two autobiographies—*I Am Spock* and *I Am Not Spock.* Nimoy suffered from COPD (chronic obstructive pulmonary disease) decades after he quit smoking. He was married twice and had two children. Leonard Nimoy lived long and prospered, and began a new trek on February 27, 2015, at the age of 83.

JAY NORTH

Most Famous TV Role: Dennis Mitchell on *Dennis the Menace;* **Network:** CBS; **Years:** 1959–1963; **Hit Recording:** none; **Label:** Colpix, Kem; **Release Year:** 1959; **Matrix:** "Little Boy Blues" (Kem #2757); *Look Who's Singing* (Kem LP #27), *Dennis the Menace* (Colpix LP #204); **Chart:** none

The not-so-menacing Jay North of *Dennis the Menace* with author Bob Leszczak at the WYUU-FM studios in St. Petersburg, Florida.

Jay Waverly North was born in Hollywood, California, on August 3, 1951. An only child, his parents split when he was four and his father never resurfaced. Young Jay was a huge TV fan, and his mother arranged for him to make an appearance on his favorite cartoon show. He was discovered by a talent scout, and he found his first work as a child model and commercial actor. He then got to audition in the nationwide search for a boy to play the title role in the TV version of the popular *Dennis the Menace* comic strip by Hank Ketcham. It took a while to make the final decision, but North was chosen to portray Dennis Mitchell on the new CBS sitcom in 1959.

During the show's run, North also recorded an album and a single for the Kem Records label. Kem was known mostly for parody and adult-themed stag party recordings, but there were several exceptions. This was one of those exceptions. The album was called *Look Who's Singing* and the 45 was "Little Boy Blues" backed with "Animal Farm." Screen Gems also jumped on the bandwagon and released an album on their Colpix label imprint called *Dennis the Menace*. None of these became big hits. The program became very popular and lasted for four seasons. However, the passing of Joseph Kearns (Mr. George Wilson) near the end of the third season, and Jay's growth spurt suddenly made the ratings plummet and the program was cancelled in 1963—and young North was very pleased. He was extremely unhappy in his work and was treated poorly by an aunt who looked after him. The heavily typecast North donned dark hair and attempted to reinvent himself as Terry Bowen in a dramatic role on NBC's *Maya* series in 1967. Despite a lot of promotion and a huge amount of buzz, the MGM adventure series only lasted 13 weeks. After this experiment, North opted to focus his attention upon voice acting for animation. In the early 1970s he was briefly married to actress Kathleen Brucher (it lasted a year). He then served in the U.S. Navy, but was teased incessantly by his shipmates because of his childhood fame. North was married twice more in the early 1990s, but each lasted only a matter of months. North had always been a fan of horror films and sought some much darker roles, but casting directors still saw him as Dennis Mitchell, and nothing ever came of that. At last report, North was working within the Florida juvenile justice system.

DON NOVELLO

Most Famous TV Role: Father Guido Sarducci on *Saturday Night Live;* **Network:** NBC; **Years:** 1977–1980; **Hit Recording:** none; **Label:** Warner Bros.; **Release Year:** 1980; **Matrix:** "I Won't Be Twisting This Christmas" (Warner Bros. #49627); **Chart:** none

Don Novello was born in Lorain, Ohio, on January 1, 1943. He studied at the University of Dayton. He created his Father Guido Sarducci character in 1973 and made a few local TV appearances in the San Francisco area that got him noticed. He became a regular on the short-lived 1975 NBC TV comeback attempt by the Smothers Brothers called *The Smothers Brothers Comedy Hour.* A short time after the cancellation of that variety show, Novello was hired as a regular on another NBC show, *Saturday Night Live* (he also wrote for the program). While on the show he released a couple of live comedy albums as the Sarducci character, including *Live at Douglas Convent* (Warner Bros. #3440), which reached number 179 on the Albums chart. Sarducci also sang on a seasonal record released in 1980 titled "I Won't Be Twisting This Christmas" (written by Novello) backed with "Parco MacArthur" (an Italian version of "MacArthur Park"). It was released on a 45, but didn't make much of a splash initially. However, it did get a lot of seasonal play as part of *The Dr. Demento Show's* holiday broadcasts. Novello also appeared in character on episodic TV programs such as *Blossom*, *Square Pegs*, *The Colbert Report*, and *Married with Children*. In 1990, Novello costarred in *The Godfather III* as Domenic Abbandando. For a while, he toured with Joe Piscopo and Victoria Jackson in a traveling salute to *SNL*.

LOUIS NYE

Most Famous TV Role: Man on the Street on *The Steve Allen Show*; **Network:** ABC, NBC; **Years:** 1956–1961; **Hit Recording:** none; **Label:** Coral, Riverside, United Artists, Wig; **Release Years:** 1957–1961; **Matrix:** "Hi-Ho Steve-O" (Coral #61836), "Emotional Newspaper" (United Artists #356), "Teenage Beatnik" (Wig #103), *Heigh-Ho Madison Avenue* (Riverside LP #842); **Chart:** none

---

Louis Neistat was born in Hartford, Connecticut, on May 1, 1913. He was not a good student, and while in high school gravitated toward something in which he did have interest—radio. He worked on the top station in Hartford for a while before finding success in New York. After serving in the U.S. Army during World War II, he found work on Broadway and eventually in television. He was very adept at sketch comedy and eventually became a popular fixture on *The Steve Allen Show*. He was most proficient at portraying snooty, wealthy, effete characters, and was also seen regularly on the "Man on the Street" feature on Allen's show. He became known for his greeting, "Hi ho, Steverino." Because of his popularity, he got to release several records during the program's run, including one for the Coral label appropriately titled "Hi Ho Steve-O" backed with "I Gotta Run." The record label credits "Louis Nye as Gordon Hathaway." There was also an album for the Riverside label, known mostly for jazz recordings, called *Heigh-Ho Madison Avenue* in 1960. None of these became big hits, but numerous others followed including "Teenage Beatnik" for the Wig label and "Emotional Newspaper" for the United Artists label. Although he found steady work on TV programs such as *The Ann Sothern Show* and *Needles and Pins*, he seemed to work best in small doses as a recurring rather than a regular character (epitomized by his irregular appearances on *The Beverly Hillbillies* and *Curb Your Enthusiasm*). Although he appeared in numerous films, his motion picture career paled in comparison to his TV successes. Nye never retired and continued to work until he was diagnosed with lung cancer. Nye died in Los Angeles at the age of 92 on October 9, 2005.

O

HUGH O'BRIAN

Most Famous TV Role: Wyatt Earp on *The Life and Legend of Wyatt Earp*;
Network: ABC; **Years:** 1955–1961; **Hit Recording:** none; **Label:** ABC-Paramount; **Release Year:** 1957; **Matrix:** "Don't Move" (ABC-Paramount #9854),
TV's Wyatt Earp Sings (ABC LP #203); **Chart:** none

Hugh O'Brian was born as Hugh Charles Krampe in Rochester, New York, on April 19, 1925. He was quite the athlete in high school, lettering in four sports. He enlisted in the U.S. Marine Corps during World War II. After his discharge, he attended UCLA and found work in stage productions where he was discovered and quickly signed to a contract with Universal Studios. In 1955 he was selected to portray Wyatt Earp in the new ABC western titled *The Life and Legend of Wyatt Earp*. The program was quite a success (westerns were immensely popular at this time), and lasted for six seasons and 226 black-and-white episodes. During the show's run, O'Brian released both a single and an album for the ABC-Paramount label. The single was called "Don't Move" backed with "I'm Walkin' Away" and the album was *TV's Wyatt Earp Sings*. Neither of them entered the charts with a bullet, and O'Brian kept his focus on his acting. He got to reprise the role in the 1990s on the short-lived series *Paradise* starring Lee Horsley. O'Brian was also one of the stars of the single-season adventure series titled *Search* in 1972 on NBC (he portrayed Hugh Lockwood). He also costarred in several motion pictures, including *Come Fly with Me, There's No Business like Show Business, In Harm's Way,* and *Ten Little Indians*. He married for the first time in his early 80s, and has a star on the Hollywood Walk of Fame.

TV's *Wyatt Earp*, Hugh O'Brian, got out of Dodge long enough to record "Don't Move" for ABC-Paramount Records.

CARROLL O'CONNOR AND JEAN STAPLETON

Most Famous TV Role: Archie (Carroll O'Connor) and Edith (Jean Stapleton) Bunker on *All in the Family*; **Network:** CBS; **Years** 1971–1983; **Hit Recording:** "Those Were the Days"; **Label:** Atlantic; **Release Year:** 1971; **Matrix:** Atlantic #2847; **Chart:** #43 *Billboard* Hot 100

John Carroll O'Connor was born in New York City on August 2, 1924. He was a Merchant Marine during World War II. He got his acting career started in Ireland. His first break in the United States came about when he was cast in the Broadway production of *Ulysses*. On television, he guest starred in countless episodic shows including *Star Trek, The Man from U.N.C.L.E., Bonanza, Gunsmoke, That Girl,* and *I Spy.* He was cast in the re-curring role of Orrin Hacker on CBS's *The Governor and J.J.* in 1969 but was replaced a short time later by Ed Platt. Coincidentally, CBS cancelled that series early in 1971 to make room for his brash new series unlike anything else on the air at the time—*All in the Family.* The program took a while to catch on, but when it finally did it became a sensation. The opening theme song, "Those Were the Days," was released as a single very late in 1971 after the program had been on the air almost a full year. It just missed the Top Forty early in 1972, peaking at number 43. The song was a duet with costar Jean Stapleton.

Jean was also born in New York City on January 19, 1923, and was a year older than O'Connor. She portrayed Archie's long-suffering dingbat of a wife, Edith Bunker, after many years of work on Broadway in *Damn Yankees, Bells Are Ringing,* and *Funny Girl.* Because of the success of the series and the theme song, an album consisting of popular scenes from the TV program (rather than singing) was released as *All in the Family* (Atlantic LP #7210). The album cover featured the cast with a pink back-ground, and it reached the Top Ten on the album chart, and earned a gold record. A sequel called *All in the Family: Second Album* (Atlantic LP #7232) only reached number 129 on that same chart. O'Connor and Stapleton re-leased another duet single, "Moments to Remember" in 1974 (RCA Victor #0962), but it was not a hit.

After *All in the Family,* Stapleton costarred with Whoopi Goldberg on a sitcom called *Baghdad Café* and had a recurring role on *Scarecrow and Mrs. King.* O'Connor starred in *Archie Bunker's Place* and *In the Heat of the Night.* O'Connor also had a recurring role as Helen Hunt's father on *Mad about You.* O'Connor was married only once and died on June 21, 2001, at the age of 76. Stapleton was also married only once and died at the age of 90 on May 31, 2013.

THE ODD COUPLE
(TONY RANDALL AND JACK KLUGMAN)

Most Famous TV Role: Felix (Tony Randall) and Oscar (Jack Klugman) on *The Odd Couple;* **Network:** ABC; **Years:** 1970–1975; **Hit Recording:** none; **Label:** London; **Release Year:** 1973; **Matrix:** *The Odd Couple Sings* (London LP #903); **Chart:** none

Tony Randall was born as Leonard Rosenberg in Tulsa, Oklahoma, on February 26, 1920. He began in radio in the 1940s on *I Love a Mystery,* and with the advent of television jumped into the new medium with both feet.

He had recurring roles on *One Man's Family* and the popular live sitcom *Mister Peepers*. He and Jack Klugman first met on the same episode of *Appointment with Adventure*, not realizing that they would work together again 15 years later.

Jack Klugman was born in Philadelphia, Pennsylvania, on April 27, 1922. His drama teacher told him that he was more suited to drive a truck, but he certainly had the last laugh. His first series, *Harris against the World*, was a bomb, but he then found success when he replaced Walter Matthau on Broadway as Oscar Madison in *The Odd Couple*. Although reluctant at first, Klugman was convinced by Garry Marshall to reprise his role on the ABC TV version.

In the middle of their five-year run, Randall and Klugman recorded an album in character called *The Odd Couple Sings* for London Records. Randall had been in numerous musicals and was able to carry a tune, but Klugman openly admitted that he was not a singer and was very uncomfortable in front of the extremely large orchestra at the recording session. The album consisted of several old standards, such as "Together Wherever We Go," "Friendship," and "Inch Worm." One of the more bizarre cuts was a cover version of Carly Simon's "You're So Vain." The most amusing cut is "The Odd Couple Opera," which takes up almost an entire side of the album. Randall and Klugman became great friends after a rocky start, and their friendship intensified after the sitcom was cancelled. Their last appearance together on an episodic TV series came in 1998 on an ABC sitcom called *Brother's Keeper* in an episode called "An Odd Couple of Days" (as garage mechanics). They also reprised their roles on stage many times and reunited in a CBS special in 1993 titled *The Odd Couple: Together Again*. This updated special had two storylines—Felix's daughter's wedding and Oscar's raspy voice (reflecting Klugman's cancerous vocal cord surgery). Randall had two other moderately successful TV shows—*The Tony Randall Show* and *Love, Sidney*. Klugman went on to a big hit show called *Quincy, M.E.*, and another sitcom titled *You Again?* Randall died May 17, 2004, at the age of 84. Surprisingly, Klugman outlived Randall and died on Christmas Eve of 2012 at the age of 90.

THE OSMOND BROTHERS

Most Famous TV Role: semiregulars on *The Andy Williams Show*; **Network:** NBC; **Years:** 1962–1967; **#1 Hit Recording:** "One Bad Apple"; **Label:** MGM; **Release Year:** 1970; **Matrix:** MGM #14193; **Chart:** #1 *Billboard* Hot 100

The Osmonds began as a barbershop quartet in their native Ogden, Utah, in 1958. At the time, the group consisted of Alan, Wayne, Merrill, and Jay.

The boys' father, George, arranged an audition with Lawrence Welk, but the group was not selected to appear on Welk's TV program. That disappointment was soon forgotten when they were discovered by Andy Williams's dad while performing at Disneyland. They were soon booked for *The Andy Williams Show* and became semiregulars. In 1963, they released their first albums on the MGM label—*Songs We Sang on "The Andy Williams Show"* (MGM LP #4146) and *A Merry Christmas* (MGM LP #4187). At this time, the group became a quintet with the addition of young Donny. Their popularity on television didn't necessarily translate into success on vinyl. The group's sound was out of date as Motown, the Beatles, the Four Seasons, and the Beach Boys ruled the record charts. They attempted to mimic the Beach Boys on a 1964 MGM 45 (#13281) written by Bobby Darin and produced by Terry Melcher called "My Mom." Even though it was quite well done, the record failed to catch on. The Osmonds jumped from label to label in search of the right sound and finally clicked upon returning to MGM in 1970. They recorded in Muscle Shoals, Alabama, and now had a much more soulful sound, not unlike the Jackson Five. A string of hits followed, capped off by the number 1 smash "One Bad Apple" featuring Donny Osmond's youthful lead vocals. Eventually, Donny found success as a solo performer, as did brother Jimmy (to a much lesser degree) and sister Marie. They then parlayed their popularity into an Osmonds Saturday morning cartoon series, and later an ABC variety series called *Donny and Marie* (she was a little bit country, and he was a little bit rock and roll). Both Donny and Marie are still popular attractions in Las Vegas and Branson. In recent years, Donny hosted a remake of the *Pyramid* game show, and Marie is the longtime spokesperson in commercials for Nutrisystem. The Osmonds have a star on the Hollywood Walk of Fame.

GARY OWENS

Most Famous TV Role: announcer on *Rowan and Martin's Laugh-In*; **Network:** NBC; **Years:** 1968–1973; **Hit Recording:** none; **Labels:** Lion, Pride; **Release Year:** 1972; **Matrix:** "Foonman Airlines" (Lion #107), "Horoscope Part 2" (Pride #1010), *Put Your Head on My Finger* (Pride LP #0302); **Chart:** none

Gary Owens was born as Gary Altman in Mitchell, South Dakota, on May 10, 1936. He started his radio career at a small local radio station, but soon jumped to larger radio markets such as St. Louis, Denver, and Dallas. He eventually landed in Los Angeles's KFWB and then KMPC. He became known for his homemade words. His booming voice was utilized for animation—cartoon characters Space Ghost and Roger Ramjet—and he served as the announcer for *The Perils of Penelope Pitstop*. He is best remembered for his time on *Rowan and Martin's Laugh-In*. He became a very familiar presence as the announcer with a hand over his ear and a clock with real hands in the background. During his five years on the program, he also got to briefly host a game show spinoff called *Letters to Laugh-In* on NBC (basically a version of *Can You Top This?* with jokes submitted by viewers). It replaced the long-running original New York City version of *The Match Game* but only lasted for 13 weeks.

During the run of *Laugh-In*, Owens released a few funny records on 45 rpm. The first was called "Foonman Airlines" on the Lion Records label, followed by "Horoscope, Part 2" for the Pride label from the *Put Your Head on My Finger* album (both the Pride and Lion labels were MGM subsidiaries). Both were issued in 1972, but neither made a big splash. There was also *The Funny Side of Bonnie and Clyde* for the Epic Records label (#26377), but it wasn't a success either. Owens briefly hosted the nighttime version of *The Gong Show* in 1976. He continued to find work in radio and later hosted a syndicated radio program titled *Soundtrack of the Sixties*. He has a star on the Hollywood Walk of Fame and was inducted into the Radio Hall of Fame. He was married only once and had two sons. Gary Owens died on February 12, 2015, at the age of 80 after a long illness. He is not to be confused with comedian Gary Owen.

P

JACK PAAR

Most Famous TV Role: host of *The Tonight Show;* **Network:** NBC; **Years:** 1957–1962; **Hit Recording:** none; **Label:** Columbia, RCA Victor; **Release Year:** 1957–1958; **Matrix:** "Good Luck, God Bless You" (Columbia #40628), "Blue Wiggle" (RCA Victor #7306); **Chart:** none

Jack Harold Paar was born in Canton, Ohio, on May 1, 1918. The family moved to Jackson, Michigan, when he was very young. He conquered a stuttering problem and became successful in local radio, and then moved on to larger markets such as Cleveland, Buffalo, and Detroit. He served in the military during World War II and loved entertaining the troops with his quick wit. Jack Benny gave Paar his big break and had him take over his radio show during the summer of 1947. He fared so well in that spot, he was soon given his own show. He appeared in a couple of motion pictures, remained in radio through the first half of the 1950s, and began to dabble in the new, burgeoning medium of television. On the small screen, he hosted a program called *Up to Paar,* and then *The Jack Paar Morning Show* in 1954.

His big TV break came when he was pegged to take over *The Tonight Show* after Steve Allen left. During his five-year stay on this legendary program, Paar also made a couple of phonograph records. The first was called "Good Luck, God Bless You" for Columbia, and then came "The Blue Wiggle" for RCA Victor. Neither of these releases made much of a splash, and no other singles followed. Paar's favorite saying was "I kid you not," and he made national headlines when he was censored over a joke about a water closet (a bathroom), and he walked off the show until NBC apologized three weeks later. In 1962, he opted to leave the show (a decision he later regretted), having grown tired of the daily grind. He was replaced a few months later by Johnny Carson. Paar then got a weekly series on NBC called *The Jack Paar Program.* Many don't remember, but he was the first to air a film of a Beatles performance—a month before they

JACK PAAR

RCA VICTOR
47-7306

A "NEW ORTHOPHONIC" HIGH FIDELITY RECORDING

BLUE WIGGLE AND FUNNY WHAT YOU LEARN FROM WOMEN

The Tonight Show's Jack Paar simply wasn't up to par on this failed single called "Blue Wiggle."

became a sensation on *The Ed Sullivan Show*. He came out of retirement a few times over the next couple of decades, but never for very long. He hosted a once-a-month program in the 1970s, but he disliked the inconsistency of a monthly broadcast and he and ABC soon parted ways. He hosted a few specials in the 1980s and made a few rare guest appearances, but he was never again a regular presence. Paar was married three times, twice to the same woman. After bypass surgery in 1998, Paar was in declining health and eventually died of a stroke on January 27, 2004, at the age of 85. I kid you not.

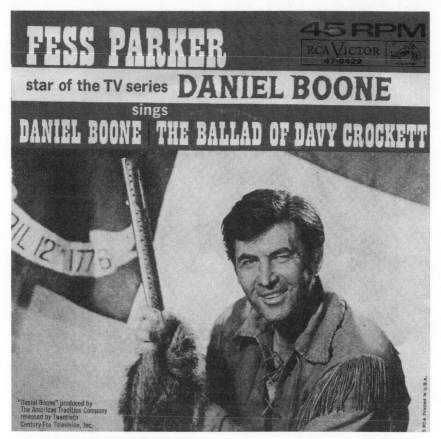

Both of Fess Parker's successful TV shows—*Davy Crockett* and *Daniel Boone*—are
represented on this RCA Victor 45.

FESS PARKER

Most Famous TV Roles: Davy Crockett on *Disneyland,* Daniel Boone on
Daniel Boone; **Networks:** ABC, NBC; **Years:** 1954–1956, 1964–1970, respec-
tively; **Hit Recording:** "Ballad of Davy Crockett"; **Label:** Columbia; **Release
Year:** 1955; **Matrix:** Columbia #40449; **Chart:** #5 *Billboard* Hot 100

Fess Elisha Parker was born in Fort Worth, Texas, on August 16, 1924. He
enlisted in the U.S. Navy during World War II, but his six-foot-six-inch
frame kept him from piloting any planes—he was just too big. After being
discharged, he studied drama at USC. Immediately after graduating, he

found work as a film extra and was eventually contracted by Warner Bros. for some minor film roles. His first big break was with the Walt Disney Company. They were seeking someone tall to portray Davy Crockett, and Parker won the role. Others considered for the role were James Arness and Buddy Ebsen. They both did OK for themselves. Parker became a success in the role as part of the *Disneyland* TV series on ABC. The Crockett character started a merchandising frenzy and even led to multiple hit versions of "The Ballad of Davy Crockett." Bill Hayes's version (Cadence #1256) reached number 1, Tennessee Ernie Ford's (Capitol #3058) reached number 5, and the version by Parker himself on Columbia also peaked at number 5. Between the three of them, the record sold millions of copies.

In the early 1960s, Parker changed directions and starred in an ABC sitcom called *Mr. Smith Goes to Washington*, loosely based upon the famous film of the same name. The show costarred country singer Red Foley, but was not as successful as the film and lasted only a single season. Parker rebounded nicely in yet another series based upon a real western hero, *Daniel Boone*. This time in living color, the series on NBC lasted for six seasons and costarred yet another famous singer, Ed Ames. Parker had the opportunity to portray *McCloud* but turned it down, and Dennis Weaver then got the nod. Parker's plans to build a Davy Crockett theme park fell apart because of funding problems, and his focus then turned to starting his own winery. Parker retired from acting and dedicated his time to the winery (its logo was a coonskin cap). He died only minutes away from the winery at his home in Santa Ynez, California, on March 18, 2010, at the age of 85.

MICHAEL PARKS

Most Famous TV Role: Jim Bronson on *Then Came Bronson*; **Network:** NBC; **Year:** 1969; **Hit Recording:** "Long, Lonesome Highway"; **Label:** MGM; **Release Year:** 1970; **Matrix:** MGM #14104; **Chart:** #20 *Billboard* Hot 100

Michael Parks was born as Harry Samuel Parks, one of five children, in Corona, California, on April 4, 1938. He got his start in television by guest starring on episodic programs such as *The Real McCoys* and *Perry Mason*. He portrayed Adam in *The Bible: In the Beginning* in 1966 and garnered a lot of attention. In 1969, he was cast as the star of his own series, *Then Came Bronson*. Mirroring his own life, the character of Jim Bronson was a drifter seeking the meaning of life. He traveled the country on his motorcycle, taking odd jobs. Parks also performed the program's theme song called "Long Lonesome Highway" for MGM Records (it was also an

MGM TV show), and reached Top Twenty on the Hot 100. He released five albums that charted—*Long Lonesome Highway* (MGM #4662), *Closing the Gap* (MGM #4646), *Blue* (MGM #4717), *Lost and Found* (Verve #5079), and *The Best of Michael Parks* (MGM #4784). The series only lasted a single season, but Parks picked up the slack by returning to guest-starring roles on prime-time TV shows and small roles in motion pictures. Although not really a household name, Parks has never been out of work and has enjoyed quite the resurgence of late in popular films such as *Kill Bill*, volumes 1 and 2; *Grindhouse*; *From Dusk 'til Dawn*; *Death Proof*; *Argo*; and *Django Unchained*. He is now pretty much a regular in films directed by Kevin Smith and especially Quentin Tarantino. Parks has been married four times. He is the father of actor James Parks.

THE PARTRIDGE FAMILY

Most Famous TV Role: Shirley Partridge (Shirley Jones), Keith Partridge (David Cassidy) on *The Partridge Family*; **Network:** ABC; **Years:** 1970–1974; **#1 Hit Recording:** "I Think I Love You"; **Label:** Bell; **Release Year:** 1970; **Matrix:** Bell #910; **Chart:** #1 *Billboard* Hot 100

The Partridge Family was a Screen Gems TV series that aired on ABC. Screen Gems had such great success with *The Monkees*, and they struck pay dirt yet again in 1970. *The Partridge Family* was actually loosely based upon the real Cowsill family who had hit singles such as "The Rain, the Park, and Other Things," "Hair," and "Indian Lake." The series starred Shirley Jones as Shirley Partridge, a widow raising five kids: Keith (David Cassidy), Laurie (Susan Dey), Danny (Danny Bonaduce), Tracy (Suzanne Crough), and Chris (Jeremy Gelbwaks and later Brian Forster). Their manager was Reuben Kincaid, played by the late Dave Madden. Only Jones and Cassidy sang on the records; all the others were lip-synching. They formed a pop music group and hit the road in a gaudy bus and toured the country. The show was a hit for the first three of its four years on the air, finishing in the Top Twenty each of those seasons. Speaking of hits, the group scored three Top Ten records—"Doesn't Somebody Want to be Wanted" (Bell #963), "I'll Meet You Halfway" (Bell #996), and the number 1 million-selling "I Think I Love You" (Bell #910). Four of their albums also reached Top Ten—*The Partridge Family Album* (Bell #6050), *Up to Date* (Bell #6059), *The Partridge Family Sound Magazine* (Bell #6064), and the number 1 *Partridge Family Christmas Card* (Bell #6066).

During the run of the show, David Cassidy (see the entry for him), Shirley Jones's real-life stepson, had one Top Ten solo hit in 1971—a remake of the Association's "Cherish" (Bell #150). He recorded on and off for the next 30 years, but never attained the same level of musical success. Perhaps his most famous vocal performance from the post-Partridge era was the theme song from NBC's *The John Larroquette Show*. Danny Bonaduce also released a few records (see the entry under his name), but his solo efforts were not successful. Screen Gems attempted a spinoff series (titled *Getting Together*, also created by Bernard Slade for Screen Gems) from the "Knight in Shining Armor" episode with guest star Bobby Sherman as down-on-his-luck songwriter Bobby Conway; the spinoff sitcom was not a success and was cancelled after only 13 weeks. The most interesting part of that series was that each episode's title was also a song title—"Why Do Fools Fall in Love?" "Blue Christmas," "Cathy's Clown," and "All Shook Up," to name a few. Shirley Jones later starred in a short-lived series called *Shirley*, David Cassidy starred in the ill-fated *David Cassidy: Man Undercover*, and Susan Dey starred in *Loves Me, Loves Me Not; Love and War*; and *L.A. Law*. Danny Bonaduce has been a successful radio personality, had his own TV talk show called *The Danny Bonaduce Show*, and was a cohost on another called *The Other Half*. Suzanne Crough surfaced briefly in the extremely short-lived *Mulligan's Stew* on NBC.

BUTCH PATRICK

Most Famous TV Role: Eddie on *The Munsters*; **Network:** CBS; **Years:** 1964–1966; **Hit Recording:** none; **Labels:** Golden, Metromedia, Rocshire; **Release Years:** 1964–1984; **Matrix:** "Gypsy Rainbow" (Metromedia #0106), "I Want Sugar All the Time" (Metromedia #251), "Little Monsters" (Rocshire #95041), *At Home with the Munsters* (Golden LP #139); **Chart:** none

Butch Patrick was born Patrick Allen Lilley on August 2, 1953, in Los Angeles, California. Before he was even 10 years old, he was amassing an amazing list of credits on episodic TV. His first recurring role was on the final season of *The Real McCoys* as Greg Howard. In 1964, he was cast as Eddie Wolfgang Munster on the iconic black-and-white classic sitcom *The Munsters*, from Revue Studios. The program was produced and written by Joe Connelly and Bob Mosher, who were also responsible for *Leave It to Beaver*. One of the episodes of *The Munsters*, titled "Far Out Munsters," featured an up-and-coming rock and roll band called the Standells. Butch Patrick elaborated, "They were really great guys. We had a lot of fun that week doing the show. It's interesting that they sing 'I Want to Hold Your Hand' and 'Come On and Ringo,' but not their big hit, 'Dirty Water.' That song was released after we filmed the episode." There was also a cast album called *At Home with the Munsters* (Golden LP #139). Everyone in the cast got a chance to perform on the album, and cuts included "Herman Says Hello," "Lily's Favorite Story," "Meet Grandpa," "Marilyn's When Will I Find a Boy for Me?" and "Eddie."

Patrick not only enjoyed working with the rock and roll group the Standells—he also got to experience the rock and roll lifestyle in the early 1970s. Patrick shared,

I was a regular on the Sid and Marty Krofft show *Lidsville* at the time, and Metromedia Records was about to drop Bobby Sherman from their recording roster. They were looking for the next Sherman, and my mother jumped at the chance and helped me get my foot in the door there. I made several records for the label—"I Want Sugar All the Time" and "Gypsy Rainbow." I got to lip-synch on *American Bandstand* on the same show with an up-and-coming Loggins and Messina. I had a wonderful time. Metromedia put a lot of money behind the project. I wish it had been more successful, but we gave it the old college try and then some. The songs were very well received. Everyone should be a rock star for a year—I highly recommend it.

Patrick got another shot a decade later and recalled, "For the small Rocshire Record label, I recorded a single with a group called Eddie and the Monsters. I was the vocalist, my brother Steve played keyboards, Reek Havoc [love the name] played drums, and Brent Black played guitar. Brent wrote the 'Little Monsters' side, and I wrote the flip, 'Whatever Happened to Eddie?' We have the distinction of being the first unsigned act ever to have a video played on MTV."

As of this writing, Butch Patrick is a regular on *Zodiac Divas with Butch Patrick* on CBS Radio in Los Angeles, and is assembling a *Munsters* book to celebrate and commemorate the program's golden anniversary. About the attempt to update *The Munsters* on TV, Patrick stated, "It was supposed to become a series called *Mockingbird Lane*, but the project was scrubbed and only the pilot aired. I was invited to be there for the last day of the shoot, and it looked like a really good idea. Too bad, but, that's show biz."

CYNTHIA PEPPER

Most Famous TV Roles: Jean Pearson on *My Three Sons*, Margie Clayton on *Margie*; **Network:** ABC; **Years:** 1960–1961, 1961–1962, respectively; **Hit Recording:** none; **Label:** Felsted; **Release Year:** 1962; **Matrix:** "Baby Blues" (Felsted #8651); **Chart:** none

Cynthia Pepper was born as Cynthia Anne Culpepper in Hollywood, California, on September 4, 1940. Her father, Jack Pepper, was an entertainer, and talent ran in the family. After several guest-starring roles on episodic shows, she snagged a recurring role on ABC's *My Three Sons*. She portrayed Jean Pearson, the romantic interest of Tim Considine's character, Mike Douglas, in numerous early episodes of that long-running series. The following year she earned her own ABC series called *Margie*. This period piece sitcom is not to be confused with *My Little Margie*. Pepper's *Margie* was set in the 1920s and showed what teenage life may have been like in that decade. During the program's run, Pepper recorded and released one single for the Felsted Records label, most famous for hits recorded by Kathy Linden, the Flares, and Kokomo. Pepper's record, "Baby Blues" backed with "A First Time Love," in 1962 failed to catch on, despite her exposure on the sitcom. No other singles followed. Despite decent ratings, and the release of a couple of *Margie* comic books and a board game, the show was not renewed for a second season. Her next big venture was playing Midge Riley in the 1964 Elvis Presley film *Kissin' Cousins*. After erratic guest-starring roles on episodic TV shows such as *The Addams Family*, *Julia*, *The Flying Nun*, and *Wagon Train*, Pepper retired from show business. However, she still appears frequently at TV autograph shows and Elvis memorabilia shows. She lives in Henderson, Nevada.

PAUL PETERSEN

Most Famous TV Role: Jeff Stone on *The Donna Reed Show*; **Network:** ABC; **Years:** 1958–1966; **Hit Recordings:** "My Dad," "She Can't Find Her Keys"; **Label:** Colpix; **Release Years:** 1962–1963; **Matrix:** "My Dad" (Colpix #663), "She Can't Find Her Keys" (Colpix #620); **Chart:** #6, #19, respectively, *Billboard* Hot 100

Paul Petersen was born on September 23, 1945, in Glendale, California. At the age of 10 he became one of TV's original Mouseketeers. His big TV break came in 1958 when he was cast as Jeff—the younger of the two Stone children on *The Donna Reed Show*. Petersen recalled,

We actually did become a close-knit family—you can see it and feel it on-screen. Shelley Fabares has always been like a sister to me. Donna Reed was always wonderful to us kids. Shelley and I became very close to Donna's own four children. Carl Betz, who played our dad, was very unlike Donna Reed's real husband, Tony Owen. Tony was a cigar-smoking sports fan, and

Paul Petersen as Jeff Stone on *The Donna Reed Show* performed this song in the episode titled "For Angie with Love," and it became a big hit.

Carl Betz was a classically trained Shakespearean actor. He was great and really got to show his talents on his later *Judd for the Defense* series. I got to debut my biggest hit, "My Dad" on the episode of the same name. To this day, it is one of my favorite episodes. The record still sells thousands of copies every year around Father's Day.

The only person in the cast of whom he wasn't fond? Petersen said, "Bob Crane, who was there for the last three seasons. He was immensely talented, but he wasn't a very good person."

About the decision to make records, Petersen shared,

We can blame it all on Ricky Nelson—he really set the whole teen idol thing in motion. Screen Gems, which was part of Columbia Pictures, decided to get Shelley and me to make records on their Colpix label. I had previously done a lot of singing as a Mouseketeer, so I liked the idea, but Shelley needed a push—she wasn't comfortable with singing in public. We recorded at United Recording Studio—usually knocking out at least six songs in about three hours' time. We were treated to the best writers in the business—Barry Mann and Cynthia Weil, Carole King and Gerry Goffin. The A&R [artist and repertoire] man for Colpix, Stu Phillips, became a great friend. We are still extremely close friends today. As far as the recordings, I fully expected to sing tender love ballads to make the girls swoon, so I was rather surprised that I was given the novelty song "She Can't Find Her Keys," which was similar in texture to "Itsy Bitsy Teenie Weenie Yellow Polka Dot Bikini." The song became a big hit, and I sang it on the show in the "For Angie, with Love" episode in January of 1962. My hit even sparked an answer record by Bet E. Martin called "I Can't Find My Keys" on Columbia's Epic label (#9414). I enjoyed performing—the screaming girls, the money. I wasn't afraid of a microphone. However, because of the schedule for *The Donna Reed Show*, I didn't get to do as much touring as I would have liked. Those Dick Clark Caravan tours were so much fun. I became good friends with a lot of the Motown acts on the tour. They came to appreciate and respect me, as I did them, and eventually I got a contract to record for the legendary Motown label. However, by this time the world was changing and I was perceived as a kind of square kid, and couldn't break out of that mold.

It is not well known, but Petersen wrote two episodes of *The Donna Reed Show*, as well as numerous well-received adventure novels. Having gone through it all himself, Petersen has become sort of a champion and guardian to child actors through his A Minor Consideration foundation, which oversees the financial, legal, and emotional protection of show business kids—past and present. As of this writing, six of the eight seasons of *The Donna Reed Show* have been made available in DVD box sets from MPI Entertainment.

REGIS PHILBIN

Most Famous TV Role: second banana on *The Joey Bishop Show*, cohost of *Live with Regis and Kathie Lee*, host of *Who Wants to Be a Millionaire?* cohost of *Live with Regis and Kelly*; **Network:** ABC; **Years:** 1967–1969, 1988–2000, 1999–2002, 2001–2011, respectively; **Hit Recording:** none; **Label:** Mercury; **Release Year:** 1968; **Matrix:** *It's Time for Regis* (Mercury LP #61169); **Chart:** none

Regis Philbin was born in the Bronx, New York, on August 25, 1931. His only sibling, a brother named Frank, was born 20 years later and died at the age of 55. Regis graduated with a degree in sociology from

Notre Dame, and after a stint in the U.S. Navy, developed an interest in broadcasting. After jobs as a page for *The Tonight Show* and host of the short-lived local San Diego TV show called *The Regis Philbin Show*, his big break came when he was named to be Joey Bishop's sidekick on ABC's late-night talk show called *The Joey Bishop Show*. During the run of that series, Philbin released an album for Mercury Records called *It's Time for Regis*. The LP was rife with old standards such as "Where or When?" "Baby Face," "Pennies from Heaven," and "The Glory of Love." The album cover contained the ABC logo and a lighted sign in the background touting *The Joey Bishop Show*. Philbin briefly walked off the show (claiming that he felt unwanted by ABC), only to be invited back a short time later. It was later revealed that the event was a planned publicity stunt to steal some of Johnny Carson's thunder.

After Bishop's show was cancelled, Philbin attempted to make it on his own. There were countless different combinations and formats until everything fell into place beginning in 1988 with ABC's *Live with Regis and Kathie Lee* (see the entry for Kathie Lee Gifford). Gifford remained until 2000 and was replaced a while later by Kelly Ripa, and the show remained intact and successful until Philbin left in 2011. During this time, Philbin also clicked with a wildly successful game show called *Who Wants to Be a Millionaire?* It was not Philbin's first game show (he'd hosted the disastrous *The Neighbors* for ABC in 1975), but this one became a sensation. However, ABC aired the game show too often, and overkill eventually wore out its welcome.

After years away from the recording studio, Philbin reignited his musical career and released numerous CDs, including *The Regis Philbin Christmas Album* (Hollywood CD #6954655), *When You're Smiling* (Hollywood CD #6776729), and *Just You Just Me* with his wife, Joy (Big Dog CD #8032898). He has a star on the Hollywood Walk of Fame, has won numerous Daytime Emmy Awards, and was inducted into the Television Hall of Fame (2006).

PHOEBE BUFFAY AND THE HAIRBALLS (LISA KUDROW)

Most Famous TV Role: Phoebe Buffay on *Friends*; **Network:** NBC; **Years:** 1994–2004; **Hit Recording:** "Smelly Cat"; **Label:** Reprise; **Release Year:** 1999; **Matrix:** Reprise #47100; **Chart:** none

Lisa Kudrow was born in Los Angeles, California, on July 30, 1963. She studied biology as Vassar College and when it came to acting, she was a late bloomer. Jon Lovitz, a family friend, realized her innate talents and urged her to pursue the performing arts. After a string of unsold pilots and the last-minute loss of the role of Roz on *Frasier*, she briefly portrayed Ursula (a waitress) on *Mad about You*. Ursula Buffay surfaced again a short time later as the twin sister of Phoebe Buffay on a new 1994 NBC sitcom called *Friends*. Phoebe was a free-spirited massage therapist who wrote and performed peculiar songs at the group's hangout called Central Perk. Her most famous song, "Smelly Cat," was even made into a music video on the show. In one episode, Phoebe teaches "Smelly Cat" to Chrissie Hynde of the Pretenders and, in fact, released a version of the song with Hynde (listed as being by Phoebe Buffay and the Hairballs) on an album called *Friends Again* in 1999. The cover pictured the six stars of the series, but only Kudrow had a cut on the album. Near the end of the show's run, she was raking in a million dollars an episode. She won an Emmy Award for the role. In her next series, *The Comeback*, she portrayed a washed-up sitcom star. Most recently, she took on the role of Dr. Fiona Wallace on *Web Therapy* and has enjoyed a long run. Kudrow has been married only once and has a grown son.

JOE PISCOPO

Most Famous TV Role: regular on *Saturday Night Live;* **Network:** NBC; **Years:** 1980–1984; **Hit Recording:** *New Jersey;* **Label:** Columbia; **Release Years:** 1982–1985; **Matrix:** "Born to Run" (Columbia #03253), "I Love Rock and Roll" (Columbia #03254), "Honeymooners Rap" (Columbia #05224), *New Jersey* (Columbia LP #40046); **Chart:** *New Jersey*—#168 *Billboard* Top Pop Albums

Joe Piscopo was born in Passaic, New Jersey, on June 17, 1951. Beginning in high school, he had a keen interest in drama and weight lifting. Against the wishes of his parents, he became a stand-up comedian (they wanted him to be a lawyer). Beginning in 1980, he became a cast member on *Saturday Night Live* along with Eddie Murphy. Piscopo was best known for his impressions, especially that of Frank Sinatra. One of his recordings during his stint on *SNL*, "I Love Rock and Roll," featured that impression. Piscopo teamed up with costar Eddie Murphy on another single, "Honeymooners Rap," in 1983 (featuring an impression of Jackie Gleason and Art Carney). Piscopo also recorded a medley of "Born to Run" and "Cold as Ice," but none of his singles charted. An album released after his run on *SNL* called *New Jersey* did make the album charts, albeit very low. After leaving the series in 1984, Piscopo appeared in several films but was not as successful in films as Bill Murray, Chevy Chase, Dan Aykroyd, John

Belushi, or Eddie Murphy. He has been married twice and still resides in New Jersey. As of this writing, he hosts a morning radio show in New York City.

MARY KAY PLACE

Most Famous TV Role: Loretta Haggers on *Mary Hartman, Mary Hartman*; **Network:** syndicated; **Years:** 1976–1978; **Hit Recording:** "Baby Boy"; **Label:** Columbia; **Release Year:** 1976; **Matrix:** Columbia #10422; **Chart:** #60 *Billboard* Hot 100

Mary Kay Place was born in Tulsa, Oklahoma, on September 23, 1947. She could do it all—act, sing, and write. Her first show business job was as a writer and production assistant for the short-lived *Tim Conway Comedy Hour* on CBS in 1970. She then got to pen scripts for some of the top shows of the day—*All in the Family, The Mary Tyler Moore Show, M*A*S*H*, and *Phyllis*. It was her recurring role as Loretta Haggers (Charlie's wife) on *Mary Hartman, Mary Hartman* that brought her the most attention. She won an Emmy for the role and also performed a song (which she composed) on said program. The song about her husband on the program, Charlie (Graham Jarvis), is called "Baby Boy." It became a fair-sized pop hit and fared even better on the Country charts. On the flip side of the single is another program-related song called "Streets of This Town." There were several follow-up singles—"Coke and Chips" backed with "Vitamin L" (Columbia #10510), and "Don't Make Love to a Country Singer" backed with "The Marlboro Man" (Columbia #10707). "Something to Brag About" (with Willie Nelson) backed with "Anybody's Darlin'" (Columbia #10644) became a Top Ten country single, but didn't cross over to the Pop charts. There were also a couple of Columbia albums—*Tonight at the Capri Lounge Starring Loretta Haggers* (Columbia LP #34353—a Top Ten country hit) and *Aimin' to Please* (Columbia LP #34908). The latter boasted big-name guest vocalists such as Dolly Parton, Emmylou Harris, and Anne Murray. She earned a key role in *The Big Chill* and a recurring role on the critically acclaimed but low-rated *My So-Called Life* TV series. She has added directing to her resume in recent years along with providing voices for animated characters. She has never been married.

PONCIE PONCE

Most Famous TV Role: Kazuo Kim on *Hawaiian Eye*; **Network:** ABC; **Years:** 1959–1963; **Hit Recording:** none; **Label:** Warner Bros.; **Release Year:** 1961; **Matrix:** "Ten Cent Perfume" (Warner Bros. #5244), *Poncie Ponce Sings* (Warner Bros. LP #1453); **Chart:** none

Poncie Ponce was born as Ponciano Hernandez in Maui on April 10, 1933. While considering becoming a welder, he got the show business bug and tried stand-up comedy. He also played several instruments—the ukulele, the trumpet, and the bongos. Ponce then moved to Los Angeles to fulfill his dreams and did well on a TV talent show called *Rocket to Stardom*. After numerous performances on the program, Ponce found work at local nightclubs. It was there that he was discovered and hired for a new Warner Bros. TV show to be called *Hawaiian Eye*, costarring Robert Conrad and Connie Stevens (see the entries for those celebrities). Ponce portrayed the smart-aleck cab driver Kazuo Kim and played ukulele often on the program. The show lasted for four seasons and had a healthy run in syndication.

During the run of the program, Ponce and many of the stars of Warner Bros. TV shows were encouraged to record for the Warner Bros. label. Ponce first appeared on a Warner Bros. holiday album collection called *We Wish You a Merry Christmas* (Warner Bros. LP #1337) in 1959. Then came *The Hawaiian Eye TV Cast Sings* (Warner Bros. LP #1355) in 1960. In 1961, Ponce became popular enough to warrant a solo single—"Ten Cent Perfume" backed with "No Hu Hu" (Warner Bros. #5244) in 1961 and a solo album—*Poncie Ponce Sings* (Warner Bros. LP #1453) in 1962. Neither of his solo efforts was very successful, and as the program neared the end of its run, no other recordings by him were released. After the TV show was cancelled, Ponce looked for parts in motion pictures. The most famous of those is as Juan Medala, a member of the pit crew, in Elvis Presley's *Speedway* from 1968. His post-*Hawaiian Eye* career was not stellar, and he found most of his work in nightclubs and an occasional engagement in Las Vegas. Ponce lived to be 80 and died in Los Angeles on July 19, 2013. He was married only once and had three children and several grandchildren.

VICTORIA PRINCIPAL

Most Famous TV Role: Pamela Ewing on *Dallas*; **Network:** CBS; **Years:** 1978–1987; **Hit Recording:** "All I Have to Do Is Dream"; **Label:** RSO; **Release Year:** 1981; **Matrix:** RSO #1065; **Chart:** #51 *Billboard* Hot 100

Many will be surprised to learn that Victoria Principal was born in Fu-
kuoka, Japan, on January 3, 1950. Her parents were stationed there at
the time; her father, Victor, was in the U.S. Air Force. The family moved
around a lot, and she attended countless schools. She eventually decided
to give acting a try and moved to Los Angeles. With only a couple of TV
commercial credits under her belt, she earned a meaty role in Paul Newman's *The Life and Times of Judge Roy Bean* for which she earned a Golden
Globe nomination. This was followed by the disaster film called *Earthquake* (in sensaround sound). Aaron Spelling took notice of Principal's
talent and put her in the pilot episode for *Fantasy Island*. She was then
cast in the megahit *Dallas*, on which she portrayed Pamela Barnes Ewing
for a decade.

During that amazing ride on CBS, Principal also attempted a musical career and recorded a duet with Andy Gibb, the younger brother of
Robin, Maurice, and Barry Gibb of the Bee Gees. This remake of the Everly
Brothers classic "All I Have to Do Is Dream" for RSO Records received
considerable airplay and promotion. Gibb and Principal performed the
song on numerous TV shows, but it didn't get as far as expected, only
reaching number 51 on the Hot 100. Principal and Gibb had a brief fling,
but his addictions led to their breakup. Gibb had previously scored six
Top Ten records of his own, but this duet marked the end for him and
he never cracked the Hot 100 again. When TNT revived *Dallas* in 2012,
Principal opted not to participate. Her Principal Secret skin care business
is wildly successful and profitable, and it keeps her very busy. She was
married twice, but is single as of this writing.

ROSEMARY PRINZ

Most Famous TV Role: Penny Hughes on *As the World Turns*; **Network:**
CBS; **Years:** 1956–1968; **Hit Recording:** none; **Label:** Pharos; **Release Year:**
1966; **Matrix:** "Penny" (Pharos #103), *TV's Penny Sings* (Pharos LP #10001);
Chart: none

Rosemary Prinz was born in New York City on January 4, 1930. Her father was an accomplished cellist, and she always wanted to be an actress.
She started her career right out of high school in summer stock. After a
stint on Broadway in *The Grey-Eyed People* in the early 1950s, she earned
a role on a TV soap opera called *First Love*. She portrayed Amy on this
short-lived show, and immediately jumped to a new CBS serial called
As the World Turns. Prinz portrayed Penny Hughes and stayed with the
successful program for a dozen years. Near the end of her run on the pro-

gram, she released a 45 rpm single for the small Pharos Records label—
"Penny" backed with "Always" in 1966. It was released from an album
titled *TV's Penny Sings* (Pharos #10001), consisting of many old standards,
such as "When I Fall in Love," "My Coloring Book," "You're Getting to
Be a Habit with Me," and "Goody Goody." Even though her character
was very popular at the time, the album and the single failed to generate
much interest and her recording career was quickly scrapped. Because of
the pressure inflicted upon her during her long run on the program, Prinz
left the series in 1968 and vowed never to do another soap opera. She did
go back on her word, however, and agreed to a few limited engagement
roles on them in later years (*All My Children, Ryan's Hope*). Except for a
brief recurring role (Sylvia Warren) on *Knots Landing* in 1981, Prinz withdrew from public view. She is still married to her second husband, Joseph
Patti (since 1967), as of this writing.

DOROTHY PROVINE

Most Famous TV Role: Pinky Pinkham on *The Roaring Twenties*; **Network:**
ABC; **Years:** 1960–1962; **Hit Recording:** *Music from "The Roaring 20s"*;
Labels: Warner Bros.; **Release Year:** 1961–1965; **Matrix:** *Music from "The
Roaring 20s"* (Warner Bros. LP #1394); **Chart:** #34 *Billboard* Top Pop Albums

Dorothy Provine was born in Deadwood, South Dakota, on January 20,
1935. She left the nest and attended the University of Washington in Seattle, where she studied drama. Her first work was in local television. She
was discovered and signed to Warner Bros. studios and did numerous
guest spots on Warner Bros. shows such as *Sugarfoot* and *Colt 45*. She was
then cast as a regular on a Warner Bros. series called *The Alaskans* in 1959.
She portrayed Rocky Shaw on this short-lived series, one of Warner's few
flops. Future James Bond Roger Moore was also in the cast. Immediately
after the demise of that series, Provine was cast in another Warner Bros.
show—a period piece called *The Roaring Twenties*. Provine, who hadn't
even been alive in the 1920s, played Pinky Pinkham. While on the show,
Provine got to release several singles and albums for Warner Bros. The al-
bums were related to the TV program—*Music from "The Roaring 20s"* and
Vamp of "The Roaring 20s" (Warner Bros. LP #1419), and the singles were
"Bye Bye Blackbird" backed with "Crazy Words, Crazy Tune" (Warner
Bros. #5202), and "Don't Bring Lulu" backed with "The Whisper Song"
(Warner Bros. #5429). Even with the additional promotion that Provine's
Top Forty album brought to the show, it was cancelled early in 1962 after
a truncated second season. Provine then found some success in a few

popular motion pictures—*That Darn Cat, The Great Race,* and *It's a Mad, Mad, Mad, Mad World,* but after marrying director Robert Day, opted to retire from acting. After many years out of the spotlight, Provine died of emphysema on April 25, 2010, in Washington State. She was married only once and had only one child.

TOMMY PUETT

Most Famous TV Role: Tyler Benchfield on *Life Goes On;* **Network:** ABC; **Years:** 1989–1992; **Hit Recording:** none; **Label:** Scotti Brothers; **Release Year:** 1990; **Matrix:** *Life Goes On* (Scotti Brothers LP #5200); **Chart:** none

Ralph Thomas Puett was born in Gary, Indiana, on January 12, 1971. He burst upon the scene and disappeared almost as quickly. He portrayed character Becca Thatcher's boyfriend Tyler Benchfield on ABC's *Life Goes On* from 1989 to 1991 while still a teenager. During this period, there was an attempt to make Puett the next teen idol, much like Shaun Cassidy and Leif Garrett. Puett was photographed countless times with his mullet haircut, and posters for teenage girls were marketed. There was also one album titled *Life Goes On* in 1990 (Scotti Brothers #5200) and a single titled "Kiss You All Over" (a remake of the song by Exile). Tommy's younger sister Devyn sang background vocals on the album. The records did not sell as well as anticipated, but Puett was still chosen to host a music show called *America's Top Ten* from 1991 to 1992. He left *Life Goes On* at this time, but his new venture was short-lived. After costarring in the 1997 motion picture *Switchback,* Puett called it a career, and today he runs a successful baseball cap company.

R

TONY RANDALL. *See* THE ODD COUPLE.

CARL REINER. *See* THE THREE HAIRCUTS.

TOMMY RETTIG

Most Famous TV Role: Jeff Miller on *Lassie*; **Network:** CBS; **Years:** 1954–1957; **Hit Recording:** none; **Label:** Coral; **Release Year:** 1956; **Matrix:** "What Is a Dad?" (Coral #61704); **Chart:** none

Thomas Noel Rettig was born in Queens, New York, on December 10, 1941. He got his start in *Annie Get Your Gun* when he was only six. Then came a laundry list of motion picture roles including *River of No Return* with Marilyn Monroe. His big break came when he was cast as Jeff Miller for a new series about a collie dog named *Lassie*. The series went through many changes and many families (and even many Lassies) during its long run. Jeff lived on a farm with his widowed mom (played by Jan Clayton), his grandfather (George Cleveland), and his dog. Wanting a normal childhood, Tommy opted out of his contract in 1957. During his three years on the show, Tommy Rettig released one single—"What Is a Dad?" backed with "What Is a Mom?" for Coral Records. The record was not a hit, but Rettig did become interested in the record business and produced a few rock and roll records, including "Oh, What a Night" backed with "Juanita" by the Tokens (not the group that recorded "The Lion Sleeps Tonight") for the Date Records label (#2737), and several others for Gene Autry's Challenge label. He was also very friendly with Dean Torrence of Jan and Dean fame and had a lot of fun during the Southern California surf music craze of the early 1960s.

Rettig surfaced on the small screen as Jojo in a short-lived daily teen soap opera called *Never Too Young* (with Tony Dow of *Leave It to Beaver*) in 1965. The program was set on Malibu Beach, and many of the music stars of the day performed on the program. With a group called the TR-4 (TR as in Tommy Rettig), he even wrote, recorded, and served as musical director for a song called "Never Too Young" (Velvet Tone #105) with hopes of it being used as the soap opera's theme song, but to no avail. Frustrated with show business, Rettig later became a motivational speaker and a computer programmer. One of his final TV appearances came on an episode of *The New Lassie* in 1991. Rettig was married only once and was felled by a heart attack at the age of 54 on February 15, 1996. Sadly, even though his *Lassie* episodes were heavily syndicated for many years as *Jeff's Collie*, he reportedly received no residuals.

ALFONSO RIBEIRO

Most Famous TV Role: Carlton Banks on *The Fresh Prince of Bel-Air*; **Network:** NBC; **Years:** 1990–1996; **Hit Recording:** "Dance Baby"; **Label:** Prism; **Release Year:** 1984; **Matrix:** Prism #99723; **Chart:** #104 *Billboard* Bubbling Under

Alfonso Ribeiro was born in the Bronx, New York, on September 21, 1971. His parents were born in Trinidad and Tobago. By the age of 12, he was on Broadway in *The Tap Dance Kid*. The following year, he found regular work as Alfonso Spears, Ricky's best friend on *Silver Spoons*. While on that sitcom, Ribeiro released a single that made the Bubbling Under charts called "Dance Baby." There was also a rap single called "Timebomb" (Prism #2006), but it was much less successful. Ribeiro also danced in one of Michael Jackson's Pepsi commercials. *Silver Spoons* lasted until 1987, and a short three years later Ribeiro landed his most famous TV role—that of Carlton Banks, the spoiled rich kid on *The Fresh Prince of Bel-Air*. The program ran for six seasons and has enjoyed a nice run in syndication. Ribeiro then found steady voice work for TV animation in *Extreme Ghostbusters* and *Are We There Yet?* As of this writing, he hosts a GSN game show called *Catch 21* and was part of season 19 of *Dancing with the Stars*. He has been married twice and has one child from each.

HOWARD RICE. *See* RICHIE'S *ROOM 222* GANG.

RICHIE'S *ROOM 222* GANG (HOWARD RICE)

Most Famous TV Role: Richie Lane (Howard Rice) on *Room 222*; **Network:** ABC; **Years:** 1969–1971; **Hit Recording:** "I'd Rather Stay a Child"; **Label:** Scepter; **Release Year:** 1971; **Matrix:** Scepter #12305; **Chart:** #48 *Billboard* R&B

Actor/singer Howard Rice was part of the original cast of the ABC sitcom called *Room 222*. The program starred Lloyd Haynes, Denise Nicholas, Michael Constantine, and perky Karen Valentine. Rice portrayed one of the more prominent students, Richie Lane. Rice had very few TV credits and seemed to disappear from public view as quickly as he appeared. He was a cast member for the first two seasons of *Room 222's* five seasons, and his brief TV popularity got him a recording deal with Scepter Records in 1971. Under the name Richie's *Room 222* Gang, a single titled "I'd Rather Stay a Child" backed with "Girls, Girls, Girls (That's All on My Mind)" cracked the R&B Top Fifty, albeit briefly. Making up the rest of the so-called gang on the record were other members of the Rice family—brothers Jerome and Alfred on guitar and cousin Dennis Hughes on piano. The series was almost cancelled after one season, but three Emmy wins earned it a renewal, and it remained on the air until 1974. Howard Rice is one of Hollywood's great mysteries. Information about him is extremely sparse and his whereabouts are unknown.

PERNELL ROBERTS

Most Famous TV Roles: Adam Cartwright on *Bonanza*, Dr. John McIntyre on *Trapper John, M.D.*; **Network:** CBS, NBC; **Years:** 1959–1965, 1979–1986, respectively; **Hit Recording:** none; **Label:** RCA Victor; **Release Year:** 1962–1963; **Matrix:** *Bonanza Ponderosa Party Time* (RCA Victor #2583), *Come All Ye Fair and Tender Ladies* (RCA Victor #2662), *Christmas on the Ponderosa* (RCA Victor #2757); **Chart:** none

Pernell Roberts was born in North Carolina on May 18, 1928, but his family moved to Waycross, Georgia, while he was still a baby. He loved music as a child, played a couple of brass instruments, and loved to perform in local plays. He served in the U.S. Marine Corps in the middle 1940s, and later attended the University of Maryland. Before graduating, he moved to New York City and found work in Broadway productions, including some Shakespearean works and a few musicals. Beginning in 1959, he was cast as Adam Cartwright on *Bonanza*. During his stay, he released an album of solo material for RCA Victor called *Come All Ye Fair and Tender Ladies*. Along with the title cut were versions of "Sylvie," "They Call the Wind Mariah," "Alberta," and "A Quiet Girl." He was also part of a couple of RCA LPs involving the *Bonanza* cast—*Ponderosa Party Time* and *Christmas on the Ponderosa*. Roberts opted to leave the hit series in 1965 to pursue other avenues of show business. Known mostly for his dramatic roles, Roberts surprised many with a guest-starring role on the sitcom *The Odd Couple* in a 1974 episode titled "Strike Up the Band or Else." Many saw his decision to leave *Bonanza* as a foolish move, but Roberts rebounded nicely when in 1979 he was cast in the role of Dr. John McIntyre decades after *M*A*S*H*. This new hour-long drama series called *Trapper John, M.D.* was quite a big hit with viewers and lasted for seven seasons. In the 1990s, he appeared in a series of TV commercials for the pain reliever Ecotrin. For quite a time, Roberts was the last surviving major *Bonanza* character. However, he was diagnosed with pancreatic cancer and died on January 24, 2010. He was married four times and had one son.

JOE E. ROSS

Most Famous TV Role: Gunther Toody on *Car 54, Where Are You?* **Network:** NBC; **Years:** 1961–1963; **Hit Recording:** none; **Label:** IPG; **Release Year:** 1963; **Matrix:** "Ooh, Ooh" (IPG #1003); **Chart:** none

Joe E. Ross was born as Joseph Roszawikz in New York City on March 15, 1914. He was a high school dropout and got a job as a singing waiter. He became popular in his job and soon graduated to stand-up comedy. His career was put on hold during World War II and he served in the U.S. Army Air Corps. After being discharged, Joe E. Ross resumed his work in comedy, and while playing in Florida nightclubs, he was discovered by Nat Hiken and Phil Silvers. He was immediately hired to portray Rupert Ritzik on *The Phil Silvers Show*. After four seasons, that classic sitcom was cancelled, but Ross was then brought over to another Nat Hiken project— a new NBC show to be called *Car 54, Where Are You?* Ross played inept Officer Gunther Toody. Ross became famous for saying, "Ooh, ooh" every time he had a great idea. "Ooh, Ooh" was also the title of a rock and roll music single by Ross released in 1963. Ross spoke his part of the song, explaining, "When you get a good idea, and you need someone to tell it to, just scratch your head and roll your eyes, and simply say Ooh Ooh." He had a group of girls and guys singing in the background and alternated calling upon them to perform their part of the song (saying, "Sing along with Joey" and "Ooh, Ooh"). The song was backed with "You're Nobody 'Til Somebody Loves You" (a song Ross sang on the Christmas episode of *Car 54, Where Are You?* titled "Christmas at the 53rd").

The following year, even though the sitcom was no longer on NBC's prime-time schedule, Ross recorded an album called *Love Songs from a Cop* (Roulette #25281). He then released a single version of "Hello, Dolly" (Roulette #4584) from the album. With his raspy voice, it was the perfect song for him, mirroring the rasp of Louis Armstrong. However, that single, backed with "Are You Lonesome Tonight?" was lost in a sea of British Invasion music in 1964 and soon forgotten. Ross then landed in another sitcom—the memorable but short-lived *It's About Time*, on which he portrayed a caveman named Gronk. He then turned to supplying voices for animation and got to reprise his Gunther Toody role in an episode of a 1974 cartoon series called *Wait 'til Your Father Gets Home*. He later portrayed Sergeant Flint in the popular animated series called *Hong Kong Phooey*. Ross suffered a massive heart attack while doing what he loved, performing stand-up comedy. He died in Van Nuys, California, on August 13, 1982 at the age of 68. He was married multiple times, and many costars were put off by his vulgar sense of humor on the set. Jay Leno delivered his eulogy.

RICHARD ROUNDTREE

Most Famous TV Role: John Shaft on TV's *Shaft* series; **Network:** CBS; **Years:** 1973–1974; **Hit Recording:** "This Magic Moment"; **Label:** Artists of America; **Release Year:** 1976; **Matrix:** Artists of America #115; **Chart:** #90 *Billboard* R&B

Richard Roundtree was born in New Rochelle, New York, on July 9, 1942. He played football in high school and is best known for his roles in what are now referred to as blaxploitation films of the 1970s—especially for his role as John Shaft in *Shaft*, *Shaft's Big Score*, and *Shaft in Africa*. The John Shaft role proved so popular, he even got to bring him to television in 1973 on CBS. The TV version of *Shaft* was 90 minutes in length and rotated on Tuesday nights with *The New CBS Tuesday Night Movies* and *Hawkins*, but it didn't translate well to the small screen. The Oscar-winning Isaac Hayes song about John Shaft ("He's a bad mother . . . hush your mouth") was also used in the series.

Speaking of songs, while on the series, Richard Roundtree attempted to parlay his screen fame into success on the record charts. He signed with MGM Records and released a single called "Man from Shaft" backed with "Tree of Life" (MGM #10696). When that record failed to catch on, he changed directions and began recording a lot of retro material, including remakes of Jesse Belvin's "Goodnight My Love" and Johnny Ace's "Pledging My Love" (MGM #14659). He tried again a couple of years later with a remake of the Tymes' "So Much in Love" backed with the Drifters' "This Magic Moment." "This Magic Moment" cracked the bottom of the R&B charts in 1976, but none of his follow-up singles had any impact. After playing Sam Bennett on *Roots* in 1977, Roundtree turned his attention to stage plays. He was diagnosed with rare male breast cancer in 1993 and had a double mastectomy and chemotherapy treatments. He has now been cancer free for over 20 years, and often speaks to men's groups about early detection. He portrayed Uncle John Shaft in the 2000 *Shaft* remake that starred Samuel L. Jackson.

IRENE RYAN

Most Famous TV Role: Granny (Daisy Moses) on *The Beverly Hillbillies;* **Network:** CBS; **Years:** 1962–1971; **Hit Recording:** none; **Label:** Nashwood; **Release Year:** 1968; **Matrix:** "Granny's Mini Skirt" (Nashwood #100); **Chart:** none

Irene Ryan was born as Jessie Irene Noblett in El Paso, Texas, on October 17, 1902. She started singing on stage in her youth, and was performing in Vaudeville in her early 20s. Her husband was comedian Tim Ryan, and they formed an act together (Tim and Irene) and made several short films. Their act was not much different from that of George Burns and Gracie Allen. Tim and Irene divorced during World War II, and Irene then began touring with Bob Hope and also performed on his radio show. In the interim, she married film producer Harold Knox. They were divorced in 1961. Both of Ryan's marriages were childless. With the advent of television, she made the rounds guest starring on episodic programs. Her first recurring role came in 1960 on the short-lived sitcom *Bringing Up Buddy* as Cynthia Boyle.

At the age of 60, she finally got her big break in the business when she was cast in the role of the cantankerous, vittle-fixing Granny on a new 1962 CBS TV series called *The Beverly Hillbillies*. The program became a ratings sensation and enjoyed a nine-season run. Merchandise related to the program included comic books, board games, and lunch boxes. There was also a cast album called *"The Beverly Hillbillies" TV Cast Sings* in 1968 (Columbia #9202). In that same year, Irene (as Granny) released a single called "Granny's Mini Skirt" backed with "Bring on the Show" for the small Nashwood Records label (its name was a combination of Nashville and Hollywood). Background vocals on the record were provided by a group called the Markleys. These novelty records weren't big sellers, but were a must for the program's most ardent fans. After 274 episodes, the program came to an end in 1971 as CBS began weeding out its many rural sitcoms. However, Irene Ryan was still a very popular entity and was cast in Broadway's *Pippin*. This will surprise many—she then released a record for the Motown label in 1972. That humorous record from the *Pippin* soundtrack, "No Time at All" backed with "Time to Believe in Each Other" (Motown #1221), credited her as Irene "Granny" Ryan. It was her final recording—Ryan died of a stroke on April 26, 1973. She was nominated for a Tony Award for the role, but lost to Patricia Elliott of *A Little Night Music*.

S

KATEY SAGAL

Most Famous TV Role: Peg Bundy on *Married with Children*; **Network:** Fox; **Years:** 1987–1997; **Hit Recording:** none; **Labels:** Valley, Virgin; **Release Years:** 1994–2004; **Matrix:** "Can't Hurry the Harvest" (Virgin #101), "I Don't Wanna Know" (Virgin #14223), *Well* (Virgin CD #39543), *Room* (Valley CD #15185); **Chart:** none

Katey Sagal was born in Los Angeles, California, on January 19, 1954. She was born into a show business family—her mom was a writer and producer, and her father a director. TV producer Norman Lear is her godfather. Sagal is a graduate of the California Institute of the Arts. She got some work in guest-starring roles on episodic TV shows, but her first regular role was as Jo Tucker on CBS's short-lived 1985 Mary Tyler Moore sitcom called *Mary*. She was then cast in the role that made her famous— that of Peg Bundy, the long-suffering wife of shoe salesman Al Bundy on the unconventional Fox sitcom *Married with Children*. The show ran on the Fox Network for a decade and has enjoyed an amazingly successful life in syndication. During the show's run, Sagal also released an album for Virgin Records titled simply *Well*. Two singles were released from the album—"Can't Hurry the Harvest" and "I Don't Wanna Know" (the latter with backing vocals from Rita Coolidge). However, neither the album nor the singles managed to make the charts, and Sagal placed recorded music on the backburner for almost a decade. She tried again while portraying Cate Hennessey on *8 Simple Rules for Dating My Teenage Daughter* in 2004 with an album titled *Room* for Valley Entertainment, but met with the same disappointing results. In recent years, Sagal has become a successful voice for animation (most notably *Futurama*) and has earned recurring roles on several series, including *Lost*, *Boston Legal*, and *Sons of Anarchy* (the latter earned her a Golden Globe Award). She has been married three times and has a star on Hollywood's Walk of Fame.

SOUPY SALES

Most Famous TV Role: host of *The Soupy Sales Show*; **Network:** ABC, syndicated; **Years:** 1955–1967; **Hit Recording:** "The Mouse"; **Label:** ABC-Paramount; **Release Year:** 1965; **Matrix:** ABC-Paramount #10646; **Chart:** #76 *Billboard* Hot 100

Soupy Sales was born Milton Supman in Franklinton, North Carolina, on January 8, 1926. His nickname as a kid was Soupbone and that later evolved into Soupy. His last name of Sales was inspired by a Vaudevillian named Chic Sale. He found work as a disc jockey, but took some time off to enlist in the U.S. Navy during World War II. After the war, he earned a master's degree in journalism and then found work as a comedian in nightclubs, as a radio disc jockey, and even hosting his own local TV show. It was at his next TV gig in Cleveland that Sales received his first of thousands of pies in his face. His next stop was Detroit, where he really honed his skills and created the type of program for which he'd become famous in the 1960s. Then opportunity knocked in Los Angeles at ABC-TV and finally at WNEW-TV in New York City with his biggest success—*The Soupy Sales Show*. The program was rife with puppets, puns, pranks, pies, and double entendre, and was syndicated to over 200 stations nationwide. The program was also very musical, and many hit makers of the day, as well as jazz greats, made guest appearances on the show.

Speaking of music, Sales even had one hit record, "The Mouse" on ABC-Paramount Records in 1965. The record was especially popular in the New York area, but did manage to chart nationally. Sales's record also incited a brief "Mouse" dance craze. The dance consisted of shaking one's hands by one's ears. Then one had to stick out his or her teeth and sneer. Sales recorded several follow-ups, including a remake of Pat Boone's "Speedy Gonzales" (ABC-Paramount #10681) and "I'm a Bird-Watching Man" (ABC-Paramount #10747), but none matched the sales of "The Mouse." There was even a *Do the Mouse* album in 1966 (ABC-Paramount #517). Sales then jumped to Capitol Records, Brunswick Records, and even Motown Records, but failed to have another hit. His antics, such as having kids send in "those little green pieces of paper in their parents' wallets" will long outlive him.

His WNEW series had begun to wear out its welcome by 1967 and eventually disappeared from the schedule. Sales quickly rebounded and became a regular panelist on the new syndicated *What's My Line?* game show, first with host Wally Bruner and then with Larry Blyden. He was also a frequent guest on other game shows, such as *The $20,000 Pyramid* and *The Gong Show*. A filmed series called *The New Soupy Sales Show* in 1978 never matched the popularity of his 1960s program, and lasted only one season. Soupy then returned to his roots, radio broadcasting, and enjoyed a nice run on WNBC-AM in New York City in the 1980s. Soupy was never quite the same after taking a bad fall in the 1990s. After a bout with cancer, Soupy died on October 22, 2009. He was married twice and has two sons who survive him. He has a star on the Hollywood Walk of Fame.

TELLY SAVALAS

Most Famous TV Role: Lieutenant Theo Kojak on *Kojak*; **Network:** CBS; **Years:** 1973–1978; **Hit Recording:** *Telly*; **Label:** MCA; **Release Years:** 1974–1976; **Matrix:** "If" (MCA #40301), "Help Me Make it through the Night" (MCA #40363), "Who Loves Ya, Baby?" (MCA #40468), *Telly* (MCA LP #436), *Who Loves Ya, Baby?* (MCA LP #2160); **Chart:** *Telly*—#117 *Billboard* Top Pop Albums

Aristotelis "Telly" Savalas was born in Garden City, New York, on January 21, 1922. His father owned a Greek restaurant. His first job was as a lifeguard and he served in the U.S. Army during World War II. He started in radio in New York in the 1950s and didn't pursue an acting career until he was already well into his 30s. He then made the rounds as a guest star on numerous prime-time drama series, such as *The Man from U.N.C.L.E.*, *Naked City*, *The Twilight Zone*, *The F.B.I.*, and *The Untouchables*. His first recurring role was as Mr. Carver on the short-lived 1961 NBC series called *Acapulco*. He shaved his head for the role of Pontius Pilate in *The Greatest Story Ever Told* in 1965, and never allowed it to grow back. After earning roles in *The Dirty Dozen* and *Kelly's Heroes*, his most famous character, Lieutenant Theo Kojak, was introduced in a 1973 TV movie called *The Marcus Nelson Murders*. The character proved popular enough to warrant a series, and the lollipop-loving detective whose catch phrase was "Who loves ya, baby?" became a hit with the public.

During the show's run, Savalas broadened his horizons and signed a recording contract with MCA Records. He released several albums and singles for the label, including an album and a 45 titled *Who Loves Ya, Baby?* Most of his albums contained cover versions of songs made popular by others, such as Bread's "If" and Mike Douglas's "The Men in My Little Girl's Life." Despite his popularity, none of his records had much of an impact in the United States, but did sell fairly well in the United Kingdom. *Kojak* was cancelled in 1978 after five years on CBS, but returned years later in a series of special TV movies. Savalas also had a long run in commercials for the Player's Club card. He continued to work even after being diagnosed with bladder cancer. He died on January 22, 1994, one day after his 72nd birthday. He was married three times.

JOHN SCHNEIDER

Most Famous TV Role: Bo Duke on *Dukes of Hazzard*; **Network:** CBS; **Years:** 1979–1985; **Hit Recording:** "It's Now or Never"; **Label:** MCA, Scotti Brothers; **Release Year:** 1981; **Matrix:** Scotti Brothers #02105; **Chart:** #14 *Billboard* Hot 100, #4 Country

John Schneider was born in Mount Kisco, New York on April 8, 1960. He had a fascination with magic and was putting on magic shows before he was 10. His interests then turned to race car driving, and his considerable driving skills helped him land the role of Bo Duke on a new TV series called *The Dukes of Hazzard*. On the series he drove the famous "General Lee," an orange 1969 Chrysler two-door muscle car. During the show's run, Schneider signed with Scotti Brothers Records and achieved instant chart success with a remake of an Elvis Presley song, "It's Now or Never," that had originally been released in 1960 (the year Schneider was born). It just missed the Top Ten on the Pop charts and peaked at number 4 Country. The *It's Now or Never* album (Scotti Brothers #37400) peaked at number 37. Schneider didn't have any big follow-up hits on the Pop charts, but he did rack up a string of successes on the Country charts—his *A Memory like You* album reached number 1 in 1985. He also scored four number 1 singles—"I've Been around Enough to Know" (MCA #52407), "Country Girls" (MCA #52510), "What's a Memory like You (Doing in a Love like This)?" (MCA #52723), and "You're the Last Thing I Needed Tonight" (MCA #52827). After the cancellation of *The Dukes of Hazzard*, Schneider remained extremely busy with recurring roles on *Dr. Quinn, Medicine Woman*; *Nip Tuck*; *90210*; *Desperate Housewives*; *Hot in Cleveland*; and *Smallville*. He's also dabbled in screenwriting, film producing, and directing. He's been married twice and is a born-again Christian.

ERIC SCOTT

Most Famous TV Role: Ben Walton on *The Waltons*; **Network:** CBS; **Years:** 1972–1981; **Hit Recording:** none; **Label:** United National; **Release Year:** 1979; **Matrix:** *Joe Conley and Eric Scott of "The Waltons"* (United National LP #1037); **Chart:** none

Eric Scott Magat was born in Los Angeles, California, on October 20, 1958. He portrayed Ben Walton first in the TV movie titled *The Homecoming: A Christmas Story* in 1971. That served as a pilot for *The Waltons* series that began a year later, and Scott was back as Ben for the series. He stayed for the entire run, and returned for the subsequent TV reunion movies. During the program's run in prime time, Scott teamed with Joe Conley, who played Ike Godsey, the storekeeper on the show, and recorded an album. Conley had a lot of prior singing experience, having been with Horace Heidt's band at one time, but this proved to be Eric Scott's only recording. The album, *Joe Conley and Eric Scott of "The Waltons,"* was released on the United National label in 1979. In that same year, the duo performed a couple of the songs from the album in an episode titled "The Obstacle." The album was not mass produced and was treated more as a souvenir and a promotional tool than a potential hit. Conley and Scott often used the record in the manner of an 8 x 10 glossy when asked for their autographs. Scott has been married three times and today has his own parcel delivery service. Other than *The Waltons*, Scott's TV credits are very few and far between. Conley was married only once, had four children, and died in Newbury Park, California, on July 7, 2013, at the age of 85.

RICKY SEGALL

Most Famous TV Role: Ricky Stevens on *The Partridge Family*; **Network:** ABC; **Years:** 1973–1974; **Hit Recording:** none; **Label:** Bell; **Release Year:** 1974; **Matrix:** "Sooner or Later" (Bell #429), *Ricky Segall and the Segalls* (Bell LP #1138); **Chart:** none

Richard Robert "Ricky" Segall was born in Plainview on Long Island, New York, on March 10, 1969. His parents were singer/songwriters who performed in local nightclubs, and by the age of three he was joining them. The young man came to the attention of Columbia Pictures, and he got to audition for the role of Ricky Stevens on *The Partridge Family* for the fourth and final season on ABC. He earned the role and his father got to write all the songs he performed on the program. During his single season on the program, Segall got to record a single for Bell Records, the same label for which David Cassidy and the Partridge Family recorded. That single, "Sooner or Later" backed with "Say Hey, Willie" (Bell #429), was not a big hit. There was also an album called *Ricky Segall and the Segalls* (Bell LP #1138), but it also sold poorly. His career on TV was very short-lived and Segall pursued a higher calling. Today he is a pastor in San Antonio, Texas. He has a wife and three children and today uses the name Rick Segall.

WILLIAM SHATNER

Most Famous TV Role: Captain James Tiberius Kirk on *Star Trek*; **Network:** NBC; **Years:** 1966–1969; **Hit Recording:** none; **Labels:** Decca, Lemli; **Release Years:** 1968–1978; **Matrix:** *The Transformed Man* (Decca LP #75043), *William Shatner Live* (Lemli LP #00001); **Chart:** none

William Shatner was born in Montreal, Canada, on March 22, 1931. He studied economics at McGill University. He became a business manager for a Canadian playhouse and then decided that he wanted to be on the stage of that playhouse and became an actor. He found work in a couple of Canadian motion pictures and TV programs before earning his first role in the United States in *The Brothers Karamazov*. He appeared in numerous episodic TV shows, including two classic episodes of *The Twilight Zone* before snagging his own series called *For the People* on CBS in 1965. Shatner portrayed district attorney David Koster in this series, and it lasted slightly over three months before being axed. Had the program been renewed for a second season, Shatner may have missed out on the role of a lifetime, that of Captain James Tiberius Kirk on *Star Trek* beginning in 1966 on NBC. Surprisingly, this program was not a ratings bonanza and struggled in each of its three seasons, only to become a sensation in reruns.

During the program's original run, Shatner got to release an album for Decca Records. The album titled *The Transformed Man* never made the charts, but became somewhat legendary in later years because of Shatner's unusual, overacted, and overzealous interpretations of classic tunes such as "Mr. Tambourine Man," "It Was a Very Good Year," and especially "Lucy in the Sky with Diamonds." When the 79 episodes of *Star Trek* took off like gangbusters in syndication, the original cast was reassembled for a series of motion pictures that continued the story and Shatner appeared in seven of them. Seemingly never out of work, Shatner starred in many different series including *Star Trek: The Animated Series*, *Barbary Coast*, *T.J. Hooker*, *$#*! My Dad Says*, and *Boston Legal*. He also had recurring roles on *3rd Rock from the Sun* and *The Practice*. He has resumed his recording career in recent years with *Has Been* in 2004, *Seeking Major Tom* in 2011, and *Ponder the Mystery* in 2013. He has been married four times and has a son and three daughters. He has a star on the Hollywood Walk of Fame. He won his only Emmy Award for *The Practice* and his only Golden Globe for *Boston Legal*.

CYBILL SHEPHERD

Most Famous TV Roles: Maddie Hayes on *Moonlighting*, Cybill Sheridan on *Cybill*; **Network:** ABC, CBS; **Years:** 1985–1989, 1995–1998, respectively; **Hit Recording:** none; **Labels:** Drive, Gold Castle, MCA, Peabody, River Siren; **Release Years:** 1974–2004; **Matrix:** *Cybill Does It* (MCA LP #25173), *Talk Memphis to Me* (Drive LP #45501), *Vanilla* (Peabody LP #102), *Somewhere Down the Road* (Gold Castle LP #71361), *At Home with Cybill* (River Siren CD #003); **Chart:** none

Cybill Shepherd was born in Memphis, Tennessee, on February 18, 1950. She was Miss Teenage Memphis at the age of 16 and was a modeling star by the age of 18. A magazine cover earned her a role in Peter Bogdanovich's *The Last Picture Show* in 1971. She became a Bogdanovich favorite and was used in several less successful films as well. Shepherd made numerous attempts at success on vinyl records, but each time was disappointed. None of her albums over 30 years managed to catch on with the record-buying public. She did succeed in television twice—first on *Moonlighting* with Bruce Willis from 1985 to 1989 on ABC, and then again a decade later on her own eponymous CBS sitcom from 1995 to 1998. An album of country, blues, jazz, and soul tunes dedicated to her hometown of Memphis (*Talk Memphis to Me*) on the Drive Entertainment label was released during her run on the *Cybill* sitcom, but her TV success did not translate into chart success. She was awarded three Golden Globe Awards—two for *Moonlighting* and one for *Cybill*. She has been married twice and has three children. Shepherd was seen most recently in a recurring role as Madeleine Spencer on USA Network's popular *Psych* series.

BOBBY SHERMAN

Most Famous TV Role: Jeremy Bolt on *Here Come the Brides*; **Network:** ABC; **Years:** 1968–1970; **Hit Recordings:** "Little Woman," "Julie Do You Love Me?"; **Label:** Metromedia; **Release Years:** 1969–1970; **Matrix:** "Little Woman" (Metromedia #121), "Julie Do You Love Me?" (Metromedia #194); **Chart:** #3, #5, respectively, *Billboard* Hot 100

Robert Cabot Sherman Jr. was born in Santa Monica, California, on July 22, 1943. He played the trumpet in his youth and took an interest in singing. He played football in high school and was part of a dance band. He became friendly with actor/singer Sal Mineo and through him eventually

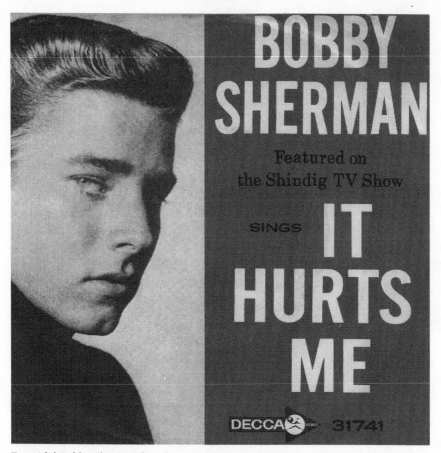

Teen idol Bobby Sherman found success on TV in *Shindig* and *Here Come the Brides*. The song pictured, "It Hurts Me," was his first charted single.

became a regular on *Shindig*. Sherman also recorded a few singles for Cameo and Decca records but only had a very minor hit with a song called "It Hurts Me" in 1965 (Decca #31741). His biggest break came in 1968 when he was cast as the shy Jeremy Bolt on ABC's *Here Come the Brides*. During the show's two-year run, Sherman scored a contract with Metromedia Records and immediately found success with a string of Top Ten hits—"Little Woman," "La La La (If I Had You)," "Easy Come, Easy Go," and "Julie Do You Love Me?" Each of these singles earned Sherman a gold record. He also scored three gold albums—*Bobby Sherman* (Metromedia #1014), *Here Comes Bobby* (Metromedia #1028), and *With Love, Bobby* (Metromedia #1032).

However, his popularity and his TV series both began to falter in 1970. *Here Come the Brides* was cancelled and ABC quickly sought another series for Sherman. He made a guest appearance as an up-and-coming songwriter on an episode of *The Partridge Family* titled "Knight in Shining Armor." That episode served as a Screen Gems pilot/spinoff for his next series, *Getting Together* in 1971. Unfortunately, by the time the program debuted, Sherman was considered passé, yesterday's news. It also didn't help that the new series was scheduled for Saturday nights on ABC against *All in the Family* on CBS. *Getting Together* only lasted for 14 weeks, and the most interesting thing about the program is that each episode shared its title with that of a famous song—"Why Do Fools Fall in Love?" "Broken-Hearted Melody," "Blue Christmas," and "All Shook Up," to name a few. *Getting Together* only spawned one very minor hit for Sherman, a song titled "Jennifer" (Metromedia #227) late in 1971, which was sung to his younger sister on the show, Jenny (portrayed by Susan Neher). After this series failed, Sherman withdrew from public view and became a member of the Los Angeles police force, where he was eventually promoted to captain. He briefly returned to TV as a member of the cast of *Sanchez of Bel-Air* in 1986 as Frankie Rondell. He has been married twice.

ROBERTA SHORE

Most Famous TV Role: Betsy Garth on *The Virginian;* **Network:** NBC; **Years:** 1962–1965; **Hit Recording:** none; **Label:** Buena Vista, Decca, Disneyland, Dot; **Release Years:** 1959–1965; **Matrix:** "Shaggy Dog" (Disneyland #123), "Happy Music" (Buena Vista #340), "A Teenage Prayer" (Dot #16189), "Rock and Roll Yodeling Guy" (Dot #16266), "Who Lies Right, Who Lies Wrong?" (Dot #16483), *The Singing Stars of "The Virginian"* (Decca LP #74619); **Chart:** none

Roberta Shore was born as Roberta Jymme Schourop in Monterey Park, California, on April 7, 1943. In the late 1950s she appeared in numerous Disney TV productions, including *Walt Disney Presents: Annette*, without ever being a Mouseketeer, and recorded several numbers for the Disneyland and Buena Vista labels—the most famous of which is "Shaggy Dog" from the film soundtrack. Shore made the rounds as a guest star on dozens of episodic TV shows such as *Father Knows Best, The Donna Reed Show, Wagon Train,* and *Laramie.* She also became a regular on *The New Bob Cummings Show* on CBS in 1961 and on *The Virginian* in 1962. While portraying Hank Gogerty on Cummings's show, she snagged a recording contract with Dot Records and released a duet with teen idol Robin Luke of "Susie Darlin'" fame. Together, they recorded "Foggin' up the Windows" backed with "A Wound Time Can't Erase" (Dot #16366) in 1961, produced by Wink Martindale. The record was not a hit but Shore got to release three other solo singles for the label in an attempt to have a chart record. Those attempts include "A Teenage Prayer" backed with "What Else Can I Do?," "Rock and Roll Yodeling Guy" backed with "Yum Yum Cha Cha," and "Who Lies Right, Who Lies Wrong?" backed with "Let There Be Peace on Earth." None of the Dot singles caught on, but Shore got another opportunity to record while she was a cast member on *The Virginian*. Paired with costar Randy Boone (see the entry for him), she released an LP of duets called *The Singing Stars of "The Virginian"* for Decca Records in 1965. After leaving *The Virginian* in 1965, Shore withdrew from public view and opted to raise a family. She's been married three times and in recent years worked for a furniture company.

MARGARITA "CHA CHA" SIERRA

Most Famous TV Role: Cha Cha O'Brien on *Surfside 6*; **Network:** ABC; **Years:** 1960–1962; **Hit Recording:** none; **Label:** Warner Bros.; **Release Year:** 1961; **Matrix:** "Cha Cha Twist" (Warner Bros. #5248); **Chart:** none

Margarita Sierra was born in Madrid, Spain, on January 5, 1936. She was a sexy singer, dancer, and nightclub performer who briefly found fame in the United States on the ABC Warner Bros. series called *Surfside 6* from 1960 to 1962. Her character's name was Cha Cha O'Brien and, like so many others on Warner Bros. TV shows, she was encouraged to record for the Warner Bros. record label. The result was "Cha Cha Twist" backed with "Pretty Baby" in 1961. Sierra performed the song a couple of times on the TV series, but it failed to crack the Hot 100. *Surfside 6* enjoyed a run in syndication on the Good Life Network from 2002 to 2003. Sierra died of a heart ailment at the age of only 27 on September 6, 1963.

RED SKELTON

Most Famous TV Role: star of *The Red Skelton Show*; **Network:** CBS, NBC; **Years:** 1951–1971; **Hit Recording:** "The Pledge of Allegiance"; **Label:** Columbia; **Release Year:** 1969; **Matrix:** Columbia #44798; **Chart:** #44 *Billboard* Hot 100

Richard Skelton was born in Vincennes, Indiana, on July 18, 1913. He was part of a traveling show beginning at the age of 10. He eventually became a Vaudeville performer and parlayed his success into a long run on radio. He also appeared in numerous motion pictures, including *Having Wonderful Time* and *Ziegfield Follies*. In television's infancy, he earned his own half-hour program on NBC in 1951 sponsored by Tide detergent. By 1954, *The Red Skelton Show* expanded to an hour in length and jumped to CBS, where it settled in for a 17-year run in prime time. During the program's storied run, Skelton recorded a single for Columbia Records (part of CBS, the Columbia Broadcasting System) on which he clarified "The Pledge of Allegiance" through the eyes and words of his teacher and principal, Mr. Lasswell. The record debuted on his CBS variety show on January 14, 1969, and when released as a single (over four minutes in length) it sold rather well and just missed the Top Forty by March of that year. The recording enjoyed a brief resurgence in airplay immediately after September 11, 2001, and was rereleased in cassette form.

In 1970, CBS began revamping its prime-time schedule and began to eliminate its many rural programs and programs that appealed mostly to an older demographic. Jackie Gleason, Ed Sullivan, and Red Skelton were in the network's crosshairs and their shows were cancelled. Even though ratings were still very decent, Skelton's show came to an end in June. It was then picked up by its original network, NBC, and was returned to its original half-hour format where it ran for one final season before leaving the airwaves for good in August of 1971. At this time, Skelton returned to live performances and was now able to find more free time to dedicate to his passion for painting. Among his final TV ventures were several HBO comedy specials in the early 1980s. After a long illness, Skelton died at the age of 84 on September 17, 1997, in the Palm Springs, California, area. He won four Emmy Awards and has two stars on Hollywood's Walk of Fame—one for radio and one for television. He was married three times and had two children.

BUFFALO BOB SMITH

Most Famous TV Role: host of *Howdy Doody*; **Networks:** NBC, syndicated; **Years:** 1947–1960, 1976; **Hit Recording:** none; **Label:** RCA Victor; **Release Year:** 1951; **Matrix:** "It's Howdy Doody Time" (RCA Victor #0296); **Chart:** none

A couple of generations grew up watching the daily fun from the peanut gallery on NBC's popular *Howdy Doody* program—one of the successes from TV's infancy. Howdy was a marionette and what we would call a "ginger" today with reddish hair and dozens of freckles. During the show's long run, Howdy and his creator and cohost Buffalo Bob Smith, released their catchy "It's Howdy Doody Time" theme song on an RCA Victor 45 (in 1951). Not unlike other singles geared toward America's youth, it was released on bright yellow vinyl. The program wore out its welcome and ended its original run in 1960. Smith attempted to revive the series with a new syndicated version in 1976, but times had changed and too few households said howdy to Doody. Smith lived to the age of 70 and died in Hendersonville, North Carolina, on July 30, 1998, only days after an appearance on the cable channel called QVC to hawk his Howdy Doody Entertainment Memorabilia Company.

REX SMITH

Most Famous TV Role: Michael Skye on *Sooner or Later*, host of *Solid Gold*; **Network:** NBC, syndicated; **Year:** 1979–1982; **Hit Recording:** "You Take My Breath Away"; **Label:** Columbia; **Release Year:** 1979; **Matrix:** Columbia #10908; **Chart:** #10 *Billboard* Hot 100

Rex Smith was born in Jacksonville, Florida, on September 19, 1955. While still in his teens he became a rock and roll performer in a group called Tricks. In 1976, he signed with Columbia Records and formed another rock band named Rex, and as Rex Smith recalled,

> We opened for Ted Nugent on the *Cat Scratch Fever Tour* and had a hard rock LP out at the time for Columbia called *Rex*. The following year, in support of my next album *Where Do We Go from Here*, I was on the road with Nugent again and this time Lynyrd Skynyrd joined the tour. After a show down south, I was having a beer with Ronnie Van Zant, the lead singer of Skynyrd. We were playing Madison Square Garden in three days. I finished my beer and said, "See you at the Garden." I never saw him again. Their tragic plane crash in 1978 affects me to this day.

Smith's life took an interesting twist because of a TV movie. Smith shared,

> On March 25, 1979, my life changed overnight. I was one of the stars of a made-for-TV movie called *Sooner or Later*, along with Barbara Feldon and Denise Miller. In the film, I was a guitar instructor, and I fell for one of my young students who lied about her age (she was only thirteen). The movie was written and directed by Bruce Hart, who also wrote the *Sesame Street* theme. The day before the movie aired, I could walk the streets without being noticed, but that next day, I was literally swamped by five hundred

girls when I tried to go shopping for clothes. Suddenly, I was this teen idol with a hit record from the film called "You Take My Breath Away," which I recorded for Columbia in one take. When it was played back in the studio I said I needed to go to the bathroom. There, crying, I just knew I'd just recorded a big, big hit record. You can just tell. It was an amazing time in my life.

The song became a Top Ten smash and garnered Smith a platinum album.

About his hit remake of Robert Knight and Carl Carlton's "Everlasting Love," Smith said, "That was a duet with the wonderful Rachel Sweet. I'm so proud of her. What a talent. She's gone on to become a great producer in partnership with Sandra Bullock. They worked on *The George Lopez Show* together." Speaking of television, shortly after that hit single in 1981, Smith became the star of an established TV show: "I stepped in to host *Solid Gold* after Andy Gibb. What a shame that was. Such a personable, talented, but self-destructive young man. Luckily, I didn't follow that path and that's why I'm still here—a father of five and now a grandfather."

Smith gave a shot to a young actor—a guest spot on his memorable series called *Street Hawk* in 1985. That actor was George Clooney. Smith's exuberance and appreciation for all the things in his life that fell into place so perfectly are contagious. Smith added, "I love to reminisce and I love to share the stories of all of the amazing happenings in my life. I've only scratched the surface in *Confessions of a Teen Idol*—a two-act autobiographical musical which began in San Diego in 2014, and is now touring the country. My music has now come full circle—from a hard rock performer to a teen idol to Broadway. I'm now in the third act of my life and the future's so bright, I gotta wear shades."

ROGER SMITH

Most Famous TV Role: Jeff Spencer on *77 Sunset Strip*; **Network:** ABC; **Years:** 1958–1963; **Hit Recording:** "Beach Time"; **Label:** Warner Bros.; **Release Year:** 1959; **Matrix:** Warner Bros. #5068; **Chart:** #64 *Billboard* Hot 100

Roger LaVerne Smith was born in South Gate, California, on December 18, 1932. His parents got him into dancing and singing lessons by the age of six. A football scholarship got him into the University of Arizona. After a stint in the U.S. Navy Reserve, he was urged to attempt success in Hollywood. He first signed with Columbia Pictures but not much happened there. His big break was in signing with Warner Bros. After good reviews for his role in the movie version of *Auntie Mame*, Warner Bros. moved

Roger Smith was the star of two Warner Bros. shows—*77 Sunset Strip* and *Mister Roberts*. He also recorded for the Warner Bros. label.

him over to their television division and a new series called *77 Sunset Strip*. He played detective Jeff Spencer on the show, and early in his run with the series he was tapped to release a couple of singles for Warner Bros.' record division. The first was "Beach Time" backed with "Cuddle Up a Little Closer" in 1959, followed by "Tick, Tick, Tick" backed with "Love of Two" (Warner Bros. #5106). Only "Beach Time" made the charts, and Smith's album titled *Beach Romance* (Warner Bros. LP #1305) didn't get very far. He left the still popular series in 1963 after five seasons for health reasons—a cerebral blood clot. He had surgery for the condition and recovered enough to star in another series in 1965—the sitcom version of *Mister Roberts* on NBC. The program was one of the early efforts produced by James Komack (see the entry in appendix A for him), who would later find success with *The Courtship of Eddie's Father, Chico and the*

Man, and *Welcome Back, Kotter. Mister Roberts* was a single-season sitcom and after its cancellation, Smith dedicated his time to his second wife's career. Her name: Ann-Margaret. His public appearances are few and far between.

DAVID SOUL

Most Famous TV Role: Detective Ken Hutchinson on *Starsky and Hutch;* **Network:** ABC; **Years:** 1975–1979; **#1 Hit Recording:** "Don't Give Up on Us"; **Label:** Private Stock; **Release Year:** 1976; **Matrix:** Private Stock #129; **Chart:** #1 *Billboard* Hot 100

David Soul was born as David Richard Solberg Jr. in Chicago, Illinois, on August 28, 1943. He had the opportunity to play for the Chicago White Sox at the age of 19, but opted to study political science instead. He switched gears again a short time later and pursued a love of music and acting. In 1966, he was already using the name David Soul, but was also known as "Covered Man" and performed folk music on several episodes of *The Merv Griffin Show.* A couple of the songs performed on Griffin's program were released as singles—"Covered Man" backed with "I Will Warm Your Heart" (MGM #13510), "Before" backed with "Was I Ever So Young?" (MGM #13589), and "Quiet Kind of Hate" backed with "No One's Gonna Cry" (MGM #13842)—but the records went nowhere fast. He was known as Covered Man because he wore a mask while performing. That alias lasted a brief time, and by 1968 as David Soul he unmasked his first regular role on the ABC series *Here Come the Brides.* Soul portrayed Joshua Bolt, and both he and costar Bobby Sherman went on to have hit records.

Several years after *Here Come the Brides* ended, he landed on another ABC series called *Owen Marshall, Counselor at Law* as Ted Warrick near the end of that show's run, replacing Lee Majors. The following year was pivotal in his career and he was cast as Detective Ken Hutchinson, the Hutch part of *Starsky and Hutch,* an Aaron Spelling police drama that ran from 1975 to 1979. During that period, Soul reignited his music career and signed with Private Stock Records in 1976. His popularity and exposure on the hit TV show aided greatly, and early in 1977 Soul scored a number 1 million-selling smash ballad called "Don't Give Up on Us." His *David Soul* album (Private Stock #2019) also became somewhat popular and reached the Top Forty. Soul's chart success was extremely short-lived, and two follow-up singles—"Going In with My Eyes Open" (Private Stock #150) and "Silver Lady" (Private Stock #163)—failed to crack the Top Fifty in the United States, but did become hits in the United Kingdom. After *Starsky and Hutch* was cancelled, he earned regular roles in several short-lived series—*Casablanca, Unsub,* and *The Yellow Rose.* His music remained popular in Europe, Asia, and South America in the 1980s, and he continued to tour there regularly. In 2004, he and former costar Paul Michael Glaser had cameo roles in the motion picture version of *Starsky and Hutch.* Soul moved to London in the late 1990s because of his lingering popularity there. He has been married five times and has a daughter and five sons.

BRENT SPINER

Most Famous TV Role: Lieutenant Commander Data on *Star Trek: The Next Generation;* **Network:** syndicated; **Years:** 1987–1994; **Hit Recording:** none; **Label:** Bay Cities; **Release Year:** 1991; **Matrix:** *Ol' Yellow Eyes Is Back* (Bay Cities CD #2004); **Chart:** none

Brent Jay Spiner was born in Houston, Texas, on Groundhog Day, February 2, 1949. He attended the University of Houston and participated in local theater productions. Upon moving to New York City, he earned a role in Stephen Sondheim's *Sunday in the Park with George.* Television was his next conquest, and he earned the recurring role of Bob Wheeler on the popular Harry Anderson sitcom called *Night Court* on NBC. Then came the role of a lifetime—that of Lieutenant Commander Data, an android, on the syndicated juggernaut called *Star Trek: The Next Generation.* While savoring a wildly successful seven-year TV run, Spiner recorded an album of old standards called *Ol' Yellow Eyes Is Back* for the Bay Cities label. The album's title was a play on Sinatra's *Ol' Blue Eyes Is Back* (Spiner's character on the show had yellow eyes). Classic songs on the album included "The Very Thought of You," "Time after Time," "Marie," "When I Fall in Love," "Embraceable You," and "More Than You Know." The CD wasn't a huge success but Spiner had a lot of fun recording it. After *Star Trek: The Next Generation* was discontinued, Spiner reprised Commander Data in four *Star Trek* motion pictures. Speaking of motion pictures, Spiner was seemingly never out of work, and earned roles in *The Aviator, Independence Day, I Am Sam, Dude Where's My Car?* and *Out to Sea.* In 2014, Spiner surfaced on Showtime as a therapist in the very popular *Ray Donovan* series. He has been married only once and has one child.

RICK SPRINGFIELD

Most Famous TV Role: Dr. Noah Drake on *General Hospital;* **Network:** ABC; **Years:** 1983–1985, 2006–2008; **#1 Hit Recording:** "Jessie's Girl"; **Label:** RCA Victor; **Release Years:** 1981–1988; **Matrix:** RCA Victor #12201; **Chart:** #1 *Billboard* Hot 100

Rick Springfield was born as Richard Lewis Springthorpe in South Wentworthville, Australia, on August 23, 1949. His interest in music began before he was a teenager, and in his teens he played and recorded with a couple of bands (Wickedy Wak and Zoot) in England, where his dad was stationed. As Zoot, the band dressed, head to toe, in pink satin, and Springfield wrote a song for the band called "Hey, Pinky" (Columbia of Australia #9169) that became popular in the United Kingdom but had no impact in the United States. Springfield first penetrated the U.S. Top Twenty with another of his compositions, "Speak to the Sky" (Capitol #3340), in 1972. With that release, Springfield got to experience a modicum of chart success, but his recording career really caught fire after he became popular as Dr. Noah Drake on ABC's *General Hospital.* He was simultaneously wearing two hats—soap star and rock star—as a song he wrote and performed called "Jessie's Girl" on RCA Victor Records soared to number 1. The album it came from, *Working Class Dog* (RCA Victor #3697), went platinum. This was followed by three more platinum LPs—*Success Hasn't Spoiled Me Yet* (RCA Victor #4125), *Living in Oz* (RCA Victor #4660), and *Hard to Hold* (RCA Victor #4935). *Hard to Hold* was also the title of a movie that starred Rick Springfield.

Suddenly, with too much on his plate, he opted to leave the soap opera role and focus upon music and his film career. However, *Hard to Hold* wasn't very well received and wasn't the box office giant the studio expected. In the new millennium, Springfield returned and settled into *General Hospital* for well over a year. A short time later, he guest starred in several episodes of *Californication.* On one of those episodes, Springfield appeared in the nude. He has also written his autobiography titled *Late, Late at Night: A Memoir.* He has been married only once and has two children. As of this writing, his latest project is a film with Meryl Streep to be called *Ricki and the Flash,* and he is said to be joining the cast of HBO's *True Detective* for its second season.

JOHN STAMOS

Most Famous TV Roles: Gino Minnelli on *Dreams*, Matt Willows on *You Again?* Jesse Katsopolis on *Full House*; **Network:** ABC; **Years:** 1984, 1986–1987, 1987–1995, respectively; **Hit Recording:** none; **Label:** Columbia; **Release Year:** 1984; **Matrix:** *Dreams TV Soundtrack* (Columbia #39886); **Chart:** none

John Stamos was born in Cypress, California, on August 19, 1963. His paternal grandparents were born in Greece. John began his acting career on *General Hospital* while still in his teens. He was introduced to prime-time viewers as one of the stars of a short-lived TV sitcom called *Dreams* in 1984 on NBC. Stamos portrayed Gino Minnelli, an aspiring musician trying to get a break into show business. An album of songs performed by the cast was released in tandem with the premiere of the program. Stamos performed three songs ("Jailhouse Rock," "I Won't Let You Take Away My Music," and "Alone") for the *Dreams* album on the Columbia label. However, the program did not perform well in the ratings and disappeared after only 12 episodes. Because of this, the album also did poorly and failed to chart. One song from the album, "Alone," written by the prolific Billy Steinberg, was covered by Heart in 1987 and became a major hit record.

Stamos's next TV venture, an NBC sitcom with Jack Klugman called *You Again?* was also a flop. The third time was the charm, and he was dealt a *Full House* in 1987 and enjoyed an eight-year run as Jesse Katsopolis. During the show's peak popularity, Stamos performed lead vocals teamed with the Beach Boys on a song called "Forever." It was released on the Beach Boys' Brothers label (PROCD #3) in 1992. The song was written by Dennis Wilson, and this version came 22 years after the Beach Boys' original. Stamos's rendition of the song was not a big hit, but he befriended the group and continued to sing with and play drums for the group on occasion. After the cancellation of *Full House*, Stamos surfaced in a couple of short-lived series—*Thieves* and *Jake in Progress*. As of this writing, he is the commercial spokesman for Oikos Greek yogurt.

JEAN STAPLETON. *See* CARROLL O'CONNOR AND JEAN STAPLETON.

CONNIE STEVENS

Most Famous TV Role: Cricket Blake on *Hawaiian Eye*; **Network:** ABC; **Years:** 1959–1963; **Hit Recordings:** "Sixteen Reasons," "Kookie, Kookie, Lend Me Your Comb"; **Label:** Warner Bros.; **Release Years:** 1959–1973; **Matrix:** "Sixteen Reasons" (Warner Bros. #5137), "Kookie, Kookie Lend Me Your Comb" (Warner Bros. #5047); **Chart:** #3, #4, respectively, *Billboard* Hot 100

Connie Stevens was born as Concetta Ingoglia in Brooklyn, New York, on August 8, 1938. Her parents were musical performers and used the surname of Stevens, which she adopted as her own. She loved singing and found some work in repertory theater in Southern California until extra roles in movies began cropping up. After larger roles in a couple of B movies, she was discovered and signed by Warner Bros. to portray Cricket Blake in a new series to be called *Hawaiian Eye*. The ABC program was a hit and lasted for four seasons.

During *Hawaiian Eye*'s run, Warner Bros. used many of the stars from its prime-time shows on its new Warner Bros. record label. In 1959, Stevens was paired with Edd Byrnes of *77 Sunset Strip* on a novelty tune called "Kookie, Kookie Lend Me Your Comb." Byrnes wasn't much of a singer, but the record caught on and became a Top Five hit. The song is most famous for the final line, "Baby, you're the ginchiest." Stevens was a much better singer and had a huge solo hit the following year called "Sixteen Reasons." Once again for Warner Bros. Records, the ballad enumerates all 16 reasons in ascending order. It became Stevens's biggest hit, peaking at number 3 in 1960.

After her run as Cricket Blake came to an end in 1963, she landed in another Warner Bros. show—a very funny but short-lived sitcom called *Wendy and Me*. Stevens was Wendy, and the "me" in the title was George Burns attempting a TV comeback after Gracie Allen's retirement. Stevens exhibited amazing comedy prowess in this ABC series, and the show has enjoyed a healthy run in syndication, despite only producing 34 episodes. Stevens continued to record for Warner Bros., but music's big changes as of 1964 rendered her singing style rather obsolete, and she never again reached the Top Forty. Even switching to Bell and MGM Records couldn't resurrect her recording career. She costarred in one other TV sitcom, *Starting from Scratch* with Bill Daily in 1988, but it lasted only one season in syndication. Today she has her own cosmetic skin care line and performs occasionally in Las Vegas. She has been married twice and has two daughters. She has stars on both the Hollywood Walk of Fame and the Palm Springs Walk of Stars.

F Troop's Larry Storch accumulated a long list of TV credits. He also made phonograph records, including this version of Frankie Lymon's "Goody Goody."

LARRY STORCH

Most Famous TV Role: Corporal Randolph Agarn on *F Troop*; **Network:** ABC; **Years:** 1965–1967; **Hit Recording:** none; **Labels:** Jubilee, MGM, Roulette; **Release Years:** 1958–1963; **Matrix:** "Vilachi Sings" (Jubilee #5462), "Pooped" (MGM #12711), "Goody Goody" (Roulette #4024); **Chart:** none

Lawrence Storch was born in New York City on January 8, 1923. He didn't complete his high school education, instead working as a comic to earn money for the family. He released a couple of comedy singles in the 1950s, including a cover version of Frankie Lymon's hit "Goody Goody." Storch's version used the same exact instrumental track—

Storch's voice was dubbed over Lymon's. He also recorded a novelty song called "Pooped" for MGM Records. Neither of these were big hits, and Storch was not yet a regular performer on television. However, in the early 1960s, Storch got very busy. He was the voice for two animated characters—"Koko the Clown" and "Mr. Whoopee" (the latter a regular on *Tennessee Tuxedo and His Tales*). He also earned a recurring role as Charlie the drunk on season two of *Car 54, Where Are You?* While doing all this, he also found time to record a single for Jubilee Records (#5462) called "Valachi Sings," parts 1 and 2. Storch is listed as the cowriter of the record—a narration. There was also a Jubilee album, *Larry Storch at the Bon Soir* (Jubilee #2033). Like his earlier efforts, none of these became hits.

Storch's biggest break came in 1965 when he was cast as the very hyper Corporal Agarn on the ABC slapstick period piece sitcom called *F Troop*. The program only lasted two seasons, but has seemingly been in syndicated reruns forever. Storch's next two sitcoms were *The Queen and I* in 1969 and *The Ghost Busters* in 1976. The latter was a CBS kids' sitcom, on which Storch was once again paired with his *F Troop* costar Forrest Tucker (see the entry for him). This series came before the blockbuster *Ghostbusters* movie and is connected in name only. He only married once and had three children. Storch makes occasional appearances at Hollywood autograph shows.

GALE STORM

Most Famous TV Roles: Margie Albright on *My Little Margie*, Susanna Pomeroy on *The Gale Storm Show*; **Networks:** ABC, CBS, NBC; **Years:** 1952–1955, 1956–1960, respectively; **Top Five Recordings:** "Dark Moon," "I Hear You Knocking," "Memories Are Made of This"; **Label:** Dot; **Release Years:** 1955–1957; **Matrix:** "Dark Moon" (Dot #15558), "I Hear You Knocking" (Dot #15412), "Memories Are Made of This" (Dot #15436); **Chart:** #4, #2, #5, respectively, *Billboard* Hot 100

Gale Storm was born Josephine Cottle, the youngest of five children in Bloomington, Texas, on April 5, 1922. Her father died before her second birthday, and her mom had to raise the five kids on her own. Young Josephine became interested in the performing arts and participated in all of her school productions. She then won first prize in a contest and in almost storybook fashion was given a one-year contract with a movie studio. It was then that her name was changed to Gale Storm. After several low-budget films, she moved to TV and from 1952 to 1960, she was never out of work. Her first sitcom, *My Little Margie*, debuted in 1952 and costarred movie star Charles Farrell as her widowed dad, Vernon Albright. The program also aired weekly on radio. Near the end of that show's run, her recording career began. Most of her releases were cover songs, but she had quite a string of big hit singles for Dot Records. She started with "I Hear You Knocking," a cover of the Smiley Lewis R&B hit, followed by a two-sided Top Ten hit—"Memories Are Made of This" backed with "Teen Age Prayer" (covers of hits by Dean Martin and Gloria Mann, respectively). Then came a remake of Frankie Lymon and the Teenagers' "Why Do Fools Fall in Love?" (Dot #15448) and a cover of Otis Williams and the Charms' "Ivory Tower" (Dot #15458).

Storm could do no wrong and immediately set sail on another sitcom venture, this time on CBS called *The Gale Storm Show* (often called *Oh, Susanna*). On this sitcom, she worked on a cruise ship and got into the wackiest situations. She also got to debut one of her biggest hits on an episode called "Sing, Susanna, Sing." That song, "Dark Moon," was a cover of a song done first by Bonnie Guitar. It became Storm's final Top Ten hit in 1957. *Oh, Susanna* lasted until 1960. The 1960s were not kind to Storm and except for a couple of guest appearances on *Burke's Law*, she disappeared from prime-time TV. She was only seen at Hollywood autograph shows. Her two hit sitcoms, however, enjoyed a long run in syndication. She was married and widowed twice and has three stars on Hollywood's Walk of Fame for radio, television, and music. She died on June 27, 2009, at the age of 87.

MARY STUART

Most Famous TV Role: Joanne Gardner Barron on *Search for Tomorrow*; **Network:** CBS, NBC; **Years:** 1951–1986; **Hit Recordings:** none; **Labels:** Bell, Columbia; **Release Years:** 1954, 1973; **Matrix:** *Joanne Sings* (Columbia LP #347), *Mary Stuart* (Bell LP #1133); **Chart:** *Joanne Sings*—#12 *Billboard* Top Pop Albums

Mary Stuart Houchins was born in Miami, Florida, on July 4, 1926. After serving as an on-screen double in countless films in the 1940s, she got to spend her entire TV career on soap operas, with 35 years clocked in on *Search for Tomorrow* alone, on which she portrayed the four-times-married Joanne Gardner Barron Tate Reynolds Vicente Tourneur. She was there from episode 1 until the finale. During that period, she twice attempted a recording career. Her first go-round was in 1954 for the Columbia label. She released a 10-inch album, *Joanne Sings*, consisting of eight songs that were also issued on 78 and 45 rpm singles—"Hush Little Baby" backed with "Pigeon House" (Columbia #40445), "What Shall We Do with the Baby?" backed with "One More River" (Columbia #40446), "More I Cannot Wish You" backed with "Lullaby and Goodnight" (Columbia #40447), and "Dance like a Lady" backed with "The Bird's Counting Song" (Columbia #40448). She was backed by the Percy Faith Orchestra on the records, and the album showed the CBS logo and a still picture from the *Search for Tomorrow* opening credits. The record fared pretty well, but Stuart didn't get another opportunity to record again until 19 years later—once again for a CBS/Columbia-related label, Bell Records. This 1973 album was called *Mary Stuart*. Two singles were released from this album—"Don't Look Back" (Bell #430) and "Let Me Be the One" (Bell #439)—but they were not hits. The cover shows Stuart in the woods, surrounded by trees, holding an acoustic guitar. Her recording career was not a whopping success, but her longevity on daytime television is quite admirable. After *Search for Tomorrow* came to a close, she still hadn't had enough and went on to portray Meta on CBS's *Guiding Light* from 1996 until her death from cancer on February 28, 2002. She was married three times.

RAVEN-SYMONÉ

Most Famous TV Role: Raven Baxter on *That's So Raven*; **Network:** the Disney Channel; **Years:** 2003–2007; **Hit Recording:** "That's What Little Girls Are Made Of"; **Label:** MCA; **Release Year:** 1993; **Matrix:** MCA #54625; **Chart:** #68 *Billboard* Hot 100, #47 R&B

Raven-Symoné Christina Pearman was born in Atlanta, Georgia, on December 10, 1985. She began appearing in commercials and print ads at the age of two. At three, she auditioned for the Bill Cosby motion picture *Ghost Dad*, but was deemed too young. Cosby took a liking to her, recognized her talent, and opted to use her on his immensely popular *Cosby Show* on NBC beginning in 1989 as Olivia Kendall. After *The Cosby Show* left the airwaves in 1992, Raven-Symoné began taking voice lessons and released an album called *Here's to New Dreams* (MCA LP #10812). The album was a flop, but a single from the album called "That's What Little Girls Are Made Of" caught on and reached both the Pop and R&B charts. It was her only single hit. There were other albums, however—*Undeniable* (Crash #417087), *This Is My Time* (Hollywood #62474—her only album to crack the Hot 100), and *Raven-Symoné* (Hollywood #176102). Even though her recording career was not overwhelmingly successful, her TV career was. *That's So Raven* enjoyed a four-year run from 2003 to 2007. On August 2, 2013, she came out as a lesbian, and is very grateful for the legalization of same-sex marriage in some states.

T

LLOYD THAXTON

Most Famous TV Role: host of *The Lloyd Thaxton Show*; **Network:** syndicated; **Years:** 1961–1967; **Hit Recording:** none; **Labels:** Capitol, Decca, Domain; **Release Years:** 1963–1965; **Matrix:** "Image of a Surfer" (Capitol #4982), "Chug-a-Lug" (Decca #31689), "Pied Piper Man" (Domain #1023), *Lloyd Thaxton Presents* (Decca LP #4594); **Chart:** none

Lloyd Thaxton was born in Memphis, Tennessee, on May 31, 1927. After serving in the U.S. Navy, he sought a career in broadcasting and moved to Los Angeles. He was an announcer and eventually got his own local show on KHJ-TV until his big break came beginning on December 29, 1961, on KCOP-TV. The program, a more skit-oriented and loosely structured version of *American Bandstand*, went through several different titles—*Lloyd Thaxton's Record Shop*, *Lloyd Thaxton's Hop*, and most famously *The Lloyd Thaxton Show*. This unique and fun local program with lots of music, dancing, and comedy eventually went national in 1964 and teens from coast to coast adored it.

During the show's run, Thaxton released a few phonograph records. The first, from 1963, was written and produced by Gary Usher, who worked extensively with the early Beach Boys. It was called "Image of a Surfer" backed with "My Name Is Lloyd Thaxton" on the Capitol label. Thaxton doesn't sing on the record, but rather uses his dulcet announcer tones with a surf rock and roll background. This novelty record was not a big hit, but when his TV program went national, he got another crack at recording—this time with Domain Records. Thaxton did sing on this one, titled "Pied Piper Man" (Domain #1023), and mentions every dance craze of the day (backed by Darlene Love and the Blossoms). It was written by David Sloane and Steve Barri, famous for composing a countless array of tunes, including "Secret Agent Man" by Johnny Rivers, "You Baby" for the Turtles, and most of the Grass Roots catalog. From there, Thaxton recorded an album for Decca Records called *Lloyd Thaxton Presents*. A cut

304

Produced by Beach Boys associate Gary Usher, Lloyd Thaxton of *The Lloyd Thaxton Show* made certain we knew his name on this 45.

from the album, a remake of Roger Miller's "Chug-a-Lug," was released as a single, but didn't rival the sales of the original.

Despite the program's continued popularity, Thaxton opted to broaden his horizons and ended his music program. He became a game show host and his first venture was called *Everybody's Talking* on ABC in 1967. A celebrity panel had to figure out what average people on the street were talking about in an edited montage of comments. The sooner they figured it out, the more points they would score. The show lasted almost a full year, but we got to see very little of the fun and funny side of Thaxton on this program. His next ABC game show showed a lot more promise—a game show from the creators of *The Hollywood Squares*, Merrill Heater and Bob Quigley, called *Funny You Should Ask*. Five celebrities were asked questions while the contestants were in soundproof rooms. When the contestants returned, they had to match the often hilarious answers with the celebrities. Once again, the show lasted close to a year before being cancelled. Sadly, Thaxton didn't get another opportunity to host a TV program. However, he did later surface behind the scenes as producer of *The Today Show*. He also worked for ABC's popular *America's Funniest People* program and toured the country seeking those humorous humans. During his career, he won five Emmys. He was married twice and had no children. He died on October 5, 2008, of multiple myeloma. He wrote a book titled *Stuff Happens (and Then You Fix It)* in 2003.

ALAN THICKE

Most Famous TV Role: Dr. Jason Seaver on *Growing Pains;* **Network:** ABC; **Years:** 1985–1992; **Hit Recording:** none; **Label:** Atlantic; **Release Year:** 1983; **Matrix:** "Thicke of the Night" (Atlantic #89701); **Chart:** none

Alan Thicke was born Alan Willis Jefferey in Ontario, Canada, on March 1, 1947. He got his show business start in Canada in the 1970s. At the time, he was married to soap opera star/singer Gloria Loring (see the entry under her name) and hosted a Canadian game show called *First Impressions*. Ever the multitasker, he was also writing theme songs for American TV sitcoms—*Diff'rent Strokes, The Facts of Life,* and *Hello, Larry*. He was simultaneously the head writer and producer for the *Mary Hartman, Mary Hartman* spinoff called *Fernwood Tonight*. Beginning in 1980 he hosted his own Canadian talk show called *The Alan Thicke Show*. Beginning in 1983, he earned his own syndicated U.S. talk show cleverly called *Thicke of the Night*. He wrote the theme song and also performed it. The song was recorded for Atlantic Records and released as a single, backed with a song called "Grandma." His talk show had been a success north of the border, but didn't translate well when it went south, and it quickly went south. Because the TV show flopped, the theme song failed to reach the charts. Thicke wasn't down for long and was soon cast in an ABC sitcom to be called *Growing Pains*. Thicke portrayed Dr. Jason Seaver, an old-fashioned Ward Cleaver-esque father with a wife and three kids. One difference between this show and others that had preceded it—dad worked at his home office while mom went off to her daily job as a reporter. The show lasted seven seasons. Thicke hosted several other programs, including *Pictionary, Animal Crackups,* and *Three's a Crowd*. He has been married three times, and his son from his first marriage to Gloria Loring, Robin Thicke, has become a musical celebrity, perhaps best known for the twerking scene with Miley Cyrus.

DANNY THOMAS

Most Famous TV Role: Danny Williams on *Make Room for Daddy/The Danny Thomas Show*; **Network:** ABC, CBS; **Years:** 1953–1964; **Hit Recording:** none; **Labels:** Columbia, Decca, MGM; **Release Years:** 1955–1960; **Matrix:** "It's Wonderful When" (Decca #29641), "Little Miss Tippy Toes" (Decca #29842), *An Evening with Danny Thomas* (MGM EP #201), *An Evening with Danny Thomas for Post Cereal* (Columbia EP #60818); **Chart:** none

Danny Thomas was born Amos Yahkoob Kairouz in Deerfield, Michigan, on January 6, 1912. He was raised in Toledo, Ohio, and referred to Toledo often on his TV shows. He attended the University of Toledo and married at the age of 24—a marriage that endured until his passing. He anglicized his name to Amos Jacobs when he began working in radio in the 1930s, and then, upon moving to Chicago, became Danny Thomas so that his family wouldn't know that he was working in nightclubs. While on radio, he found small recurring roles on *The Bickersons* and *The Baby Snooks Show*. Then came his film career in the early 1950s—*I'll See You in My Dreams* with Doris Day and a remake of *The Jazz Singer* with Peggy Lee.

While enjoying an 11-year run in the sitcom *Make Room for Daddy* (later known as *The Danny Thomas Show*), he released several singles for Decca Records. Danny Thomas played nightclub entertainer Danny Williams on the show and sang often. However, "It's Wonderful When" backed with "Bring Back Our Beale Street" and "Little Miss Tippy Toes" backed with "Nobody Knows But the Lord" failed to make the charts. He also released a few extended play 45s, but they met a similar fate. He didn't need a hit record—his TV show survived two wives (Jean Hagen and Marjorie Lord) and numerous other cast changes (not to mention a jump from ABC to CBS and a title change). In fact, Thomas wanted the series to end and only appeared in a select few episodes in the final two seasons. Finding another hit series, however, proved elusive. There was *The Danny Thomas Hour*, *Make Room for Granddaddy*, *The Practice*, *I'm a Big Girl Now*, and *One Big Family*, but none achieved success. Thomas's production company however produced numerous successes—*The Dick Van Dyke Show*, *The Andy Griffith Show*, *The Mod Squad*, and *The Real McCoys*. His daughter, Marlo, found success in an ABC sitcom called *That Girl*, and it ran for five seasons. Thomas championed St. Jude's Hospital and was their familiar spokesperson for decades until his passing on February 6, 1991, at the age of 79. Daughter Marlo has picked up where her dad left off and continues to embrace the cause. A commemorative forever postage stamp with Danny Thomas's picture was issued in January of 2012.

PHILLIP MICHAEL THOMAS

Most Famous TV Role: Detective Ricardo Tubbs on *Miami Vice;* **Network:** NBC; **Years:** 1984–1989; **Hit Recording:** none; **Label:** Atlantic; **Release Year:** 1985–1988; **Matrix:** *Living the Book of My Life* (Atlantic LP #90468), *Somebody* (Atlantic LP #90960); **Chart:** none

Phillip Michael Thomas was born in Columbus, Ohio, on May 26, 1949. His acting career began in the early 1970s with guest-starring roles on the ABC drama series *Toma* and the CBS sitcom *Good Times.* After a string of less-than-stellar roles in such forgettable motion pictures as *Blackfist, Coonskin,* and *Death Drug,* he snagged his most famous role on NBC's *Miami Vice*—that of Detective Ricardo Tubbs, a former cop seeking the man who killed his brother. Both he and his costar Don Johnson attempted to parlay their sudden TV fame into hit phonograph records. Johnson was by far the more successful of the two (see the entry for him). Thomas released an album in 1985 titled *Living the Book of My Life* for Atlantic Records. It was not a big seller and didn't produce any hit singles. He got to try again three years later with the *Somebody* album, but nobody bought *Somebody* and he was dropped by the Atlantic label.

Miami Vice began losing its cool by 1989 and was cancelled after five years on NBC. In the 1990s Thomas made a couple of guest appearances on Don Johnson's other popular series, *Nash Bridges* on CBS. He also found consistent work supplying the voice for the character named Lance Vance in a series of video games. He was also briefly the spokesperson for the Florida-based Psychic Reader's Network.

THE THREE HAIRCUTS
(SID CAESAR, HOWARD MORRIS, CARL REINER)

Most Famous TV Role: regulars on *Your Show of Shows* and *Caesar's Hour;* **Network:** NBC; **Years:** 1950–1954, 1954–1957, respectively; **Hit Recordings:** "You Are So Rare to Me" as by the Three Haircuts; **Label:** RCA Victor; **Release Year:** 1955; **Matrix:** RCA Victor #6149; **Chart:** Top Ten hit in Buffalo, New York

Sid Caesar was born as Isaac Sidney Caesar on September 8, 1922, in Yonkers, New York. While working in his parents' luncheonette, he became proficient in copying the dialects of the clientele and used that talent,

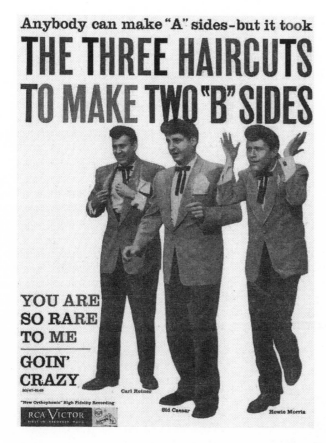

Anybody can make "A" sides–but it took

THE THREE HAIRCUTS TO MAKE TWO "B" SIDES

YOU ARE
SO RARE
TO ME

GOIN'
CRAZY

"New Orthophonic" High Fidelity Recording

RCA VICTOR

Carl Reiner

Sid Caesar

Howie Morris

In a parody of the vocal group known as the Crew Cuts, *Caesar's Hour* stars Carl Reiner, Sid Caesar, and Howard Morris had a minor hit as the Three Haircuts.

along with his innate comedic abilities, during the advent of television. He and Imogene Coca made their mark on a landmark 90-minute weekly variety/sketch comedy series titled *Your Show of Shows*. It was later shortened to a 60-minute weekly show and retitled *Caesar's Hour*. It was during that second version of the series that Caesar, along with costars Carl Reiner and Howard Morris, assembled a vocal group to make sport of the pop and rock and roll records of the day. As a direct parody of the group the Crew Cuts, most famous for "Sh-Boom," Caesar's group was called the Three Haircuts, and in 1955 they released a fun, repetitive ditty titled "You Are So Rare to Me" on the RCA Victor label. To their surprise, the record caught on in some U.S. cities, Buffalo in particular, where it reached Top Ten on local radio. The trio performed the song on *Caesar's Hour* several times and sported tall, greasy pompadours for the skit. The flip side, "Goin' Crazy," also got some airplay, but no follow-up singles were released.

Carl Reiner went on to an amazing multiple award-winning TV and movie career (most notable is his work on- and offscreen on *The Dick Van Dyke Show*) and, as of this writing, has a recurring role on TV Land's *Hot in Cleveland*. This kind and generous man has published two wonderful memoirs—*I Just Remembered* and *I Remember Me*. Howard Morris went on to portray Ernest T. Bass on *The Andy Griffith Show* and provided cartoon voices for popular animated favorites such as *Atom Ant*, Mr. Peebles on *Magilla Gorilla*, and dozens of others—mostly for Hanna-Barbera Productions. Morris died of pneumonia on May 21, 2005. Sid Caesar lived to be 91, dying after a brief illness on February 12, 2014.

LILY TOMLIN

Most Famous TV Role: cast member on *Rowan and Martin's Laugh-In*; **Network:** NBC; **Years:** 1970–1973; **Hit Recording:** none; **Label:** Polydor; **Release Years:** 1973–1976; **Matrix:** "20th Century Blues" (Polydor #14180), "Detroit City" (Polydor #14283); **Chart:** none

Lily Tomlin was born as Mary Jean Tomlin in Detroit, Michigan, on September 1, 1939. While attending Wayne State University, her interest in the performing arts blossomed. After graduation, she attempted stand-up comedy and got a booking on *The Merv Griffin Show*—her TV debut in 1965. She then became a regular on the very short-lived 1966 comeback attempt by Garry Moore, once again called *The Garry Moore Show*. Contrary to popular belief, she wasn't one of the original cast members of *Rowan and Martin's Laugh-In* when it debuted on NBC in 1968. Instead, she was hosting a weekly 45-minute ABC program called *The Music Scene*. Tomlin was asked to join *Laugh-In* beginning in 1970 and remained until the program's end in 1973. Her characters such as Ernestine the telephone operator, the little girl in the big chair named Edith Ann, and the very stuffy Tasteful Lady, among others, became popular regular fixtures on the program.

Near the end of the show's run, Tomlin had success with her comedy albums, especially *This Is a Recording* as Ernestine the operator on the Polydor label (#4055). It reached number 15 on the album chart in 1971 and garnered her a Grammy for Best Comedy Album. Tomlin's *And That's the Truth* album as Edith Ann (Polydor #5023) just missed the Top Forty. She did *sing* on a couple of 45 rpm releases for Polydor—"20th Century Blues" (Polydor #14180) in 1973 and then "Detroit City" (Polydor #14283) in 1976, but neither one was a big success. After *Laugh-In* Tomlin aired a couple of high-quality, Emmy-winning TV specials and also made numerous popular motion pictures, including *Nashville*, for which she was nominated for an Oscar. Other big screen highlights include *The Late Show, Nine to Five, The Incredible Shrinking Woman*, and *All of Me*. She conquered Broadway and won a Tony Award for *The Search for Intelligent Life in the Universe* written by her life partner, Jane Wagner. She recently returned to television in the short-lived Reba McEntire sitcom titled *Malibu Country* as Lillie Mae. She had a recurring role on *Desperate Housewives* as Roberta, and at press time, she was getting ready to costar in a new Netflix comedy series titled *Grace and Frankie*.

JOHN TRAVOLTA

Most Famous TV Role: Vinnie Barbarino on *Welcome Back, Kotter*; **Network:** ABC; **Years:** 1975–1979; **Hit Recordings:** "Let Her In," "Summer Nights," "You're the One That I Want"; **Labels:** Midland, RSO; **Release Years:** 1976–1978; **Matrix:** "Let Her In" (Midland #10623), "Summer Nights" (RSO #906), "You're the One That I Want" (RSO #891); **Chart:** #10, #5, #1, respectively, *Billboard* Hot 100

John Travolta was born in Englewood, New Jersey, on February 18, 1954. His father was of Italian descent and his mother of Irish descent. The youngest of six children, he dropped out of high school, moved to New York City, and soon earned a role in a touring production of *Grease*. Things really fell into place when he was cast as the dimwitted ladies' man Vinnie Barbarino on *Welcome Back, Kotter* beginning in 1975 (the same year he became interested in Scientology). His role in the original *Carrie* movie with Sissy Spacek in 1976 got a lot of attention, and this was followed by two huge successes—*Saturday Night Fever* and the motion picture version of *Grease*. He could seemingly do no wrong. He even scored several hit records—a solo ballad called "Let Her In" for the Midland label in 1976, and then two more Top Ten smashes in *Grease* duets with Olivia Newton-John ("You're the One That I Want" and "Summer Nights"). All good things must come to an end, and for Travolta, that came to fruition in the 1980s when his career hit a huge lull. Except for *Look Who's Talking*, there were no big conquests at the box office for the entire decade. That all changed in 1994 with a whopper of a comeback incited by *Pulp Fiction*. He won a Golden Globe Award for *Get Shorty*. He's been married to Kelly Preston since 1991 and is an experienced pilot.

FORREST TUCKER

Most Famous TV Role: Sergeant Morgan O'Rourke on *F Troop*; **Network:** ABC; **Years:** 1965–1967; **Hit Recording:** none; **Label:** Dot; **Release Year:** 1965; **Matrix:** "Dan's Girl" (Dot #16812); **Chart:** none

Forrest Tucker was born in Plainfield, Indiana, on February 12, 1919. By the age of 14 he was performing as a singer at the Chicago World's Fair. Then he became an emcee at a burlesque theater, despite being underage. In 1940, Tucker moved to Los Angeles to try his luck in the motion picture industry. He got *very* lucky and was signed to Columbia Pictures. Then came World War II, and the movie career was put on hold until 1946. By 1949, he jumped over to Republic Pictures where he was instantly cast in John Wayne's *The Sands of Iwo Jima*. After several action pictures, he moved over to the small screen and a syndicated series called *Crunch and Des*. Tucker played Crunch Adams and Sandy Kenyon was Des Smith. The syndicated series was set in the Bahamas. After the series was cancelled, he enjoyed a nice run in the national production of *The Music Man*. He also found work on Broadway in *Fair Game for Lovers*. After this came his second and more successful shot at television success. He was cast as Sergeant Morgan O'Rourke on ABC's F Troop.

While starring on this period piece sitcom, Tucker also attempted a recording career. His 1965 single, produced by Charles Grean for the Dot label, "Dan's Girl" backed with "Just Plain Dog," was not a big hit and failed to make the charts. The recording career was abruptly abandoned. *F Troop*'s first season was filmed in black and white, but its second was in color. There were only two seasons and 65 episodes, but it has run continuously since 1967 in syndication. Tucker didn't release any other singles, but did land in other TV comedy shows. In 1973, Tucker portrayed Callahan and Bob Denver played Dusty in *Dusty's Trail*, a syndicated sitcom that was, for all intents and purposes, *Gilligan's Island* set in the old West. It even had *Gilligan's Island*'s producer, Sherwood Schwartz. It lasted for one season. Then in 1975 Tucker was reunited with his former *F Troop* costar Larry Storch (see the entry under his name) on a Saturday morning kids' comedy show, *The Ghost Busters*. It preceded the blockbuster film and, except for the title and the subject matter, was not connected. His final recurring role on a TV series came in the sitcom *Filthy Rich*, which aired briefly on CBS during the 1982–1983 TV season. In his final years in the business, Tucker found work on stage and in films. It's no secret that Tucker was a heavy smoker and drinker, and was eventually diagnosed with lung cancer and emphysema and died on October 25, 1986. He was married four times and two of his wives were named Marilyn.

V

DICK VAN DYKE

Most Famous TV Role: Rob Petrie on *The Dick Van Dyke Show*; **Network:** CBS; **Years:** 1961–1966; **Hit Recording:** none; **Labels:** Columbia, Jamie, RCA Victor, United Artists; **Years:** 1961–1968; **Matrix:** "Three Wheels on My Wagon" (Jamie #1178), "Hushabye Mountain" (United Artists #50486); **Chart:** none

Richard Van Dyke was born in West Plains, Missouri, on December 13, 1925, but was raised in Danville, Illinois. For a time, he considered a career in the ministry, but gravitated toward the performing arts. He enlisted in the U.S. Army Air Corps during World War II and briefly put his career aspirations on hold, but did perform radio announcements. Speaking of radio, after his discharge Van Dyke and his girlfriend, Margerie, were married on a weekly series called *Bride and Groom* in 1948. They remained married until 1984.

Van Dyke's first break in television came in the middle 1950s when he hosted a kids' show called *CBS Cartoon Theater*. He then got to host a couple of short-lived TV game shows—*Mother's Day* and *Laugh Line*. Along with this, he appeared on Broadway in *The Girls against the Boys* and *Bye Bye Birdie*. After getting noticed for his comic timing in guest appearances on *The Phil Silvers Show*, he was tapped to portray comedy writer Rob Petrie on a CBS sitcom. Originally, Carl Reiner was to play the role and indeed did in the pilot called *Head of the Family*. The program was recast from head-to-toe and evolved into the Emmy Award–winning *Dick Van Dyke Show*. The program debuted in 1961 and did poorly in the ratings, but caught on in its second year and came to be considered one of the finest sitcoms of all time, and many scriptwriters consider it a tutorial on how it should be done.

During that low-rated first season, Van Dyke released a song written by Bob Hilliard (lyrics) and Burt Bacharach (music) called "Three Wheels

313

Dick Van Dyke, star of the legendary eponymous sitcom, jumped on the recording bandwagon with "Three Wheels on My Wagon."

on My Wagon" backed with "One Part Dog, Nine Parts Cat" for Philadelphia's Jamie Records label (it was issued with a picture sleeve). During his sitcom's run, Van Dyke also costarred in two immensely popular motion pictures—*Mary Poppins* and the big screen version of *Bye Bye Birdie*. Each motion picture spawned a successful soundtrack album (*Mary Poppins*—Disneyland LP #4026; *Bye Bye Birdie*—RCA Victor LP #1081), and Van Dyke was convinced that he should concentrate on making more films. Because of that, he opted to end the still very successful and popular *Dick Van Dyke Show* after only five seasons. His decision was likely premature, as only *Chitty Chitty Bang Bang* was a bona fide hit. A song from that film called "Hushabye Mountain" for United Artists Records was released as a single by Van Dyke in 1969, but was not a sensation. After numerous lackluster follow-up films, he returned to television with

The New Dick Van Dyke Show and the Emmy-winning but short-lived variety series called *Van Dyke and Company*, which introduced many to the antics of one Andy Kaufman. After one other ill-fated sitcom called *The Van Dyke Show*, he landed in another hit—*Diagnosis: Murder* from 1993 to 2001. His son Barry was also a regular on the program. Van Dyke married makeup artist Arlene Silver in 2012—a woman many years his junior. He has a star on the Hollywood Walk of Fame and his proficiency with physical comedy has inspired millions.

JERRY VAN DYKE

Most Famous TV Role: assistant coach Luther Van Dam on *Coach*; **Network:** ABC; **Years:** 1989–1997; **Hit Recording:** none; **Label:** Columbia; **Release Year:** 1965; **Matrix:** "It Kinda Makes Yuh Wonder" (Columbia #43198), "My Mother the Car" (Columbia #43585); **Chart:** none

Jerry Van Dyke was born in Danville, Illinois, on July 27, 1931. He became a stand-up comedian in his early 20s but put his career on hold in 1954 when he joined the air force, where he performed at countless military bases. Upon being discharged, he earned his own morning TV show for an Indiana station. He guest starred on numerous episodes of his older brother's *Dick Van Dyke Show* as the shy, sleepwalking, banjo-playing Stacey Petrie. He briefly got to host his own prime-time CBS game show called *Picture This* in 1963. It was a summer replacement for *The Jack Benny Program*. At least one episode has survived and is available for viewing at the UCLA TV and Film Archives in Los Angeles, California. Van Dyke was briefly a regular on the highly touted but short-lived *Judy Garland Show* in that same year. He then had a decision to make—a starring role in a TV sitcom about a talking car or a sitcom about seven stranded castaways on an uncharted island. He chose the former, the much maligned *My Mother the Car* and passed on *Gilligan's Island*. On *My Mother the Car*, lawyer David Crabtree buys a broken down 1928 Porter automobile that he is convinced is the reincarnation (or rein-*car*-nation) of his deceased mother. He has the vehicle restored and, despite his wife's protests, uses it as the family car. His mother, the car, only speaks to him. The bizarre premise lasted only one season on NBC. The opportunity he turned down, the much more famous *Gilligan's Island*, ran for three seasons on CBS and has never been out of syndication.

During the run of *My Mother the Car*, Van Dyke released a couple of 1965 singles for the Columbia label—"It Kinda Makes Yuh Wonder"

Jerry Van Dyke performs the theme song for his much-maligned sitcom about rein-*car*-nation called *My Mother the Car.*

backed with "I Wanna Say Hello" and "Weeping Willow" backed with "My Mother the Car." The latter, Van Dyke's version of his TV show's theme, was not used for the series (Paul Hampton performed it for the opening and closing credits). Van Dyke's Columbia singles were not big sellers. This series was not the right "vehicle" for him, and he kept trying with *Accidental Family*, *Headmaster*, and *13 Queens Blvd*. These were even less successful than *My Mother the Car*. It took until 1989 for him to finally land in a hit series—ABC's *Coach*. Jerry was the ideal assistant coach and second banana on the show, and enjoyed an eight-season run and lots of residuals in syndication. He was nominated for four Emmy Awards during the show's run, but didn't win. After *Coach*, he had recurring roles on *You Wish* and *Yes, Dear*. He also had a long run as the TV spokesperson for Big Lots stores in the 1990s. He has been married twice, has three children, loves playing poker, and lives in Arkansas.

HERVE VILLECHAIZE

Most Famous TV Role: Tattoo on *Fantasy Island*; **Network:** ABC; **Years:** 1978–1983; **Hit Recording:** none; **Label:** Epic; **Release Year:** 1980; **Matrix:** "Why?" (Epic #50947); **Chart:** none

Herve Villechaize was born in Paris, France, on April 23, 1943. He was raised by his stepfather, a surgeon. Young Herve ceased growing after reaching 3 feet, 11 inches, and none of his stepdad's attempts to correct this were effective. Because of his lack of height, Villechaize was teased incessantly but found comfort in painting and also some modeling work. He later parlayed modeling into work in off-Broadway shows. Work in films and television was scarce, and for a time he lived in his car until things broke his way.

After some minor roles in films and some work on *Sesame Street*, Villechaize landed the role that would make him famous—that of Tattoo on ABC's *Fantasy Island*. Smack dab in the middle of the show's run, he got to record a single for Epic Records—"Why?" backed with "When a Child Is Born" in 1980. He was no singer, and the record was not a hit but was included as a cut on an Epic album called *Children of the World* (Epic #36769) in that same year. His relationship with costars and the show's producers and directors was said to be contentious, and he was eventually fired after five seasons (he also asked for a salary on par with Ricardo Montalban's). The program continued for one more season after having its Tattoo removed, but faltered in the ratings and was cancelled. After a few guest-starring roles on episodic TV shows and a run in a series of Dunkin' Donuts TV commercials, Villechaize became depressed over personal health issues and died of a self-inflicted gunshot wound on September 4, 1993. The final days of Villechaize's life are to be tackled in an upcoming film from Mandate Pictures to be titled *My Dinner with Herve*, starring actor Peter Dinklage.

W

JACK WAGNER

Most Famous TV Role: Frisco Jones on *General Hospital*; **Network:** ABC; **Years:** 1983–1991, 1994–1995, 2013; **Hit Recording:** "All I Need"; **Label:** Qwest; **Release Year:** 1984; **Matrix:** Qwest #29238; **Chart:** #2 *Billboard* Hot 100, #1 Adult Contemporary

Peter John Wagner was born in Washington, Missouri, on October 3, 1959. He played football and baseball in high school. He then studied drama at the University of Arizona. His youthful good looks got him cast on *General Hospital* in his early 20s as Frisco Jones. He had several stints on the show, and early in his first run he signed with Quincy Jones's Qwest Records label and in 1984 scored a huge ballad called "All I Need," which made it all the way to number 2 on the Hot 100. The *All I Need* album (Qwest LP #25089) just missed the Top Forty. Wagner stayed with the label for several years but never again penetrated the Top Forty on the singles chart. After his first go-round on *General Hospital*, Wagner surfaced as Warren Lockridge on *Santa Barbara* in the early 1990s, followed by a prime-time run on *Melrose Place* as Peter Burns. This was followed by almost a decade as Nick Marone on *The Bold and the Beautiful*. He recently reprised his role as Frisco Jones (2013) in a few episodes of his original soap, *General Hospital*. He is an avid golfer, he participated in season 14 of *Dancing with the Stars* (finishing in eleventh place), and he has been married only once.

CLINT WALKER

Most Famous TV Role: Cheyenne Bodie on *Cheyenne*; **Network:** ABC; **Years:** 1955–1962; **Hit Recording:** none; **Label:** Warner Bros.; **Release Year:** 1959; **Matrix:** "Silver Bells" (Warner Bros. #5133), "I Believe" (Warner Bros. #5135), *Inspiration* (Warner Bros. LP #1343); **Chart:** none

The man from *Cheyenne*, Clint Walker, released a few records for Warner Brothers, backed by the Sunflower Serenaders.

Clint Walker was born as Norman Eugene Walker in Hartford, Illinois, on May 30, 1927. He was a Merchant Marine during the latter part of World War II. Standing six feet, six inches tall, he worked for a time as a nightclub bouncer. He briefly used the name Jett Norman and earned a few minor roles in motion pictures. He was discovered by the powers-that-be at Warner Bros. and cast in their new western series to be called *Cheyenne*. Now called Clint Walker, he portrayed Cheyenne Bodie—a wandering cowboy in the years after the Civil War. He sang on the program on occasion, and Warner Bros. capitalized on his vocal talents with an album called *Inspiration* in 1959 and a couple of singles—"I Believe" backed with "The Kentuckian Song" and, from the *We Wish You a Merry Christmas* album (Warner Bros. #1337), "Silver Bells" backed with "Love at Home." The records weren't big hits, but the TV program was and ran for seven years.

After the series came to a close in 1962, Walker found roles in motion pictures such as *Send Me No Flowers*, *None but the Brave*, and *The Dirty Dozen*. He also guest starred in two episodes of *The Lucy Show* as Frank Winslow in the middle 1960s. He returned to series television in 1974 on an ABC series set in Alaska called *Kodiak*. Walker's return was less than stellar, and his role as Cal "Kodiak" McKay was pummeled in the ratings by *Sanford and Son* and gone after only five weeks. He also had a long run in Kal Kan dog food commercials. He has been married three times and has a star on the Hollywood Walk of Fame.

JIMMIE WALKER

Most Famous TV Role: J.J. Evans on *Good Times*; **Network:** CBS; **Years:** 1974–1979; **Hit Recording:** none; **Label:** Buddah; **Release Years:** 1975–1976; **Matrix:** "Abbadabba Honeymoon" (Buddah #529), *Dyn-o-Mite* (Buddah LP #5635); **Chart:** *Dyn-o-Mite*—#139 *Billboard* Top Pop Albums

Jimmie Walker was born as James Carter Walker in the South Bronx, New York, on June 25, 1947. In his teens he had dreams of becoming a basketball star. At one time, he was a vendor at Yankee Stadium. His show business career began in radio, first in New York City and then Los Angeles. His stand-up comedy really got him noticed, and he was then cast in a *Maude* spinoff to be called *Good Times*. Director John Rich recommended the use of the word *dyn-o-mite* in every episode, and Walker's character became so popular, he even recorded an album for Buddah Records called *Dyn-o-Mite* in 1975. He also released a remake of the standard "Abbadabba Honeymoon" backed with "I Know" with a picture sleeve of Walker with a sock puppet monkey, and also an EP for Buddah Records. None of these became big hits, but "Abbadabba Honeymoon" was reissued as the B-side of a 1996 single by a rock band known as Spazz on the Slap-a-Ham label (#31). Only about 1,000 copies were pressed up. After the cancellation of *Good Times* in 1979, Walker returned to doing stand-up after finding that he was typecast in the J.J. role. His three series during the 1980s (*B.A.D. Cats*, *At Ease*, and *Bustin' Loose*) were all short-lived. He has never been married. His memoirs are called *Dyn-o-Mite! Good Times, Bad Times, Our Times—a Memoir*.

Good Times star Jimmie Walker attempted success as a recording star with an updated version of the old standard "Abbadabba Honeymoon." The honeymoon was over very quickly.

BURT WARD

Most Famous TV Role: Robin on *Batman*; **Network:** ABC; **Years:** 1966–1968; **Hit Recording:** none; **Label:** MGM, Soultown; **Release Year:** 1967; **Matrix:** "Boy Wonder, I Love You" (MGM #13632), "I've Got Love for You, Baby" (Soultown #12); **Chart:** none

Burt Ward was born Bert Gervis Jr. in Los Angeles, California, on July 6, 1945. He grew up as a lover of superhero comic books. He was quite the athlete as a young man and lettered in track, football, and wrestling. At the age of 19, he auditioned for the role of Robin using his mother's maiden name, Ward. He had to be able to do his own stunts, and his audition for the role can be viewed on YouTube. His athleticism came in very handy, and he beat out all of the others. Both Ward and his costar, Adam West (see the entry for him), released 45 rpm records during the TV program's peak popularity. One of Ward's releases, "Boy Wonder I Love You" backed with "Orange Colored Sky" on the MGM label, was written, arranged, and conducted by Frank Zappa, greatly enhancing its value and collectability. Ward recites the words on the "Boy Wonder, I Love You" side under the guise of reading fan mail. It's very obvious why "Orange Colored Sky" is the B-side. Ward attempted to sing the tune but is obviously tone deaf (few could intentionally sing that off key). He got one more chance at a hit record, this time on the Soultown label ("I've Got Love for You, Baby"). It never got past the promotional copy phase. The *Batman* series became so popular that ABC began airing it twice a week. There was also *Batman: The Movie* in 1966. It proved to be too much of a good thing, and the series lasted only two and a half seasons. During its heyday, however, it was a ratings and merchandising bonanza, and made big stars of Ward and West. Ward wrote his autobiography in 1995—*Boy Wonder: My Life in Tights*. Finding work after *Batman* was rough on Ward, and he was typecast in the role. He and his costar have remained close friends all these years. He's been married four times and has two children. He is a regular fixture at Hollywood autograph shows.

BEVERLY WASHBURN

Most Famous TV Role: Kit Wilson on *Professional Father*, Vickie Massey on *The New Loretta Young Show*; **Network:** CBS; **Years:** 1955, 1962–1963, respectively; **Hit Recording:** "Ev'rybody Loves Saturday Night"; **Label:** Smash; **Release Year:** 1963; **Matrix:** Smash #1855; **Chart:** none

Beverly Washburn was born in Los Angeles, California, on November 25, 1943. In the 1950s, as a child, she regularly appeared on an abundant amount of anthology drama programs on prime-time network television. Her first series was called *Professional Father*, and she portrayed Kit Wilson, the daughter of a child psychologist played by Steve Dunne. Her mother on the program was played by future June Cleaver actress Barbara Billingsley. The filmed series lasted only 18 episodes and never found an audience. One of her biggest claims to fame came in 1957 when she portrayed Lisbeth Searcy in the classic motion picture *Old Yeller*. Her next series came in 1962, again on CBS, as Loretta Young attempted a TV comeback in *The New Loretta Young Show*. Most programs with *new* in the title fail to catch on, and this one followed that rule. Beverly portrayed Lo-

While a costar on *The New Loretta Young Show*, actress Beverly Washburn attempted success on the pop charts with "Ev'rybody Loves Saturday Night" on the Smash label, but it wasn't a smash.

retta's daughter Vickie on that single-season dramedy. During the show's run, Beverly got to record a single for the Smash Records label and had a minor hit with "Ev'rybody Loves Saturday Night." For some reason it was released with two different flip sides—"The Heart You Break May Be Your Own" and also "Wartime Blues." It failed to chart, but received a fair amount of airplay and enjoyed some regional success in some parts of the United States. Beverly's most famous guest-starring role came on the original NBC version of *Star Trek* as Lieutenant Arlene Galway in the episode titled "The Deadly Years." Among her other guest-starring roles are two episodes of *Gidget*, one episode of *The Patty Duke Show*, and three episodes of *Streets of San Francisco*. Today she is a journalist and resides in Henderson, Nevada.

DENNIS WEAVER

Most Famous TV Role: Chester Goode on *Gunsmoke*, Tom Wedloe on *Gentle Ben*, Sam McCloud on *McCloud*; **Networks:** CBS, NBC; **Years:** 1955–1964, 1967–1969, 1970–1977, respectively; **Hit Recording:** *Dennis Weaver*; **Labels:** Cascade, Century City, Eva, Impress, Ovation, Warner Bros.; **Release Years:** 1959–1975; **Matrix:** "Girls Wuz Made to Be Loved" (Cascade #5906), "Chicken Mash" (Eva #103), "Prairie Dog Blues" (Ovation #1056), "One More Road" (Ovation #1440), "Sinking of the Reuben James" (Warner Bros. #5352), *Gentle Ben: The Bear Facts* (Century City LP #70101), *Dennis Weaver* (Impress LP #1614); **Chart:** *Dennis Weaver*—#191 *Billboard* Top Pop Albums

William Dennis Weaver was born in Joplin, Missouri, on June 4, 1924. He wanted to be an actor beginning in his childhood. He was on the track team and studied drama at the University of Oklahoma. During World War II he served in the U.S. Navy. He got married right after his discharge—a marriage that lasted until his death. He understudied for several Broadway shows and, with the help of Shelley Winters, got a contract with Universal Studios. His big break came when he landed the role of Chester Goode on *Gunsmoke* beginning in 1955. While on the show, he released a single for the small Cascade label, "Girls Wuz Made to Be Loved" backed with "Michael Finnigan" (1959), and for the Eva label— "Chicken Mash" backed with "Apes" (1963). Also in 1963, he released one single for Warner Bros.—"Sinking of the Reuben James" backed with "Genesis through Exodus." These didn't make a lot of noise and were quickly forgotten.

After almost a decade with *Gunsmoke*, Weaver left to star in a new NBC sitcom called *Kentucky Jones* with costar Harry Morgan, but it only lasted one season. Weaver rebounded nicely in 1967 with an adventure series set in Florida's Everglades about a friendly and lovable 600-pound black bear named *Gentle Ben*. That series ended in 1969, and Weaver quickly landed in a new show titled *McCloud* on NBC the following year. As part of the rotating *NBC Mystery Movie*, the series enjoyed a seven-year run. Sam McCloud was an out-of-place western crime fighter working among New York's police department while on temporary assignment. Weaver was nominated for two Emmys for the role, but did not win. During this show's long run, Weaver released a couple of singles (in Quadrophonic sound) for the Ovation Records label—"Prairie Dog Blues" backed with "Hubbardsville Store" and "One More Road" in 1975 (the latter never made it past the promotional copy phase). Weaver was extremely busy at this time in his career, and served as the Screen Actors Guild president from 1973 to 1975. Even with three hit shows under his belt, he wanted more and starred in three short-lived series in the 1980s—*Stone, Emerald Point N.A.S.,* and *Buck James*. He was a vegetarian, he had three children, and he earned a star on the Hollywood Walk of Fame. He died in his Colorado home on February 24, 2006, after a bout with cancer.

JACK WEBB

Most Famous TV Role: Sergeant Joe Friday on *Dragnet;* **Network:** NBC; **Years:** 1952–1959, 1967–1970; **Hit Recording:** *Pete Kelly's Blues;* **Label:** Warner Bros.; **Release Years:** 1958–1967; **Matrix:** "Try a Little Tenderness" (Warner Bros. #5003), *Pete Kelly's Blues* (RCA Victor LP #1126), *You're My Girl* (Warner Bros. LP #1207); **Chart:** *Pete Kelly's Blues*—#2 *Billboard* Top Pop Albums

Jack Webb was born as John Randolph Webb in Santa Monica, California, on April 2, 1920. His father split before he was born, and the two never met. Webb's lifelong interest in jazz music was incited by a neighbor in his youth. He was an art major at St. John's University, and after a stint in the air force, Webb became a radio announcer in San Francisco. *Dragnet* started on radio utilizing real cases as subject matter. For a while it ran on both radio and television. The program's first TV run was on NBC from 1952 to 1959, and during that time Webb released an album (1958) of "romantic reflections" called *You're My Girl* for Warner Bros. Records. Webb didn't sing, but rather narrated the lyrics to each song with Billy May and His Orchestra in the background. The album cover features a smiling Webb in the foreground with a lit cigarette in hand. In the background is a blurred image of a young woman in a white dress. Songs include "When Sunny Gets Blue," "Stranger in Town," "You're My Girl," and "Try a Little Tenderness." This rather unusual album was not a success, but an album credited to him called *Pete Kelly's Blues* (from the movie of same name) reached number 2. Webb had very little to do with the album—it was the Warner Bros. Orchestra and Matty Matlock and His Jazz Band performing each cut. There was also an RCA Victor EP (#3199) called "The Christmas Story." The audio was taken from an episode of the series about a young Hispanic boy who steals a statue of the Christ child from a manger on a church altar. This episode, a favorite of Webb's, was filmed in color and then remade when the series was resurrected in the late 1960s.

During the run of those latter episodes (1967–1970), a single of Webb's, "Try a Little Tenderness," was rereleased because of that song's resurgence in hit versions by Otis Redding and Three Dog Night. Webb's

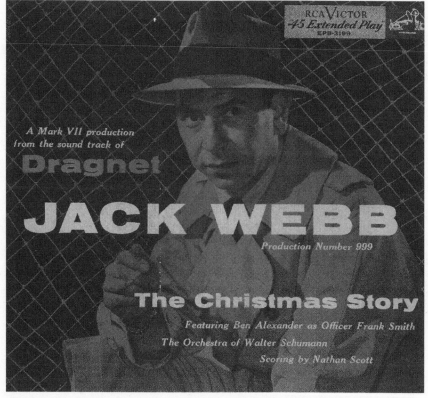

Bum-ba-dum-bum. Just the facts, ma'am. *Dragnet*'s Jack Webb released several phonograph records.

version was sadly out of date and out of touch and went absolutely nowhere. Webb was a stickler for attempting to create realism on the program, but nowadays his very stiff portrayal of Los Angeles police sergeant Joe Friday appears as anything but realistic. The program became well known for its opening narration by George Fenneman—"The story you are about to see is true, the names have been changed to protect the innocent"—as well as Webb's own lines, "This is the city—Los Angeles, California" and "Just the facts, ma'am."

In the 1960s, Webb was credited with bringing about the downfall of *77 Sunset Strip*. He completely changed the show's direction, leading to its quick cancellation. Another of his programs, a western called *Temple Houston* in 1963, was a flop. However, he redeemed himself when his *Adam-12* series was a hit and ran for seven seasons on NBC from 1968 to 1975, followed by the equally successful *Emergency!* The latter oddly starred his ex-wife, Julie London, and her new husband, Bobby Troup. Webb was married four times and was working on a revival version of *Dragnet* in 1982 when he succumbed to a heart attack on December 23, 1982. He has two stars on the Hollywood Walk of Fame—one for radio and one for television. Joe Friday's badge number 714 was retired by the Los Angeles Police Department in his honor.

ADAM WEST

Most Famous TV Role: Bruce Wayne on *Batman*; **Network:** ABC; **Years:** 1966–1968; **Hit Recording:** none; **Label:** 20th Century Fox; **Release Year:** 1966; **Matrix:** "Miranda" (20th Century Fox #627); **Chart:** none

Adam West was born William West Anderson in Walla Walla, Washington, on September 19, 1928. He graduated from Whitman College with a degree in literature. He was drafted into the U.S. Army and utilized his dulcet tones to become an announcer for the Armed Forces Network. After his discharge he moved to Hollywood and changed his name to Adam West. He scored a goodly amount of guest-starring roles on TV westerns such as *Lawman, Colt 45, The Rifleman,* and *Sugarfoot*. His first regular role came on *The Detectives Starring Robert Taylor* on NBC in 1961. West portrayed Sergeant Steve Nelson for the program's third and final season. In 1966, a new prime-time *Batman* series was being pitched, and it was between Lyle Waggoner and Adam West for the title role. West won and he was paired with Burt Ward as Robin (see the entry for him). The campy tongue-in-cheek program was a huge success and eventually aired twice a week on ABC. *Batman* merchandise was plentiful, and West was hastily brought into the recording studio with a Lee Pockriss and Paul Vance composition titled "Miranda." Pockriss and Vance are probably best known for writing "Itsy Bitsy Teenie Weenie Yellow Polka Dot Bikini" for singer Brian Hyland and "Catch a Falling Star" for Perry Como. "Miranda" was performed in character. Batman falls in love with Miranda in the song, but she wants him to remove his mask. After she badgers him, he finally removes the mask, but Miranda asks him to put it back on. Oddly, he calls Robin "Boy Genius" instead of "Boy Wonder" throughout the song. The record was backed with "You Only See Her." West hit a few flat notes on the record and it wasn't a big hit, but was within his "Miranda" rights to record it, and it is highly collectible today—especially with the picture sleeve showing West as Bruce Wayne and as Batman.

After the series ended in 1968, both West and Ward were typecast and had a hard time finding serious acting roles. After numerous guest-starring roles on episodic TV shows, West finally landed another series—the extremely short-lived sitcom called *The Last Precinct* in the spring of 1986 on NBC. He frequently voiced the Batman character in numerous animated incarnations of the comic superhero. For a time in the late 1980s, West was the spokesman for the Nick at Nite cable channel, and in recent years has enjoyed a long run as the voice for Mayor Adam West on Fox's animated *Family Guy* series. He has a star on the Palm Springs Walk of Stars and the Hollywood Walk of Fame. He has been married three times and has six children. He frequently appears at Hollywood autograph conventions.

LISA WHELCHEL

Most Famous TV Role: Blair Warner on *The Facts of Life*; **Network:** NBC; **Years:** 1979–1988; **Hit Recording:** *All Because of You*; **Label:** Nissi; **Release Year:** 1984; **Matrix:** Nissi LP #4606; **Chart:** #17 *Billboard* Contemporary Christian Albums

Lisa Whelchel was born in Littlefield, Texas, on May 29, 1963. Her parents divorced while she was still a teenager and her mother remarried. She's been a born-again Christian since the age of 10. A short time later she was selected to be a Mouseketeer on *The New Mickey Mouse Club*. After that show came to an end, she was cast as Blair Warner on the new NBC sitcom called *The Facts of Life* and settled in for a nine-year stay. In the middle of the show's run, Whelchel recorded a pop gospel album called *All Because of You* on the Nissi label. Among the cuts on the album are "Cover Me Lord," "Good Girl," "Love Believer," and "Just Obey." The album became a surprise hit on the Contemporary Christian charts, peaking at number 17. Whelchel was nominated for a Grammy Award, but did not win. Despite the album's success, there wasn't a follow-up. She participated in the 2001 *Facts of Life Reunion* and was also present for the program's salute at the TV Land Awards in 2011 along with Charlotte Rae. In 2012, she was a contestant on *Survivor: Philippines* and finished in second place. She has written several books about motherhood and is a motivational speaker. She has been married only once and has three children.

JOHNNY WHITAKER

Most Famous TV Role: Jody Davis on *Family Affair*; **Network:** CBS; **Years:** 1966–1971; **Hit Recording:** none; **Labels:** Chelsea, United Artists; **Release Years:** 1968–1973; **Matrix:** "Every Little Boy Can Be President" (United Artists #50296), "Friends" (Chelsea #0056); **Chart:** none

Johnny Whitaker was born in Van Nuys, California, on December 13, 1959. He is the fifth of eight children born to Thelma and John O. Whitaker Sr. Young John was acting and singing by the age of three. Both he and Brian Keith had roles in *The Russians Are Coming, the Russians Are Coming* in 1966. Later that year, Keith and Johnny Whitaker were reunited in a new Don Fedderson sitcom to be called *Family Affair*. Whitaker recalled, "The role of Jody Davis was originally set for a ten-year-old boy, but Brian Keith suggested that they see me for the role, and so my agent contacted casting director Virginia Martindale for an audition for the Jody role. It was thought that Anissa Jones and I looked like twins, and so the original concept for the part of Jody was changed to accommodate me. However, during the show's five-year run, I grew a lot but Anissa didn't, so for a time they considered dropping the word *twins*, but that never did happen."

The program bore a striking resemblance to *Bachelor Father*—a wealthy playboy takes care of his deceased sibling's offspring. Both programs even had a housekeeper/manservant, and both lasted for five seasons. The only difference—Uncle Bill Davis on *Family Affair* took care of three children while Uncle Bentley Gregg on *Bachelor Father* only cared for one. During *Family Affair*'s run on CBS, Whitaker shared, "I got to record a single for United Artists Records. The A-side was 'Every Little Boy Can Be President' backed with 'The Garden Song.'" The record was well timed, as 1968 was a presidential election year, and the song was featured in a *Family Affair* episode titled "The Unsound of Music." Whitaker also performed the tune live on ABC's *Hollywood Palace*. The 45 was issued with a picture sleeve and the artist was listed as Johnny (Jody) Whitaker. He also garnered quite a bit of attention for his role as Michael in the 1969 TV movie *The Littlest Angel* and sang on the soundtrack album. Whitaker added,

I performed on numerous soundtrack albums. Between *Family Affair* and *Sigmund and the Sea Monsters*, I made several Disney films—*The Biscuit Eater, Napoleon and Samantha* [with Jodie Foster], *Snowball Express*, and *Mystery in Dracula's Castle*—the latter was a Disney movie made for television. Most people think *Tom Sawyer* was a Disney film but it was actually distributed by United Artists. Originally, I was going to lip-synch to the tunes for the film recorded by Donny Osmond, but Arthur P. Jacobs's wife, Natalie Trundy, wanted to see if I could sing the songs myself on film and on the soundtrack album. She was sold on me because of the cry and sniffle I placed in the perfect spot in the song "If'n I Was God" and told her husband that "he wouldn't get any" if he didn't let me sing most of the songs myself. Turns out that the only song I didn't sing was "Freebootin." My role in *Tom Sawyer* convinced Sid and Marty Krofft that I'd be perfect for their new series called *Sigmund and the Sea Monsters* on NBC's Saturday morning schedule. It ran for two seasons, and I portrayed Johnny Stuart.

During the program's run, Whitaker released a *Sigmund and the Sea Monsters* album (Chelsea LP #0332) and a couple of songs he performed on the program—"Friends" backed with "You You" were placed on a single in 1973. Whitaker said, "'You You' is a bonus cut that wasn't on the album. The only way to get it is on the 45. On the A-side, 'Friends,' there's a segment of the song intended to sound like a party. I pointed out that all of the voices at the party were male and that it needed a female presence, too."

About the recording session for the album, he shared, "One of the cuts, 'Lovin' Ain't Easy' has one 'you' that is a very low note. I was fourteen at the time and my voice was changing. I simply could not hit that bottom 'you,' and so singer/songwriter Bobby Hart jumped up to the microphone and sang it. The whole album took a couple of days to record and was a lot of fun."

Whitaker later got to costar in a TV movie that served as the pilot episode for a series called *Mulligan's Stew*. Whitaker played Mark Mulligan, but he remembered, "NBC wanted to go another way and nixed me from the series. The role was given to Johnny Doran when the pilot became a very short-lived series." About his recordings, Whitaker mused, "Looking back, I wish they had given me more direction in the studio. I'd been singing since I was a toddler, but with a bit more coaching I think the records may have been bigger hits."

As of this writing, he is portraying the judge in the Judson Theatre Company's production of *To Kill a Mockingbird* in Pinehurst, North Carolina. He is fluent in five languages and also performs some very rewarding work as a drug counselor and as a counselor for the California State Prison in Lancaster, California, preparing those soon to be released for reentry into society (with more information available at the website www .pasoporpaso.org). He also shares some great film clips, photographs, and career highlights at his official website www.johnnywhitaker.com.

ANSON WILLIAMS

Most Famous TV Role: Warren "Potsie" Weber on *Happy Days*; **Network:** ABC; **Years:** 1974–1983; **Hit Recording:** "Deeply"; **Label:** Chelsea; **Release Year:** 1977; **Matrix:** "Deeply" (Chelsea #3061); **Chart:** #93 *Billboard* Hot 100

Anson Williams was born Anson William Heimlich in Los Angeles, California, on September 25, 1949. He is, indeed, related (second cousins) to Dr. Henry Heimlich, famous for the Heimlich maneuver treatment for choking victims. He lettered in track in high school and participated in all of the school stage productions. At the age of 22, he first portrayed the naive and well-meaning Potsie Weber in a segment of ABC's *Love American Style* titled "Love and the Happy Days." The segment that aired on February 25, 1972, served as a pilot, and almost two years later, it became a series and debuted on ABC on January 15, 1974. There were some changes, however—Howard Cunningham was now played by Tom Bosley instead of Harold Gould and the characters of Ralph Malph (Donny Most) and Fonzie (Henry Winkler) were added. Anson Williams reprised his role as Potsie Weber and sang on many episodes of the show. During the show's run, he also got to make a 45 rpm record for the Chelsea label. That 1977 single, "Deeply" backed with "I Want to Believe in This One," was released with a picture sleeve. Despite the popularity of the program and his character, the record was a very minor hit and no others followed. He also cowrote the closing theme song for the short-lived 1979 NBC sitcom titled *Brothers and Sisters*.

After *Happy Days* ended its run during the summer of 1984, Anson turned his attentions behind the camera and became a rather prolific director for programs such as *Melrose Place*, *Beverly Hills 90210*, *Sabrina the Teenage Witch*, *Charmed*, and *7th Heaven*. He also founded his own cosmetics company, Starmaker Products. He and his costars won a big lawsuit against CBS, which owns the program, for merchandising revenues for which they hadn't received payment. He has been married twice and has six children.

CINDY WILLIAMS. *See* LAVERNE AND SHIRLEY.

GUY WILLIAMS

Most Famous TV Roles: Zorro on *Zorro*, John Robinson on *Lost in Space*; **Networks:** ABC, CBS; **Years:** 1957–1959, 1965–1968, respectively; **Hit Recording:** none; **Labels:** Assault, Romano; **Release Year:** 1958; **Matrix:** *Presenting Señor Zorro* (Disneyland LP #102), *Cancion del Zorro* (RCA Victor LP #1416); **Chart:** none

Guy Williams was born Armand Joseph Catalano in New York City on January 14, 1924. His parents were born in Sicily. He was a good student and was in the chess club and on the football team. While working at several menial jobs, on a whim he sent his picture to a modeling agency. They were taken with his height and good looks, and suddenly a career was born. Williams moved to Hollywood and found small roles in a few motion pictures, but soon returned to New York where he was able to find more work as a print model. In the new medium of television, he found a few small recurring roles on programs such as *The Mickey Rooney Show*, *Men of Annapolis*, and *Highway Patrol*. In 1957, the Disney Corporation was seeking an actor to star in their new *Zorro* series, and the actor now known as Guy Williams got the nod. *Zorro* was a big hit and would have continued through more than two seasons, but a legal dispute between Disney and ABC led to the popular program being discontinued. During *Zorro's* run, Guy Williams released an album for the Disneyland label called *Presenting Señor Zorro*. It was popular with kids but didn't chart. Williams also recorded an album of songs for RCA Victor Records called *Cancion del Zorro*, released only in Argentina, where he spent a good deal of his later life.

After *Zorro*, Williams earned a recurring role (five episodes) as Will Cartwright on NBC's *Bonanza*. Then came his most memorable role—that of John Robinson on CBS's sci-fi hit called *Lost in Space*. The program lasted for three seasons, and after it ended in 1968, Williams opted to retire. He had made many very savvy investments and decided to enjoy his considerable wealth. He was married only once and had two children. He died of a brain aneurysm in Argentina on April 30, 1989, at the age of 65. He got a star on Hollywood's Walk of Fame in 2001, posthumously. A biography was released in 2005 titled *Guy Williams: The Man behind the Mask* by Antoinette Girgenti.

MASON WILLIAMS

Most Famous TV Role: musician and writer on *The Smothers Brothers Comedy Hour*; **Network:** CBS; **Years:** 1967–1969; **Hit Recording:** "Classical Gas"; **Label:** Warner Bros.; **Years Active:** 1968–present; **Matrix:** Warner Bros. #7190; **Chart:** #2 *Billboard* Hot 100

Mason Williams was born on August 28, 1938, in Abilene, Texas. However, he moved around a lot as a child and recalled,

> My parents divorced when I was young, and my mom took up with a serviceman and we relocated to Mount Clemens, Michigan, for a time (around 1945 or '46). Then it was back to Texas and a very small town known as Rule before settling in Oklahoma City in 1947. I became interested in music very

early on, and loved to imitate the falsetto singers of the 1950s—especially the songs of the Platters. I also developed an early affinity for comedy, and loved to write parodies of the songs of the day (such as "Cry" by Johnnie Ray and "The Ballad of Davy Crockett" by Bill Hayes). My biggest influences, however, were sitar player Ravi Shankar, and especially the folk musicians the Kingston Trio and Theodore Bikel. Once I entered Oklahoma City University, the emphasis of course was on classical, but I maintained my love of folk music and its wonderful chord changes and lyrics.

At this same time, I was learning jokes, and the art of telling jokes. This came in very handy because by 1960, I was recording for the Mercury label ["Little Billy Blue Shoes" backed with "Run Come See"—Mercury #71676]. Oklahoma City had its own unique folk music scene, and to be a good folk music performer, one had to be able to entertain the audience with more than just a jukebox list of songs. This scene began with a group of local performers in a living room, and grew to the stage of a local club known as the Gourd. In 1961, I became a folk singer in the navy, and while that was happening, I absorbed every song in every music book and on every album on which I could get my hands. Upon my return to civilian life, in 1964 I recorded an album titled *Them Poems* for Vee Jay Records. The Beatles were on Vee Jay at this same time with releases initially rejected by Nick Venet at Capitol Records, a move later dubbed Nick Venet Syndrome. Every cut on *Them Poems* began with the word "Them."

While still making great music, Williams gravitated to writing comedy for TV, and secured gigs with *The Roger Miller Show*, and specials starring Petula Clark and Andy Williams. Some of his fondest memories and greatest successes came with writing for *The Smothers Brothers Comedy Hour* alongside an up-and-coming Steve Martin. Williams said,

> We had all the big name musical acts of the day on the show—the Turtles, the Buckinghams, the Mamas and the Papas, and both Tommy [Smothers] and I knew they were as sick of singing their current big hit as we were of hearing it, so we used to encourage that they sing another cut from their album or a flip side. That worked out really well, and made big hits out of many of those songs because of the exposure. That made a lot of record labels very happy, and in fact, Warner Bros. asked Tommy if there was anything they could do for *him*. He suggested that they record *me*, and the rest is history. I performed my "Classical Gas" song several times on the program, and even though I didn't tour with the song, that exposure made it a hit. It garnered me a Grammy. "Classical Gas" has the distinction of being the most played instrumental song of all time.

How does he feel about his music being used in movie soundtracks and TV shows such as *The Sopranos* and *Fringe?* Williams chimed in, "It's great—very flattering. The song is like a time machine—great for setting a mood. It was a hit in the summer of 1968—a very turbulent period in

American history. In fact, Bobby Kennedy was scheduled to appear on the program to promote his antismoking campaign. I was very busy writing jokes for him to use on the show just as the news about his assassination was broadcast—an amazing coincidence." Speaking of campaigns, Williams added, "Tommy and I came up with the whole Pat Paulsen campaign for president. That was a lot of fun—there were so many good lines that are still fondly remembered today. The best part of those shows were the surprises—the audience was never sure what was coming next."

Williams continued to write material for the Smothers Brothers, including their new series in 1975, and numerous TV specials. When asked about any writing jobs he didn't enjoy, Williams stated, "*Saturday Night Live*. I didn't like it. It was 1980, and the impression I got immediately from New York was that it was too aggressive—they wanted you to fail. The writers in Los Angeles were very helpful, but in New York everyone was out for themselves. I only did about six shows there and wanted out. I was too naive—too much a country boy. They wanted me to be more like them."

Speaking of his naïveté, Williams shared, "I attribute a good deal of my success to being naive, but still being creative. I made the most of my limitations—and I have so goddamn many."

Has he kept in touch with Steve Martin? Williams replied, "Yes, indeed. He's so very busy so I don't like to bother him very often, but when I do, I always get a very kind and complimentary response."

Williams's latest CD is the Grammy-nominated *Electrical Gas* (Skookum #1008), and for more information on obtaining a copy, check out his website—www.masonwilliams-online.com/home.html.

ROBIN WILLIAMS

Most Famous TV Role: Mork from Ork on *Mork and Mindy*; **Network:** ABC; **Years:** 1978–1982; **Hit Recording:** none; **Labels:** Boardwalk, Casablanca; **Release Years:** 1980–1981; **Matrix:** "I Yam What I Yam" (Boardwalk #5701), "Elmer Fudd Sings Bruce Springsteen" (Casablanca #2367); **Chart:** none

Robin Williams was born in Chicago, Illinois, on July 21, 1951. He was painfully shy as a kid and his joining the drama club in high school helped him break out of that. He earned a scholarship at the Juilliard School, as his undeniable talents became very obvious very early. This bundle of energy then sought success as a stand-up comic. He was discovered by George Schlatter and tapped to join the cast for a revival of *Laugh-In* in 1977. The new *Laugh-In* bombed but Williams's abilities were evident, and he was then cast as the lead in a new Paramount sitcom to be called *Mork and Mindy* (after a memorable guest appearance as Mork in an episode of *Happy Days* called "My Favorite Orkan"). He became an instant star, and *Mork and Mindy* enjoyed a four-season run on ABC from 1978 to 1982.

During this time, Williams was snagged for several motion picture roles, including that of *Popeye*. In 1980, the Boardwalk Records label released a single of his performance of "I Yam What I Yam" backed with costar Shelley Duvall's "He Needs Me." It was released with a picture sleeve but wasn't a big seller. The following year, while still filming *Mork and Mindy*, Williams's performance of Bruce Springsteen's "Fire" as it would be done by Elmer Fudd was released as a single on Casablanca Records. Officially called "Elmer Fudd Sings Bruce Springsteen," the single got some airplay because of Williams's immense popularity, but it didn't chart. However, several of his stand-up comedy albums were big sellers and three earned Grammy Awards—*Reality . . . What a Concept* (Casablanca LP #7162), *A Night at the Met* (Columbia LP #40541), and *Robin Williams Live* (Columbia LP #86977). *Reality . . . What a Concept* also earned Williams a gold record.

The sitcom ran out of steam after four seasons, and Williams then focused on his stand-up, HBO specials, and motion pictures. Among his most famous films are *Good Morning, Vietnam*; *Mrs. Doubtfire*; *Dead Poets Society*; *Awakenings*; *Aladdin*; *Happy Feet*; *The Birdcage*; and *Good Will Hunting*—the latter garnering him an Oscar. He also won numerous Emmy and Golden Globe Awards. He attempted a return to TV in 2013 in *The Crazy Ones* on CBS, but it never did find an audience. After years of battling depression, possibly exacerbated by the cancellation of his CBS series, Williams tragically took his own life on August 11, 2014. He was married three times and had three children. As a tribute, "Robin Williams, rest in peace, make God laugh" was placed on the marquee of Hollywood's Laugh Factory immediately after the sad news broke.

BRUCE WILLIS

Most Famous TV Role: David Addison on *Moonlighting*; **Network:** ABC; **Years:** 1985–1989; **Hit Recording:** "Respect Yourself"; **Label:** Motown; **Release Year:** 1987; **Matrix:** Motown #1876; **Chart:** #5 *Billboard* Hot 100

Walter Bruce Willis was born in Idar-Oberstein, West Germany, on March 19, 1955, while his father, David, was in the military. Bruce is the eldest of four children. The family moved to New Jersey in 1957. He had a stutter as a child, but worked through it and gravitated toward the performing arts. He then enrolled in the drama program at Montclair State University. He earned a few off-Broadway roles in the late 1970s and very early 1980s. He then packed up and headed west, seeking work in television. After a few guest starring roles, he landed one of the lead roles in ABC's *Moonlighting* opposite Cybill Shepherd (see the entry for her). The program became popular very quickly, and Willis won an Emmy for playing David Addison, and earned a very lucrative contract with Seagrams to promote its line of wine coolers.

From there, he began his immensely successful motion picture career, and the original *Die Hard* really put him on the map. He also ventured into making phonograph records, and was successful there, too (albeit briefly). An album he released on the legendary Motown label called *The Return of Bruno* (Motown LP #6222) reached the Top Twenty and earned a gold record. A single from the album, a remake of the Staple Singers' classic "Respect Yourself," became an even bigger hit than the original version, peaking at number 5. A very clever and popular music video showing Willis at numerous famous musical events and concert venues aided its success. Other remakes from the album—the Coasters' "Young Blood" (Motown #1886) and the Drifters' "Under the Boardwalk" (Motown #1896)—failed to match the success of "Respect Yourself," and Willis focused on his acting alone and found roles in many famous ones: *Pulp Fiction, Sixth Sense, The Whole Nine Yards, Looper, Moonrise Kingdom, Armageddon,* and countless *Die Hard* sequels. He won another Emmy for the recurring role of Paul Stevens on *Friends* in 2000. He was a cofounder of Planet Hollywood along with Sylvester Stallone and Arnold Schwarzenegger. Willis has been married twice—first to Demi Moore with three children and in 2009 to Emma Heming with two children.

PAUL WINCHELL

Most Famous TV Role: host of *Winchell Mahoney Time;* **Network:** ABC, NBC, syndicated; **Years:** 1950–1961, 1965; **Hit Recording:** none; **Labels:** Decca, X; **Release Year:** 1954; **Matrix:** "Anything You Can Do" (X #0025), "Hooray Hooray (It's Winchell Mahoney Time)" (Decca #88203); **Chart:** none

Paul Winchell was born as Paul Wilchinsky in New York City on December 21, 1922. He had aspirations of becoming a doctor, but the family's hard financial times put the kibosh on medical school and he took an interest in ventriloquism. Jerry Mahoney, a homemade puppet, was named after one of his teachers. After lots of practice, he took part in *Major Bowes' Amateur Hour* on radio at the age of 16, and came in first place. His act didn't work all that well on radio for obvious reasons, but with the advent of television Winchell had a long run with mostly children's programming. He and his puppets, Knucklehead Smiff and Jerry Mahoney, also made a few records throughout the 1950s and 1960s, but most were skits. However, Winchell was a decent singer, and he recorded a duet with Jerry Mahoney in 1954 for RCA Victor's X label subsidiary. Paul and Jerry's picture was emblazoned on the label for this release—Irving Berlin's "Anything You Can Do" backed by (with tongue in cheek) "You're So Much a Part of Me." There was also one for the Decca label called "TV Clubs Songs" issued with a picture sleeve featuring the songs "Friends, Friends, Friends" and "Hooray Hooray (It's Winchell Mahoney Time)." Winchell also hosted a kids' game show called *Runaround* in the early 1970s. He provided numerous voices to animated characters on *Wacky Races, Dastardly and Muttley in Their Flying Machines, The Smurfs, The Adventures of the Gummi Bears,* and *The New Adventures of Winnie the Pooh* (the latter as Tigger). He was also Fleabag, the slovenly dog in the animated version of *The Odd Couple* called *The Oddball Couple.* He is also responsible for some 30 patents, including the artificial heart and the disposable razor. In a strange coincidence, Winchell died on June 24, 2005, one day before John Fiedler, the voice of piglet in those same animated *Winnie the Pooh* motion pictures and specials. His original puppets are housed in the Smithsonian. He was married three times and had three children, with whom he was not close.

WOLFMAN JACK

Most Famous TV Role: host of *The Midnight Special;* **Network:** NBC; **Years:** 1973–1981; **Hit Recording:** "I Ain't Never Seen a White Man"; **Label:** Wooden Nickel; **Release Year:** 1973; **Matrix:** Wooden Nickel #0108; **Chart:** #106 *Billboard* Bubbling Under

Robert Weston Smith was born the younger of two children in Brooklyn, New York, on January 21, 1938. His parents separated when he was very young, and to help him through this trying time, his father bought him a radio. This radio became his favorite toy, and Robert grew up loving R&B and the personalities that presented it. His first job was at a radio station in Newport News, Virginia. His next stop was Shreveport, Louisiana, where he met and married Lucy Lamb, nicknamed "Lou." They had two children together and it was the Wolfman's only marriage. He became

Wolfman Jack because of inspiration from "the Moondog," Alan Freed, and blues singer Howlin' Wolf, and a passion for horror films.

He made his big splash in radio when he moved to the West Coast. He landed at a super-powered station XERF in Mexico near the California border. He was heard everywhere and became a West Coast radio star with his gravelly voice, his wolfman howl, double entendre references, and fun and sexy R&B music. In the early 1970s, he became a national star when he was tapped to portray himself in George Lucas's blockbuster called *American Graffiti*. He also portrayed himself in an episode of *The Odd Couple* called "The Songwriter." At this same time, he was named as the announcer for NBC's weekly Friday night concert series called *The Midnight Special*, and also made a few of his own records for the Wooden Nickel label. The company cleverly pictured a wooden nickel on the label, and the A- and B-sides of the record were listed as "heads" and "tails," respectively. The Wolfman made the charts with one record—"I Ain't Never Seen a White Man" backed with "Gallop"—and it bubbled under the Hot 100 for six weeks. After a few more singles and two albums for Wooden Nickel, he moved over to RCA Victor Records and released a cover version of the old Five Keys R&B doo-wop song "Ling Ting Tong" (RCA Victor #0117) with a picture sleeve, but it wasn't a big hit.

Wolfman stayed with *The Midnight Special* until it ended in 1981. He also worked for WNBC-AM radio in New York City—first in 1973 and then again in a pretaped broadcast in 1984. In that same year, he voiced an animated version of himself on a cartoon show called *Wolf Rock TV*. Wolfman was immortalized in a Top Ten hit by Canada's Guess Who called "Clap for the Wolfman" (RCA Victor #0324) in 1974. Wolfman's voice is heard on that major hit record. His final radio job came with a weekly live broadcast from Washington DC's Hard Rock Café originating on WXTR-FM (XTRA 104.1). Wolfman, a chain smoker with a nagging cough, flew home to North Carolina after one of these live broadcasts to see his loving wife, Lou. He suffered a massive heart attack in his driveway and died while greeting her on July 1, 1995.

PAT WOODELL

Most Famous TV Role: Bobbie Jo Bradley on *Petticoat Junction*; **Network:** CBS; **Years:** 1963–1965; **Hit Recording:** none; **Label:** Colpix; **Release Year:** 1965; **Matrix:** "What Good Would It Do?" (Colpix #772); **Chart:** none

Patricia Joy Woodell was born in Winthrop, Massachusetts, on July 12, 1944. In her teens, she attempted to make a go of it as an actress and earned a few guest starring roles on episodic TV shows such as *Hawaiian*

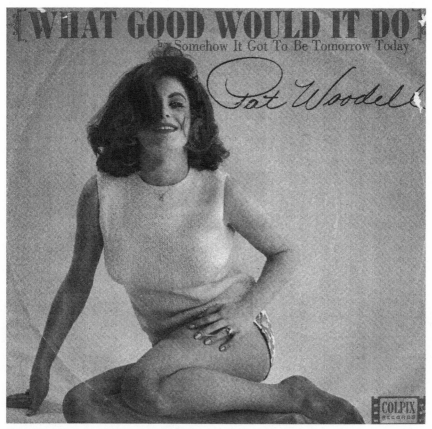

During her brief juncture on *Petticoat Junction*, Pat Woodell recorded a couple of less-than-successful "tracks" for the Colpix label.

Eye, Cheyenne, and *77 Sunset Strip.* Then she landed a regular role on a new CBS sitcom called *Petticoat Junction* in 1963 as the bookworm named Bobbie Jo, one of the three Bradley Sisters at the Shady Rest Hotel. The show became a hit, and during the show's run Woodell attempted to get her recording career started and released a single for Colpix Records called "What Good Would It Do?" backed with "Somehow It Got to Be Tomorrow Today." She had a decent voice, but her singing style was reminiscent of an earlier era and the single bombed. Even a photo of Woodell on the picture sleeve didn't help sales. However, she opted to leave the series to pursue her dream of becoming a recording star and the role of Bobbie Jo went to Lori Saunders for the rest of the show's run. In 1973, after a few uneventful roles in unheralded motion pictures, Woodell retired from show business. She was married only once, to actor Gary Clarke. That marriage ended in divorce.

SHEB WOOLEY

Most Famous TV Role: Pete Nolan on *Rawhide*; **Network:** CBS; **Years:** 1959–1965; **#1 Hit Recording:** "The Purple People Eater"; **Label:** MGM; **Release Years:** 1955–1968; **Matrix:** MGM #12651; **Chart:** #1 *Billboard* Hot 100

Shelby "Sheb" Wooley was born in Erick, Oklahoma, on April 10, 1921. He was a true cowboy and worked the rodeo circuit for many years before his acting and singing career came into focus. The hard work led him to try something else, and he took acting lessons and scored with the role of Ben Miller in the 1952 western classic *High Noon*. He also made a couple of records for the tiny Bullet Records label to no avail. It would take a few years, but he would find success on TV and on vinyl at the same time. He was cast as Pete Nolan in a new CBS western called *Rawhide*, alongside Clint Eastwood (see the entry for him), and also scored with a rock and roll novelty song on the MGM label called "The Purple People Eater," reaching number 1. He never again made Top Ten, but he did place quite a few songs in the Hot 100, including several country music parodies under the alias of Ben Colder, the last one coming in 1968 called "Harper Valley P.T.A., Later That Same Day" (MGM #13997). In 1969 he was, briefly, a *Hee Haw* cast member, and continued to record until 1973 when he pretty much went into retirement. He was diagnosed with leukemia in 1996 and died on September 16, 2003, at the age of 82. He was married only once and had two children.

TOM WOPAT

Most Famous TV Role: Luke Duke on *The Dukes of Hazzard*; **Network:** CBS; **Years:** 1979–1985; **Hit Recordings:** "The Rock and Roll of Love," "A Little Bit Closer"; **Labels:** Capitol, Columbia, EMI, Epic; **Release Years:** 1983–1991; **Matrix:** "The Rock and Roll of Love" (Columbia #8364), "A Little Bit Closer" (EMI/Manhattan #50112); **Chart:** #16, #18, respectively, *Billboard* Country

Tom Wopat was born in Lodi, Wisconsin, on September 9, 1951—the fifth of eight children born to Albin and Ruth Wopat. Tom studied at the University of Wisconsin and a short time later made his TV debut on *One Life to Live* on ABC. He was then an understudy for Broadway's *I Love My Wife* in 1977. He finally landed a starring role beginning very early in 1979 on a program called *The Dukes of Hazzard*. It was lambasted by the critics, but became a quick and enduring hit with viewers and remained on CBS's prime-time schedule through the summer of 1985. It even spawned a short-lived spinoff called *Enos*. The program's popularity allowed Wopat to kick off his recording career. His first album came in 1983 and was simply titled *Tom Wopat* (Columbia LP #38592). It was not a whopping success. But his next album, *A Little Bit Closer* (EMI America LP #17270), became his biggest and spawned two Top Twenty country singles—the title cut, and "The Rock and Roll of Love." He continued recording into the 1990s with *Don't Look Back* (Capitol LP #90121) and *Learning to Love* (Epic LP #47874). He landed in another hit series in 1995. This time around it was a sitcom called *Cybill*, and again on CBS. Wopat portrayed Cybill's ex-husband Jeff Robbins, a stuntman who was living on her sofa. His stay, however, was brief and by 1996 his appearances were few and far between. Wopat participated in all of the popular *Dukes of Hazzard* TV reunions and was seen most recently in Quentin Tarantino's *Django Unchained*. He has been married twice. His latest album, *I've Got Your Number*, is available only through his website, www.tomwopat.com.

JO ANNE WORLEY

Most Famous TV Role: cast member on *Rowan and Martin's Laugh-In*; **Network:** NBC; **Years:** 1968–1970; **Hit Recording:** none; **Label:** Reprise; **Release Year:** 1968; **Matrix:** "Why Won't You Come Home?" (Reprise #0782); **Chart:** none

Jo Anne Worley was born the third of five children, the middle child, in Lowell, Indiana, on September 6, 1937. She was known for her loud voice in school and was considered the class clown. She majored in drama at Midwestern State University in Texas but left a short time later to continue her studies at the Pasadena Playhouse. She eventually found some understudy work on Broadway and created a nightclub act that caught the attention of talk show host Merv Griffin. She guest starred on Griffin's show over 40 times, and it was those memorable appearances that got her cast as a regular on *Rowan and Martin's Laugh-In* beginning in 1968. On the program she often made reference to her husband named Boris, but she was single at the time (she did marry actor Roger Perry in 1975). She only stayed with the program until 1970 before moving on to other things. She performed in countless regional theater productions and was a frequent guest on TV variety and game shows. She made frequent returns to the Broadway stage, most recently as Madame Morrible in *Wicked*. She is very active in animal rights causes and frequently provides voices for animation. She and Roger Perry divorced in 2000 and they had no children (he is currently married to Joyce Bulifant). Her lone 45 rpm release was titled "Why Won't You Come Home?," and it was not a hit.

Y

TINA YOTHERS

Most Famous TV Role: Jennifer Keaton on *Family Ties*; **Network:** NBC; **Years:** 1982–1989; **Hit Recording:** none; **Label:** Tri Tab; **Release Year:** 1987; **Matrix:** "Baby, I'm Back in Love Again" (Tri Tab #1); **Chart:** none

Kristina Louise Yothers was born in Whittier, California, on May 5, 1973. Her father was a TV producer, and she and her three male siblings all appeared in commercials as children. At the age of nine, Tina snagged the role of the youngest Keaton child on a new NBC sitcom titled *Family Ties*. Although she was overshadowed by Michael J. Fox's meteoric rise to stardom, she grew up on the program during its seven-year stay. During its run, she recorded a single called "Baby, I'm Back in Love Again" on the Tri Tab label with "Girlie Girlie" on the B-side. She got to lip-synch to the record on a 1987 episode of the sitcom titled "Band on the Run." She also performed the song on the popular *Solid Gold* musical program, but despite its exposure the record failed to catch on. The series ended in 1989, and after several years out of the spotlight, Yothers attempted musical success again in a group called Jaded along with her brother Cory Yothers. Their CD called *Confessions* was released in 2000 on the Harvest Products label (#200). Tina and Cory also wrote many of the songs on the album, but it was not a major success, even though she had distanced herself from her sitcom days by letting her hair return to its natural brunette color. Tina is married to an electrician and has two children.

Z

JOHN ZACHERLEY

Most Famous TV Role: host of *Shock Theater*; **Network:** WCAU-TV, Philadelphia; WABC-TV (Channel 7), WOR-TV (Channel 9), WPIX-TV (Channel 11), New York City; **Years:** 1957–1958; **Hit Recording:** "Dinner with Drac"; **Label:** Cameo; **Release Year:** 1958; **Matrix:** Cameo #130; **Chart:** #6 *Billboard* Hot 100

John Zacherle was born in Philadelphia, Pennsylvania, on September 26, 1918. He majored in English literature at the University of Pennsylvania. He served in the U.S. Army during World War II, and after his discharge sought work in local theater productions. He found local TV work on WCAU-TV Channel 10 beginning in 1954, and by 1957 became host of a program called *Shock Theater*. He dressed as an undertaker for the program and introduced old horror films. He became quite popular and early in 1958 recorded a spooky novelty number for the local Cameo Records label titled "Dinner with Drac." It was released in March of that year, half a year away from Halloween, and yet the record became a hit, and even though Zacherley was just a local celebrity, it still made Top Ten nationally. The lyrics were narrated but set to a rock and roll beat. Allegedly Dick Clark thought the lyrics were too gruesome, but it became a big hit nonetheless. Zacherley released numerous eerie follow-ups such as "Eighty-Two Tombstones" backed with "Lunch with Mother Goose" (Cameo #139), "Hurry Bury Baby" backed with "Dinner with Drac" (Parkway #853), "I Was a Teenage Caveman" backed with "Dummy Doll" (Cameo #145), "Surfboard 109" backed with "Clementine" (Parkway #885), and "Monster Monkey" backed with "Scary Tales from Mother Goose" (Parkway #888).

Nicknamed "The Cool Ghoul," Zacherle then moved on to New York City's WABC-TV Channel 7. It was there that a *y* was added to his surname, and he became John Zacherley. His new show was almost a carbon copy of *Shock Theater*, but was now titled *Zacherley at Large*. He jumped

343

around often between New York City TV stations, and was seen for a while on WOR-TV Channel 9 and WPIX-TV Channel 11—the latter as host of *Chiller Theater*. For a time in the middle 1960s he even hosted, in costume, a live rock and roll dance show on UHF (WNJU-TV Channel 47 in Newark, New Jersey) called *Disc-o-Teen*. Zacherley is a nonagenarian and retired as of this writing, but on occasion he still surfaces for horror TV specials, documentaries, and fan/autograph shows.

EFREM ZIMBALIST JR.

Most Famous TV Roles: Stuart Bailey on *77 Sunset Strip*, Inspector Lewis Erskine on *The F.B.I.*; **Network:** ABC; **Years:** 1958–1974; **Hit Recording:** none; **Label:** Warner Bros.; **Year:** 1959; **Matrix:** "Adeste Fideles" (Warner Bros. #5126); **Chart:** none

Efrem Zimbalist Jr. was born in New York City on November 30, 1918. His father was a concert violinist and his mother an opera singer. Surprisingly, his career focus was on acting, with music only as an afterthought. Efrem Jr. attended Yale University and served in the U.S. Army during World War II. After his discharge, he pursued his love for acting and earned a role alongside Spencer Tracy on Broadway in *The Rugged Path*. His first regular role on television came with a short-lived NBC series in 1954 titled *Concerning Miss Marlowe* with costar Ross Martin. In 1956 he signed with Warner Bros. Studios and the following year starred in a Warner Bros. television show called *77 Sunset Strip*. He is the only cast member to stay for all six seasons. While the show was in its heyday, Warner Bros. was very keen upon having its TV stars record for its record company. Zimbalist got to record a couple of cuts for the company's *We Wish You a Merry Christmas* album (Warner Bros. LP #1337). His two cuts were also released as a single in 1959—"Adeste Fideles" backed with "Deck the Halls with Boughs of Holly" (Warner Bros. #5126).

The year 1959 was a big one for Zimbalist—he also won a Golden Globe for Most Promising Newcomer. In 1963, *77 Sunset Strip* was revamped, but the changes alienated viewers and the show was cancelled in 1964. Zimbalist didn't mind too much and the following year he earned a role in yet another long-running program, *The F.B.I.* The show was a Quinn Martin Production and ran for nine years on ABC. It has been alleged that the cast had to go through a background check before portraying FBI agents. He received numerous awards from the FBI itself for his portrayal. Despite having musical genes from both his mother and father's

While starring as Stuart Bailey on *77 Sunset Strip*, Efrem Zimbalist Jr. was on Warner Bros.' Christmas list.

side, he didn't record or release any other singles. Zimbalist remained active through the 1980s and '90s with recurring roles in such series as *Remington Steele*, *Hotel*, and *Babylon 5*. He also found a goodly amount of voice work for animated programs such as *The Legend of Prince Valiant*, *Batman: The Animated Series*, *Spider Man*, and *Justice League*. He was married three times and has three children, including popular actress Stephanie Zimbalist. He died at the age of 95 in Solvang, California, on May 2, 2014.

Appendix A:
Honorable Mentions

This appendix contains a list of TV stars who released recordings outside the window of their TV fame, but merited inclusion.

BILL ANDERSON

Most Famous TV Role: host of *The Bill Anderson Show* and *The Better Sex*; **Network:** syndicated; **Years:** 1965–1974, 1977–1978, respectively; **Hit Recording:** "Still"; **Label:** Decca; **Release Year:** 1963; **Matrix:** Decca #31458; **Chart:** #8 *Billboard* Hot 100

James William "Bill" Anderson III was born on November 1, 1937, in Columbia, South Carolina. He earned his college degree in journalism with aspirations of becoming a sports writer. However, while working as an on-air radio personality to put himself through journalism school, Anderson's singing and songwriting talents became his primary focus. The first song he penned, "City Lights," was recorded by the legendary Ray Price (Columbia #41191). However, still bigger things, including over 40 studio albums, were ahead for the man who became known as "Whispering" Bill Anderson, who shared, "While my Top Ten crossover hit, 'Still' (Decca #31458) likely contributed to the nickname, it was actually given to me by a comedian named Don Bowman on my television show because in many of my songs, I would sing a bit and talk a bit. My voice is just naturally soft, and therefore lent itself to the nickname."

Speaking of the syndicated *Bill Anderson Show*, Anderson recalled, "It was in production for nine years—1965 to 1974. It had several different producers during its lifetime. At one time, it was syndicated on almost two hundred stations nationwide. Regular members of the cast were Jan Howard, Jimmy Gately, and my Po' Boys Band. Guest stars included virtually everyone from within the field of country music—Johnny Cash, Dolly Parton, Waylon Jennings, and a thirteen-year-old Tanya Tucker among them. Outside of country, we featured R&B icon Ivory Joe Hunter, folk-rocker Don McLean, and actor Cliff Robertson. Sadly, there are very few copies of the show still in existence."

A short time after *The Bill Anderson Show* ended its run, another great television opportunity cropped up. Anderson added, "I started going to California in the 1970s, and doing guest appearances on Goodson and Todman game shows such as *The Match Game, Password Plus,* and *Tattletales.* Mark Goodson took a liking to me and encouraged me to try out for a role as male host on a new show he was developing called *The Better Sex.* After many trips to California and many, many auditions, I was awarded the job. Sarah Purcell was the female host [this was the first major game show with male and female cohosts] and a delight to work with. It was very much a fun show to be a part of."

Are there any classic outtakes of his TV shows? Anderson smiled and said, "There were many funny moments on both shows. For example, there was the time on *The Bill Anderson Show* that Johnny Cash told me that Jan Howard could teach me to sing. On *The Better Sex,* a male contestant walked off the set because, 'There ain't no woman ever beat me at anything!' We put it right on TV for the whole world to see—those moments actually aired. Those shows provided me with a lifetime of wonderful memories."

What's Anderson up to nowadays? Anderson stated, "I have a new CD called *Life,* and as the name implies, it's a collection of songs drawn from a wide variety of lifetime experiences. My tour schedule is posted regularly on my website—www.billanderson.com."

LUCIE ARNAZ

Most Famous TV Role: Kim Carter on *Here's Lucy;* **Network:** CBS; **Years:** 1968–1974; **Hit Recording:** none; **Label:** Casablanca; **Release Year:** 1979; **Matrix:** "If You Really Knew Me" (with Robert Klein, Casablanca #971), *They're Playing Our Song* (Casablanca LP #7141); **Chart:** none

Lucie Desiree Arnaz was born July 17, 1951, only a few months before the debut of her mom and dad's legendary *I Love Lucy* series. It was a given that she, and younger brother Desi Jr., would pursue careers in show business. Young Lucie made her TV debut in several episodes of *The Lucy Show* in the 1960s. She and her brother became regulars on their mother's new series, *Here's Lucy,* beginning in 1968 (as Kim and Craig Carter, respectively). The series had a six-season run on CBS. Arnaz also amassed a very impressive list of guest-starring roles on episodic TV, as well as two of her own shows—the eponymous *The Lucie Arnaz Show* (as advice columnist Jane Lucas) and *Sons and Daughters* (as Tess Hammersmith). She also garnered acclaim in movies such as *The Jazz Singer*, *Down to You*, and *Who Is the Black Dahlia?* Arnaz was also up for the role of Betty Rizzo in the motion picture version of *Grease*, but because of contractual issues, it went to Stockard Channing. However, we did get to hear her sing when she signed with the red hot Casablanca Records label in 1979. While there, she recorded a Carole Bayer Sager and Marvin Hamlisch composition titled "I Still Believe in Love," and a duet with Robert Klein titled "If You Really Knew Me" backed with "Workin' It Out" from the Casablanca LP titled *They're Playing Our Song*.

Nowadays residing in Palm Springs, California, Arnaz provided the voice of Henry's mom for the animated 2014 motion picture *Henry and Me*. She has been married to actor Laurence Luckinbill since 1980.

DESI ARNAZ JR.

Most Famous TV Role: Billy Simmons on *The Lucy Show*, Craig Carter on *Here's Lucy*; **Network:** CBS; **Years:** 1962–1965, 1968–1971, respectively; **Hit Recording:** "I'm a Fool"; **Label:** Reprise; **Release Year:** 1965; **Matrix:** Reprise #0367; **Chart:** #17 *Billboard* Hot 100

Desiderio Alberto Arnaz IV was born in Los Angeles, California, on January 19, 1953. Having two of the most famous parents on earth certainly doesn't hurt one's career aspirations. When Lucy Ricardo on *I Love Lucy* was "expecting," she was carrying Desi Jr. and it was written into the script. Little Ricky and Desi Jr. were born on the very same day, and Lucy's real baby appeared on the cover of the very first issue of *TV Guide*. Desi Jr. later guest starred in five episodes of his mother's early 1960s sitcom titled *The Lucy Show* (as Billy Simmons), and did three guest appearances with his bandleader father on *The Mothers-in-Law* in 1967 and 1968. Desi Sr. produced that sitcom and portrayed a bullfighter on several episodes. Following in Desi Sr.'s footsteps, Jr. also had a keen interest in music, and teamed with Dean Martin's son, Dino, and a high school friend named Billy Hinsche in a pop vocal group called Dino, Desi and Billy. The trio's first release, "I'm a Fool," reached the Top Twenty and became their biggest hit. For all intents and purposes, "I'm a Fool" was "Hang On, Sloopy" with different lyrics. Their follow-up, "Not the Lovin' Kind" (Reprise #0401), was penned by Lee Hazlewood. After these two successes, they were never able to again penetrate the Top Fifty. They disbanded in 1968, and Arnaz was cast in his mom's new CBS sitcom, *Here's Lucy*. He portrayed Lucy's son, Craig Carter, and his real-life sister,

Lucie Arnaz, portrayed his sister, Kim Carter, on the show. Arnaz stayed with the show for the first three of its six seasons. He later portrayed his famous father in the 1992 film *The Mambo Kings*. He reformed his band as Ricci, Desi and Billy (after the death of Dean Martin's son, Dino), and they toured from 1998 to 2010. The Ricci was Dean Martin's youngest son, Ricci Martin. Today, Arnaz and his wife, Laura, live in Boulder City, Nevada, and own the Boulder Theatre.

JIM BACKUS

Most Famous TV Role: Thurston Howell III on *Gilligan's Island*; **Network:** CBS; **Years:** 1964–1967; **Hit Recording:** "Delicious"; **Label:** Jubilee; **Release Year:** 1958; **Matrix:** Jubilee #5330; **Chart:** #40 *Billboard* Hot 100

Jim Backus was born February 25, 1913, in Cleveland, Ohio. Jim's father was a mechanical engineer, and the family was rather well-heeled, akin to the lifestyle of Thurston Howell III, a character Jim later portrayed on *Gilligan's Island*. He became quite adept at playing that kind of character, and utilized those well-honed skills frequently. Along with movie roles in *Rebel without a Cause, Pat and Mike,* and *It's a Mad, Mad, Mad, Mad World*, Backus found steady work in television, beginning with *I Married Joan* on NBC from 1952 to 1955. He portrayed Judge Bradley Stevens, the long-suffering husband of the zany character of Joan Stevens portrayed by Joan Davis. His popularity on that series led to a recording contract with Jubilee Records in 1958. While there, he scored a unique Top Forty novelty record simply called "Delicious." The song features a couple at a restaurant getting more and more tipsy on each sip of champagne. Backus had a couple of follow-up singles for the label—"Why Don't You Go Home for Christmas?" (Jubilee #5351) and "Cave Man" (Jubilee #5361)—but neither made the charts. Backus then jumped to the Dico Records label for another yuletide single—"I Was a Teenage Reindeer" (Dico #101)—but it, too, failed to chart.

Backus wasn't too disappointed, however, and in 1960 he starred in his own eponymous single-season sitcom set in the office of a newswriting service (also known as *Hot off the Wire*). Simultaneously, Backus began providing the voice for the nearsighted cartoon character named Mr. Magoo, and secured a goodly amount of TV and commercial work as a result. In 1964, Backus earned his most famous role—that of millionaire Thurston Howell III, one of those stranded on *Gilligan's Island* for three prime-time seasons and never-ending reruns. Backus also cowrote several humor books. He remained busy doing voice work until he contracted pneumonia as a result of having Parkinson's disease and died on July 3, 1989.

ROBBY BENSON

Most Famous TV Role: Professor Witt on *American Dreams*; **Network:** NBC; **Years:** 2002–2003; **Hit Recordings:** none; **Labels:** Arista, Bell, MCA, Warner Bros.; **Release Years:** 1974–1980; **Matrix:** "Rock and Roll Song" (Arista #100), "Hey, Everybody" (Bell #45611), "Memories of Sarah" (MCA #41027), "Far Side of a Dream" (Warner Bros. #49211); **Chart:** none

Robby Benson was born as Robin David Segal in Dallas, Texas, on January 21, 1956. Benson was his mother's maiden name, and he affixed it to his own name when his acting career began at age 10. Benson is best known for his TV and big-screen movies (such as *Ice Castles* in 1978), but he also performed both behind and in front of the camera in episodic TV. His first recurring role was on the CBS soap opera *Search for Tomorrow* as Bruce Carson in the early 1970s. At this same time, his teen idol status, it was thought, would be perfect fodder for hit records. He never was able to crack the Hot 100, but not for a lack of trying. In the early to middle 1970s he released two pop singles, beginning with "Hey, Everybody" on the Bell label and then "Rock and Roll Song" on Arista. Another media blitz in the late 1970s with "Memories of Sarah" on MCA and "Far Side of a Dream" on the Warner Bros. label failed to yield any hits. Benson attempted to become a sitcom star as Detective Cliff Brady in *Tough Cookies* on CBS in 1986, but the series only lasted six episodes. Benson found that his bailiwick was behind the scenes as a director (*Friends, Evening Shade, Sabrina the Teenage Witch,* and *Ellen*). He also found a modicum of success as a character voice for animated series such as *The Adventures of Prince Valiant* (1991–1994) and *House of Mouse* (2001–2002). He supplied the voice of Vincent to the 1997 episode of *Seinfeld* titled "The Comeback." Benson returned to television in the flesh in the recurring role of Professor Witt on the NBC period drama titled *American Dreams* from 2002 to 2003. He has been married to Karla DeVito since 1982. They have two children.

LISA HARTMAN BLACK

Most Famous TV Role: Cathy Geary Rush on *Knots Landing*; **Network:** CBS; **Years:** 1982–1986; **Hit Recording:** "When I Say I Do"; **Label:** RCA Nashville; **Year:** 1999; **Matrix:** RCA #0876367823; **Chart:** #1 *Billboard* Country

Lisa Hartman was born June 1, 1956, in Houston, Texas. Hartman's first regular role on TV was in the short-lived ABC *Bewitched* spinoff titled

Tabitha. The program aired erratically, and fans of the show were never certain when and where to find it, and it was quickly cancelled. At this same time, Hartman made her first attempts at a recording career and released several singles for Don Kirshner's Kirshner label—"Pickin' Up the Pieces" (Kirshner #4260), "So Glad I Found You" (Kirshner #4262), "Kentucky Rainbows" (Kirshner #4265), "100 Different Ways" (Kirshner #4275), and "Walk Away" (Kirshner #4283). None of these singles caught on, and Hartman jumped over to RCA Victor in the early 1980s, just as she scored a recurring role on CBS's popular *Knots Landing.* Actually, it was two roles—rock singer Ciji Dunne, and after her death on the program, her lookalike named Cathy Geary. After two singles for RCA—"Hidin' from Love" (RCA #13251) and a remake of "Where the Boys Are" (RCA #13804)—Hartman jumped to Atlantic Records, but her three releases for the label failed to chart. It would take until 1999 for Hartman to have a hit record—a duet with her husband, country singer Clint Black, called "When I Say I Do." It reached number 1 on the country chart and garnered a CMA Award for "Vocal Event of the Year." It was also nominated for a Best Country Collaboration Grammy, but didn't win. Hartman and Black have been married since 1991 and have one daughter named Lily.

JIMMY BOYD

Most Famous TV Role: Howard Meechim on *Bachelor Father*; **Networks:** CBS, NBC; **Years** 1958–1961; **#1 Hit Recording:** "I Saw Mommy Kissing Santa Claus"; **Label:** Columbia; **Release Year:** 1952; **Matrix:** Columbia #39871; **Chart:** #1 *Billboard* Hot 100

Jimmy Boyd was born in McComb, Mississippi, on January 9, 1939. His biggest success came at age 13 with a holiday classic that hit number 1 called "I Saw Mommy Kissing Santa Claus" for Columbia Records and Mitch Miller. As an adult he gravitated toward acting, and earned the regular role of Howard Meechim, Kelly Gregg's boyfriend on *Bachelor Father* from 1958 to 1962. He was briefly married to future Batgirl, Yvonne Craig. Boyd died of lung cancer on March 7, 2009.

RUTH BROWN

Most Famous TV Role: Leona Wilson on *Hello, Larry*; **Network:** NBC; **Years:** 1979–1980; **Biggest Hit Recording:** "Teardrops from My Eyes"; **Label:** Atlantic; **Release Year:** 1950; **Matrix:** Atlantic #919; **Chart:** #1 *Billboard* R&B

Rhythm and blues legend Ruth Brown brought her "Lucky Lips" to the small screen as Leona Wilson on *Hello, Larry.*

Ruth Brown was born as Ruth Weston in Portsmouth, Virginia, on January 12, 1928. After singing in USO shows and in nightclubs, she got to audition for Atlantic Records and was an instant success in rock and roll's infancy. She scored five number 1 singles on the R&B charts for Atlantic with the biggest being "Teardrops in Your Eyes" in 1950 and the most famous being "Mama, He Treats Your Daughter Mean" (Atlantic #986) in 1953. In the 1960s she took some time off to raise a family, only to return in the late 1970s on McLean Stevenson's *Hello, Larry* as the sassy neighbor Leona Wilson on NBC. She then also found great success on Broadway, and won a Tony for *Black and Blue* and a Grammy for her *Blues on Broadway* album (Fantasy LP #9662). Brown was inducted into the Rock and Roll Hall of Fame in 1993, and died of complications of a heart attack and stroke on November 17, 2006, at the age of 78.

GEORGE BURNS

Most Famous TV Role: himself on *The George Burns and Gracie Allen Show;* **Network:** CBS; **Years:** 1950–1958; **Hit Recording:** "I Wish I Was Eighteen Again"; **Label:** Mercury; **Release Year:** 1980; **Matrix:** Mercury #57011; **Chart:** #49 *Billboard* Hot 100

George Burns was born as Nathan Birnbaum in New York City on January 20, 1896. His first wife and show business partner was named Hannah Siegel, and their union last only a matter of weeks. While he was in vaudeville, he met Gracie Allen and they clicked instantly and were successful on stage, in the movies, on radio, and most memorably on television. Their CBS sitcom began as a live program in 1950, but was eventually a filmed weekly show, and those classic episodes, sponsored by the Carnation Company, are still in syndication. *The George Burns and Gracie Allen Show* had to be among the most difficult programs for its writers because of Allen's frequent use of malapropisms. Because of failing health, Allen bowed out of the TV series after eight seasons, and Burns then attempted to make it on his own in *The George Burns Show* in 1958. The rest of the cast was there, except for one element, Allen, and the show was cancelled. Burns tried again in 1964 and found a new Allen in Connie Stevens for a funny but low-rated sitcom called *Wendy and Me* on ABC. Allen died shortly after a few episodes were filmed, and Burns buried himself in his work to persevere. The series lasted only one season.

Burns always liked to sing, but a running joke on all of his shows was that no one wanted to hear him doing it. That didn't stop him from releasing several albums—*George Burns Sings* (Buddah LP #5025), *A Musical Trip with George Burns* (Buddah LP #5127), and in 1980 *I Wish I Was Eighteen Again* (Mercury LP #5025). A novelty hit, the title cut from the latter reached the Top Fifty on the Pop charts. A couple of years later, he went to the well again with "Young at Heart" (Mercury #76149), but it didn't work a second time. Burns remained a popular attraction in Las Vegas and on late-night talk shows, and made a comeback on the silver screen when the films *The Sunshine Boys* and *Oh, God* became big hits in the middle 1970s. A fall in the bathtub at the age of 98 was devastating to Burns. He loved to work and lived to work, but he was never the same after the injury and died two years later at the age of 100 on March 9, 1996. He has three stars on the Hollywood Walk of Fame—for live performance, film, and TV.

MICHAEL CALLAN

Most Famous TV Role: Peter Christopher on *Occasional Wife*; **Network:** NBC; **Years:** 1966–1967; **Hit Recording:** none; **Label:** Reprise; **Release Year:** 1962; **Matrix:** "Mix Master" (Reprise #20172); **Chart:** none

Michael Callan was born as Martin Calinieff in Philadelphia, Pennsylvania, on November 22, 1935. Known affectionately as "Mickey" in Hollywood, he first appeared on Broadway in *The Boy Friend* and *West Side Story* in the middle 1950s. He signed with Columbia Pictures in 1959, and earned roles in *Gidget Goes Hawaiian* and later *Cat Ballou*. He also got the opportunity to record a single for Reprise Records in 1962—"Mix Master" backed with "Nancy Lovin'"—but nothing much came of it and his

Michael Callan, the star of *Occasional Wife*, also released an occasional 45.

only other record was as part of the cast album for the 1968 TV version of *Kiss Me, Kate*. He is best known to television audiences as the bachelor named Peter Christopher on *Occasional Wife*. Peter's boss at a baby food company demanded that his managers be married, so to placate said boss, Peter cooked up a scheme that his pretty blonde neighbor who lived two flights above him would pose as his bride "occasionally," when needed. For the favor, he paid for her education, and comedy and much confusion ensued. During the program's single season, Callan fell in love in real life with his costar Patricia Harty and they were married, albeit briefly. After this, Callan went the guest-star route, and his list of credits runs a mile long. He has been "occasionally" married three times (all ending in divorce) and has three children.

LES CRANE

Most Famous TV Role: host of *The Les Crane Show*; **Network:** ABC; **Years:** 1964–1965; **Hit Recording:** "Desiderata"; **Label:** Warner Bros.; **Release Year:** 1971; **Matrix:** Warner Bros. #7520; **Chart:** #8 *Billboard* Hot 100

Les Crane was born as Lesley Stein in Long Beach, New York, on December 3, 1933. He was an English major who started in radio in San Antonio, Texas, but made his mark in San Francisco, California, with his confrontational talk show. He was then hired for a national talk show on ABC called *The Les Crane Show* to compete with Johnny Carson's *Tonight Show*. It wasn't a success and lasted only five months. He made a big comeback in 1971 with a Top Ten hit for Warner Bros. Records called "Desiderata." It was a narration of the old Max Ehrmann poem of the 1920s with musical accompaniment and a female chorus, and it garnered him a Grammy. Crane was briefly married to Tina Louise of *Gilligan's Island*. Coincidentally, one of his other wives (he had five) was named Ginger. Crane died July 13, 2008, in the San Francisco area. No complete episode of *The Les Crane Show* is known to exist (only a few clips).

The Les Crane Show was never in the Top Ten, but his single called "Desiderata" was in 1971.

JAMES DARREN

Most Famous TV Roles: Dr. Tony Newman on *The Time Tunnel*, Officer Jim Corrigan on *T.J. Hooker*; **Networks:** ABC, CBS; **Years:** 1966–1967, 1983–1986, respectively; **Top Ten Recordings:** "Goodbye Cruel World," "Her Royal Majesty"; **Label:** Colpix; **Release Years:** 1961–1962; **Matrix:** "Goodbye Cruel World" (Colpix #609), "Her Royal Majesty" (Colpix #622); **Chart:** #3, #6, respectively *Billboard* Hot 100

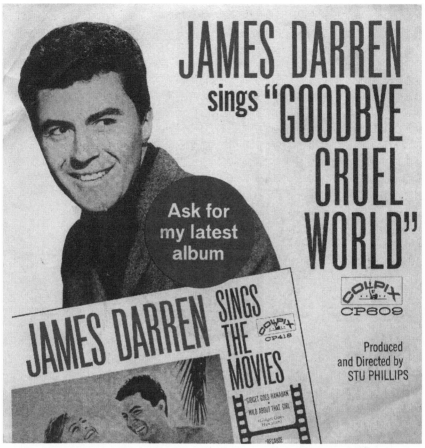

Utilize "the time tunnel" and go back to 1961 for James Darren's biggest hit.

James Darren was born as James Ercolani in Philadelphia, Pennsylvania, on June 8, 1936. He began his show business career as Moondoggie in the *Gidget* film of 1959 with Sandra Dee. His first single to reach the charts was the title song from the film (Colpix #113), and it just missed the Top Forty. It took more than two years after that release to crack the Top Ten, and Darren did it twice—once with "Goodbye Cruel World" late in 1961, complete with circus references and sound effects, and once with "Her Royal Majesty," written by the prolific Carole King and Gerry Goffin. He reached number 11 with his next single, "Conscience," penned by another prolific Brill Building team—Barry Mann and Cynthia Weil. None of Darren's follow-ups ever came close to the Top Ten again, and he began to focus on his acting career.

He got to star in an Irwin Allen sci-fi series in the 1966–1967 TV season. Darren was Dr. Tony Newman on the popular but short-lived *Time Tunnel* series—a program still fondly recalled by many. After a career lull, Darren was back in a series called *T.J. Hooker* with William Shatner on ABC and then CBS. Darren portrayed Officer Jim Corrigan for three of the show's five seasons. After this, he began working behind the camera and directed episodes of *The A-Team*, *Hunter*, *Melrose Place*, and *Beverly Hills 90210*. In 1998, he returned on-screen in holographic form as a singer named Vic Fontaine on the popular sci-fi series *Star Trek: Deep Space Nine*. Darren continues to record, and sings mostly old standards today when performing in Atlantic City and Las Vegas.

Soul singer Hannah Dean was a regular cast member in the short-lived Paramount sitcom *Out of the Blue* on ABC.

HANNAH DEAN

Most Famous TV Role: Gladys on *Out of the Blue*; **Network:** ABC; **Year:** 1979; **Hit Recording:** none; **Label:** Columbia; **Release Year:** 1962; **Matrix:** "Itty Bitty Love" (Columbia #41768), "High Noon" (Columbia #42862); **Chart:** none

Hannah Dean was born in Los Angeles, California, on March 2, 1933. While still in her 20s, she recorded a couple of early soul singles for Columbia Records—"Itty Bitty Love" backed with "So Little Time" and "High Noon" backed with "You, You, You." Neither single sold well, and Dean then focused on acting, but only a small handful of opportunities presented themselves in television. She guest starred on a couple of episodes of *Sanford and Son* in the middle 1970s and earned roles in a couple of long-forgotten motion pictures—*Panic in Echo Park*, *The World's Greatest Lover*, and *The Black Six*. Her only regular TV role came in a single season sitcom for Paramount called *Out of the Blue* in 1979 on ABC. She portrayed Gladys, the housekeeper. Dean died in Compton, California, on May 6, 2004.

RICK DEES

Most Famous TV Role: host of *Solid Gold* and *Into the Night*; **Networks:** ABC, syndicated; **Years:** 1984–1985, 1990–1991, respectively; **#1 Hit Recording:** "Disco Duck"; **Label:** RSO; **Release Year:** 1976; **Matrix:** RSO #857; **Chart:** #1 *Billboard* Hot 100

Rick Dees was born as Rigdon Osmond Dees in Jacksonville, Florida, on March 14, 1950. After graduating from the University of North Carolina at Chapel Hill, he sought radio work and jumped from market to market until landing his first big gig in Memphis, Tennessee. While there, he composed and recorded "Disco Duck"—a number 1 novelty hit on the RSO label, the same label on which the Bee Gees were having monumental success. It proved to be his only hit, and the follow-up called "Disco-Rilla" (RSO #866) failed to catch on. A novelty song about Elvis Presley's considerable weight gain called "He Ate Too Many Jelly Donuts" (RSO #870) was ill timed in its 1977 release that coincided with "the King of Rock and Roll's" surprise passing. Dees also recorded for the legendary

Stax and Atlantic labels. For the latter, he released another somewhat popular novelty song called "Eat My Shorts" (Atlantic #89601) in 1985.

In the meantime, Dees had left Los Angeles's popular KHJ-AM for KIIS-FM, where he stayed for over 20 years (he was eventually replaced by Ryan Seacrest). During his run at KIIS, Dees also hosted the syndicated *Solid Gold* music program, and in 1990–1991 snagged his own short-lived late night talk show called *Into the Night*. Dees's bandleader was the man famous for "At this Moment," Billy Vera (see the entry for him in this appendix). Dees was quite the multitasker, also hosting the *Weekly Top 40* syndicated radio program (heard on dozens upon dozens of stations each week) and performed a small role in the popular motion picture *La Bamba*. He has a star on the Hollywood Walk of Fame and has been inducted into the Radio Hall of Fame. He has been married twice and has one son.

DICK DODD

Most Famous TV Role: Mouseketeer on *The Mickey Mouse Club*; **Network:** ABC; **Year:** 1955; **Hit Recording:** "Dirty Water"; **Label:** Tower; **Release Year:** 1966; **Matrix:** Tower #185; **Chart:** #11 *Billboard* Hot 100

Dick Dodd was born Joseph Richard Dodd Jr. in Hermosa Beach, California, on October 27, 1945. At the tender age of nine, he became one of the original 1955 TV Mouseketeers on ABC's *Mickey Mouse Club*. He stayed with the show for one year. Despite having the same surname, he was not related to that show's Jimmie Dodd. A true rock and roll fan, Dodd purchased a used drum set and by the early 1960s was active in the burgeoning surf rock scene. He was a member of the Belairs, who had a minor hit in 1961 with "Mr. Moto" (Arvee #5034) and Eddie and the Showmen, most famous for the 1963 surfing song about hanging 10 called "Toes on the Nose" (Liberty #55566). His biggest claim to fame came with the garage rock group known as the Standells. Before even having a hit, the group performed on an episode of *The Munsters* titled "Far Out Munster" and in a 1964 motion picture titled *Get Yourself a College Girl*. The group's only venture into the Top Twenty is a very memorable one—"Dirty Water" on the Tower label from 1966. Despite its negative comments about Boston, the song has been embraced by the town and is played regularly at Boston sporting events. Dodd plays drums and sings on the record, which, as of this writing, is the theme song for the new CBS sitcom *The McCarthys*. They also released one single as by the Sllednats (Standells spelled backward) titled "Don't Tell Me What to Do" (Tower #312), but never again captured the magic of "Dirty Water." He even released a few solo singles for Tower as Dick Dodd, but nothing much came of that venture. Dodd died of cancer on November 29, 2013, shortly before the group was to set out on its first U.S. tour in decades. He was married twice and had a daughter.

LEIF GARRETT

Most Famous TV Roles: Leonard Unger on *The Odd Couple*, Endy Karras on *Three for the Road*; **Networks:** ABC, CBS; **Years:** 1974–1975, 1975, respectively; **Top Ten Hit Recording:** "I Was Made for Dancing"; **Label:** Scotti Brothers; **Release Year:** 1978; **Matrix:** Scotti Brothers #403; **Chart:** #10 *Billboard* Hot 100

Leif Garrett was born Leif Per Nervik in Hollywood, California, on November 8, 1961. He became Leif Garrett and began finding acting roles while still a child. He played Felix's son Leonard Unger on two episodes of *The Odd Couple* with Tony Randall and Jack Klugman, he was Zack on *Family*, and he portrayed Endy on the short-lived MTM series called *Three for the Road*. Influenced by the success of Shaun Cassidy, young Leif also sought teen idol stardom and succeeded, albeit briefly. He and Cassidy even shared the same producer, Michael Lloyd. Garrett only scored one Top Ten hit, "I Was Made for Dancing" on the Scotti Brothers label, but also came very close with remakes of Dion's "Runaround Sue" (Atlantic #3440) and the Beach Boys' "Surfin' USA" (Atlantic #3423) in 1977. Two of his albums earned gold records—*Leif Garrett* (Atlantic LP #19152) and *Feel the Need* (Scotti Brothers LP #7100). His battles with drug addiction later in life are well documented, and Garrett appeared on the fourth season of *Celebrity Rehab with Dr. Drew*. In recent years, Garrett has attempted to resurrect his musical career, but thus far to no avail.

BARRY GORDON

Most Famous TV Role: Charlie Harrison on *Fish*, Gary Rabinowitz on *Archie Bunker's Place*; **Networks:** ABC, CBS; **Years:** 1977–1978, 1981–1983, respectively; **Hit Recording:** "Nuttin' for Christmas"; **Label:** MGM; **Release Year:** 1955; **Matrix:** MGM #12092; **Chart:** #6 *Billboard* Hot 100

Barry Gordon was born in Brookline, Massachusetts, on December 21, 1948. He was performing at the age of three and was soon finding work as a guest star on episodic TV shows such as *The Jack Benny Show*, *Alfred Hitchcock Presents*, and *The Ann Sothern Show*. At the age of six he became one of the youngest people ever to reach the Top Ten with a cute holiday novelty song titled "Nuttin' for Christmas" late in 1955. In the lyrics, Gordon reveals that he's been a very mischievous boy all year long, thus the lyric "I'm gettin' nuttin' for Christmas cause I ain't been nuttin' but bad." A follow-up single called "Rock around Mother Goose" (MGM #12166) just missed the Top Fifty. Gordon remained in show business, eventually landing roles in programs such as *The New Dick Van Dyke Show*, *Fish*, *A Family for Joe*, and *Archie Bunker's Place*. He also became extremely prolific at providing voices for animation on programs such as *Tarzan Lord of the Jungle*, *Pole Position*, *Gravedale High*, and *Teenage Mutant Ninja Turtles*. He was also the longest serving president of the Screen Actors Guild from 1988 to 1995. Most recently, he hosted a popular internet talk show titled *Left Talk*. He has been married only once.

ANDY GRIFFITH

Most Famous TV Role: Andy Taylor on *The Andy Griffith Show*, Benjamin L. Matlock on *Matlock*; **Networks:** ABC, CBS, NBC; **Years:** 1960–1968, 1986–1995, respectively; **Hit Recording:** "What It Was Was Football"; **Label:** Capitol; **Release Year:** 1954; **Matrix:** Capitol #2893; **Chart:** #9 *Billboard* Hot 100

Andy Griffith was born in Mount Airy, North Carolina, on June 1, 1926. He was an only child and very shy. He found a way out of his shyness when he joined his school's drama club. He also had a passion for music and played the trombone, and had a penchant for storytelling. The latter talent led to a big hit record in 1954. That record, "What It Was Was Football," is the story of a naive hayseed who attempts to make sense of football, after seeing his very first game. It was originally released on the local Colonial label (#3) in 1953, but when it began to catch on nationally, it was leased to Capitol Records for distribution and became a Top Ten hit. Griffith reached Top Thirty again with "Make Yourself Comfortable" the following year (Capitol #3057), but turned his focus to the silver screen and found starring roles in two gems—*A Face in the Crowd* in 1957 and *No Time for Sergeants* in 1958. He had already conquered the music charts and the box office, and television was next. *The Andy Griffith Show* began on an episode of *The Danny Thomas Show* called "Danny Meets Andy Griffith." It served as a pilot for Griffith's beloved series that ran from 1960 to 1968. It would have run even longer, but Griffith bowed out after eight seasons (the program was number 1 in the ratings in that final season). After a couple of attempts to return to the small screen in *Headmaster* and *The New Andy Griffith Show* (two huge flops), he rebounded as country lawyer Benjamin L. Matlock in 1986 and settled in for another long run. He died of a heart attack on July 3, 2012. He was married three times and had two adopted children.

BILL HAYES

Most Famous TV Role: Doug Williams on *Days of Our Lives*; **Network:** NBC; **Years:** 1970–1984, 1993–1996, 1999–present; **#1 Hit Recording:** "The Ballad of Davy Crockett"; **Label:** Cadence; **Release Year:** 1955; **Matrix:** Cadence #1256; **Chart:** #1 *Billboard* Hot 100

Bill Hayes was born in Harvey, Illinois, on June 5, 1925. His first big break came as a regular singer on Sid Caesar and Imogene Coca's *Your Show of Shows* from 1950 to 1953. In 1955, while not a member of any series, Hayes scored his only hit record, "The Ballad of Davy Crockett" on the Cadence label. It was the theme for the hit TV series starring Fess Parker. In fact, Parker also had a hit version of the song (Columbia #40449), as did Tennessee Ernie Ford (Capitol #3058), but only Hayes's version reached number 1. Hayes returned to episodic TV with a long run on the daytime soap opera *Days of Our Lives* as Doug Williams beginning in 1970. He married his costar, Susan Seaforth, on the program and in real life in 1974. Hayes worked steadily on the program until 1984 and got to perform regularly on the show as a lounge singer. He returned to the program frequently, often for months, even years at a time. He and Seaforth wrote a joint autobiography in 2005 titled *Like Sands through the Hourglass* about their long-enduring Hollywood marriage. He has five children from a previous marriage to Mary Hobbs.

BURL IVES

Most Famous TV Role: Walter Nichols on *The Bold Ones*; **Network:** NBC; **Years:** 1969–1972; **Top Ten Hit Recordings:** "On Top of Old Smoky," "Funny Way of Laughin'," "A Little Bitty Tear"; **Label:** Columbia, Decca; **Release Years:** 1951–1962; **Matrix:** "On Top of Old Smoky" (Columbia #39328), "Funny Way of Laughin'" (Decca #31371), "A Little Bitty Tear" (Decca #31330); **Chart:** #10, #10, #9, respectively, *Billboard* Hot 100

Burl Ivanhoe Ives was born into a family of seven children in Jasper County, Illinois, on June 14, 1909. Burl took an interest in singing as a young child, and as a young adult began touring. He attended the Juilliard School when he was almost 30, and a short time later had his own music-oriented radio program. After being drafted into the army during World War II, he resumed his radio career and parlayed that into the role of a singing cowboy in the motion picture titled *Smoky* in 1946. He also appeared in much more famous films such as *East of Eden, Cat on a Hot Tin Roof,* and *The Big Country,* for which he won an Academy Award. Although he had some success with Columbia Records in the early 1950s, his recording career really took shape in the early 1960s with three consecutive Top Twenty hits for the Decca label—"A Little Bitty Tear," "Funny Way of Laughin'" (for which he won a Grammy), and "Call Me Mr. In-Between" (Decca #31405). In 1964, Ives performed many of the songs in the perennial holiday classic *Rudolph the Red-Nosed Reindeer* TV special (including the title song and "A Holly Jolly Christmas"). Ives tried his hand at a sitcom in 1965—the short-lived and very forgettable *O.K. Crackerby.* He had a bit more success with his role as Walter Nichols on *The Lawyers*—one of the rotating programs on the series known as *The Bold Ones* from 1969 to 1972. After years of smoking cigars and pipe tobacco, Ives developed oral cancer and died on April 14, 1995, at the age of 85. He was married twice.

MABEL KING

Most Famous TV Role: Mrs. Mabel Thomas on *What's Happening?;* **Network:** ABC; **Years:** 1976–1979; **Hit Recording:** none; **Label:** Amy, Rama; **Release Years:** 1956, 1962; **Matrix:** "I'm Gonna Change" (Rama #200), "Symbol of Love" (Rama #204), "Lefty" (Amy #851), "Love" (Amy #874), "I Could Cry" (Amy #886); **Chart:** none

Mabel King was born as Mabel Washington in Charleston, South Carolina, on Christmas Day in 1932. The family moved to Harlem, New York, when she was very young. She started as a gospel singer and in her 20s released a few records for George Goldner's Rama Records label. She was backed by the legendary Harptones on a few of the cuts. First came "I'm Gonna Change" backed with "Alabama Rock and Roll," followed by "Symbol of Love" backed with "Second Hand Love." These singles were very well done but they were not big sellers. In the early 1960s she signed with Amy Records and released three singles—"Lefty" backed with "Go Back Home to Your Fella," "Love" backed with "When We Get the Word" (backed by the Harptones again), and "Why Can't We Get Together"

Although all of her singles were quite good, Mabel King, the matriarch on *What's Happening?* never "happened" as a recording star.

backed with "I Could Cry." She was quite a good singer, but none of the singles made the charts. She then gravitated toward acting in the middle 1960s when she was already well into her 30s, and soon found work on Broadway in *Hello, Dolly* and then *Don't Play Us Cheap*. She later earned the role of the Wicked Witch of the West in *The Wiz*. Then came success on television as Mabel Thomas (a.k.a. Mama) on the popular sitcom *What's Happening?* Mabel Thomas was the mother of Raj (Ernest Thomas) and sarcastic young Dee (Danielle Spencer). Mabel also found a few movie roles in Steve Martin's *The Jerk* and *The Jerk, Too*, as well as Bill Murray's *Scrooged*. Mabel battled diabetes for years and eventually suffered a stroke and loss of several of her limbs. She died at the age of 66 on November 9, 1999.

GLADYS KNIGHT

Most Famous TV Role: Diana Richmond on *Charlie & Co.*; **Network:** CBS; **Years:** 1985–1986; **#1 Hit Recording:** "Midnight Train to Georgia"; **Label:** Buddah; **Release Year:** 1973; **Matrix:** Buddah #383; **Chart:** #1 *Billboard* Hot 100

Gladys Knight was born in Oglethorpe, Georgia (near Atlanta), on May 28, 1944. She was already singing at the age of seven and was a winner on *Ted Mack's Original Amateur Hour*. Named for a cousin whose nickname was "Pip," she and several relatives formed a vocal group known as the Pips. They remade a song called "Every Beat of My Heart," written by Johnny Otis and originally recorded by the Royals. In 1961, it became their first of many Top Ten hits. After leaping from label to label, they scored with Motown's Soul label and had a string of hits, capped off by the first version of "I Heard It through the Grapevine" (Soul #35039) in 1967. After several other big hits for Motown, Knight and the group jumped ship and moved to Buddah Records. There they scored their only number 1 hit—a song about Knight's home state, "Midnight Train to Georgia." The popular group earned a summer replacement series called *Gladys Knight and the Pips* on NBC in July of 1975. As an actress, Gladys played Flip Wilson's wife on a short-lived CBS sitcom called *Charlie & Co.* during the 1985–1986 season. The show was set in Chicago, and Gladys portrayed teacher and housewife Diana Richmond. She also earned a role in Tyler Perry's *I Can Do Bad All by Myself* in 2009 and as of this writing was working on a project for the Lifetime network. She has been married four times and has three children.

JAMES KOMACK

Most Famous TV Roles: Harvey Spencer Blair on *Hennesey*, Norman Tinker on *The Courtship of Eddie's Father*; **Networks:** ABC, CBS; **Years:** 1959–1962, 1969–1972, respectively; **Hit Recording:** none; **Labels:** Coral, RCA Victor; **Release Year:** 1956–1957; **Matrix:** "The Nic-Name Song" (Coral #61809), "The Way She Talks" (RCA Victor #6452); **Chart:** none

James Komack was born in New York City on August 3, 1924. Komack did it all in show business. He was a stand-up comic, he performed in *Damn Yankees* on Broadway and on the silver screen, and he was also in Frank Capra's *A Hole in the Head*. He possessed a gravelly voice and

Multitasker James "Jimmie" Komack created *Welcome Back, Kotter* and *Chico and the Man*. He also created several less-than-successful records and performed the "Girls, Girls, Girls" theme song for TV's *Sugar Time*.

singing was not his forte, but he did release a couple of records in the 1950s—"The Nic-Name Song" for Coral Records and "The Way She Talks" (cowritten by Komack) for RCA Victor. When neither single went anywhere, Komack focused on television. He had a recurring role as Harvey on *Hennesey* on CBS from 1959 to 1962 and as Norman Tinker on *The Courtship of Eddie's Father* on ABC from 1969 to 1972. He also directed a few episodes of *The Dick Van Dyke Show*. Komack is best known for the programs he produced—*Mister Roberts*; *Chico and the Man*; *Welcome Back, Kotter*; and *The Courtship of Eddie's Father*. Among those many successes were some really big flops, such as *The Roller Girls*, *Me and Maxx* (inspired by his only daughter, Maxx), *Another Day*, *Mr. T. and Tina*, and *Sugar Time*.

Komack performed the theme song for the latter. He also wrote for and directed numerous episodes of the programs he produced and created. He was married only once. Komack died on Christmas Eve of 1997 of heart failure.

L. L. COOL J.

Most Famous TV Role: Sam Hanna on *NCIS: Los Angeles*; **Network:** CBS; **Years:** 2009–present; **#1 Hit Recordings:** "I Need Love," "Luv U Better"; **Label:** Def Jam; **Release Years:** 1987, 2002, respectively; **Matrix:** "I Need Love" (Def Jam #07350), "Luv U Better" (Def Jam #063956); **Chart:** both #1 *Billboard* R&B

L. L. Cool J. was born as James Todd Smith in Bay Shore, New York, on January 14, 1968. As a teenager, he was making his own demo recordings and they caught the attention of the Def Jam label. Smith changed his name to L. L. Cool J. (and that stood for Ladies Love Cool James) and released his first single, "I Need a Beat" (Def Jam #001). It sold well and put him on the map in 1984, but it would take a few years for him to reach Top Ten on the R&B charts. That came in 1987 with "I'm Bad" (Def Jam #07120). That set him up for a long and healthy run on the R&B charts well into 2003. He earned his own TV sitcom in 1995 called *In the House* on NBC (he portrayed the landlord Marion Hill on the show). He also costarred in the motion pictures *Wildcats*, *Krush Groove*, *Toys* (with Robin Williams), and *Any Given Sunday*. His biggest break came when he was cast as Sam Hanna on the *NCIS* spinoff called *NCIS: Los Angeles*. To date, he has released 13 studio albums.

PATTI LABELLE

Most Famous TV Role: Chelsea Paige on *Out All Night*; **Network:** NBC; **Years:** 1992–1993; **#1 Hit Recordings:** "Lady Marmalade," "On My Own"; **Labels:** Atlantic, Epic, MCA, Newtown, Parkway; **Matrix:** "Lady Marmalade" (Epic #50048), "On My Own" (MCA #52770); **Chart:** both #1 *Billboard* Hot 100

Patti LaBelle was born as Patricia Louise Holte in Philadelphia, Pennsylvania, on May 24, 1944. People took notice of her considerable vocal talents at a very young age while she was singing in the church choir. Inspired by the local doo-wop music scene, young Patti formed a girl group called the Bluebelles and scored a couple of fair-sized hits with "I Sold My Heart to the Junkman" (Newtown #5000—credited to the Bluebelles, but actually a Chicago R&B girl group called the Starlets), "You'll Never Walk Alone" (Parkway #896), and "Down the Aisle" (Newtown #5777). The Bluebelles became known as simply LaBelle in the 1970s and reached the top of the charts with the first hit version of the classic "Lady Marmalade." A short time later, Patti opted to go solo and continued to conquer the charts with major hits such as "New Attitude" (MCA #52517) and "On My Own" (the latter, a duet with Michael McDonald). During this time, she also expanded her horizons and pursued an acting career, and found roles in several TV movies such as *Unnatural Causes* and *Fire and Rain* before scoring the recurring role of Adele Wayne on NBC's *A Different World*. Her stint on that sitcom led to a starring role in her own—the short-lived *Out All Night* on which she portrayed Chelsea Paige from 1992 to 1993. LaBelle has a star on the Hollywood Walk of Fame, and she has garnered two Grammy Awards and numerous gold records during her stellar career.

MICHELE LEE

Most Famous TV Role: Karen Fairgate MacKenzie on *Knots Landing*; **Network:** CBS; **Years:** 1979–1993; **Hit Recording:** "L. David Sloane"; **Label:** Columbia; **Release Year:** 1968; **Matrix:** Columbia #44413; **Chart:** #52 *Billboard* Hot 100

Michele Lee Dusick was born in Los Angeles, California, on June 24, 1942. Immediately after graduating high school, she began auditioning for stage work and was on Broadway a short time later in *How to Succeed in Business without Really Trying* (followed by the motion picture version of same). The year 1968 was a great one for Michele: she costarred in one of the top grossing films, *The Love Bug*, and had a fair-sized hit record called "L. David Sloane" for Columbia Records—a song about trying to forget an old lover. It became her only chart single. It peaked at number 52, but was a much bigger Top Forty hit in numerous pockets of the United States. She also released an album called *L. David Sloane and Other Hits of Today* (Columbia LP #9682), but it failed to chart. For a time, she was on the game show panel circuit and guest starred on countless episodic TV shows. Her most famous role, that of Karen Fairgate MacKenzie on *Knots Landing*, began in 1979. She stayed for the program's entire 14-season run. She was married to late actor James Farentino from 1966 to 1983 and Fred Rappaport from 1987 to present. She got her star on the Hollywood Walk of Fame in 1998.

#55269

Julie London

In The Wee Small Hours
OF THE MORNING
and TIME FOR LOVERS

LIBERTY

Emergency! star Julie London released numerous singles and LPs for Liberty Records. They are popular among collectors as much for the record jackets as for the music.

JULIE LONDON

Most Famous TV Role: Nurse Dixie McCall on *Emergency!*; **Network:** NBC; **Years:** 1972–1977; **Hit Recording:** "Cry Me a River"; **Label:** Liberty; **Release Year:** 1955; **Matrix:** Liberty #55006; **Chart:** #9 *Billboard* Hot 100

Julie London was born as Gayle Peck in Santa Rosa, California, on September 26, 1926. Her parents were vaudevillian performers, and she opted to follow in their footsteps. Young Gayle sang on radio for the first time at age three, and by her early teens was in motion pictures as Julie London. She and *Dragnet* star Jack Webb were married in 1947 but their union dissolved by 1954. She and future husband Bobby Troup worked together on one of the first rock and roll movies made in color, *The Girl Can't Help It*, in 1956. London's biggest hit, the torch song "Cry Me a River," was featured in the film. London's many albums have become very collectible over the years, not only for the music, but also for the sultry poses of London on the album covers. Although Bobby Troup professed disdain for rock and roll music, he wrote several of the rock and roll songs included in the film. London and Troup were married a few years later in 1959—truly one of Hollywood's longest lasting. She made dozens of guest appearances on prime time shows, but she and Bobby Troup got to work together on NBC's *Emergency!* from 1972 to 1977 (although they weren't husband and wife on the show). Apparently, London and her ex-husband, Jack Webb, parted on good terms because he was the executive producer of *Emergency!* Troup died in 1999, and London was never the same after; she had suffered a stroke in 1995, and then she died on October 18, 2000—coincidentally, on what would have been Troup's 82nd birthday. She has a star on the Hollywood Walk of Fame.

TINA LOUISE

Most Famous TV Role: Ginger Grant on *Gilligan's Island*; **Network:** CBS; **Years:** 1964–1967; **Hit Recording:** none; **Labels:** Concert Hall, United Artists; **Release Years:** 1957–1958; **Matrix:** "I'll Be Yours" (United Artists #127), *It's Time for Tina* (Concert Hall LP #1521); **Chart:** none

Tina Louise was born as Tina Blacker in New York City on February 11, 1934. She was an only child and she was raised by her fashion model mom. By her teen years, she knew she wanted to be an actress and studied drama in New York City. She began her acting career with modeling jobs and performances in musical stage productions. A short time later she was on Broadway and was making guest appearances on dramatic TV programs such as *Studio One*. At this same time, she got to release an album for the Concert Hall Records label titled *It's Time for Tina*. The album was chock-full of old standards such as "Hands across the Table," "Embraceable You," "I'm in the Mood for Love," and "Hold Me." It wasn't a big hit, but Tina got another shot a year later for a larger label, United Artists. "I'll Be Yours" backed with "In the Evening" on 45 rpm also failed to make the charts, but it did come with a sexy picture sleeve. Speaking of which, her pictures in *Playboy* garnered a lot of attention in the late 1950s. In 1964 she costarred with Bob Denver in a beach party film titled *For Those Who Think Young*. Later that same year, she and Denver found themselves stranded on an uncharted desert island with five others. Louise left her role on Broadway in *Fade in, Fade Out* when she got the part on the show. She had the opportunity to sing often on that program titled *Gilligan's Island*. Her most popular number on the show was "I Want to Be Loved by You," always topped off with some very sensuous "boop boopy doos." The program lasted for three seasons in prime time, but since its 1967 cancellation, has been wildly successful in syndication. For a time she was married to talk show host Les Crane. Louise's most famous TV role is part of the ongoing "Ginger or Maryann?" conundrum.

JAMES MACARTHUR

Most Famous TV Role: Detective Danny "Danno" Williams on *Hawaii Five-O*; **Network:** CBS; **Years:** 1968–1979; **Hit Recording:** "Ten Commandments of Love"; **Label:** Scepter; **Release Year:** 1963; **Matrix:** Scepter #1250; **Chart:** #94 *Billboard* Hot 100

James Gordon MacArthur was born in Washington DC (but raised in Nyack, New York) on December 8, 1937. His father was playwright Charles MacArthur and his mother by way of adoption was legendary actress Helen Hayes. Young James was quite the athlete and excelled at basketball, baseball, and football. He was also a member of the drama club and performed in many local stage plays. He and a classmate, up-and-coming actress Joyce Bulifant, married in 1958. About that same time, MacArthur had the opportunity to appear in several Walt Disney films, and left Harvard University in favor of making these movies (*Swiss Family Robinson* and *Kidnapped*). He also had the opportunity to release a few 45 rpm records on the Scepter Records label (famous for records by the Shirelles, Dionne Warwick, and B. J. Thomas). He made the charts (albeit, near the bottom) with a remake of Harvey and the Moonglows' classic "Ten Commandments of Love." MacArthur's version featured a female vocal group in the background while he recited all "Ten Commandments of Love." Some of the original lyrics from the hit Moonglows version were changed for this remake. MacArthur's take on the song was also much shorter than the Moonglows' almost four-minute rendition.

After filming several other motion pictures, including *Spencer's Mountain*, MacArthur got remarried, this time to Melody Patterson of *F Troop*. In that same year, MacArthur was cast as Detective Danny "Danno" Williams on a new police drama called *Hawaii Five-O* on CBS. He was second banana to Jack Lord's Steve McGarrett for 11 of the show's 12 seasons. Countless episodes during that period ended with McGarrett saying, "Book him, Danno." Helen Hayes portrayed his Aunt Clara in an

TV's Danno was "booked" for a few releases on the Scepter Records label. This one cracked the Hot 100.

episode titled "Retire in Sunny Hawaii Forever" in 1975. After leaving the long-running series, MacArthur performed mostly stage work. He had a genuine passion for golf, and in fact his third and final marriage was to LPGA member Helen Beth Duntz. He has a star on the Hollywood Walk of Fame and was honored in a 2010 episode of the new *Hawaii Five-O* titled "Ho'apono" shortly after his death on October 28th of that year at the age of 72.

PATTY MCCORMACK

Most Famous TV Role: Ingeborg on *Mama*, Torey Peck on *Peck's Bad Girl*, Anne Brookes on *The Ropers*, Liz LaCerva on *The Sopranos*; **Networks:** ABC, CBS, HBO; **Years:** 1953–1956, 1959, 1979–1980, 2000–2006, respectively; **Hit Recording:** none; **Label:** Dot; **Release Year:** 1958; **Matrix:** "Bubble Gum" (Dot #15762); **Chart:** none

Patty McCormack was born as Patricia Ellen Russo in Brooklyn, New York, on August 21, 1945. She was modeling at the age of four, and performing on television by the age of seven. At eight, she earned the recurring role of Ingeborg on the long-running *Mama* on CBS. In that same year, she played her most famous role—that of Rhoda Penmark in *The Bad Seed*. She was nominated for an Oscar for that role, but did not win. McCormack then attempted to make her mark in popular music with a release on the Dot Records label. That record was "Bubble Gum" backed with "Kathy-O." The latter is from a motion picture of the same name, in which McCormack portrayed Kathy O'Rourke. The single was not a hit, and no other recordings were released. In 1959, McCormack starred in a short-lived TV sitcom called *Peck's Bad Girl*. Even with David Susskind as executive producer of the show, it failed to find an audience and disappeared after 14 weeks. She continued to make movies and guest appearances on episodic television until earning her next regular role as Anne Brookes on the *Three's Company* spinoff called *The Ropers*. Years later, she snagged the recurring role of Liz LaCerva on HBO's popular *The Sopranos* series. She was married only once and has a star on the Hollywood Walk of Fame.

MARILYN MICHAELS

Most Famous TV Role: a regular on *The Kopykats*; **Network:** ABC; **Year:** 1972; **Hit Recording:** "Tell Tommy I Miss Him"; **Label:** RCA Victor; **Release Year:** 1960; **Matrix:** RCA Victor #7771; **Chart:** #110 *Billboard* Bubbling Under

Marilyn Michaels was born Marilyn Sternberg into a very musical family in New York City on February 26, 1944. Michaels shared, "I was so lucky that my dad was a basso with the chorus for the Metropolitan Opera. He guided me vocally, as did my mom. Actually, I performed on the Yiddish stage from the age of seven. I was a child prodigy." She was also found to have an impressive amount of artistic talent, and developed an affinity for painting, and for a while was unsure whether to pursue the stage or the easel. Music and performing won out, and Michaels recalled,

> In 1959, I was pounding the pavement at the famous Brill Building. And the first door I opened—they signed me to a recording contract (Ray Rainwater and his famous country singing brother, Marvin). At that time I was Toni Michaels, and I recorded "Let It Rain" backed with "I'm Gonna Build a Mountain" on the Debbie Record label [#1407]. By the way, the engineer on that record was the legendary Phil Ramone. They couldn't afford a string section, so Phil recorded the violin part by himself, then overdubbed it, and voila—we had a string section. Phil passed away not long ago. Luckily, I connected with him before he took ill and we did a lot of reminiscing. From there, I somehow got to producers/songwriters Hugo [Peretti] and Luigi [Creatore] at RCA Victor. I aced an audition for them playing piano and singing "Padre." I developed quite a crush on Luigi. While there at RCA, I recorded the answer to Ray Peterson's "Tell Laura I Love Her" called "Tell Tommy I Miss Him" [RCA Victor #7771]. I was seventeen with lots of talent and guts.

Michaels recalled performing regularly in the Borscht Belt (the Catskills), "It was great and exciting. Some folks did three shows a night. My folks didn't allow me to be overworked, so I usually did two shows. I was making good money when other girls were thinking about college. I got about fifty dollars per show—not bad for weekends in 1961."

Before long, she garnered guest appearances on *The Ed Sullivan Show* and *The Tonight Show with Johnny Carson*. Jules Styne caught one of her performances, and cast her for the touring company of *Funny Girl*. Besides being a proficient singer, Michaels became very famous for her dead-on impressions of Carol Channing, Joan Rivers, and especially Barbra Streisand. Did she ever meet Streisand? Michaels said, "Yes, I met her while doing *Funny Girl*. She was doing it on Broadway at the time. We had a night out on the town with her entourage. She was unusual. Very interested in me, the new girl on the block, and very insecure when a reporter directed his attention to me. An indomitable, driven woman. I adore her."

Michaels's proficient impressions led to her becoming part of the repertory company of *The ABC Comedy Hour* in 1972 (later retitled *The Kopykats* in syndication). The program also featured George Kirby, Frank Gorshin, Rich Little, Fred Travalena, and Charlie Callas. Michaels stated, "There are many, many stories about that experience. I'll save those for my book, but the program was directed by the best team in variety television—Gary Smith and Dwight Hemion. They did all the Streisand specials, and so much more." Michaels also became a frequent guest star on numerous episodic TV programs, game shows, and variety shows, and did voiceover work for PBS's *Reading Rainbow*, about which Michaels added, "That was fun, but I had to talk very slowly. It was for kids, so I did all of the character voices very slowly."

She continues to tour and record. Her latest CD is called *Marilyn Michaels: Wonderful at Last*, featuring songs written by Michaels. The CD (autographed, if you like) can be found on her website, www.marilyn michaels.com. While there, get an eyeful of her exquisite and colorful artwork. Speaking of works of art, Michaels said, "My personal favorite of all of my recordings has to be the 'Danny Boy/Sonny Boy' medley from the CD *A Mother's Voice*. Marvin Hamlisch gave me that song. That, to me, is the best singing I have ever done."

Good Morning, Miss Bliss star Hayley Mills scored one Top Ten hit titled "Let's Get Together" as a result of her dual role in *The Parent Trap*.

HAYLEY MILLS

Most Famous TV Role: Miss Bliss on *Good Morning, Miss Bliss*; **Network:** Disney Channel; **Years:** 1987–1989; **Hit Recording:** "Let's Get Together"; **Label:** Buena Vista; **Release Year:** 1961; **Matrix:** Buena Vista #385; **Chart:** #8 *Billboard* Hot 100

Hayley Mills was born in London, England, on April 18, 1946. She began her acting career while still very young and was considered a newcomer with a lot of promise. *Pollyanna* in 1959 put her on the map. Her most famous film role was the dual role of Sharon and Susan in *The Parent Trap* in 1961. A song from the film, "Let's Get Together," was released as a single in 1961 on Disney's Buena Vista Records label and became a Top Ten smash. Mills released several other records, but she never again attained hit status. She continued to make motion pictures, such as *That Darn Cat* and *The Trouble with Angels*. In the 1980s, she made the move to television and appeared in numerous episodes of *The Love Boat*. In 1987, she was cast as Miss Bliss on *Good Morning, Miss Bliss*—a show that later evolved into the very popular *Saved by the Bell*. Mills also took part in two TV movie sequels to her most popular film role—*Parent Trap II* and *Parent Trap III*. Most recently, Mills scored a recurring role in the series titled *Wild at Heart* on ITV1. She has been married once, has two sons, and is a breast cancer survivor.

BILL MUMY

Most Famous TV Role: Will Robinson on *Lost in Space*; **Network:** CBS; **Years:** 1965–1968; **Hit Recording:** "Fish Heads"; **Label:** Lumania; **Release Year:** 1979; **Matrix:** Lumania (no number) **Chart:** none

Born on February 1, 1954, Billy Mumy (as he was known in his youth) knew what he wanted to be at a very early age. He wanted to be an actor and pressured his parents to get him in front of the camera. They obeyed his wishes, and beginning in the late 1950s, he began amassing a long list of movie and TV credits, highlighted by appearances in three very memorable episodes of *The Twilight Zone*—"Long Distance Call," "In Praise of Pip" (with Jack Klugman), and "It's a Good Life" as the monster child known as Anthony Fremont (with Cloris Leachman). A short while later, over a series of 84 episodes, Mumy portrayed Will Robinson—as in

"Danger, danger Will Robinson"—in the iconic sci-fi sensation called *Lost in Space*. Years later, coming full circle, Mumy costarred in yet another successful sci-fi program—*Babylon 5*.

However, there was another side to Mumy most fans hadn't yet seen. We got to see a glimpse of his musical chops in the short-lived 1975 comedy/drama called *Sunshine*, in which Mumy portrayed Weaver—a member of a Canadian rock band led by Sam Hayden (Cliff DeYoung—see the entry for him in the main section). Now known as *Bill* Mumy, his focus switched to music. Mumy shared, "Although I started acting professionally when I was five years old, it wasn't until I was the old age of ten that I started playing guitar. By the time I was eleven I'd started writing songs. Since then, music has driven me. Whether writing and recording my solo projects, making novelty music with Barnes and Barnes, performing live or recording with America or many, many other artists, music is my true home."

The Barnes and Barnes comedy/novelty songs (Mumy with Robert Haimer) have outrageous and memorable titles such as "Party in My Pants," "Making Love in a Subaru," and of course, "Fish Heads" on the Lumania, Brylen, and Rhino record labels. "Fish Heads" was a mainstay on Dr. Demento's radio shows, and also the *Kids America* radio program. Barnes and Barnes also made a popular video for the song, and it aired often on MTV (when they still played videos, that is). Mumy also worked with the Igloos, the Be Five, and the Jenerators. He composed music for television programs such as *The Universe and I* and *Adventures in Wonderland*—the latter garnering him an Emmy nomination. Mumy is also a prolific voice-over announcer in commercials and voice actor for animated series such as *Animaniacs* and *Ren and Stimpy*. He's been married only once and has two children.

OZZIE NELSON

Most Famous TV Role: Ozzie Nelson on *The Adventures of Ozzie and Harriet*; **Network:** ABC; **Years:** 1952–1966; **#1 Hit Recording:** "And Then Some"; **Label:** Brunswick; **Release Year:** 1935; **Matrix:** Brunswick #7464; **Chart:** #1 *Billboard* Music Hit Parade

Oswald Nelson was born in Jersey City, New Jersey, on March 20, 1906. He was a boy scout and a football player, and he took up the saxophone to earn money. He eventually became quite a proficient musician and was the leader of the Ozzie Nelson Band. He recorded for RCA Victor, Bluebird, Vocalion, and Brunswick. He scored a number 1 hit on Brunswick called "And Then Some" in 1935. In that same year he married the band's vocalist, Harriet Hilliard. In the 1940s, *The Adventures of Ozzie and Harriet* debuted on radio and their sons were portrayed by actors. However, when the show moved to ABC Television in 1952, David and Ricky, their real sons, were used. Nelson was far from the laid-back presence we saw on TV. He was rather quite a hands-on taskmaster and had say in every aspect of the long-running TV show (14 seasons). His son Ricky became the second generation Nelson to score number 1 hits (see the entry for him), and then Ricky's sons, Gunnar and Matthew, followed suit in 1990 with "Can't Live without Your Love and Affection" (DGC #19689). After the original series ended in 1966, Ozzie and Harriet returned to television with *Ozzie's Girls* in 1973 and utilized the same old TV set, but with boarders (two college girls) renting out the boys' room upstairs. The program was about to be renewed for a second season in syndication when Ozzie took ill and died a while later of liver cancer on June 3, 1975. He has a star on the Hollywood Walk of Fame.

JOE PESCI

Most Famous TV Role: Rocky Nelson on *Half Nelson*; **Network:** NBC; **Year:** 1985; **Hit Recording:** none; **Labels:** Jamison, Mainstream, Topic; **Years:** 1958–1972; **Matrix:** "Tell Me" (Jamison #864), "Can You Fix the Way I Talk for Christmas?" (Mainstream #5531), "Let's Exchange Graduation Rings" (Topic #9120); **Chart:** none

Joseph Pesci was born in Newark, New Jersey, on February 9, 1943. He was a stage performer beginning at a very young age, but worked for a time as a barber. Influenced by the many doo-wop vocalists from his neighborhood, he was a member of the group called the DuBarrys for a time. The group released two flop singles for small labels—"Let's Exchange Graduation Rings" backed with "Movin' Around" for the Topic label, and "Tell Me" backed with "I Must've Been Crazy" for Jamison Records of Newark. The group's style was actually more like that of the Four Aces than most of the doo-wop groups of the era. Without a hit, the group quickly disbanded. Pesci sometimes filled in for absent members of Joey Dee and the Starliters, and in fact has an uncredited cameo in that group's rock and roll motion picture titled *Hey, Let's Twist*. He was also associated, for a time, with the Four Seasons (and that association is captured in *The Jersey Boys*). Pesci then recorded a solo album in 1968 called *Little Joe Sure Can Sing* on the Brunswick label (#754135), featuring covers of numerous Beatles and Bee Gees songs of the day.

Joe Pesci of *Half Nelson* made several unsuccessful records with some "good fellas" known as the DuBarrys.

From there, he recorded a Christmas novelty cut as Vincent and Pesci for Mainstream Records in 1972. Pesci performed the song "Can You Fix the Way I Talk for Christmas?" as Porky Pig (very convincingly). The flip side was an instrumental called "Little People Blues." In 1985, he starred as Rocky Nelson in the short-lived TV series called *Half Nelson*. More than making up for his lack of success on vinyl and TV, Pesci scored over and over again on the silver screen with *Raging Bull*, *The Goodfellas*, *Home Alone*, *JFK*, *My Cousin Vinny*, *Casino*, and *A Bronx Tale*. In 1998, Pesci released his second album, *Vincent LaGuardia Gambini Sings Just for You* (Columbia CD #69518)—an album that encompassed jazz, rock, and even hip hop. He has been married and divorced three times. Today he is in semiretirement.

DELLA REESE

Most Famous TV Role: Tess on *Touched by an Angel*; **Network:** CBS; **Years:** 1994–2003; **Biggest Hit Recording:** "Don't You Know"; **Label:** RCA Victor; **Release Year:** 1959; **Matrix:** RCA Victor #7591; **Chart:** #2 *Billboard* Hot 100

Della Reese was born as Delloreese Patricia Early in Detroit, Michigan, on July 6, 1931. She began singing in church at the age of 6, and by 13 she was performing with gospel singer Mahalia Jackson. After working at numerous odd jobs, she signed with Jubilee Records and scored her first big hit with "And That Reminds Me" (Jubilee #5292) in 1957. This led to a contract with RCA Victor, and her biggest hit—"Don't You Know" (an adaptation of "Musetta's Waltz" from *La Boheme*). A follow-up called "Not One Minute More" (RCA Victor #7644) also reached Top Twenty. She then tried her hand at television and movies. Her first series was a groundbreaking syndicated talk show called *Della*. It ran from 1969 to 1970. She then joined *Chico and the Man* midstream in 1976 as Della Rogers. In 1989, she earned a memorable costarring role in the Richard Pryor motion picture *Harlem Nights*, and got a big laugh with the line, "Kiss my entire ass." Her biggest break came in 1994 when she landed the role of an angel named Tess on CBS's long running Sunday night juggernaut *Touched by an Angel*. In recent years (2010), Reese was ordained as a minister.

BURT REYNOLDS

Most Famous TV Role: Wood Newton on *Evening Shade*; **Network:** CBS; **Years:** 1990–1994; **Hit Recording:** "Let's Do Something Cheap and Superficial"; **Label:** MCA; **Release Year:** 1980; **Matrix:** MCA #51004; **Chart:** #88 *Billboard* Hot 100

Burton Reynolds was born in Lansing, Michigan, on February 11, 1936. His dad was in the army and he traveled a lot as a child, eventually landing in Riviera Beach, Florida. His father became chief of police there. Burt received a football scholarship at Florida State University, but injuries soon put the kibosh on a career in professional sports. At this juncture, he pursued an interest in theater.

After some stage and stuntman work, Reynolds got his big break in a TV series called *Riverboat* in the 1959–1960 season (as Ben Frazer) on NBC. Several years later he starred in the short-lived police dramas *Hawk* in 1966 and *Dan August* (a Quinn Martin Production) in 1970 (both on ABC). He also enjoyed a stint on *Gunsmoke* as Quint Asper—a blacksmith (1962–1965). He became better known for his motion pictures—especially *Deliverance* and the *Smokey and the Bandit* series of films. A country song he performed in *Smokey and the Bandit* titled "Let's Do Something Cheap and Superficial" was released as an MCA single in 1980 and cracked the Hot 100 for five weeks. He wasn't a great singer, but the song was humorous and fun and he was able to put it over. Burt received a lot of press because of a nude spread in *Cosmopolitan*, and he became a big star and a popular guest on talk and game shows. He returned to television in 1990 in a sitcom with a superstar cast called *Evening Shade*. Burt portrayed Wood Newton, garnered an Emmy Award for his role, and enjoyed a four-season run. Shortly after the series ended, Burt won a Golden Globe Award for his role in *Boogie Nights*. He was married twice and has a star on the Hollywood Walk of Fame.

KURT RUSSELL

Most Famous TV Role: Jamie McPheeters on *The Travels of Jamie McPheeters*; **Network:** ABC; **Years:** 1963–1964; **Hit Recording:** none; **Label:** Capitol; **Release Year:** 1970; **Matrix:** *Kurt Russell* (Capitol LP #492); **Chart:** none

Kurt Russell was born in Springfield, Massachusetts, on March 17, 1951. At the age of 12, he was the star of his own TV series on ABC titled *The Travels of Jamie McPheeters*, based upon a novel by Robert Lewis Taylor. It only lasted one season, and Russell found motion pictures to be his forte. He had a small role in Elvis Presley's *It Happened at the World's Fair*, but soon became a darling for the Disney Company and guest starred numerous times on *Disney's Wonderful World of Color* on TV, as well as Disney pictures such as *Follow Me Boys*, *The Computer Wore Tennis Shoes*, *The Barefoot Executive*, and *Now You See Him, Now You Don't*. At this same time, there was an attempt to make him the next teen idol singing star, a la Bobby Sherman and David Cassidy. He released one album simply titled *Kurt Russell* at the age of 19 in 1970 for Capitol Records, but it failed to catch on (even though he performed several of the songs from the album on *Disney's Wonderful World of Color*). Cuts on the album included a cover of the Archies' "Sugar, Sugar," and a remake of Tommy Roe's "Dizzy." He also had aspirations at this same time to play professional baseball, but an injury to his shoulder ended that quest. Speaking of *Quest*—that was the title of a short-lived NBC TV series from 1976 on which he portrayed Morgan Beaudine. Luckily, he was able to graduate to more mature roles in *Escape from New York*, *Silkwood*, and *Miracle*. For a time he was married to actress Season Hubley, but has been partnered with Goldie Hawn since 1983. Most recently, he has appeared in Quentin Tarantino's *Death Proof* and *Grindhouse*.

SUSAN SILO

Most Famous TV Role: Rusty on *Harry's Girls*; **Network:** NBC; **Years:** 1963–1964; **Hit Recording:** none; **Labels:** Bell, Candlelight; **Release Year:** 1956; **Matrix:** "Mr. Wonderful" (Bell #1122), "Dear Diary" (Candlelight #1005); **Chart:** none

Harry's Girls costar Susan Silo scored a minor hit with this teen ballad called "Dear Diary."

Susan Silo has been performing since the age of 4; she was playing the Palace at the age of 12. Born in New York, but based in Los Angeles since her teens, Silo recalled, "Two people, in particular, took me under their wing and were very important to my career. I became a protégé to comedian Jerry Lewis, and performed on his very first TV special. We stayed in touch and he came to see me when I was in *West Side Story*. He took the whole cast out afterwards. Bandleader Larry Clinton was also very important—especially for my recording career. He was a great promoter." Among Silo's most successful recordings—"Mr. Wonderful" backed with "Poor People of Paris" for the Bell Record label (#1122) in 1956. Silo shared, "We always had a big orchestra for the songs I recorded. It wasn't done piecemeal as it is today. We were all in the recording studio together and if one person made a mistake, we had to start all over again."

Silo got to perform her biggest hit on *American Bandstand*. Silo recalled, "That was a song titled 'Dear Diary' on the small Candlelight label of New York. I did two records for them, but 'Dear Diary' was the biggest one. In fact, it sold so well, the tiny record label couldn't handle it. Because it was a rock and roll record, initially I wasn't welcome on *The Tonight Show*. Jack Paar hated rock and roll, but his daughter loved it, and that was my 'in.'"

Silo parlayed her musical success into achievements in television. She was a regular on the 1963 Larry Blyden sitcom titled *Harry's Girls* (Silo portrayed Rusty)—a great showcase for Silo's song-and-dance prowess. A couple of years later, she had a recurring role as Vera on the NBC sitcom *Occasional Wife*, with Michael Callan (see the entry for him) and Patricia Harty. Silo appeared on many other episodic television shows, such as *The Love Boat*, *Bonanza*, *The Wild Wild West*, *McHale's Navy*, and then was the Riddler's girlfriend, Mousey, on the original *Batman* series (and we've only scratched the surface). Silo's continued success has been with television voice-over and film animation (as well as radio and TV commercials). Silo stated, "Beginning with an animated special called *Hey, It's the King*, followed by the role of Sue in the *Pac-Man* series (both with Hanna-Barbera), I settled in for a long career as a voice actress." She also found steady work in animated shows such as *Biker Mice from Mars*, *Curious George*, *Where's Waldo? Garfield and Friends*, *The Tick*, and *Xiaolin Showdown*. Silo added, "And I'm still going strong. Most recently, I've worked on *Turbo*, *Fast and Furious*, and I have a recurring role on *Avatar: The Legend of Korra*. I'm so fortunate—all of my life I've gotten to do what I like. Not everyone can say that."

THE SMOTHERS BROTHERS

Most Famous TV Roles: Tom (an angel) and Dick Smothers on *The Smothers Brothers Show*, hosts of *The Smothers Brothers Comedy Hour*; **Network:** CBS; **Years:** 1965–1966, 1967–1969, respectively; **Hit Recording:** "Jenny Brown"; **Label:** Mercury; **Release Year:** 1963; **Matrix:** Mercury #72182; **Chart:** #84 *Billboard* Hot 100

The Smothers Brothers were born on Governor's Island where their father, a U.S. Army officer, was stationed. Tom was born February 2, 1937, and Dick on November 20, 1939. Their dad died during World War II, and they were raised by their mom in Southern California. Both brothers developed an affinity for folk music and formed an act. They played at numerous nightclubs and had their big break on *The Jack Paar Show* in 1961. They signed a contract with Mercury Records in 1962 and had a minor chart hit in 1963 with a single called "Jenny Brown." It was their third of eight singles for Mercury. A couple of years later they starred in their own TV sitcom while still recording for the label. The sitcom from Four Stars Studios featured Tom as an angel who came back from the dead to help folks on earth who needed it. He moved in with his younger brother, Dick, and sent Dick's life into total upheaval. However, they were very out of their comfort zone on this series—they didn't get to sing or do their regular comedy shtick. The series lasted only a single season, and the brothers were very grateful when it ended. Their next series on CBS made them famous—*The Smothers Brothers Comedy Hour*. However, despite their popularity, their edgy and antiwar segments led to the high-rated program's cancellation in 1969. They attempted numerous TV comebacks but never again captured the magic of their CBS variety series. They have remained an immensely popular and always entertaining presence on the Las Vegas and Atlantic City circuit.

MARCIA STRASSMAN

Most Famous TV Role: Julie Kotter on *Welcome Back Kotter*; **Network:** ABC; **Years:** 1975–1979; **Hit Recording:** "The Flower Children"; **Label:** Uni; **Release Year:** 1967; **Matrix:** Uni #55006; **Chart:** #105 *Billboard* Bubbling Under

Marcia Strassman was born in New York City on April 28, 1948. She made her first TV appearance on an episode of *The Patty Duke Show*. In 1967, she recorded a single called "The Flower Children" for the Uni Records label.

That record became a big hit in California and was in the Top Ten in many West Coast cities. However, nationally, it failed to crack the Hot 100 and her recording career stalled without any follow-ups making the charts. She rebounded a few years later and earned the recurring role of Margie Cutler in the early episodes of *M*A*S*H*. Her most famous role came on James Komack's *Welcome Back, Kotter* from 1975 to 1979 on ABC. She was the straight man to Gabriel Kaplan's Gabe Kotter character, and endured all the jokes about the eccentric members of his family. She later earned regular roles on a couple of short-lived series—*Good Time Harry* with Ted Bessell in 1980, *Booker* in 1989, and *Tremors* in 2003. She portrayed Rick Moranis's wife in *Honey, I Shrunk the Kids* and all of its sequels. After a long bout with breast cancer, Strassman died at the age of 66 on October 25, 2014.

PAUL SYLVAN

Most Famous TV Role: Woody Warshaw on *Busting Loose*; **Network:** CBS; **Years:** 1977; **Hit Recording:** *Good Paul Sylvan*; **Label:** Colossus; **Release Year:** 1969; **Matrix:** Colossus LP #1008; **Chart:** none

Paul Sylvan was born July 29, 1941, in New York City. His passions for music and motion pictures led to his pursuing dual careers as a vocalist and an actor (and he became quite proficient at both). Being a native of the East Coast, he was influenced by the doo-wop vocal groups of his youth, such as Frankie Lymon and the Teenagers, the Channels, the Charts, and Dion and the Belmonts. Sylvan said,

> I made my first record in 1958 when I was seventeen with an a cappella group called the Four Crowns. It was covered by the Mystics of "Hushabye" fame. While at Ithaca College, I got into another a cappella group called Harvey and the Classics. That opened the door for me to get hooked up with a band called the Thrashers, and we became very popular as a frat party band. The Thrashers later turned into the Bitter Seed Blues Band, and while playing at the Café Wha in Greenwich Village, we borrowed the guitar player from another band known as Curtis Knight and the Squires. His name was Jimmy James and he was a great guitar player, but I couldn't get to the mic as much as I should have. Jimmy just kept on playing. Yes, that was Jimi Hendrix just before he left for England and worldwide fame.

Then came Sylvan's solo venture for Jerry Ross's Colossus Records label, about which he shared,

Busting Loose costar Paul Sylvan released a few singles as Good Paul Sylvan, including "Ophelia."

The *Good Paul Sylvan* album was a combined effort of a group of friends. Alan Gordon, cowriter of "Happy Together" by the Turtles and "Celebrate" by Three Dog Night penned most of the songs. The album has an all-star list of musicians playing on it. The album was pretty good for the time, but the demos that we did to sell it were sensational. Alan and I played drums on them, Jerry Friedman played guitar and keyboard, Andy Muson played bass, and we all did the background vocals. It was a blast being in the studio with those guys. We were all really close friends and it was a true labor of love. The album got me an audition for the original Broadway cast of *Jesus Christ Superstar*, which I did for a bit more than a year. Then I moved to Hollywood and got lucky.

To appeal to the female record-buying demographic, Sylvan is pictured shirtless on the front and back covers of the *Good Paul Sylvan* album.

Sylvan then quickly assembled a healthy list of credits on episodic TV programs such as *The Blue Knight, Police Story, The Streets of San Francisco, The Rockford Files, CPO Sharkey, Archie Bunker's Place, Charlie's Angels,* and *Laverne and Shirley.* Sylvan stated, "I did a guest starring role on the fifth episode of *Laverne and Shirley* as Sal Malina. Mark Rothman and Lowell Ganz were executive producers of the show and wrote the pilot for *Busting Loose.* They called me in to read for the role of Woody Warshaw, the guy that got the girls while his friends watched in awe. Worked for me. We did twenty-three episodes and I had a great time. If I got laid in real life as much as Woody got laid, I'd probably be missing an extremely important (and quite frisky) appendage."

Sylvan added, "We never really became an ensemble—ours was not the happiest cast on the Paramount lot." Sylvan won a coveted Clio Award for his Foamy Shaving Cream commercial, and said, "It ran for eleven years on television. One day of work put food on the table for over a decade. That was an amazing and wonderful period of my life."

In recent years, Sylvan has switched gears, and adopted the role of acting coach. He offers his services at www.paulsylvan.com.

TRACEY ULLMAN

Most Famous TV Role: host of *The Tracey Ullman Show,* host of *Tracey Takes On;* **Networks:** Fox, HBO; **Years:** 1987–1990, 1996–1999, respectively; **Hit Recording:** "They Don't Know"; **Label:** MCA; **Release Year:** 1984; **Matrix:** MCA #52347; **Chart:** #8 *Billboard* Hot 100

Tracey Ullman was born as Trace Ullman in Slough, Berkshire, England, on December 30, 1959. Her father died of a heart attack when she was just a toddler, and she was raised by her mother. Despite hard times, her mother's positive attitude and humor rubbed off. Young Tracey began imitating friends, neighbors, and relatives and became quite proficient at it. This wasn't her only talent—she could also sing and dance rather well, and soon found work in musical productions such as *Grease* and *Gigi.* She then graduated to the small screen. Her first TV series were the short-lived *Mackenzie* and *Girls on Top.* While on the latter, she recorded an album called *You Broke My Heart in 17 Places* (MCA LP #5471). It reached the Top Forty, and the album spawned a Top Ten remake of Kirsty Mac-Coll's "They Don't Know." The song got a nice extra push because Paul McCartney made a cameo appearance in the MTV video.

The hit song really put her on the map, and before long she was approached about having her own comedy sketch show. From 1987 to 1990,

The Tracey Ullman Show showcased her many characters, garnering four Emmy Awards. However, the program is best remembered as the springboard for *The Simpsons*, which ran in prime time for over a quarter of a century. She was given even more room to create on her next show, *Tracey Takes On* on HBO from 1996 to 1999. She has provided countless voices for animation in recent years and enjoyed a nice run on another sketch comedy series, *State of the Union*, from 2008 to 2010 on the Showtime network. She has been married only once—to Allan McKeown for 29 years until his passing in December of 2013.

MIYOSHI UMEKI

Most Famous TV Role: Mrs. Livingston on *The Courtship of Eddie's Father*; **Network:** ABC; **Years:** 1969–1972; **Hit Recording:** none; **Label:** Mercury; **Release Years:** 1956–1961; **Matrix:** "How Deep Is the Ocean?" (Mercury #70838), "Little Lost Dog" (Mercury #70880), "Mountains beyond the Moon" (Mercury #71215), "Sayonara" (Mercury #71216); **Chart:** none

Miyoshi Umeki was born in Otaru, Japan, on May 8, 1929. The youngest of nine children, she briefly used the name Nancy Umeki as a nightclub singer. She loved American pop music and was quite an accomplished vocalist. She was recording for RCA Victor's Japanese subsidiary beginning in the very early 1950s. In the middle 1950s she signed with Mercury Records in the United States and rose quickly in show business. She won an Oscar for her role in the motion picture *Sayonara*, and was nominated for a Tony for her portrayal of Mei-Li in the Broadway production of *Flower Drum Song*, and then a Golden Globe for the film version. Despite the quality of her singles on the Mercury label, none of them penetrated through the rock and roll ruling the Hot 100, and her career hit a lull until 1969 when she was cast as the housekeeper to "Mr. Eddie's father" on *The Courtship of Eddie's Father* and held the role for the show's three seasons on ABC. Unfortunately, she didn't sing on the show and an entire generation missed out on her considerable vocal talents. Umeki was married twice. She died of cancer on August 28, 2007.

BILLY VERA

Most Famous TV Role: orchestra leader for *Into the Night Starring Rick Dees*; **Network:** ABC; **Years:** 1990–1991; **#1 Hit Recording:** "At This Moment"; **Label:** Alfa, Atlantic, Rhino, Rust; **Years:** 1962–present; **Matrix:** Alfa #7005 and Rhino #74403; **Chart:** #1 *Billboard* Hot 100

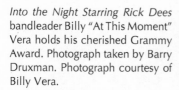

Into the Night Starring Rick Dees
bandleader Billy "At This Moment"
Vera holds his cherished Grammy
Award. Photograph taken by Barry
Druxman. Photograph courtesy of
Billy Vera.

Billy Vera was born on May 28, 1944, into a show business family in Riverside, California (but raised in New York). His father, Bill McCord, was a golden-voiced TV announcer for vintage programs such as *Tic Tac Dough*, *Concentration*, and *Twenty One*. His mom, Ann Ryan, was a regular on-camera background singer on one of the many incarnations of *The Perry Como Show*. Young Billy followed in their footsteps and successfully conquered a TV and musical career. Influenced by jazz, R&B, and doo-wop greats of the 1940s and 1950s, he formed his own vocal group called Billy Vera and the Contrasts, and recorded "My Heart Cries" backed with "All My Love" for the Laurie subsidiary called Rust Records (#5051) in 1962. Truly a multitasker (before the term existed), he found a lot of session work through the 1960s and can be heard on countless recordings by a very diverse group of performers. He penned numerous songs for big name performers such as Rick Nelson ("Mean Old World"—Decca #31756) and Barbara Lewis ("Make Me Belong to You"—Atlantic #2346). Speaking of Atlantic Records, Vera got to record for that legendary label as well—both *with* Judy Clay and as a solo performer—having a total of six charted singles during his stay.

Jumping ahead to 1979, Vera assembled a new 10-piece R&B band called the Beaters and soon found himself back on the charts with singles recorded for the Alfa Records label—"I Can Take Care of Myself" and "At This Moment" (Alfa #7002 and #7005, respectively). The latter was a bit of a sleeper hit, but thanks to its use in a couple of episodes of the popular Michael J. Fox sitcom titled *Family Ties*, it was rereleased and soared to number 1. Vera recalled,

> At this same time, director Bobby Roth had the Beaters and me perform six songs for his TV movie called *Tonight's the Night*. One of the songs was "At this Moment," which was, simultaneously, quickly climbing the charts. Because of the song's success, an additional scene—an acting scene was written for me. A couple of years later, when the Beaters and I became the house band for *Into the Night Starring Rick Dees*, some of my scenes from the movie were used in promos for Dees's show. I cowrote the program's theme song, and got to perform songs I wrote on the show each week. It was a nice steady paycheck for both me and the Beaters. It was most fun when recording stars such as Dion, Frankie Valli, Henry Mancini, Paul Anka, and Merle Haggard were the musical guests. I also made a sitcom pilot for Dick Clark Productions. It was never picked up to become a series, but it starred Frankie Avalon as an aging teen idol, and soap opera star Michael Damian as a young man who dropped out of med school to become a rock star. Dick Clark was great to work with, very loyal, and always very good to me. I miss his great laugh.

It should be noted that Vera also performed the theme songs for the long-running sitcoms *Empty Nest* and *The King of Queens*.

Among the many highlights of Vera's storied, charmed life? He said,

> Getting to perform on *The Tonight Show with Johnny Carson*. I heard from Johnny's bodyguard that I was Johnny's second favorite singer, after Tony Bennett, which is an overwhelming honor. I was presented with the gold record for "At This Moment" on his show. I also had a recurring role as Duke Weatherill on the original *Beverly Hills 90210* on Fox. Then I got to reunite with the *Family Ties* cast on a recent *TV Land Awards Show*, where I performed "At This Moment" live. What class. TV Land treated us like kings—first class accommodations from beginning to end. Very fun and memorable.

As of this writing, Billy and the Beaters continue to perform 52 weeks a year and are enjoying great success with their latest CD titled *Big Band Jazz* for Robo Records. Vera's long-awaited yet-untitled memoirs are coming soon, and "At This Moment" is enjoying a huge resurgence in popularity because of its inclusion on Michael Bublé's CD titled *Crazy Love* (143 Records #520733). Vera recently garnered a Grammy Award for his liner notes on the Ray Charles CD box set, and in 1988 got a star on the Hollywood Walk of Fame.

ADAM WADE

Most Famous TV Role: host of *Musical Chairs*; **Network:** CBS; **Year:** 1975; **Hit Recordings:** "Writing on the Wall," "Take Good Care of Her," "As If I Didn't Know"; **Label:** Coed; **Release Year:** 1961; **Matrix:** "Writing on the Wall" (Coed #550), "Take Good Care of Her" (Coed #546), "As If I Didn't Know" (Coed #553); **Chart:** #5, #7, #10, respectively, *Billboard* Hot 100

Adam Wade was born Patrick Henry Wade in Pittsburgh, Pennsylvania, on March 17, 1935. It's interesting to note that he was a laboratory assistant for Dr. Jonas Salk in his quest for a polio vaccine before switching gears and opting to seek fame as a recording artist. He sounded a lot like Johnny Mathis and was signed to Coed Records beginning in 1959. His best year was 1961 with three Top Ten hits—"The Writing on the Wall," "As If I Didn't Know," and "Take Good Care of Her." The latter was covered by Elvis Presley years later. When the hits stopped coming, he concentrated on his acting and appeared in numerous TV commercials and blaxploitation films. He made history in 1975 when he became the first African American game show host on a musical CBS show called *Musical Chairs*. Also on the program were the Spinners, the Tokens, and Irene Cara. Wade has been married twice and has three children from his first marriage. He continues to work in local theater productions, often near his home in New Jersey.

ROBERT WAGNER

Most Famous TV Role: Alexander Mundy on *It Takes a Thief*, Jonathan Hart on *Hart to Hart*; **Network:** ABC; **Years:** 1968–1970, 1979–1984, respectively; **Hit Recording:** none; **Label:** Liberty; **Release Year:** 1957; **Matrix:** "So Young" (Liberty #55069); **Chart:** none

Robert Wagner was born in Detroit, Michigan, on February 10, 1930. His film career began at the age of 20 with *The Happy Years*. He was contracted to 20th Century Fox for the entire decade of the 1950s and attempted to become a teen idol in 1957 with a single for the new Liberty Records label of Southern California. Wagner wasn't yet a household name, and his record, "So Young" backed with "Almost Eighteen," received very little airplay and failed to make the charts. Wagner signed with Columbia Pictures in the 1960s, but really made his mark in television. He starred as

Alexander Mundy from 1968 to 1970 on ABC's *It Takes a Thief*—a program that still runs in syndication. Next came a CBS series called *Switch*. Wagner portrayed Pete T. Ryan on the show and his costar was Eddie Albert. His longest-running series, *Hart to Hart*, teamed him with the beautiful Stephanie Powers on ABC. In recent years, Wagner has enjoyed recurring roles on *Two and a Half Men* and *NCIS*. Wagner has been married four times—two of which were to Natalie Wood. Every few years, interest in the mysterious death of Wood incites new but inconclusive information. As of this writing, Wagner is still seen regularly in reverse mortgage TV commercials. He has two children.

ROBERT WALDEN

Most Famous TV Role: Joe Rossi on *Lou Grant*; **Network:** CBS; **Years:** 1977–1982; **Hit Recording:** none; **Label:** JDS; **Release Year:** 1960; **Matrix:** "Girls Were Made for Boys" (JDS #5001); **Chart:** none

Robert Walden was born Robert Wolkowitz in New York City on September 25, 1943. His first taste of show business came in 1960 when he was a member of the doo-wop group known as Bobby Roy and the Chord-a-Roys. They recorded one single for the JDS label called "Girls Were Made for Boys" backed with "Little Girl Lost." The label was better known for a hit record by the Videls called "Mister Lonely," and when their single tanked, the disillusioned Chord-a-Roys disbanded. Ten years later, Walden attempted to conquer television and the movies. His first regular TV role came as Dr. Cohen in the final season of *The New Doctors*—a rotating segment of *The Bold Ones* on NBC. His next TV role as Joe Rossi on *Lou Grant* from 1977 to 1982 is his most famous, although he later surfaced on *Brothers* on Showtime, and most recently on *Happily Divorced* on TV Land. Today he is a distinguished teacher of acting at the New School for Drama in New York City.

DEBORAH WALLEY

Most Famous TV Role: Susie Buell on *The Mothers-in-Law*; **Network:** NBC; **Years:** 1967–1969; **Hit Recording:** none; **Label:** Dee Gee; **Release Year:** 1963; **Matrix:** "So Little Time" (Dee Gee #3006); **Chart:** none

Deborah Walley was born in Bridgeport, Connecticut, on August 12, 1941. Her parents were skaters with the Ice Capades. Deborah performed in all of her high school plays and also worked in summer stock. She was discovered on stage and cast in the title role in *Gidget Goes Hawaiian* in 1961. Most of her work on the silver screen was in light fare, such as beach movies and Elvis Presley's *Spinout*. She also attempted to become a recording star in 1963 with a single titled "So Little Time" backed with "Sometimes in the Darkest Hour" on the Dee Gee Records label. Walley recited the lyrics on the record, and it received very little airplay. It was her only 45. She then earned a recurring role on television in the zany and popular sitcom titled *The Mothers-in-Law* with seasoned pros Eve Arden and Kaye Ballard on NBC from 1967 to 1969. In the 1970s, Walley took time off to raise a family and eventually turned her attention to children's theater. From 1962 to 1968 she was married to actor/singer John Ashley (see the entry for him in the main section). Walley had three sons and died young of cancer of the esophagus on May 10, 2001.

TUESDAY WELD

Most Famous TV Role: Thalia Menninger on *The Many Loves of Dobie Gillis*; **Network:** CBS; **Years:** 1959–1960; **Hit Recording:** none; **Label:** Plaza; **Release Year:** 1962; **Matrix:** "Are You the Boy?" (Plaza #508); **Chart:** none

Tuesday Weld was born as Susan Ker Weld in New York City on August 27, 1943. Her father died when she was only four, and to help make ends meet, her mother found modeling work for her daughter a short time later. In her early teens, she starred in Alan Freed's black-and-white rock and roll motion picture titled *Rock, Rock, Rock*. Weld lip-synchs to a yet unknown Connie Francis's vocals in the film. At the age of 16, she earned her first regular role on television as the lovely and fickle snob Thalia Menninger on *The Many Loves of Dobie Gillis*. She was the girl for whom Dobie (and most teenage boys watching) pined. The role earned her a Golden Globe Award as the Most Promising Newcomer. She didn't stay for the program's four-season run, but rather opted to make motion pictures with Bing Crosby (*High Time*) and Elvis Presley (*Wild in the Country*). At this same time she recorded a single for Southern California's Plaza Records label. She wasn't much of a singer (the reason she lip-synched in *Rock, Rock, Rock*), but it was thought that her on-screen popularity would help sell tens of thousands of copies of "Are You the Boy?" backed with "All Through Spring and Summer," but the label miscalculated and the record bombed. Weld didn't ever try again. In her 30s, she graduated to more grown-up roles, such as Katherine in *Looking for Mr. Goodbar*. She has been married and divorced three times—most notably to Dudley Moore from 1975 to 1980. She has two children.

MARIE WILSON

Most Famous TV Role: Irma Peterson on *My Friend Irma*; **Network:** CBS; **Years:** 1952–1954; **Hit Recording:** none; **Label:** Design; **Release Year:** 1957; **Matrix:** *Gentlemen Prefer Marie Wilson* (Design LP #76); **Chart:** none

Marie Wilson was born as Katherine Elisabeth White in Anaheim, California, on August 19, 1916. She was a dancer on Broadway before earning the role of Irma Peterson—a role that defined her and personified every single "dumb blonde" joke ever told. She portrayed *My Friend Irma* first on radio, then in the motion picture series, and eventually on live early television. Many different actresses portrayed her level-headed female friend and roommate over the years, but Peterson was always Irma. The TV version lasted for three seasons and was sponsored by Kool Cigarettes. After the TV version ended in 1954, Wilson found that the role was to typecast her for the rest of her career, and she attempted to cash in on that fact with an album for Design Records titled *Gentlemen Prefer Marie Wilson*. In character, the album was chock-full of silly songs such as "If We Didn't Have Worms," "Rock the Wolf," and "Lettuce." She wasn't much of a singer, but these novelty tunes didn't require much of a voice. She was married four times, and she has three stars on the Hollywood Walk of Fame—for radio, movies, and television. She died young, at the age of 56, on November 23, 1972.

HATTIE WINSTON

Most Famous TV Role: Margaret Wyborn on *Becker*; **Network:** CBS; **Years:** 1998–2004; **Hit Recording:** none; **Label:** Parkway; **Release Year:** 1964–1965; **Matrix:** "Pictures Don't Lie" (Parkway #928), "Pass Me By" (Parkway #956); **Chart:** none

Hattie Winston was born in Lexington, Mississippi, on March 3, 1945. She began her career as a teenager making soul records for Philadelphia's Parkway Records label. She released two singles for the prolific label—

"Pictures Don't Lie" backed with "Please Write Back to Me" and "Pass Me By" backed with a rerelease of "Pictures Don't Lie." Unfortunately, she landed at the label just a bit after their heyday and her singles were not hits. However, "Pass Me By" is today a prime want by serious soul 45 collectors, and has been known to fetch in excess of $200. Winston more than made up for this early setback and enjoyed a long run on PBS's *Electric Company* as Valerie the librarian and also Sylvia from 1973 to 1977. She is best known for her role as Dr. John Becker's sassy receptionist Margaret on *Becker* from 1998 to 2004 on CBS. She has also provided many character voices for animated programs such as *Rugrats* and *All Grown Up*. Most recently, she earned a recurring role on TV Land's *Soul Man* as Miss Pearly. She is married to Harold Wheeler, the musical director for *Dancing with the Stars*.

EDWARD WOODWARD

Most Famous TV Role: Robert McCall on *The Equalizer*; **Network:** CBS; **Years:** 1985–1989; **Hit Recording:** none; **Labels:** Columbia, DJM; **Release Years:** 1971–1975; **Matrix:** "The Way You Look Tonight" (DJM #232), "It Had to Be You" (DJM #249), "Champagne Charlie" (DJM #614), "Only a Fool" (Columbia #8547); **Chart:** none

Edward Woodward was born in Croyden, Surrey, England, on June 1, 1930. After attending Kingston College, he worked on stage in England and on Broadway in the United States. As much as he longed to be an actor, he also yearned to play professional soccer in his youth. He never did become a soccer star and relied upon his acting skills. His first Broadway success was in *High Spirits* in 1964—a musical that garnered three Tony Awards. A very accomplished singer, Woodward attempted success on vinyl in the 1970s. He recorded mostly show tunes and old standards and came up empty in the hit department. He found a lot of work and success on television in Great Britain, and in 1985 starred as Robert McCall in a very popular detective show on CBS called *The Equalizer*. The network moved the show around on its schedule often, but it still managed to last for four seasons. Woodward earned a Golden Globe Award for his role on the program. Many fans of the series would be amazed to learn of Woodward's musical roots and skills. He was married twice and had four children. He was felled by prostate cancer on November 16, 2009, at the age of 79. Inspired by the TV series, *The Equalizer* became a moderately popular motion picture in 2014 starring Denzel Washington.

CHUCK WOOLERY

Most Famous TV Role: host of *Wheel of Fortune, Love Connection, Scrabble,* and *Lingo;* **Networks:** GSN, NBC, syndicated; **Years:** 1975–1981, 1983, 1984–1990, 2002–2007, respectively; **Hit Recording:** "Naturally Stoned"; **Label:** Columbia; **Release Year:** 1968; **Matrix:** Columbia #44590; **Chart:** #40 *Billboard* Hot 100.

Chuck Woolery was born in Ashland, Kentucky, on March 16, 1941. After high school he served in the U.S. Navy. Teamed with a friend named Elkin Fowler, a group called the Avant-Garde was born in the late 1960s. The pop folk group signed with Columbia Records in 1967 and scored one Top Forty hit called "Naturally Stoned" (#44590), written by Woolery. After a couple of less successful singles, Woolery opted to go solo and released several others while still under contract with Columbia including "Heaven Here on Earth" (Columbia #45135) and "Your Name Is Woman" (Columbia #45225). When these failed to catch on, he began to pursue other avenues of show business success and in 1975 became the original host of *Wheel of Fortune* on NBC. At that time the program was only hanging in the ratings by its very fingertips. It became wildly successful when Pat Sajak took the reins beginning late in 1981.

In that year, Woolery again attempted a singing career, this time with Columbia's Epic subsidiary, but his single called "The Greatest Love Affair" (Epic #50897) flopped and Woolery jumped back into game shows with both feet, finding success with *The Love Connection, Scrabble,* and most recently *Lingo* on GSN. He is a born-again Christian and has been married four times, with a total of six children.

Appendix B:
Debunked TV Stars' Records

This appendix lists various TV stars to whom recordings have been misattributed in one way or another.

DON ADAMS

Most Famous TV Role: Maxwell Smart on *Get Smart;* **Networks:** CBS, NBC; **Years:** 1965–1970; **Hit Recording:** none; **Label:** United Artists; **Release Year:** 1967; **Matrix:** *Don Adams Live* (United Artists LP #3604); **Chart:** none

Don Adams was born as Donald James Yarmy in New York City on April 13, 1923. He is best known for his work on television—*The Bill Dana Show, Check It Out, Don Adams' Screen Test, The Partners,* and especially as the bumbling spy named Maxwell Smart on *Get Smart.* He also provided the voice for the animated characters *Tennessee Tuxedo* and *Inspector Gadget.* This Don Adams did release a comedy album in 1967 called *Don Adams Live* for United Artists Records. It's his stand-up routines captured on vinyl. Two of the cuts from the album, "Golfers Are All Crazy" backed with "Non-Sched Airline," were released on a 45 (United Artists #50197). This Don Adams didn't sing on record. However, a country singer named Don Adams did sing and released singles and albums on numerous labels such as Ariola, Liberty, and Musicor (to name but a few). These releases are often erroneously attributed to TV's Don Adams. Adding to the confusion is the fact that Don Adams the country singer also released an album for United Artists Records in 1972 titled *The Black Voice* (United Artists #29210). TV's Don Adams was married three times and died of a lung infection on September 25, 2005, at the age of 82.

A comedy 45 by *Get Smart*'s Don Adams—not to be confused with the country singer of the same name.

WALLY COX

Most Famous TV Roles: Robinson J. Peepers on *Mister Peepers*, the voice of *Underdog*, occupied the upper left square on *The Hollywood Squares*; **Network:** NBC; **Years:** 1952–1955, 1964–1966, 1965–1973, respectively; **Hit Recording:** none; **Label:** RCA Victor, Waldorf; **Release Years:** 1953–1955; **Matrix:** "What a Crazy Guy" (RCA Victor #5278), "The Pushcart Serenade" (Waldorf Music Hall #218); **Chart:** none

Wally Cox, the actor, was the star of TV's *Mister Peepers* and *The Adventures of Hiram Holliday*. He was also a regular on the original *Hollywood Squares*, and the voice of the animated superhero known as *Underdog*. Although he did make records, he is not to be confused with the prolific-but-obscure soul singer of the 1960s of the same name who recorded for the Cordon, Lama, Orchestra, and Wand labels. (See the entry for Wally Cox in the main section.)

DONNA DOUGLAS

Most Famous TV Role: Elly May Clampett on *The Beverly Hillbillies*; **Network:** CBS; **Years:** 1962–1971; **Hit Recording:** none **Label:** Miracle, Oak; **Release Year:** early 1970s; **Matrix:** "Never Ending Song of Love" (Oak Records—no number on label), "At the End of the Rainbow" (Miracle #1002); **Chart:** none

Donna Douglas is best known for her nine-year run as Elly May Clampett on *The Beverly Hillbillies*. She did indeed release several single recordings in the 1970s, but is not to be confused with the British Donna Douglas who recorded "He's So Near" for the Arlen Records label in 1962. (See the entry for Donna Douglas in the main section.)

LINDA EVANS

Most Famous TV Role: Krystle Jennings Carrington on *Dynasty*; **Network:** ABC; **Years:** 1981–1989; **Hit Recording:** "Don't You Need"; **Labels:** Ariola, Watts Sound; **Release Years:** 1973–1979; **Matrix:** "Don't You Need" (Ariola #7739); **Chart:** #70 *Billboard* R&B, #55 Dance

The Linda Evans on record is not the Linda Evans of *The Big Valley*, *Hunter*, and *Dynasty*, but rather an African American R&B singer. Linda Evans the singer is best known for her disco song "Don't You Need" backed with "You Got Me Dreaming" (Ariola #7739) from 1979. She also recorded "A Woman Has Taken Her Place" backed with "I've Gotta Get Myself Together" in 1973 for the Watts Sound label (#700187). Linda Evans the actress does lip-synch a song called "He's My True Love" in *Beach Blanket Bingo* (actually performed by singer Jackie Ward), and likely that is responsible for part of the confusion.

BRIAN KEITH

Most Famous TV Role: Uncle Bill on *Family Affair*, Judge Milton G. Hardcastle on *Hardcastle and McCormick*; **Networks:** ABC, CBS; **Years:** 1966–1971, 1983–1986, respectively; **Hit Recording:** none; **Label:** Page One; **Year:** 1969; **Matrix:** "When the First Tear Shows" (Page One #21014); **Chart:** none

Brian Keith was born as Robert Alba Keith in Bayonne, New Jersey, on November 14, 1921. He began his acting career as a toddler in silent films. He starred in the motion picture *The Parent Trap* in 1961, and numerous TV series—*The Crusader, The Westerner, Family Affair, The Little People* (a.k.a. *The Brian Keith Show*), *Hardcastle and McCormick, Heartland*, and *Walter and Emily*. During the run of *Family Affair*, a British singer named Brian Keith released a single (in 1968) for a subsidiary of Bell Records, the Page One label, written by a young and yet unknown Elton John. The record was "When the First Tear Shows." Same name, totally different performer. The *actor* Brian Keith was a longtime smoker (in fact, he was often seen smoking on camera in his first series, *The Crusader*, which had Camel for a sponsor), and he developed emphysema and lung cancer. Depressed over these developments, Keith took his own life on June 24, 1997, at the age of 75. He has a star on Hollywood's Walk of Fame.

CHUCK NORRIS

Most Famous TV Role: Cord Walker on *Walker, Texas Ranger*; **Network:** CBS; **Years:** 1993–2001; **Hit Recording:** none; **Labels:** Aladdin, Atlantic, Imperial; **Release Years:** 1950–1953; **Matrix:** "I Know the Blues" (Aladdin #3081), "Messin' Up" (Atlantic #994), "I Love You Baby Blues" (Imperial #5049); **Chart:** none

Carlos Ray Norris was born in Ryan, Oklahoma, on March 10, 1940. He served in the U.S. Air Force and made a name for himself as a martial arts expert. He parlayed that area of expertise into a motion picture and television career—most famous for *Delta Force* on the silver screen, and *Walker, Texas Ranger* on the small screen. He may be proficient at many things, but he did not make records. The Chuck Norris that recorded for R&B labels such as Aladdin, Atlantic, and Imperial was an African American bluesman. He was sometimes called Charles Norris, but was more often billed as the Chuck Norris Band. Most cuts are R&B instrumentals from rock and roll's infancy. Chuck Norris the actor has been married twice and has five children.

Appendix C: Vinyl Releases from Animated and Costumed Character Shows

THE ARCHIES

Network: CBS, NBC; Years: 1968–1978; #1 Hit Recording: "Sugar, Sugar"; Label: Calendar; Release Year: 1969; Matrix: Calendar #1008; Chart: #1 *Billboard* Hot 100

This animated, long-running Saturday morning series was based on the popular comic strip. The program had a myriad of different titles over its 10-year run. The early years emphasized music, and with the help of producer Don Kirshner and the vocals of Ron Dante, the Archies scored a number 1 smash with "Sugar, Sugar" in 1969. For a brief time, cardboard copies of their singles were available on the backs of Post Cereal boxes.

THE BANANA SPLITS

Network: NBC; Years: 1968–1970; Hit Recording: none; Label: Decca; Release Year: 1968; Matrix: *We're the Banana Splits* (Decca LP #75075); Chart: none

The Banana Splits Adventure Hour from Hanna-Barbera Productions featured the live action costumed characters/animals named Fleegle, Snorky, Bingo, and Drooper. Together, they formed a rock and roll band and attempted to parlay the program's popularity into record sales. The result was an album for Decca Records called *We're the Banana Splits* in 1968. It didn't chart, but quite a few copies were sold to ardent young fans of the TV show. A couple of singles from the album were released by Decca—"The Tra La La Song" (Decca #32429) and the title cut "We're the Banana Splits" (Decca #32391). In 1970, the Splits split.

BARNEY AND FRIENDS

Network: PBS; **Years:** 1992–2008; **Hit Recording:** *Barney's Favorites*, volumes 1 and 2; **Labels:** EMI, SBK; **Release Years:** 1993–1994; **Matrix:** SBK LP #27114, EMI LP #28338; **Chart:** #9, #66, respectively, *Billboard* Top Pop Albums

Barney and Friends was a highly successful PBS program geared toward very young children. Barney was a purple and green dinosaur (a costumed character) with an overtly friendly and positive attitude. Songs from the program were included in two albums released early in the program's run. Both *Barney's Favorites: Volume 1* and *Barney's Favorites: Volume 2* attained platinum status, with volume 1 reaching the Top Ten. Of course, everyone knows Barney's most famous number, "I Love You." The program was maligned by many critics who failed to see any educational value in it.

THE BEAGLES

Network: ABC, CBS; **Years:** 1966–1968; **Hit Recordings:** none; **Label:** Columbia; **Release Year:** 1966; **Matrix:** "Looking for the Beagles" (Columbia #43789); **Chart:** none

The Beagles was an animated parody of the Beatles featuring two beagle dogs named Stringer and Tubby in a rock band (voiced by Mort Marshall and Allen Swift, respectively). The program ran for one season on CBS's Saturday morning lineup, and then aired for one more season in reruns on ABC. A single called "Looking for the Beagles" backed with "I Wanna Capture You" was issued in 1966. It was thought that all episodes of this Total Television production were lost, but they were found years later in a warehouse.

THE BUGALOOS

Network: NBC; **Years:** 1970–1972; **Hit Recording:** "For a Friend"; **Label:** Capitol; **Release Year:** 1970; **Matrix:** Capitol #2946; **Chart:** #128 *Billboard* Bubbling Under

The Bugaloos was a live-action costumed Saturday morning series about a vocal group consisting of four insects named Joy (Carolyn Ellis), Courage (John Philpott), Harmony (Wayne Laryea), and I. Q. (John McIndoe). The program was created by Sid and Marty Krofft, and in the show's first season, the group released an eponymous album featuring all four costumed members in flight on the cover. Only "For a Friend" made the charts, albeit very low. Other songs on *The Bugaloos* album (Capitol LP #621) include "If You Become a Bugaloo" and "Fly Away with Us." The show ran for two seasons on NBC. When ratings began to slip, NBC used a big can of Raid.

CASPER, THE FRIENDLY GHOST

Network: ABC; **Years:** 1963–1969; **Hit Recording:** none; **Label:** Golden; **Release Year:** 1964; **Matrix:** *Casper, the Friendly Ghost* (Golden LP #113); **Chart:** none

Harvey Comics gave us *Casper, the Friendly Ghost*—a long-running cartoon series featuring a good-natured ghost that frightened away almost everyone he encountered. All episodes had a happy ending with the other characters coming to the realization that Casper only wanted to be their friend. A new batch of cartoons was unveiled in *The New Casper Cartoon Show*, also on ABC. Casper released an album for Golden Records in 1964 titled *Casper, the Friendly Ghost*. It consisted of a dozen short and ghostly adventures.

FAT ALBERT. *See* BILL COSBY in the main section.

THE FLINTSTONES

Network: ABC; **Years:** 1960–1966; **Hit Recordings:** "Open Up Your Heart (Let the Sunshine In)," "Daddy"; **Label:** HBR; **Release Years:** 1965–1966; **Matrix:** "Open Up Your Heart" (HBR #449), "Daddy" (HBR #484); **Chart:** none

Known as "the modern stone age family," the Flintstones "starred" in an eponymous long-running animated ABC prime-time series that featured Fred and Wilma Flintstone and their neighbors Barney and Betty Rubble (all patterned after *The Honeymooners*). Fred and Wilma's natural daughter, Pebbles, befriended Barney and Betty's adopted son, Bamm-Bamm, and formed a duet. "Open Up Your Heart (Let the Sunshine In)" debuted in a 1965 episode of the series titled "No Biz like Show Biz." It didn't chart, but did sell a lot of copies on Hanna-Barbera's own HBR records label. Another single called "Daddy" (set to B. J. Thomas's song called "Mama") became a regional hit in Boston and Baltimore. Countless variations on the original *Flintstones* concept emerged on television during the 1970s and '80s. A moderately popular motion picture version starring John Goodman was released in 1994.

THE GROOVIE GOOLIES

Network: CBS; **Years:** 1970–1972; **Hit Recording:** none; **Label:** RCA Victor; **Release Year:** 1970; **Matrix:** *The Groovie Goolies* (RCA Victor LP #4420); **Chart:** none

The Groovie Goolies qualifies as a cartoon spinoff. The characters began on a series titled *Sabrina and the Groovie Goolies*. The next season, the Goolies had top billing. They were musical monsters, and their musical "haunt" was Horrible Hall. RCA Victor released an eponymous album of songs from the series in 1970. Songs included "Bumble Goolie," "Goolie Garden," and "The Goolie Get-Together Theme." There were also a couple of *Groovie Goolies* comic books released during this period by Gold Key. Reruns of the animated series were shown on Saturday mornings by ABC during the 1975–1976 season.

H.R. PUFNSTUF

Network: NBC; **Years:** 1969–1971; **Hit Recording:** none; **Label:** Capitol; **Release Year:** 1969; **Matrix:** *Sing Along with H.R. Pufnstuf* (Capitol EP #57); **Chart:** none

H.R. Pufnstuf was the rotund mayor of Living Island on this program that combined costumed Sid and Marty Krofft characters with a human character named Jimmy (played by Jack Wild). The single-camera Saturday morning children's program employed a laugh track, and quite a bit of music. An EP 45 of music from the show was released in 1969 by Capitol Records, and consisted of the Pufnstuf theme song along with "How Lucky I Am," "I'm So Happy to Be Here," and "A Bucket of Sunshine." A Universal motion picture titled *Pufnstuf*, based upon the TV series, was released in 1970.

HECTOR HEATHCOTE

Network: NBC; **Years:** 1963–1965; **Hit Recording:** none; **Label:** RCA Camden; **Release Year:** 1963; **Matrix:** *The Hector Heathcote Show* (RCA Camden LP #1053); **Chart:** none

Hector Heathcote was a Terrytoons cartoon character with a time machine who took young viewers on a fun history lesson. His cohorts were Sidney the Elephant and judo expert Hashimoto-San the Mouse. During their two-year run on NBC, an LP was released by RCA's Camden division and called *The Hector Heathcote Show*. The album consisted of a mixture of music and adventures, but was not a big seller.

HUCKLEBERRY HOUND

Network: syndicated; **Years:** 1958–1962; **Hit Recording:** none; **Label:** Colpix; **Release Years:** 1959–1961; **Matrix:** *Huckleberry Hound: The Great Kellogg's TV Show* (Colpix LP #202), *Here Comes Huckleberry Hound* (Colpix LP #207); **Chart:** none

This Emmy Award–winning Hanna-Barbera cartoon series had a four-year run in syndication. Daws Butler provided Huckleberry's voice, inspired by a North Carolina neighbor with a heavy southern drawl. Huckleberry's favorite song was "Clementine," and he sang a bit of the song in most episodes of the series. During the early part of the program's run, two albums were released for the Colpix label (LP #202 and #207, respectively) called *Huckleberry Hound: The Great Kellogg's TV Show* and *Here Comes Huckleberry Hound*. Huckleberry's cartoons have been seen most recently on the Boomerang TV network.

THE JETSONS

Network: ABC; **Years:** 1962–1963; **Hit Recording:** none; **Label:** Golden; **Release Year:** 1963; **Matrix:** *New Songs of the TV Family of the Future* (Golden LP #98); **Chart:** none

William Hanna and Joseph Barbera had such great success with *The Flintstones*, they went to the well a couple more times with *The Roman Holidays* set in first century Rome, and the much more successful *Jetsons*, set well into the 21st century. The original series only lasted one season in prime time, but it has enjoyed an amazing life in reruns. In the 1980s, numerous new episodes were added to the syndication package. During the show's original run, an album of songs was released for kids on the Golden Records label. Among the songs were the program's theme song and another titled "Eep Opp Ork" from the episode titled "A Date with Jet Screamer." But, "rut row," it did not make the album charts. A movie based on the cartoon series was released in 1990 from Universal Pictures.

JONNY QUEST

Network: ABC, CBS, NBC; **Years:** 1964–1981; **Hit Recording:** none; **Label:** HBR; **Release Year:** 1965; **Matrix:** *Jonny Quest—20,000 Leagues under the Sea* (HBR LP #2030); **Chart:** none

This was a long-running Hanna-Barbera cartoon starring young Jonny Quest, who accompanied his scientist father on worldwide adventures. Actor Tim Matheson provided Jonny's voice. This durable program also spawned a record album on Hanna-Barbera's own HBR label in 1965. Along with the show's theme song, both sides of the album called *Jonny Quest—20,000 Leagues under the Sea* featured Quest's latest adventure. In 1993, the still popular franchise enjoyed an update in an animated movie titled *Jonny's Golden Quest*.

JOSIE AND THE PUSSYCATS. See CHERYL LADD in the main section.

LINUS THE LIONHEARTED

Network: ABC, CBS; **Years:** 1964–1969; **Hit Recording:** none; **Label:** General Foods; **Release Year:** 1964; **Matrix:** *Linus the Lionhearted* (General Foods LP #10); **Chart:** none

This popular cartoon series enjoyed a two-year run on CBS on Saturday mornings from 1964 to 1966, and then on ABC on Sunday mornings from 1966 to 1969. Set in Africa, this cartoon series was canceled because it was, for the most part, a half-hour commercial for Post breakfast cereals. All of the characters had their own cereals—Lovable Truly touted Alpha-Bits, Sugar Bear hawked Sugar Crisp, and Linus was the poster lion for Crispy Critters. General Foods/Post even had a record label, albeit briefly, on which the *Linus the Lionhearted* album was released in 1964. It contained a mixture of music and adventures. Voices for the series included Carl Reiner, Sheldon Leonard, and Ruth Buzzi.

MIGHTY MOUSE

Network: CBS; **Years:** 1955–1966; **Hit Recording:** none; **Label:** Lion; **Release Year:** 1959; **Matrix:** *Terrytoons' Mighty Mouse Playhouse* (Lion LP #70115); **Chart:** none

Mighty Mouse was Terrytoons' most successful cartoon creation—a rodent that wore a cape and fought crime. Not only did he fly, but he also sang "Here I come to save the day" in an operatic fashion. During the program's long run the Lion label released an album titled *Terrytoons' Mighty Mouse Playhouse* featuring numerous adventures narrated by Tom Morrison. An updated version of the series titled *Mighty Mouse: The New Adventures* had a brief run on CBS in the latter part of the 1980s.

THE NEW ZOO REVUE

Network: syndicated; **Years:** 1972–1975; **Hit Recording:** none; **Label:** Disneyland; **Release Year:** 1972; **Matrix:** *The New Zoo Revue* (Disneyland LP #3807); **Chart:** none

New Zoo Revue was a popular syndicated daily half-hour live action costumed character series featuring Freddie the Frog (Yanco Inone), Henrietta Hippo (Larri Thomas), and Charlie the Owl (Sharon Baird). Early in its run an album of songs from the show was released on the Disneyland label. Songs included "Stay in School," "In the Arts," and "Cheer Up." The LP was not hugely successful and there were no follow-up releases.

QUICK DRAW MCGRAW

Network: syndicated; **Years:** 1959–1962; **Hit Recording:** none; **Label:** Colpix; **Release Year:** 1960; **Matrix:** *Quick Draw McGraw: Original TV Soundtrack Voices* (Colpix LP #203); **Chart:** none

Quick Draw McGraw was an equine cowboy, accompanied by his deputy—a burro named Baba Looey. Together, they fought crime in the old
west. Daws Butler provided the voices for both Hanna-Barbera characters.
In some episodes, Quick Draw took on the alter ego of El Kabong, a caped
crime fighter who caught the bad guys with a loud "kabong" on their
head with his guitar. During the show's run, Colpix Records released
an album of adventures on *Quick Draw McGraw: Original TV Soundtrack
Voices*. After a three-year run in syndication, the cartoons jumped to CBS's
Saturday morning schedule from 1963 to 1966, sponsored by Kellogg's.

RUFF AND REDDY

Network: NBC; **Years:** 1957–1964; **Hit Recording:** none; **Label:** Golden; **Release Year:** 1959; **Matrix:** "Ruff and Reddy and Professor Gizmo" (Golden
#558); **Chart:** none

This was the first successful cartoon series for Hanna-Barbera. Ruff was
a cat and Reddy was a dog. Ruff was the brains of the duo. Reddy was a
good egg, but not particularly bright. Together, they helped launch a cartoon franchise. During the run of *The Ruff and Reddy Show*, they released a
Golden 45 rpm record geared for children with the A-side of the 45 titled
"Ruff and Reddy," and the B-side called "Professor Gizmo" (a diminutive
recurring character on the show).

SESAME STREET

Network: PBS; **Years:** 1969–present; **Hit Recording:** "Rubber Duckie"; **Label:** Columbia; **Release Year:** 1970; **Matrix:** Columbia #45207; **Chart:** #16
Billboard Hot 100

Sesame Street is considered by many to be the most important children's
show in TV's long history. It was the brainchild of Joan Ganz Cooney of
the Children's Television Workshop as early as 1967, but finally came to
fruition in November of 1969. It went on to win Clio, Peabody, and Emmy
awards. Jim Henson's Muppets were the biggest part of the program—
most being puppets (Kermit the Frog, Bert, Ernie, Miss Piggy, Cookie
Monster, Oscar the Grouch). Big Bird, however, was the exception, being
a costumed character. The program contained a goodly amount of music,

including Kermit's lament about "Bein' Green," but the show's biggest hit came in 1970 from Ernie. It was a song about bath time and his love for his "Rubber Duckie." The single became a surprise hit in that year and narrowly missed the Top Ten. Jim Henson's other hit single, "The Rainbow Connection" (Atlantic #3610), came in 1979, but was from the soundtrack of *The Muppet Movie*.

SIGMUND AND THE SEA MONSTER. *See* JOHNNY WHITAKER in the main section.

WALLY GATOR

Network: syndicated; **Year:** 1963; **Hit Recording:** none; **Label:** Golden; **Release Year:** 1963; **Matrix:** "TV Theme Songs of Wally Gator" (Golden #701); **Chart:** none

Wally Gator, much like Magilla Gorilla, didn't mind his keeper and was always getting into fixes outside the confines of the zoo. Wally, much less successful than many other Hanna-Barbera series, briefly had his own TV program. During that window of opportunity, he released one single for the Golden Records label. The A-side was the "Wally Gator Theme," and the B-side featured the theme for a regular segment on Wally's show, "Lippy and Hardy Har Har."

YOGI BEAR

Network: syndicated; **Years:** 1961–1963; **Hit Recording:** none; **Label:** Colpix; **Release Year:** 1961; **Matrix:** *Yogi Bear and Boo Boo* (Colpix LP #205); **Chart:** none

Yogi Bear resided in fictional Jellystone Park, and along with his cohort and conscience named Boo Boo, he was notorious for snatching picnic baskets from park visitors (much to the dismay of Ranger Smith). Yogi became so popular that he also became the subject of a Top Ten record by the Ivy Three (Shell #720) and the star of an animated motion picture called *Hey There, It's Yogi Bear* in 1964. There was also a record album titled *Yogi Bear and Boo Boo* on the Colpix label, featuring four of Yogi's mischievous picnic basket-swiping adventures.

Further Reading

Lofman, Ron. *Goldmine's Celebrity Vocals.* Iola, WI: Krause Publications, 1994.

Osborne, Jerry, ed. *Rockin' Records: Buyers-Sellers Reference and Price Guide.* Port Townsend, WA: Osborne Enterprises, 2014.

Whitburn, Joel. *Hot R&B Songs.* 6th ed. Menomonee Falls, WI: Record Research, 2010.

Whitburn, Joel. *Top Pop Albums.* 7th ed. Menomonee Falls, WI: Record Research, 2010.

Whitburn, Joel. *Top Pop Singles.* 14th ed. Menomonee Falls, WI: Record Research, 2012.

Index

About the Author

Bob Leszczak was born and raised in Elizabeth, New Jersey. An only child, Bob turned to the television set and the phonograph, which became his favorite toys before the age of two, and his passion for both has never diminished. He is a lifetime vinyl record collector and music historian. Bob got his bachelor's degree in communication at Seton Hall University in South Orange, New Jersey, and while still in college, he toured as a member of the vocal group the Duprees, most famous for the Top Ten hit called "You Belong to Me." He also released recordings with numerous vocal ensembles, such as the Infernos, the Autumns, Retrospect, and the James Myers Quintet. At the same time, Bob was paying his dues in radio broadcasting and eventually became a popular on-air personality in great radio markets such as Boston, Washington DC, Tampa/St. Petersburg (where he garnered a coveted Air Award in 1999), Orlando, Hartford, Denver, and Riverside/San Bernardino (as Bob O'Brien). He was also a panelist on the weekly TV talent show titled *Lucky Break* in 2006, and in 2013 he was an extra in the Emmy- and Golden Globe–winning HBO motion picture called *Behind the Candelabra*. Bob was the writer/producer of a weekly five-hour music trivia program called *Solid Gold Scrapbook* for the United Stations Radio Network in the 1980s. In recent years, Bob has returned to writing and is the author of *Single Season Sitcoms 1948–1979: A Complete Guide*; *Who Did It First? Great Rhythm and Blues Cover Songs and Their Original Artists*; *Who Did It First? Great Pop Cover Songs and Their Original Artists*; *Who Did It First? Great Rock and Roll Cover Songs and Their Original Artists*; and *"The Odd Couple" on Stage and Screen: A History with Cast and Crew, Profiles, and an Episode Guide*. He is an avid jogger and a fervent fan of football and baseball. He has recently returned to the Garden State and currently works on-air at 100.1 WJRZ-FM, playing the greatest hits of the 1960s, '70s, and '80s. Thomas Wolfe was wrong—you *can* go home again.